The Poor's Struggle for Political Incorporation

This book offers an innovative perspective on the ever-widening gap between the poor and the state in Latin American politics. It presents a comprehensive analysis of the main social movement that mobilized the poor and unemployed people of Argentina to end neoliberalism and to attain incorporation into a more inclusive and equal society. The *piquetero* (picketer) movement is the largest movement of unemployed people in the world. This movement has transformed Argentine politics to the extent of becoming part of the governing coalition for more than a decade. Rossi argues that the movement has been part of a long-term struggle by the poor for socio-political participation in the polity after having been excluded by authoritarian regimes and neoliberal reforms. He conceptualizes this process as a wave of incorporation, exploring the characteristics of this major redefinition of politics in Latin America.

Federico M. Rossi is a Research Professor of CONICET at the School of Politics and Government of the National University of San Martín, Argentina. Rossi received his PhD in Political and Social Sciences from the European University Institute in Florence. Rossi's research interests focus on the relational study of social movements – state dynamics and on the historical analysis of strategy-making. His work has been published in more than fifteen edited volumes, in *Latin American Politics and Society*, *Latin American Perspectives*, *Social Movement Studies*, *Mobilization*, *International Sociology*, *Desarrollo Económico*, and *América Latina Hoy*, among others. He is the co-editor of *Social Movement Dynamics: New Perspectives on Theory and Research from Latin America* (2015). Rossi has been Global Visiting Scholar at New York University, Postdoctoral Fellow at Tulane University and the European University Institute, and Visiting Researcher at the Universidade de Brasília and Singapore Management University.

Cambridge Studies in Contentious Politics

Books in the Series

Rina Agarwala, *Informal Labor, Formal Politics, and Dignified Discontent in India*
Ronald Aminzade, *Race, Nation, and Citizenship in Post-Colonial Africa: The Case of Tanzania*
Ronald Aminzade et al., *Silence and Voice in the Study of Contentious Politics*
Javier Auyero, *Routine Politics and Violence in Argentina: The Gray Zone of State Power*
Phillip M. Ayoub, *When States Come Out: Europe's Sexual Minorities and the Politics of Visibility*
Amrita Basu, *Violent Conjunctures in Democratic India*
W. Lance Bennett and Alexandra Segerberg, *The Logic of Connective Action: Digital Media and the Personalization of Contentious Politics*
Nancy Bermeo and Deborah J. Yashar, *Parties, Movements, and Democracy in the Developing World*
Clifford Bob, *The Global Right Wing and the Clash of World Politics*
Clifford Bob, *The Marketing of Rebellion: Insurgents, Media, and International Activism*
Charles Brockett, *Political Movements and Violence in Central America*
Marisa von Bülow, *Building Transnational Networks: Civil Society and the Politics of Trade in the Americas*
Valerie Bunce and Sharon Wolchik, *Defeating Authoritarian Leaders in Postcommunist Countries*
Lars-Erik Cederman, Kristian Skrede Gleditsch, and Halvard Buhaug, *Inequality, Grievances, and Civil War*
Christian Davenport, *How Social Movements Die: Repression and Demobilization of the Republic of New Africa*
Christian Davenport, *Media Bias, Perspective, and State Repression*
Gerald F. Davis, Doug McAdam, W. Richard Scott, and Mayer N. Zald, *Social Movements and Organization Theory*
Donatella della Porta, *Clandestine Political Violence*

(*continued after index*)

The Poor's Struggle for Political Incorporation

The Piquetero *Movement in Argentina*

FEDERICO M. ROSSI
CONICET – UNSAM

CAMBRIDGE
UNIVERSITY PRESS

CAMBRIDGE
UNIVERSITY PRESS

University Printing House, Cambridge CB2 8BS, United Kingdom

One Liberty Plaza, 20th Floor, New York, NY 10006, USA

477 Williamstown Road, Port Melbourne, VIC 3207, Australia

4843/24, 2nd Floor, Ansari Road, Daryaganj, Delhi – 110002, India

79 Anson Road, #06–04/06, Singapore 079906

Cambridge University Press is part of the University of Cambridge.

It furthers the University's mission by disseminating knowledge in the pursuit of education, learning, and research at the highest international levels of excellence.

www.cambridge.org
Information on this title: www.cambridge.org/9781107110113
DOI: 10.1017/9781316273180

First published 2017

Printed in the United States of America by Sheridan Books, Inc.

A catalogue record for this publication is available from the British Library.

ISBN 978-1-107-11011-3 Hardback

Contents

Figures

Maps

Tables

Preface

Over the past 20 years, major transformations have come to pass in Latin American politics, with an ever-widening gap between the popular sectors and the state and the rise of left and populist governments in response to this gap. This book's primary theoretical aim is to understand these transformations and, in particular, the role of poor people's movements in effecting them. These transformations represented as much a desperate claim for dignity as a politically driven attempt on the part of many groups to achieve specific political goals. The question of how to characterize this process and the struggle of social movements led me to revisit Collier and Collier's masterpiece *Shaping the Political Arena* (1991) and ask whether recent developments in some Latin American countries might in fact signal a *reshaping* of the political arena. This book provides an affirmative answer to this question through my argument that a second incorporation of the popular sectors has taken place since the early 2000s.

The argument of the second wave of incorporation is the first main theoretical contribution of this book and is presented in Chapter 1. The waves of incorporation signal the recognition and inclusion of poor people's organized interests in the socio-political arena. The concept of popular incorporation refers to the recognition of the claims of politically active poor people's movements as well as the creation or reformulation of formal and informal rules and regulations that govern their participation in politics and their connection to the policy process.

The first wave of incorporation, dating back to the 1930s–50s, focused on the legitimation and legal regulation of the labor movement. Corporatism emerged as the primary form of popular interest intermediation, with trade unions as the politically dominant representatives of popular sectors (Collier and Collier 1991). The aftermath of first incorporation was one of exclusion or disincorporation, as a result of the application of economic and political reforms that reduced the political power of the popular sectors and marginalized them from the socio-political arena. However, disincorporation was not absolute – there was no return to the conditions of the nineteenth and early twentieth centuries. Disincorporation sparked widespread resistance and the mobilization of poor people for their reincorporation. A long relational process – analyzed in detail in this book – led to a second wave of incorporation of the popular sectors in the socio-political arena.

The second wave of incorporation is different from the first in that it is not corporatist and that the central actors are social movements aiming to *expand* initial incorporation centered on unions to include territorially organized poor people. This has led me to focus my attention on conceptualizing a specific type of movement that emerges in response to exclusionary neoliberal policies and that is vital to an understanding of the second wave of incorporation: the reincorporation movement.

If social movements are central actors in the second incorporation process, then it is necessary to analyze the goals and strategies of these movements in order to understand the dynamics that constitute the subject of this book. This concern with the strategies of movements underpins the second main theoretical goal of this book, presented in Chapter 2: the need for bridging the relationship between the pace of long-term historical processes and the expectations and strategies of the actors involved in them.

I propose a relational perspective that draws on social movement and historical institutionalist literatures in my analysis of the macro-process of second incorporation. In doing so, I contribute to a promising cross-fertilization between these approaches. Building upon the foundational work of Bourdieu (1998, 2000) and, mainly, Tilly (1986, 2006, 2008), I propose two concepts – "repertoire of strategies" and "stock of legacies" – that aim at complementing the structuralist tendencies of many macro-historical studies while avoiding explanations that are limited by the assumptions of rational choice theory. These two concepts are important because they incorporate agency to the second incorporation process. In this way, the struggle of social movements can be located as part of a long-running historical process.

In addition to these theoretical objectives, this book has an empirical focus: it conducts an in-depth analysis of Argentina's *piquetero* (picketers) movement, the main movement of unemployed people of the contemporary world. This social movement emerged to organize the victims of neoliberalism as they struggled to reverse their exclusion from the socio-political arena. Beginning with the pioneering book by Svampa and Pereyra (2003), this movement garnered considerable academic attention in its earlier years. Although this attention has waned of late, a profound understanding of this movement's historical role in the reshaping of Argentina's socio-political arena continues to be of prime importance. Hence, this book offers a process-tracing analysis of the struggle of the *piquetero* movement in Argentina leading to the partial achievement of a second incorporation of the popular sectors into the socio-political arena (1996–2009).

The theoretical and empirical objectives of this book – with its focus on both the process of second incorporation and the repertoire of strategies developed by the *piqueteros* – are reflected in its structure, which combines narration and theory. In Chapters 3 to 6, I apply the toolkit proposed in the two opening chapters to a dynamic narration of the *piqueteros*' struggle for reincorporation. The narrative chapters follow a strict chronology. However, there is a partial, coincidental overlap between the reincorporation stages and the development of the *piquetero* movement, and the synchronization of these is crucial in explaining the different pathways of each *piquetero* social movement organization (SMO) as well as heuristically relevant for further cross-national comparisons (carried out at the end of the book).

Chapter 3 traces the origins of the *piquetero* movement and the introduction of the first national policies directed at the victims of neoliberalism. I argue that the emergence of the *piquetero* movement as the main organizer of poor people in their quest for reincorporation was the result of a combination of economic and political changes. In the latter sections of this chapter I study the emergence of a new "social question" stemming from the socioeconomic consequences of neoliberalism. Chapter 4 analyzes the period between March 1999 and December 2001, which spanned the state's recognition of the *piqueteros*' claim up to the eventual legitimation of the entire movement as a new political actor. I also investigate the dynamics that led to the collapse of the national government in December 2001.

Chapters 5 and 6 examine how the *piqueteros* came to be incorporated into the socio-political arena between 2002 and 2009. Chapter 5 analyzes the period that starts in 2002 with the first moves toward incorporation and the demobilization of the *piquetero* movement during January 2002–May 2003 and its later failure. The focus of Chapter 6 is the continuation of this stage with the more successful partial incorporation of the *piquetero* movement during May 2003–December 2008. Chapter 6 closes with an analysis of the end of second incorporation following the March–July 2008 rural lockout.

After the narrative sections, Chapter 7 evaluates the aftermath (2009–15) of second incorporation and the socio-political transformations produced by the *piquetero* movement in Argentina.

Since I propose that the second wave of incorporation is not a process unique to Argentina and the *piqueteros*, in Chapter 8 I compare the Argentine case with those of other Latin American reincorporation struggles. In particular, I study the indigenous and coca growers' movements in Bolivia and the movement of landless peasants in Brazil – the other main Latin American reincorporation movements.

The book also includes one appendix containing two flowcharts that synthesize the historical development of the organizations, parties, and unions implicated in the emergence and evolution of the *piquetero* movement.

In the concluding chapter, I summarize the book's main contributions to the study of the recursive expansion and contraction of the socio-political arena in Latin America and consider its theoretical implications for the general scholarship on social movements. My hope is that this book will stimulate future comparative studies involving collective and historical analysis of strategies while inserting social movements into the macro history of decisive transformations of the polity.

Acknowledgments

The research process can be a solitary activity, involving several months of work in libraries and archives and sitting at a desk typing. Fortunately, as scholars of human activities our lives invariably intertwine with those of others. In this way this process of self-imposed distancing that we must pursue in our line of work also leads to the forging of social relationships and sometimes even long-standing friendships. In writing this book, I experienced both feelings of solitude and companionship and luckily survived the whole process. A series of people must be thanked for this achievement.

This book is the result of ten years of research. I started my work on this topic in 2006 as a PhD candidate in the Department of Political and Social Sciences at the European University Institute at the gorgeous Badia Fiesolana in the hills of Florence. In addition, through the research period I was fortunate in being able to take up postdoctoral or visiting scholar posts at three different institutions. Firstly I was Junior Visiting Researcher at the Political Science Institute (IPOL) at the University of Brasília (September–December 2008) and then Graduate Global Visiting Scholar at the Graduate School of Arts and Sciences at New York University (January–June 2009). My debates with IPOL colleagues – above all Marisa von Bülow – as well as with those of the Department of Sociology at NYU – and in particular Neil Brenner's and Manu Goswami's students – were more important than they can know for the theoretical sections of this book. Finally, between August 2012 and August 2014 I was a Postdoctoral Research Fellow at the Center for Inter-American Policy and Research (CIPR) at Tulane University. The much-needed time this provided to reflect and write, the wonderfully collegial atmosphere, and the generous support of the CIPR's director Ludovico Feoli were invaluable to the success of this book.

This book has much greater significance to me than merely what is described in these pages. I was transformed as a person and a citizen by the conversations I had with so many amazing individuals. Needless to say, this research was made possible thanks to the generosity of these people who I interviewed. I hope that the narrative and analytic framework I am proposing in this book will be useful for them too.

Most of these interviews, as well as my ability to access crucial first-hand material, would never have been possible without the support of several people. I must thank Federico Schuster, Sebastián Pereyra, Germán Pérez, Martín Armelino, Ana Natalucci, and Melina Vázquez, members of the Research Team on Social Protest and Collective Action at the "Gino Germani" Research Institute at the University of Buenos Aires. Others were also very important in helping me gain access to social movement organizations, in particular Carina Balladares, María Cecilia Ferraudi Curto, and Alejandro Grimson of the National University of San Martín and Luciana Ghiotto, Shirley Medina, Federico Montero, Jimena Ponce de León, and Julio Quiroga. Journalists at the newspaper *Página/12* also facilitated access to this complex terrain of investigation: Martín Piqué and Laura Vales in particular were of great help for accessing the more arcane corners of the state. Admission to the *Página/12* archives was also crucial, where I worked for several weeks benefiting from the marvelous resources and support of archive staff. Germán Lodola and my great friend and colleague Sebastián Mauro also gave up their time to discuss various issues and ideas concerning my research and fieldwork, which greatly enhanced and focused my fieldwork. Though not responsible for my mistakes and biases, they are definitely responsible for many of the positive results of my research. Finally yet importantly, I also had the luck of receiving the assistance of Tim Peace, Mona-Lynn Courteau, Felipe Ponce de León, and Lucas Rossi, who did very professional jobs. My brother Lucas also produced the maps and images that this book contains in record time.

As my research unfolded I had the chance to share my results at different conferences as well as with colleagues and friends at the European University Institute and elsewhere. I presented earlier versions of this book at the XXIV Convegno della Società Italiana di Scienza Politica (Università IUAV di Venezia, September 16–18, 2010); the conference "Latin America and the Caribbean: Beyond Neoliberalism?" (University of Groningen, November 18–19, 2010); the Sixth General Conference of the European Consortium for Political Research (University of Iceland, August 24–27, 2011); the Young Scholars in Social Movements Conference at the Center for the Study of Social Movements, University of Notre Dame (May 4, 2012); the Pittsburgh Social Movement Forum, University of Pittsburgh (November 2, 2012); the conferences "From Resisting Neoliberalism to the Second Wave of Incorporation" and "Rethinking State-Society Relations in Contemporary Latin America" I organized at the CIPR, Tulane University (October 24–25, 2012, and May 24, 2013); the conference "Contentions Against Neoliberalism: Reconstituting the Social Fabric in the Developing World" (Department of International Development, University of Oxford, June 27–28, 2013); and the Fourth Annual Conference of the Sociology of Development Section of the American Sociological Association (Watson Institute for International and Public Affairs, Brown University, March 13–15, 2015).

Parts of my research were previously published elsewhere, and I would like to thank Wiley, Springer, and Taylor & Francis for the authorization to reproduce passages from the following texts: "*Piqueteros* (Workers/Unemployment Movement in Argentina)," in David Snow, Donatella della Porta, Bert Klandermans, and Doug McAdam (2013) (eds.), *The Wiley-Blackwell Encyclopedia of Social and Political Movements* (volume 3; Oxford: Wiley-Blackwell), 929–32; "The Second Wave of Incorporation in Latin America: A Conceptualization of the Quest for Inclusion Applied to Argentina," *Latin American Politics and Society* (2015), 57 (1), 1–28; "Beyond Clientelism: The Piquetero Movement and the State in Argentina," in Paul Almeida and Allen Cordero Ulate (2015) (eds.), *Handbook of Social Movements across Latin America* (New York: Springer), 117–28; and "Conceptualizing Strategy Making in a Historical and Collective Perspective," in Federico M. Rossi and Marisa von Bülow (2015) (eds.), *Social Movement Dynamics: New Perspectives on Theory and Research from Latin America* (The Mobilization Series on Social Movements, Protest and Culture; Farnham: Ashgate), 15–41.

The outstanding conversations with my great friends and fellows Amr Adly and Jess Rich presented me with memorable intellectual challenges that changed my perspective on crucial topics. At the same time, various rough ideas, first drafts, and full chapters were improved thanks to comments provided by Rebecca Neara Abers, Paul Almeida, Gustavo Alares López, Javier Alcalde Villacampa, Javier Auyero, Stephanie Arnett, Benjamín Arditi, Lúcia Avelar, Leonardo Avritzer, Miguel De

Luca, Özge Ertem, Lorenza Fontana, Mayo Fuster Morrell, Roberto Gargarella, Jeff Goodwin, Matthew Johnson, Hank Johnston, Mimi Keck, Andrés Malamud, John Markoff, Mattea Musso, Gabriel Ondetti, David Ortiz, Nicky Owtram, Leigh Payne, Tim Peace, Enrique Peruzzotti, Ken Roberts, Philippe Schmitter, Sid Tarrow, Alexander Treschel, Marisa von Bülow, Jonas Wolff, and – obviously – Donatella della Porta. Finally yet importantly, two anonymous reviewers provided me with constructive comments that helped me improve this book.

Some persons must also be thanked for their vital support and presence in difficult moments. Most importantly, Ken Hulley, my grandparents Vicenza "Gina" Di Martino and Jorge González, my aunt Laura González, and my cousins Manuel, Ignacio, and Francisco Romero provided decisive support when it was urgently needed. In particular, Donatella and Sid made constant and substantial suggestions while supporting my research ambitions as a student.

This book is dedicated to my parents Gustavo Rossi and Silvia González, my great friend Carolina Barrionuevo, and my dear wife Mattea Musso. They were the ones who kept the foundations firmly under foot when it seemed they were sitting on quicksand. They are, in some ways, the unwitting co-authors of this book.

Abbreviations

ANTOD	*Asamblea Nacional de Trabajadores Ocupados y Desocupados* (National Assembly of Employed and Unemployed Workers)
ATE	*Asociación de Trabajadores del Estado* (State Workers' Association)
BPN	*Bloque Piquetero Nacional* (National *Piquetero* Block)
CBCs	Christian-based communities
CC-ARI	*Coalición Cívica – Alianza por una República de Iguales* (Civic Coalition – Alliance for a Republic of Equals)
CCC	*Corriente Clasista y Combativa* (Classist and Combative Current)
CDES	*Conselho de Desenvolvimento Econômico e Social* (Economic and Social Development Council [Brazil])
CES	*Consejo de Emergencia Social* (Council for Social Emergency)
CGT	*Confederación General del Trabajo* (General Labor Confederation)
CIC	*Centros Integradores Comunitarios* (Community Integration Centers)
CIDOB	*Central de Pueblos y Comunidades Indígenas del Oriente Boliviano* (Confederation of Indigenous Peoples of Eastern Bolivia)

CNBB	*Conferência Nacional dos Bispos do Brasil* (National Commission of Brazilian Bishops)
CONAIE	*Confederación de Nacionalidades Indígenas del Ecuador* (Confederation of Indigenous Nationalities of Ecuador)
CONALCAM	*Coordinadora Nacional por el Cambio* (National Committee for Change [Bolivia])
CONAMAQ	*Consejo Nacional de Ayllus y Markas del Qullasuyu* (National Council of Ayllus and Markas of Qullasuyu [Bolivia])
CONTAG	*Confederação Nacional dos Trabalhadores na Agricultura* (National Confederation of Agricultural Workers [Brazil])
CSUTCB	*Confederación Sindical Única de Trabajadores Campesinos de Bolivia* (Unified Confederation of Rural Workers of Bolivia)
CTA	*Central de Trabajadores de la Argentina* (Argentine Workers Union)
CTD "Aníbal Verón"	*Coordinadora de Trabajadores Desocupados "Aníbal Verón"* (Coordinator of Unemployed Workers "Aníbal Verón")
CTD "Trabajo y Dignidad"	*Coordinadora de Trabajadores Desocupados "Trabajo y Dignidad"* (Coordinator of Unemployed Workers "Work and Dignity")
CTD of Tartagal	*Coordinadora de Trabajadores Desocupados de Tartagal* (Coordinator of Unemployed Workers' of Tartagal)
CTERA	*Confederación de Trabajadores de la Educación de la República Argentina* (Argentine Confederation of Education Workers)
CUBa	*Coordinadora de Unidad Barrial* (Neighborhood Unity Coordinator)
CUT	*Central Única dos Trabalhadores* (Unitary Workers' Union [Brazil])
ECLAC	Economic Commission for Latin America and the Caribbean

EZLN	*Ejército Zapatista de Liberación Nacional* (Zapatista Army of National Liberation [Mexico])
FAA	*Federación Agraria Argentina* (Argentine Agrarian Federation)
FG	*Frente Grande* (Broad Front)
FOL	*Frente de Organizaciones en Lucha* (Front for Organizations Engaged in Struggle)
FOP	*Frente de Organizaciones Populares* (Popular Organizations Front)
FPDS	*Frente Popular "Darío Santillán"* (Popular Front "Darío Santillán")
FpV	*Frente para la Victoria* (Front for Victory)
FRENAPO	*Frente Nacional contra la Pobreza* (National Front against Poverty)
FREPASO	*Frente por un País Solidario* (Front for a Country in Solidarity)
FTNyP	*Frente Transversal Nacional y Popular* (National and Popular Transversal Front)
FTV	*Federación de Trabajadores por la Tierra, Vivienda y Hábitat* (Workers' Federation for Land, Housing and Habitat)
H.I.J.O.S.	*Hijos por la Identidad y la Justicia contra el Olvido y el Silencio* (Sons and Daughters for Identity and Justice against Oblivion and Silence)
IADB	Inter-American Development Bank
IMF	International Monetary Fund
INCRA	*Instituto Nacional de Colonização e Reforma Agrária* (National Institute for Colonization and Agrarian Reform [Brazil])
INDEC	*Instituto Nacional de Estadística y Censos* (National Institute of Statistics and Censuses)
IU	*Izquierda Unida* (United Left)
MAS (Argentina)	*Movimiento al Socialismo* (Movement Toward Socialism)
MAS (Bolivia)	*Movimiento al Socialismo* (Movement for Socialism [Bolivia])

MG	*Movimiento Guevarista* (Guevarist Movement)
MIC	*Movimiento Inter-sindical Clasista* (Inter-union Classist Movement)
MIJD	*Movimiento Independiente de Jubilados y Desocupados* (Independent Movement of the Retired and Unemployed)
MIJP	*Movimiento Independiente de Jubilados y Pensionados* (Independent Movement of Retired and Pensioners)
MILES	*Movimiento Integración Latinoamericana de Expresión Social* (Latin American Integration for Social Expression Movement)
MIP	*Movimiento Indígena Pachakuti* (Pachakuti Indigenous Movement [Bolivia])
MNR	*Movimiento Nacionalista Revolucionario* (Nationalist Revolutionary Movement [Bolivia])
MP	*Medida Provisória* (Provisional Measure [Brazil])
MPN	*Movimiento Popular Neuquino* (Neuquén People's Movement)
MPR "Quebracho"	*Movimiento Patriótico Revolucionario "Quebracho"* (Patriotic Revolutionary Movement "Quebracho")
MPSL	*Movimiento Político-Sindical Liberación* (Politico-Syndical Liberation Movement)
MPU "Quebracho"	*Movimiento de Unidad Popular "Quebracho"* (Popular Unity Movement "Quebracho")
MST (Argentina)	*Movimiento Socialista de los Trabajadores* (Socialist Workers Movement)
MST (Brazil)	*Movimento dos Trabalhadores Sem Terra* (Rural Landless Workers Movement [Brazil])
MST "Teresa Vive"	*Movimiento Sin Trabajo "Teresa Vive"* (Jobless Movement "Teresa Is Alive")
MTA	*Movimiento de Trabajadores Argentinos* (Argentine Workers' Movement)

MTD "Aníbal Verón"	*Movimiento de Trabajadores Desocupados "Aníbal Verón"* (Unemployed Workers Movement "Aníbal Verón")
MTD of La Juanita	*Movimiento de Trabajadores Desocupados de La Juanita* (Unemployed Workers Movement of La Juanita)
MTD of Solano	*Movimiento de Trabajadores Desocupados de Solano* (Unemployed Workers Movement of Solano)
MTL (Argentina)	*Movimiento Territorial Liberación* (Territorial Liberation Movement)
MTL (Brazil)	*Movimento Terra, Trabalho e Liberdade* (Land, Work and Freedom Movement [Brazil])
MTP	*Movimiento Todos por la Patria* (All for the Motherland Movement)
MTR	*Movimiento de Trabajadores Desocupados "Teresa Rodríguez"* (Unemployed Workers' Movement "Teresa Rodríguez")
MUP "May 29"	*Movimiento de Unidad Popular "29 de Mayo"* (Movement for Popular Unity "May 29")
OB "Tupac Amaru"	*Organización Barrial "Tupac Amaru"* (Neighborhood Organization "Tupac Amaru")
PAC	*Programa de Aceleração do Crescimento* (Growth Acceleration Program [Brazil])
PCA	*Partido Comunista de la Argentina* (Communist Party of Argentina)
PC-CE	*Partido Comunista – Congreso Extraordinario* (Communist Party – Extraordinary Congress)
PCR	*Partido Comunista Revolucionario* (Communist Revolutionary Party)
PEC	*Programa de Empleo Comunitario* (Community Employment Program)
PEL	*Programa de Emergencia Laboral* (Labor Emergency Program)
PI	*Portaria Interministerial* (Interministerial Ordinance [Brazil])

PJ	*Partido Justicialista* (Justicialist Party)
PJJHD	*Programa Jefes y Jefas de Hogar Desocupados* (Unemployed Heads of Household Program)
PO	*Polo Obrero* (Workers' Pole)
PR	*Peronismo Revolucionario* (Revolutionary Peronism)
PRO	*Propuesta Republicana* (Republican Proposal)
PRT-ERP	*Partido Revolucionario de los Trabajadores – Ejército Revolucionario del Pueblo* (Revolutionary Workers' Party – People's Revolutionary Army)
PSOL	*Partido Socialismo e Liberdade* (Socialism and Freedom Party [Brazil])
PT	*Partido dos Trabalhadores* (Workers' Party [Brazil])
SEOM	*Sindicato de Empleados y Obreros Municipales* (Union of Municipal Workers and Employees)
SERPAJ	*Servicio de Paz y Justicia* (Peace and Justice Service)
SMO	social movement organization
SRA	*Sociedad Rural Argentina* (Argentina Rural Society)
UCR	*Unión Cívica Radical* (Radical Civic Union)
UGTT	*Unión General de Trabajadores del Transporte* (Transport Workers General Union)
UNDP	United Nations Development Program
UOM	*Unión Obrera Metalúrgica* (Metallurgy Workers' Union)
UTD of Mosconi	*Unión de Trabajadores Desocupados de Mosconi* (Union of Unemployed Workers of Mosconi)
YPF	*Yacimientos Petrolíferos Fiscales* (Treasury Petroleum Fields)

PART I

THEORETICAL FRAMEWORK

I

Introduction: A Theory for the Popular Sectors' Quest for Inclusion in Latin America

"We want to return to factories. We said to the [national Labor] Ministry that we are socialists; that we question the private ownership of the means of production; that we struggle for a workers' state – but that we won't wait for the revolution to return to the job market. We want to be exploited by a capitalist again."
– Néstor Pitrola, national *piquetero* leader of the Trotskyist Workers' Pole social movement organization (*La Nación*, April 6, 2004)

What did it take to bring a key national Trotskyist leader to demand that the government allow workers to be exploited by capitalists *again*? Although it may seem contradictory at first glance, this social movement leader's request was the logical result of the effects of neoliberal reforms on Latin American politics and society. Neoliberalism has been defined as crucial to the reformulation of state–society relations in many parts of the world.[1] In Latin America, neoliberal reforms have also caused the socio-political exclusion or *disincorporation* of the popular sectors[2] (cf. Tokman and O'Donnell 1998; Portes and Hoffmann 2003; Reygadas and Filgueira 2010). However, exclusion was intensely resisted by social movements mobilizing the popular sectors, such as the landless peasants in Brazil, the indigenous in Bolivia and Ecuador, and the unemployed in

[1] For a discussion of the multiple dimensions that compose the definition of "neoliberalism," cf. Lee Mudge (2008), and about the crucial differences between neoliberalism in the Global South and the North-West, cf. Connell and Dados (2014).

[2] This book uses the terms "popular sectors," "workers," "laborers," and "urban/rural poor" interchangeably to refer to the poor and/or marginalized strata in society, which in Spanish is commonly rendered as *sectores populares*.

Argentina (Almeida 2007; Ondetti 2008; Silva 2009; Becker 2011), contributing to a resurgence of the left.

A growing body of literature has examined the turn toward leftist governments in the region in the past ten years (Panizza 2009; Cameron and Hershberg 2010; Weyland et al. 2010; Levitsky and Roberts 2011). Some scholars associate what might be considered as the end of neoliberalism with the accession to power of left-wing or populist parties in Argentina, Bolivia, Brazil, Ecuador, Uruguay, and Venezuela in the 1990s and 2000s (Grugel and Riggirozzi 2009, 2012). While the accession to power of left-wing or populist parties seems to lead to the implementation of inclusionary policies (Huber and Stephens 2012), as yet there has been no systematic study of how this has played out. In order to accomplish such a study, we need to add extra layers of empirical detail and theoretical density to the "left turn" thesis to explain the complexity of the macro-process of transformation in Latin America's socio-political arena and how it relates to the capacity of poor people's movements to influence the political agenda to include their interests.[3]

In the quest to empirically trace the historical path that gives sense to demands such as the one quoted at the beginning of this chapter, this book addresses the following questions: How did the struggle from below contribute to the halt of neoliberalism in part of Latin America? And how has the socio-political arena been expanded to include the interests of the poor and excluded strata of society? The starting point for the answer this book offers is to put poor people's movements into the long-term perspective of the societal transformations produced by neoliberalism. We still need to learn more about the relationship between macro-processes of transformation and social movements (McAdam et al. 2001).

This book proposes an explanation for the major process of transformation behind the Latin American left turn: *the second wave of incorporation of the popular sectors*. For "second wave of incorporation" I mean the second major redefinition of the socio-political arena, caused by the broad and selective inclusion of the popular sectors in the polity after being excluded or disincorporated by military authoritarian regimes and democratic neoliberal reforms. The second wave of incorporation is the result of the accumulation of transformations that were carried out to deal with the contentious struggle for reincorporation by the popular sectors,

[3] The concept of "poor people's movement" is used following the original definition of Piven and Cloward (1979) and interchangeably with "popular movement," its equivalent for the Latin American tradition in social movement studies.

organized in territorialized social movements. The emergence of left-wing or populist parties in government is one of the by-products of two decades of struggle against disincorporation.[4]

This book presents a relational study of twenty years of a poor people's movement's pressure for inclusion and the state mechanisms for institutional change that this pressure has produced. I conceptualize the dynamics of the popular sectors' struggle for their reincorporation into the socio-political arena and analyze the role played by the main political actor related to this historical process in Argentina, the *piquetero* (picketer) movement. Given that the *piqueteros* emerged as a by-product of the transformations caused by neoliberalism, this movement of unemployed people represents a paradigmatic case of a specific type of movement I will conceptualize in this chapter: the *reincorporation movement*. This definition considers the *piquetero* movement as part of a long-term quest on the part of the poor people of Argentina for socio-political participation in the polity.

The *piquetero* movement is a key case for social movement scholars as well as students of Latin American politics because it represents the largest movement of unemployed people in the contemporary world.[5] The *piqueteros* was the main national social movement in the struggle to shape a post-neoliberal arena in Argentina.[6] Since 1996, the *piquetero* movement

[4] When dealing with "(re)incorporation" as a concept, I am following Collier and Collier (1991) rather than social movement scholars' conceptualization of this term (Giugni 1998a). This is because rather than considering incorporation as an immediate outcome of social movement struggles, I understand it – like Luna and Filgueira (2009) and Reygadas and Filgueira (2010) – as a Latin American macro-historical process.

[5] Reiss and Perry (2011) offer several historical examples of other unemployed workers' movements.

[6] I follow the definition of post-neoliberalism proposed by Grugel and Riggirozzi (2012: 3–4): "we understand it to embody a different conceptualization of the state from that which reigned in the high period of neoliberalism, based on a view that states have a moral responsibility to respect and deliver the inalienable (that is, not market-dependent) rights of their citizens (see Almeida and Johnston 2006: 7) alongside growth. Politically, post-neoliberalism is a reaction against what came to be seen as excessive marketization at the end of the twentieth century and the elitist and technocratic democracies that accompanied market reforms. ... It is, as such, part of an unfinished debate over what constitutes the transition to democracy (Peruzzotti 200[5]: 209). But changes to the portfolio of state responsibilities and a vision of a more equal distribution of national income sit alongside strong continuities from the recent past, in particular the retention of the export axis and commitment to a degree of fiscal restraint that are seen as essential for economic stability. ... Crucially, in much of Latin America it is emerging in the context of an unprecedented export bonanza that permits the adoption of more expansive public spending than has been the case since the 1980s."

has mobilized the poor and unemployed people of Argentina, providing organizational structure to their quest to end neoliberalism and see themselves incorporated into a more inclusive and equal society. Moreover, this movement influenced national politics to such an extent that it became part of the governing coalition. This is the first time that a movement made up of unemployed people has come to occupy such a central position in Latin American politics.

This book offers an analysis and conceptualization of the dynamics of the second incorporation in Argentina: from the emergence of the *piquetero* movement as a means of resisting the social, economic, and political exclusion of the poor in the 1990s to the development – partially as a result of this movement – of a series of policies enabling the partial inclusion of the poor into the socio-political arena in the 2000s. To do so, this analysis applies a qualitative process-tracing method based on the triangulation of interviews with key actors, newspaper data, and archival material to study the process (the second wave of incorporation) and actor (the reincorporation movement) that have partially reshaped the socio-political arena in Argentina, and perhaps elsewhere in the region.

This book links historical institutionalism and social movement studies to improve our relational analyses of social movements as part of macro-processes of socio-political change. On the one hand, I introduce the importance of considering timing and sequence as a manifestation of the thoroughness required by historical institutionalism (Aminzade 1992; Pierson 2000, 2004; Sewell 2005, 2008) that supplies the need – as claimed by some scholars – for dynamic studies of social movements (Tilly 1995, 2004; McAdam et al. 2001; Tilly and Tarrow 2006). On the other hand, the second incorporation process included the re-routinization of rules and procedures. Based on institutions and practices of the previous context, on the movement side the second incorporation process was built through the use of a predominant repertoire of strategies, which transcended contentious politics and implied mid- and long-term goals (conceptualized in Chapter 2). In Argentina, this happened within a mostly trade unionist strategy in combination with other strategies coming from left-wing traditions. To analyze and conceptualize the historical process of strategy making and performing of social movements we need to recover the school of historical analysis of Charles Tilly while at the same time escaping from the structuralist trap of most macro studies. In other words, the concepts I will propose in Chapter 2 provide us with the elements for studying in detail how social movements' strategies differ from or coincide with the ones of the elites and also enrich the social movement literature by contributing elements for studying what happens when contentious politics is not taking place.

This book builds on and expands previous studies of the neoliberal period in Latin America (Cavarozzi and Garretón 1989; Oxhorn 1998; Roberts 2002, 2008; Almeida 2014) by outlining what happened after the period of resistance to recommodification ended. It also complements the analyses of post-neoliberalism that have focused on trade unions (Etchemendy and Collier 2007), political parties (Levitsky and Roberts 2011; Flores-Macías 2012; Roberts 2013), and community organizations and NGOs (Collier and Handlin 2009a), along with the role played by social movements (Auyero 2003; Lucero 2008; Burdick et al. 2009; Silva 2009).

The main argument of this book is that, between 1996 and 2009, the Argentine socio-political arena was reshaped according to non-corporatist logic. Neoliberal reforms, carried out under authoritarian and democratic regimes as of the 1970s, had led to the gradual disincorporation of the popular sectors from the political and socioeconomic arenas. This consequence of the neoliberal program led to the emergence in the 1990s of the *piqueteros*, a movement of unemployed people seeking a halt to neoliberal reforms and reincorporation into the socio-political arena. However, transformations were not immediate. The state responded to the challenge posed by the *piquetero* movement with some innovations in policing at protest events but also with incremental changes and additions to social policies addressing some of the *piqueteros*' demands. In other words, the state identified a new "social question" as a result of the protests of the *piqueteros*, devising institutional responses in a bid to calm social unrest. The dynamics of interaction between claims for reincorporation and the accumulation of gradual changes on the part of the state to deal with the new "social question" were the elements that two decades later led to the rise of post-neoliberalism in Argentina.

However, this second wave of incorporation was not done through the trade union system as it had been in the 1940s but through the legitimation of a new political actor, the *piqueteros* – a territorially organized movement. As a result, once the *piqueteros* succeeded in stopping neoliberal policies, a portion of the movement began to participate in the governing coalitions.

Why does this book propose a dynamic analysis of a social movement rather than a structuralist analysis to study a macro-process like the second wave of incorporation? Because, for both periods of incorporation, the interactions of the actors involved unfolded in a pattern that led to long-term consequences and effects that – in many cases – had not been foreseen *a priori*. However, this book does not propose a path-dependent argument: on the contrary, agency, in particular from below, is the crucial explanatory element for the second wave of incorporation in Argentina, and – as analyzed in Chapter 8 – also elsewhere. In Argentina, governmental decisions were important, but much less than what could be expected from a study that primarily focuses on the elites.

Each historical period has been associated with different types of popular movements leading the efforts for social change. During the liberal period (1870s–1930s) that preceded the first incorporation in Latin America (1930s–50s), the labor and/or peasant movements were the main organizers of the popular sectors in their claim for well-being through reform or revolution. For the second incorporation (2000s–10s), a different type of movement emerged in Latin America during the neoliberal period (1970s–90s) as the central popular actor in the drive to reverse the exclusionary consequences of authoritarianism and neoliberalism and claim the reincorporation of the popular sectors as citizens and wage-earners. The emergence of what I define as the "reincorporation movement" – a type of movement that has built upon, but also decentered, labor-based actors – is the result of important transformations that took place in the socio-political arena between the two waves of incorporation of the popular sectors.

THE TWO WAVES OF INCORPORATION OF THE POPULAR SECTORS

In Argentina, the first incorporation was a corporatist process that unfolded between 1943 and 1955.[7] It involved a combination of the mobilization of popular claims by the labor movement at the factory level and the application of populist Peronist party policies for channeling these claims into corporatist institutions.[8] The first incorporation in

[7] "Corporatism can be defined as a system of interest representation in which the constituent units are organized into a limited number of singular, compulsory, non-competitive, hierarchically ordered and functionally differentiated categories, recognized or licensed (if not created) by the state and granted a deliberate representational monopoly within their respective categories in exchange for observing certain controls on their selection of leaders and articulation of demands and supports" (Schmitter 1974: 93–94).

[8] Briefly, Peronism is the national-populist movement that first incorporated workers into the nation's politics. The establishment of the dominant labor tradition in Argentina is intimately related to the Peronist movement. Peronism has an emblem, a hymn, and a stable of intellectuals and is the hegemonic popular political culture of the Argentine poor

Argentina (and Latin America) has been defined as "[t]he first sustained and at least partially successful attempt by the state to legitimate and shape an institutionalized labor movement" (Collier and Collier 1991: 783).[9] This was done through the gradual creation of social policies for addressing the claims of the increasingly unionized popular sectors. The origins of first incorporation may be traced to the collapse of economic and political liberalism, the ruin of the western European and US economies in the 1930s, and decades of accumulated protests for inclusion by popular movements across most of Latin America since the late nineteenth century (Piven and Cloward 1979; Collier and Collier 1991; French 1992; Hobsbawm 1994; Botana and Gallo 1997; Gotkowitz 2007; Kurtz 2013).

The second incorporation was a territorially based process that happened between 2002 and 2009 after an extended period of disincorporation of the popular sectors. This new wave originated from the inherited institutions and actors of the first incorporation. In addition, the two waves of incorporation were *partial* and *selective*, redefining the relationship between the popular sectors and the state. Like the first, the second incorporation was a predominantly urban and industrial process; rural peasants, of marginal relevance in Argentine national politics, were not included. However, in this second wave, the main actor mobilizing the claims of the poor and excluded was the *piquetero* movement, organizing the disincorporated popular sectors at the territorial level. A Peronist party was again in charge of developing the policies for channeling these new claims, but in this case, they were not the old corporatist institutions but new or reformulated institutions conceived in response to the territorialized nature of the claims that emerged with the *piqueteros* and as a result of the weakening of corporatism caused by neoliberalism.

Incorporation waves represent major and prolonged historical processes of struggle among socioeconomic and political groups for the expansion or reduction of the socio-political arena. In analytical terms, I define the second incorporation process as sharing the same basic requisites identified by Collier and Collier (1991: 783) for the first

since the 1940s (Germani 1973; Brennan 1988; James 1988; Torre 1990; Auyero 2000; Plotkin 2003; Karush and Chamosa 2010; Rossi 2013a).

9 This process was not exclusive to Argentina. In Brazil, the first incorporation was done for demobilization purposes, while in Bolivia, Venezuela, and – mainly – Argentina, incorporation implied the mobilization of the labor movement. In Bolivia and Venezuela, the first incorporation also included peasants, and in Ecuador, incorporation was done by a military reformist regime with a weak labor movement (Collier and Collier 1991; French 1992; Klein 2003; Yashar 2005; Gotkowitz 2007).

TABLE 1.1 *Historical Sequence of Stages in the Popular Sectors' Struggle for Incorporation in Argentina, 1915–2009*

Years	Stage
1915–43	Reform
1943–55	Party corporatist incorporation
1955–62	Aftermath – Heritage – Coup
1962–76	Equilibrium/ Zero-sum game
1976–96	Coup – Disincorporation
1996–2002	Recognition – Legitimation
2002–9	Party territorial reincorporation

Sources: The stages for the period 1915–62 were taken from Collier and Collier (1991). Reproduced from Rossi (2015b).

incorporation process: it "occurs in relatively well defined policy periods, which we frequently refer to as the 'incorporation period'. These periods emerge as part of a larger program of political and economic reform ... " If we apply this long-term perspective to the analysis of poor people's movements, the historical sequence of stages in the popular sectors' struggle for incorporation in Argentina can be synthesized as shown in **Table 1.1**. While according to Collier and Collier (1991: 22, figure 0.1) the initial incorporation process in Argentina followed a logic of Reform – Incorporation – Aftermath – Heritage – Coup, I suggest the following as the logic of the second incorporation process: Disincorporation – Recognition – Legitimation – Reincorporation.

Rather than a linear understanding of the progress of society, the Machiavellian recursive logic of history is the one that better grasps the dynamic of the eternal reshaping of the polity. The historical process of the first incorporation in Argentina is not the focus of this book, as this has already been successfully analyzed by Collier and Collier (1991). This book focuses on the historical continuation of what these authors studied, that is, the stages that compose the second wave of incorporation: from neoliberal disincorporation to the recognition of the claim for reincorporation (Chapter 3), the struggle for legitimation of the reincorporation movement as a new political actor (Chapter 4), and the second incorporation phase (Chapters 5 and 6). However, the advances (1943–55), stalemates (1962–76), and setbacks (1976–96) of the popular sectors' quest for inclusion in Argentine politics that link the first and second incorporations should be viewed as stages of the same historical process.

The "Social Question" Then and Now

As part of the recurring dynamics of incorporation, both waves had some elements in common in terms of the steps leading to incorporation. Both incorporation periods were preceded by a (neo)liberal phase that created a new "social question." This "social question" in both cases evolved into a *political* question with a contentious actor that was gradually recognized and legitimated. In the 1990s and 2000s, the emergence of recommodification and marginalization (unemployment, impoverishment, exclusion, etc.) as a new "social question," the modification of policing techniques, and the creation of massive social programs can be seen as a process equivalent to that of the pre-incorporation dynamics. Between the 1870s and the 1930s, anarchists, syndicalists, and socialists posing the "social question" pushed the elites to create anti-immigration and security laws (Isuani 1985; Suriano 1988) to recognize the claim to social rights and later the actor behind this new claim, the labor movement (Suriano 2000). Concerning social policies, the first-wave process, begun in 1935, eventually led to the creation of the Secretariat of Employment and Social Security in 1943 (Gaudio and Pilone 1983, 1984) and, later, the enactment of comprehensive social rights policies and constitutional reform before ending in 1955.[10] During the second wave, the process led to the creation of the Ministry of Social Development in 1999 and the establishment of wide-ranging cash-transfer policies and universal citizenship income rights policies, mainly since 2002.[11]

These transformations do not imply that the relationship between popular movements and the elites have been harmonious. The first incorporation divided movements, some supporting governments, while others becoming critical or even suffering persecution and repression. In the first wave, the labor movement maintained a conflictive relationship with Juan

10 Furthermore, Collier and Collier (1991: 155) argue that the connection between the period of 1935–43 and the later labor populism incorporation of 1943–55 under the first two Perón governments is "that the 'institutionalization' of this state role did not occur until Perón period – though Perón's policies should definitively be viewed as the product of a progressive 'sedimentation' of these earlier informal practices [of the process]."

11 The Ministry of Social Development existed during the aftermath and coup stages of the first incorporation as the Ministry of Social Welfare or Social Action, from 1966 (the start of Juan Carlos Onganía's authoritarian regime) to the end of 1982. Before this, from 1955 it had been a subsidiary division of the Ministry of Health. With the neoliberal disincorporation phase and redemocratization, the Ministry of Social Welfare was again downgraded to a secretariat, until 1999 when the Ministry of Social Development was restored in response to the *piqueteros*' struggles for reincorporation (Chapters 4, 5, and 6).

Domingo Perón's governments in Argentina (James 1988).[12] This holds also true for the second wave of incorporation. The question of how to deal with the Néstor Kirchner (2003–7) and Cristina Fernández de Kirchner (2007–15) Peronist administrations divided the *piquetero* movement into one sector that was supportive of them and another that was critical.[13] However, this is just half of the story. Cooperation with, and participation in, the coalition in government was very important, with thousands of middle- and lower-ranking members of social movements coming to office, most of them in secondary roles in state departments related to social policies (Chapter 6).

While these parallels allow us to talk about two waves of incorporation, they do not mean that history has repeated itself. There are elements of iteration and innovation in a process that is, as such, like a collage. Some crucial differences with the second incorporation are a consequence of the effects produced by the disincorporation phase (1976–96). These distinctive characteristics must be considered as defining the dynamics of the second incorporation as unique and different from the first incorporation, while the similar characteristics are the product of the historical heritage of the first incorporation. The conditions of the second incorporation that are similar to those of the first are the lack of any regulatory system (laws, institutions, etc.) for the new political actor and thus the lack of a routinized formal or informal mechanism for dealing with the specific "social question" of the reincorporation struggle in Argentina: in the case of the second, the "*piquetero* question."

It is also important to bear in mind that waves of incorporation should be equated *not* with the constitution of a more equal society or the creation of a welfare state but rather with the reshaping of the sociopolitical arena by redefining and expanding the number of legitimate political actors. In some countries, the urban and rural poor were first incorporated into very unequal societies, as in Brazil under Getúlio Vargas (Cardoso 2010), while in other countries, a more equal society and some

[12] In Brazil rural incorporation was also conflictive (Welch 1999), while trade unions resisted some of the control mechanisms associated with urban incorporation (French 1992). In Bolivia, Gotkowitz (2007) argues that peasants and indigenous movements were very important in building the conditions for first incorporation but later were the main losers of incorporation policies during the Revolution of 1952.

[13] In Ecuador, the Confederation of Indigenous Nationalities of Ecuador (CONAIE) had a very conflictive relationship with Rafael Correa's government (Becker 2011), and the Rural Landless Workers Movement (MST) was disappointed with the modest advances of agrarian reform during the Luiz Inácio Lula da Silva and Dilma Rousseff presidencies (Chapter 8).

welfare policies emerged as a result of incorporation, as in Argentina under Perón (Torre and Pastoriza 2002).

From Neo-corporatism to Territorialism

There is another crucial distinction between the first and second incorporation waves, this one related to the path taken by the popular sectors in each historical moment. While the first incorporation was characterized by massive unionization and corporatist state arrangements, the second incorporation followed a territorialized logic that went hand in hand with an overall territorialization of Argentine politics.

The process of contemporary territorialization of politics in Argentina has its origins in the 1976–83 authoritarian regime as part of a failed attempt to gradually democratize from the local to the national level and the application of neoliberal fiscal decentralization policies (Prévôt-Schapira 1993; Falleti 2011). The increased territorialization of politics is intimately related to the provincial-centric nature of party politics (De Luca et al. 2002) that produced a political arena with territorially concentrated and personalized leaderships where local political programmatic agendas are more important than those at the national level (Calvo and Escolar 2005). For poor people's movements, territorialization means the centrality of "*basismo*" (organization of the popular sectors through territorially based grassroots assemblies) since its emergence in the 1960s (Prévôt-Schapira 1999).

Territorialization includes patronage and clientelism but is not a synonym of either. I define the territorialization of politics as the dispute for the physical control of space, be it a municipality, province, or portion of land, within one or more politically constituted entities. The territorialization of politics does not mean the emergence of a new regime type but rather the process through which the territory *re-emerges* as a new cleavage after neoliberal reforms and authoritarian regimes have weakened or dissolved neo-corporatist arrangements for the resolution of socio-political conflicts in society. It is a cleavage because central political divisions are produced as a result of the physical encounter of or distance between political actors and of the dispute for the control of a territory for socio-political goals and causes that are not always territorially defined. For this reason, what differentiates the political actors is not their ideology or class but rather their geographical location, modifying their alliances and "loyalties" based on the latter. In the intertwining of contentious and routine politics, territorialization refers to the spatial interfusion of the grassroots actors involved in the political struggle. For this reason, it is a crucial element of governability, the one which since the mid-1990s has been under the control of Peronist party and union organizations and disputed by the *piquetero* movement.

This second wave was "territorial" because the incorporation of the popular sectors was predominantly done through institutions created or reformulated for the articulation of actors that were *not* functionally differentiated. This was a result of the emergence of contentious claims for reincorporation outside the trade union system. Instead, urban and peri-urban land occupations, neighborhoods, and shantytowns became central spaces for claim-making for the organized poor people (Cerrutti and Grimson 2004; Merklen 2005) once neoliberal reforms and authoritarian regimes had weakened or dissolved neo-corporatist arrangements for resolving socio-political conflicts (Oxhorn 1998; Collier and Handlin 2009b). For this reason, the social policies to reincorporate the popular sectors were not function- or class-based but territory-based (i.e., defined by the physical location of the actors).[14] This was an important shift from the functionalist logic of corporatism, which had articulated the popular sectors' claims through trade unions as their sole representative actor and through the Ministry of Labor as their exclusive state department. To sum up, because they were not seen as serving a clear "function" for institutions with a corporatist logic, the disincorporated popular sectors were targeted by policies based on where they were located and the multiplicity of needs associated with their situation and not only as workers without jobs or peasants without land. However, that the second incorporation was mainly defined by territory-based logics did not mean that corporatist arrangements were abandoned altogether.

Consequently, the second incorporation path differed from the first because the government and the movement were not dealing with an inter-corporatist system of relations as they had done after the first incorporation. **Table 1.2** schematically synthesizes the main differences between both waves. As I will show in Chapters 3 to 6, the second incorporation in Argentina followed a multi-level game (local, provincial, national) of territorialized interactions. The specificities of the second incorporation are due to the disincorporation consequences of neoliberal reforms.

[14] For example, the social policies related to housing and habitat (Cravino 2013).

TABLE 1.2 *Main Differences between the First and Second Incorporation Waves in Argentina*

	First Incorporation (1943–55)	**Second Incorporation (1996–2009)**
Main type of state–popular sectors relationship	Neo-corporatist	Territorially based
Main political actor organizing the popular sectors	Labor movement	Reincorporation movement
Main national state department for the articulation of the claims for incorporation	Ministry of Labor	Ministry of Social Development

NEOLIBERAL DISINCORPORATION

The neoliberal reforms that started the process of recommodification of relations in the 1970s can be interpreted as a process of disincorporation, thereby redefining the main populist versus conservative political cleavage (Roberts 2002, 2008) as well as the roles of political actors involved in the first incorporation process of the 1950s. However, neoliberal disincorporation does not entail a total rupture with the past, as there are certainly elements of continuity.

In concrete terms, after the end of corporatist inclusion (1943–55), consolidated through the import substitution industrialization (ISI) model, Argentina went through a period of stalemate between the Peronist movement and the other political actors (O'Donnell 1973). This situation collapsed after the bureaucratic–authoritarian state model was imposed during the military regime of 1966–73 (O'Donnell 1988; Collier and Collier 1991), only to re-emerge after a short democratic spring (1973–76). Indeed, a new and more resolutely oppressive military coup in 1976 definitively initiated a disincorporation process by systematically applying repressive policies so as to demobilize the popular sectors and leftist groups – with the extrajudicial killing of thousands of activists – while concurrently dismantling the ISI model in favor of a more neoclassical, liberalized economy (Epstein 1987; Oxhorn 1998; Schvarzer 1998; Novaro and Palermo 2003).

Democratization in 1983 brought with it both pluralism and an expectation of the recovery of welfare through the relaunching of ISI. During Raúl Alfonsín's mandate (1983–89), representing the Radical Civic Union

(UCR), the Professional Associations Law was reformed, and this allowed the corporate structure of the Peronist General Labor Confederation (CGT) to be maintained and the labor confederation to reassert itself against other corporate structures, such as the Argentine Industrial Union, the Catholic Church, and the military. By the end of the Alfonsín presidency, the CGT had essentially maintained its monopoly of one union per industry, won back its rights to collective bargaining by sector, and regained control of its social welfare network. However, with the failure of the Austral economic stabilization plan, ISI was rapidly dismissed. At the same time, the Latin American debt crisis contributed to a 7.2 percent contraction of Argentina's economy between 1983 and 1985. The hyperinflation crisis of 1989–91 exacerbated the gravity of the situation (Smith et al. 1994; Acuña 1995; Saad-Filho et al. 2007: 10).

Beginning in 1991, a heterodox, neoliberal reform program was implemented during the presidency of Carlos Menem, of the Peronist Justicialist Party (PJ), with the urgent intention of resolving the hyperinflation crisis (Palermo and Novaro 1996). These reforms were applied in two stages. The first stage was to introduce stabilization policies to solve the debt and fiscal crises and hyperinflation. The focus was on the privatization of state-owned companies and the liberalization of ISI regulations, with a neoclassical economic perspective (Haggard and Kaufman 1995; Oszlak 2003). The second stage focused on the restructuring of the public sector through the decentralization and reformulation of social policies, moving from a universalist to an individualistic approach (Orlansky 1998; Oxhorn 1998; Tokman and O'Donnell 1998). Foremost among the mixed results of the neoliberal reforms in Argentina was a rapid phase of deindustrialization. Although in 1989, 31 percent of GDP was based on manufactured products, by 2001 the rate was just 17 percent (Saad-Filho et al. 2007: 24). This led to an increase in the number of precarious and informal types of labor arrangements and a more uneven distribution of income (Beccaria and López 1996; Altimir and Beccaria 2001; Portes and Hoffmann 2003); this was related to a concomitant increase in unemployment from a historical average of 5 percent to 18.4 percent in 1995 – with a peak of 21.5 percent in 2002.[15]

In Argentina, the labor movement has traditionally been strong and well organized by the Peronist movement. The collapse of ISI and its replacement by a neoliberal model strongly affected the link between the

[15] Statistics of the National Institute of Statistics and Censuses (INDEC) for 1974–2003 (www.indec.gob.ar/nuevaweb/cuadros/4/shempleo1.xls, viewed August 15, 2010).

main Peronist organizations and the popular sectors.[16] The same was true for equivalent labor-based movements elsewhere in the region.[17]

Neoliberalism was also related to the metamorphosis of the dominant labor-based party – Peronist PJ – into a clientelistic and patronage machine (McGuire 1997; Levitsky 2003b; Torre 2004: xiv). The state mechanisms for the resolution of societal conflicts were also redefined, from a corporatist regime with a hegemonic Peronist CGT to a pluralized, segmented corporatist system (Etchemendy and Collier 2007). A key change in the political arena was the emergence of the *piquetero* movement as a national political actor, mobilizing a growing constituency of disincorporated popular sectors as they struggled to recover their place in wage-earning society (Chapter 3).

THE STRUGGLE FOR REINCORPORATION

Neoliberal reforms have produced a change in the focus of protest in Latin America: since the 1980s it mainly occurs in the quest for recognition by the state (Delamata 2002; Auyero 2003). This quest for recognition is part of what I call the *struggle for (re)incorporation.*[18] I use this term because although most actors in this quest present discourses of radical societal transformation, those discourses have actually unfolded as types of collective action that can be deemed "bridging with the state" (apart from the

16 Several wide-ranging reforms affected labor relations and corporatist mechanisms; for a description of these reforms, cf. Cook (2007).

17 In this sense, Roberts (2002: 19) argues, "neoliberal critical junctures produced sharp discontinuities in the labor-mobilizing systems. More than a simple epiphenomenon of economic crisis, this discontinuity reflects the collapse of a mode of political organization and representation that was deeply embedded in the previous development model and is increasingly out of sync with the socioeconomic landscape carved out by the process of free-market reforms. The stratified (or at least semi-stratified) cleavage structures and corporatist organizational practices of labor-mobilizing systems have been undermined by the individualizing logic of the neoliberal era, eroding class cleavages ... "

18 Honneth (1995: 165) argues that "the models of conflict that start from collective feelings of having been unjustly treated are those that trace the emergence and the course of social struggles back to moral experiences of social groups who face having legal or social recognition withheld from them. In the first case, we are dealing with the analysis of competition for scarce goods, whereas in the second case, we are dealing with the analysis of a struggle over the intersubjective conditions for personal integrity." Hobson (2003), by contrast, contends that the materialistic struggle is neither detached from nor opposed to the struggle for recognition. Moreover, "Recognition struggles often involve making claims for resources, goods, and services through state policies ... But claims in recognition struggles are also connected to membership and inclusion in the polity" (Hobson 2003: 3).

unintended transformations produced by the incorporation of the actors). By "bridging with the state," I mean types of collective action that aim to (re)connect excluded segments of society with state institutions to recover – or, for the first time, gain – access to rights and benefits that the state has failed or ceased to secure or provide. The *piqueteros*' claim to unemployment subsidies, housing, and other benefits is an example of this "bridging" collective action because it reconnects the popular sectors with the state as a provider of some benefits and rights.

Much of the initial research conducted on the *piqueteros* came about because of interest in this "quest for recognition" from governments that had previously ignored the poor and unemployed. However, this literature has overlooked a crucial question: if the state is the main institution structuring social relations in a society, what exactly should movements challenge when the state reduces its structuring role? It seems that it is the absence of – or lack of due regard for – the structuring of certain types of social relations that movements must challenge. Protest is thus a substantial and moral tool for popular sectors to form a bridge between the state as it actually is and the state as it should be. In other words, what the *piqueteros* struggle for, like the landless peasants in Brazil, is the presence of the state as more than a merely repressive institution. In this sense, reincorporation struggles are linked in history to the heritage of the incorporation of the first laborers into the political arena. The consequences of the neoliberal reforms explain the demand for a return of the state presence as an articulator of social relationships.

So what differentiates recognition struggles from those for (re)incorporation? I argue that the two are intimately related. The pursuit of recognition might be defined as the initial quest linked to the popular sectors' disruptive emergence in protest. After some degree of recognition has been achieved (e.g., unemployment subsidies, media attention), the claim organized as a movement will usually lead to socioeconomic conflicts and the quest for incorporation. In societal terms, a popular sector's struggle for recognition might lead to a struggle for incorporation – or reincorporation – as a subject and member of society that merits esteem and is entitled to some of the rights that the (neoliberal) context has (abruptly) altered. In this sense, it is both a moral economy issue and a specific process attached to the constitution of the polity through its expansion or contraction.

Another reason for defining recognition and reincorporation as intimately linked struggles is that no quest for reincorporation can emerge without a prior claim for recognition; it is that first claim that constitutes a new "social question." However, the quest for recognition does not necessarily evolve into one for reincorporation, as it can be a goal in itself (e.g., claims for a multilingual society). In other words, when discussing popular sector movements, struggles for recognition should be considered as the first stage of the legitimation of both the claim and the actor. If organized into a movement, this process will evolve toward the dynamics of incorporation. The *piquetero* movement can be defined as a type of actor that is particular to the consequences of neoliberalism and one that is related to equivalent processes of disincorporation and reincorporation in Latin America since the 1980s.

Definition of Reincorporation Movements

Reincorporation movements share many of the longstanding characteristics of the popular sector movements' drive for social transformation through inclusion, by revolution or reform. At the same time, they have specific attributes that mark them as particular expressions of the historical process of struggle for incorporation that emerged with neoliberalism (at least in Latin America). As such, reincorporation movements use the repertoire of strategies and legacies accumulated in the initial incorporation period while pushing for the reestablishment of the tie between the popular sectors and the socio-political arena in the quest for reintegration into the polity. In Argentina, this tie reconstruction was executed through the intertwining of preexisting practices in a new scenario with somewhat different actors: a social movement (albeit heavily influenced by trade unionist practices) and a state prepared to deal only with already established neo-corporatist actors. This new context for the inherited repertoire led to the recycling of strategies with new claims; for example, trade union-style negotiations for food distribution (Chapter 2). A pattern of interaction between government and movement was thus established through new institutions or the redefinition of roles of existing institutions.

Therefore, "reincorporation movements" can be defined as a gestalt composed of six categories.[19] Two of these are central and universal, with

[19] For this conceptual proposal, I have followed the logic of Collier and Mahon (1993: 851, n. 8) for the formation of radial categories: "with radial categories it is possible that two members of the category will not share all of what may be seen as the defining attributes ... with radial categories the overall meaning of a category is anchored in a 'central subcategory,' which corresponds to the 'best' case, or prototype, of the category. In the process of cognition, the central subcategory functions as a gestalt, in that it is constituted

four subcategories that logically depend on the first two and must be adapted to each cluster of cases studied to explain more specific national or regional patterns. The two central categories in this definition of reincorporation movements are the following:

1. *Period of emergence.* These movements are by-products of the disincorporation process that started in the 1970s and a result of the crisis of party communities and mass-based labor parties set up in the 1980s and 1990s.[20]
2. *Demands.* Claims for inclusion predominate, even though these could be framed by the leaders as "revolutionary" in their long-term goals.[21]

Reincorporation movements are also defined by the following non-central categories, which can be seen to have these common attributes:

3. *Method and locus of protest.* Radical methods of protest, such as insurrectional direct actions, tend to be used, while the movements are contemporaneously open to negotiation with government. Their locus of protest is generally the territory.
4. *Leadership.* Leaders come mainly from trade unions, Christian-based communities, and former guerrilla organizations.
5. *Organizational format.* These movements are loose, territorialized networks of highly vertical organizations.

by a bundle of traits that are learned together, understood together, and most quickly recognized when found together. 'Non-central subcategories' are variants of the central one. They do not necessarily share defining attributes with each other but only with the central subcategory – hence the term radial, which refers to this internal structure" (Collier and Mahon 1993: 848).

[20] Manin (1992) defines the "crisis of party communities" as the metamorphosis of political representation. Representation changed from a form based on programmatic parties reflecting the concerns of social classes or communities to a more personality-based form of politics, in which a multidimensional society is represented through governing elites that attempt to interpret public opinion.

[21] This means that reincorporation movements can follow multiple goals simultaneously, but incorporation must be the main medium-term focus. The use of "revolutionary" (or other) rhetoric by movements struggling for the second incorporation of the popular sectors does not mean that movement leaders are confused or uncertain about movement goals. Instead, it means that a movement can be defined as a "reincorporation movement" by its relation to a macro-historical process of *dis-* or *re*incorporation, even though the main long-term goal for some organizations might be something else. Thus, following this definition, all movements that have struggled for the popular sectors' incorporation since neoliberal state reforms were applied can be defined as reincorporation movements, be this a short-, medium-, or long-term goal within "revolutionary," "reformist," or "conservative" rhetorical forms.

6. *Perception of democracy*. These movements make a positive re-evaluation of the value of democracy as a political regime, insofar as it is perceived as necessary and reforms are, in some cases, achieved by electoral means.

To summarize, the basic assumption underlying the historicist definition proposed here is that the second wave of incorporation is attached to the emergence of a specific type of political actor. Therefore, many movements are not of the reincorporation type because, even though they may share some of the non-central categories, they are not explained by at least one of the central categories. Examples of this are cultural or counter-cultural movements, environmental movements, anti-immigration or xenophobic movements, and separatist or pro-independence movements. The benefit of defining a type of movement as associated with a particular historical period in a region is that this (historical and geographical) context allows for conceptualizations that encompass the distinctiveness of these types of movements.

THE PIQUETEROS AND REINCORPORATION STRUGGLES IN ARGENTINA

Since 1996, the *piquetero* movement has mobilized the poor and unemployed people of Argentina. For almost two decades, the *piqueteros* has been the main contentious actor in the resistance to the social consequences of neoliberal reforms and in the struggle for the reincorporation of the popular sectors in Argentina's socio-political arena. The name "*piqueteros*" (picketers) is based on the type of protest action that brought the movement to the public's awareness: the picketing/blocking of the country's main roads in their demand for jobs, unemployment subsidies, food, etc.[22]

The *piqueteros*, as a collection of actors, fulfills all the basic requisites to be considered a social movement.[23] Since the emergence of the first

[22] As will be made clearer in Chapter 2, this does not mean that the *piquetero* movement only organizes pickets. Naming an actor after one of its ways of making a claim may seem confusing, but preserving in political and academic debates the name that is most well known and widely applied to this actor is a linguistically pragmatic choice to allow for a clear understanding of the movement being studied.

[23] I define a social movement as informal networks of conflict-oriented interactions composed of individuals, groups, and/or organizations that, based on shared solidarities, are provided with a collective political identity and use protest as a means – among others – to present themselves in the public arena (Melucci 1989; Diani 1992; della Porta and Diani 1999: 13–16; Snow et al. 2004: 3–15; Rossi 2006: 243–46).

unemployed workers' protests in Argentina, the movement has become increasingly organized as a network of conflict-oriented actors that almost two decades later continues to be active. As with any movement, the *piquetero* movement is composed of a number of social movement organizations (SMOs) (**Table 1.3**). The movement was founded by three main SMOs as part of a dynamic political network, their number expanding gradually over time (cf. Figures A and B in Appendix). The founding SMOs were the Guevarists and autonomists Unemployed Workers Movements (MTDs), the Maoist Classist and Combative Current (CCC), and the Liberation Theology-inspired Workers' Federation for Land, Housing and Habitat (FTV). Concerning identity, notwithstanding the disparity of ideologies held by the various SMOs that make up the movement, all participating SMOs recognize themselves (and are recognized by their opponents and allies) as part of a movement called "*piqueteros*" (cf. Svampa and Pereyra 2003: ch. 4), defined by the struggle of unemployed people for socio-political reincorporation as citizens and wage-earners. Finally, the use of protest is a constant and crucial dimension of this movement.

The relevance of this movement for Argentine politics placed it at the core of social movement studies for several years in Argentine academia. The pioneering studies of Scribano (1999), Oviedo (2000, 2004), Svampa and Pereyra (2003), and Auyero (2003) were mostly motivated by the search for explanations for the origin of the movement and its first decade of existence. However, the debate about the origin of the movement has failed to connect a long-term perspective on the quest for inclusion of poor people's movements of Argentina with the role of the left in national politics and the specific claims and grievances of the popular sectors in the 1990s (but see Benclowitcz 2013, for a study focusing on the North-East of Argentina). This will be one of the main goals of Chapter 3.

Like Oviedo in the two editions of his widely read book (2000, 2004), many other activist-scholars analyzed the *piqueteros* (Sánchez 1997; Alderete and Gómez 1999; Kohan 2002; MTD de Solano and Colectivo Situaciones 2002; Mazzeo 2004; Pacheco 2004; Flores 2005b, 2006). The importance of the FTV, CCC, and MTDs for the movement also prompted some interesting academic studies about the specificities of these SMOs (Calvo 2006; Torres 2006; Motta 2009), as well as about other cases, such as the Trotskyist Workers' Pole (PO) (Delamata 2004) and the indigenist Neighborhood Organization "Tupac Amaru" (hereafter OB "Tupac Amaru") (Battezzati 2012), among many others.

TABLE 1.3 *The* Piquetero *Movement (December 2008)*

Main Social Movement Organizations	Related Political Organizations	Ideology	Main Geographical Location (Province)
Classist and Combative Current (CCC)	Communist Revolutionary Party (PCR)	Maoist	Buenos Aires, Salta and Jujuy
Coordinator of Unemployed Workers (CTD) "Aníbal Verón"	Revolutionary Popular Movement (MPR) "Quebracho"	National-populist	Buenos Aires
"Evita" Movement	None	Left-wing Peronist	Buenos Aires
Independent Movement of the Retired and Unemployed (MIJD)	None	National-populist	Buenos Aires, Chaco and Salta
Jobless Movement "Teresa Is Alive" (MST "Teresa Vive")	Socialist Workers' Movement	Trotskyist	City of Buenos Aires
Neighborhood Organization (OB) "Tupac Amaru"	CTA since 2003	National-populist and indigenist	Jujuy and Mendoza
Popular Front "Darío Santillán" (FPDS)	None	Autonomist	Buenos Aires
Neighborhoods Standing Up (*Barrios de Pie*)	Free Homeland – Southerners' Freedom Movement	National-populist	Buenos Aires and Córdoba
Territorial Liberation Movement (MTL)	Communist Party of Argentina (PCA)	Marxist-Leninist	City of Buenos Aires
Union of Unemployed Workers (UTD) of Mosconi	None	Syndicalist	Salta
Unemployed Workers Movement (MTD) "Aníbal Verón"	Guevarist Movement	Guevarist	Buenos Aires
Unemployed Workers Movement (MTD) of La Juanita	Civic Coalition – Alliance for a Republic of Equals (CC–ARI) since 2007	Social-democratic	Buenos Aires
Unemployed Workers Movement (MTD) of Solano and allies	None	Autonomist	Buenos Aires and Río Negro
Unemployed Workers' Movement "Teresa Rodríguez" (MTR) – Neighborhood Unity Coordinator (CUBa)	Guevarist Movement and Liberation Revolutionary Party	Guevarist and Trotskyist	Buenos Aires
Workers' Federation for Land, Housing and Habitat (FTV)	Argentine Workers Union (CTA) until 2006	Liberation Theology and national-populist	Buenos Aires and Santa Fe
Workers' Pole (PO)	Workers' Party	Trotskyist	Buenos Aires and Salta

Source: Adapted from Rossi (2013b).

In their struggle for reincorporation, the *piqueteros* needed to deal with a wide array of actors, such as elected and appointed public officials, informal party and union brokers, the police, churches, and NGOs. Some authors presented studies of politics in the shantytowns and neighborhoods where the *piqueteros* have been disputing power with other political groups (Auyero 2003; Ferraudi Curto 2006; Quirós 2006) as part of a well-developed Argentine tradition of ethnographic research of politics from below. As these studies and others show (Pereyra et al. 2008; Rossi 2015b), the struggle of the *piquetero* movement cannot be explained through co-optation- or clientelism-based accounts of *piquetero*–government interactions; the process is more complex than these may suggest. This is confirmed by all quantitative research done to date, which concedes – though to varying degrees – that the gains in state social programs achieved by the *piqueteros* were more a result of protest than anything else (Lodola 2005; Weitz-Schapiro 2006; Giraudy 2007; Franceschelli and Ronconi 2009). I take this up in Chapters 4, 5, and 6, where I demonstrate that the relational pattern of reincorporation is a multi-level process that is based on two main elements: the evolution of public policies and the territorially based disputes between the movement and other political actors.

The accession to power of many leaders and grassroots members of the *piquetero* movement in the 2010s has sparked a new (and still developing) line of studies analyzing what has happened with the *piqueteros* in government (Massetti 2009; Perelmiter 2012; Pérez and Natalucci 2012). However, very few of the studies about the *piqueteros* published to date have been in English (Auyero 2003; Alcañiz and Scheier 2007; Wolff 2007; Motta 2009), and none has yet proposed a process-tracing analysis of the macro-process of transformation associated with the *piqueteros*. This book is an attempt to fill the gap of the macro question in the scholarship on the *piqueteros*.

THEORETICAL CONTRIBUTIONS FOR SOCIAL MOVEMENT STUDIES

Chapter 2 presents the second main theoretical contribution of this book. Although dialogue between social movement scholars and historical institutionalists is quite rare (but see Aminzade et al. 2001), I draw on both literatures in my analysis of the macro-process of second incorporation. In doing so, I contribute to a promising cross-fertilization between these approaches. In social movement studies, there is a tendency to apply concepts created in specific contexts in a universal manner (Goodwin and Jasper 2012). This standpoint sometimes produces conceptual stretching that a more historically grounded approach, such as that favored by historical institutionalism, would avoid. By contrast, historical institutionalism has a tendency to produce structurally determinist studies that do not acknowledge human agency until rational choice is added into the analysis (Mahoney and Thelen 2010: 6–8). Combining the two approaches takes advantage of the empirically and conceptually rich debates on collective action within the social movement literature and allows for the preservation of the historical focus of historical institutionalism while avoiding the pitfalls of determinist structuralism and rational choice. In this same sense, Thelen (1999: 388) argues that institutions are enduring legacies of political struggles, and Pierson (2000) says that relatively small or contingent events may have far-reaching consequences. This is particularly important when analyzing how pressure from popular movements might have prompted changes to social policies and policing techniques.

The historical institutionalists that study Latin America (Collier and Collier 1991; Mahoney 2001; Roberts 2002, 2008) provide social movement scholars with long-term historical contextualization of contentious and routine dynamics performed by social movements that is generally overlooked by scholars of contentious political dynamics. In this way, social movements can be placed against a long-term historical background, as called for by Tilly (1984, 2008)[24] and as I proposed with my definition of reincorporation movements.

The social movement literature is the best suited for avoiding the structuralist trap of theory-guided narratives. However, while the introduction of contentious political dynamics into routine politics (and vice versa) can enrich the literature on historical institutionalism, the scholarship on social movements considers that the definition of the relationship between contentious and routine politics is still underdeveloped (Aminzade et al. 2001; Auyero 2003, 2007; Goldstone 2003; Tarrow

[24] "We should build concrete and historical analyses of the big structures and large processes that shape our era. The analyses should be concrete in having real times, places, and people as their referents and in testing the coherence of the postulated structures and processes against the experiences of real times, places and peoples. They should be historical in limiting their scope to an era bounded by the playing out of certain well-defined processes, and in recognizing from the outset that time matters – that *when* things happen within a sequence affects *how* they happen, that every structure or process constitutes a series of choice points. Outcomes at a given point in time constrain possible outcomes at later points in time" (Tilly 1984: 14; italics in original).

2012). In this sense, Tilly's (1986, 1995, 2006, 2008) concept of "repertoire of contention" has allowed us to study public and disruptive events and their slow pace of change as part of what is known as "contentious politics." However, when studying the interaction of the *piqueteros* or any social movement with the state, allies, and antagonists, the public and contentious dimension of this interaction is just one part of the story. There are many other strategic activities performed by social movements as part of their effort to influence political decisions that are not contentious and public. In Chapter 2, I propose two concepts for the study of social movements' strategic interactions with the state. In doing so I aim to help bridge contentious and routine politics, linking events that happen in the public arena with those happening in semi-public and private arenas. To complement Tilly's "repertoire of contention," I propose the concepts of "repertoire of strategies" and "stock of legacies." These two concepts are important because they correspond to the element of agency that is part of the macro-historical process of second incorporation. Together, the first two chapters of this book present my joining of the structure-based approach of historical institutionalism with the agency-based approach of social movement studies. Chapter 2 closes with a synthesis of the main strategies used by the *piquetero* movement from 1996 to 2009.

In a Tillyian relational approach to social change, the strategies of movements are also linked to what is happening with the elites. The best suited concept for analyzing this from a social movement perspective is Tarrow's (1994) concept of political opportunities.[25] I apply this concept framed within a broader debate about the configuration of the political context, with the hope of avoiding some of the universalizing stretching tendencies in the literature (McAdam 1982, 1996; Tarrow 1994, 1998; Goodwin and Jasper 1999, 2012; Meyer and Minkoff 2004). In my use of Tarrow's definition, the concept of political opportunities refers specifically to the less stable, more dynamic, and eventful shifts and changes of the political context. As Gamson and Meyer (1996: 283) argue, the relatively more stable elements of the context delimit the arena where a series of actors engage in struggles and try to define the opportunities. Therefore, a divided elite creates an opportunity for movements but also affects the intensity of elite divisions and

[25] Defined as "consistent – but not necessarily formal or permanent – dimensions of the political environment that provide incentives for people to undertake collective action by affecting their expectations for success or failure" (Tarrow 1994: 18).

TABLE 1.4 *Horizontal and Vertical Political Opportunities*

Political Opportunities	Definition	Example
Horizontal	Divisions across functions/actors within the same scale of action.	Single-level dispute between national ministries of the same governing coalition over who will control a policy area.
Vertical	Divisions across scales of action (multi-level).	Multi-level dispute between the national cabinet, the governorship, and local authorities in the same district for the resolution of a conflictive issue.

intra-elite conflicts, which result from horizontal (*intra*-scalar) and vertical (*inter*-scalar) political opportunities (schematically shown in **Table 1.4**). Political opportunities are crucial for understanding the interplay between actors within specific configurations of the political context. Horizontal and vertical political opportunities generally work together, but it is not uncommon for them to branch into different and sometimes contradictory directions. In brief, actors making use of a predominant repertoire of strategies (Chapter 2) are the contenders that struggle for resources, positions, and the redefinition of the issues being disputed, producing and dealing with intra-elite functional and/or multi-level junctural divisions.

METHODOLOGICAL MATTERS AND SOURCES

In his short story "Del rigor en la ciencia," Jorge Luis Borges (1996 [1960]: 119) puts forth the idea that it is impossible for the human sciences to analytically reconstruct the world because this would imply the reproduction of the world itself. In this story, the attempt of cartographers to construct the most detailed map of an entire empire in all its dimensions represents not only a task that is impossible to achieve but also one that will always produce an outdated result. Any reconstruction of the world is a reconstruction of a world *as it was*. As such, any analytic historical reconstruction represents an incomplete assemblage of events based on selective memory. Continuing along these lines, could it be said that history is but the sequence of events selected by actors when reconstructing a story? This question emerged when I was faced with the challenge of historically reconstructing the *piquetero* movement. Having read some of the literature produced about them, the *piqueteros* and some movement's antagonists have come across accounts of their own stories. Is the overlap between the accounts actors give of themselves and the subsequent academic production a result of the actors' interpretation of the research about themselves, or do the actors redefine their story as they read their own history? I recur to methodological triangulation in order to avoid the excessive thoroughness of the Borgean imperial cartographers in attempting to solve this puzzle. As the aim of this research is also historical, I provide a detailed account of some of the forgotten voices in narrating this crucial process in recent Argentine politics.

I used several data sources for my research. I consulted around 2,000 newspaper articles and archival material collected from 27 commercial and alternative newspapers and magazines, publications produced by the SMOs, websites of the movement and related institutions, quantitative data on protest events, and interviews with the main actors involved. The mass-media commercial sources were collected at the *Página/12* newspaper archive in Buenos Aires.

An important part of the data collection for this research is the forty open-ended, in-depth interviews that I carried out with almost all the main *piquetero* leaders and key state brokers in the *piquetero* public policy domain – mayors, ministries, informal brokers, and so on. These interviews, which lasted between one and a half and four hours each, were conducted in situ in the cities of Buenos Aires (the national capital) and La Plata (the capital of Buenos Aires province) as well as in some Greater Buenos Aires districts (Florencio Varela, La Matanza, Quilmes, and Tres de Febrero) over four fieldwork periods: June–October 2007, September–October 2008, December 2008, and July–August 2013. The focus of this research was the city of Buenos Aires and its suburban periphery because this is where the *piquetero* movement has mostly been concentrated: it is only in Buenos Aires that the *piquetero* movement has become a national actor with relevant links with the state, with the exception of the pioneering Union of Unemployed Workers (UTD) of Mosconi in Salta and also, since 2003, the OB "Tupac Amaru" in Jujuy.[26] The fieldwork periods also included direct observation of

[26] Herrera (2008: 183, table 11) has quantitatively shown how between 1991 and 2002 the main sites for *piquetero* protests were the Buenos Aires, Salta, Santa Fe, Neuquén, and Río Negro provinces. Studies by the *Centro de Estudios para la Nueva Mayoría* show that in 2006, 30 percent of all pickets were staged in Buenos Aires (Chapter 3).

protest events, visits to SMO branches, and participation in movement assemblies and public governmental meetings.

I used purposive sampling as the method for selecting the persons to be interviewed. This method was used because of the relatively small number of actors with the relevant knowledge and expertise as well as crucial political positioning for the aims of this research. Starting from these sources, the sample was expanded through snowballing until I had covered almost the totality of the *piquetero* national SMOs, allies, and crucial state brokers at the national and provincial level (Buenos Aires) and in the main two local sites of contention (the Florencio Varela and La Matanza municipal governments). This did not mean always interviewing exactly the same category of actors but rather those who were functionally equivalent. In those cases where the public official (three cases), union leader (two cases), or *piquetero* leader (three cases) refused to be interviewed, alternative sources were used to track down statements made by them in interviews with journalists and other academics (mainly the collection of extensive interviews published in Germano [2005]). Substitutes were also sought as alternative interviewees, such as other officials with equal or equivalent expertise in the same ministry or other union or *piquetero* leaders of the same trade union or SMO.

The use of interviews was the only available tool for understanding, in non-ethnographic terms, what the media has ignored and what has not yet been presented in other historical accounts. Because of this methodological choice, I was faced with the Borgean cartographers' problem of full reconstruction, in relation to the actors' selective use of memory[27] in telling their own story. In process-tracing analysis there is a debate about the role played by actors' own accounts of the events that are to be historically reconstructed. As George and McKewon (1985: 35) noted: "As we understand process-tracing, it involves both an attempt to reconstruct actors' definitions of the situation and an attempt to develop a theory of action. The framework within which actors' perceptions and actions are described is given by the researcher, not by the actors themselves." This dual aim is present in this book as, while the actors' voices are overtly present, I propose a narrative that is not the depiction of any

[27] By "memory" I mean a socially built process as defined by Traverso (2006: 12): "Memory – that is, the collective representation of the past as it is forged in the present – structures social identity by inscribing it on a historical continuum and attributing meaning to it, that is, content and direction."

one particular voice. With this methodological conundrum in mind, this book is historically minded in Tilly's sense (1984). As such, this book is the result of a theoretically guided process-tracing case study of the actors' and media narration of a social movement's pattern of interaction considered to be a paradigmatic case of a reincorporation movement. As a type of within-case analysis (Mahoney 2000: 409), I adopted process-tracing to build a detailed narrative that could provide an explanation of the second incorporation process and its relational path in Argentina through the case of a crucial actor in this story – the *piquetero* movement.

My research is also historical because the sequence of events is crucial for understanding the claims of this book.[28] Thus, although the *why* and *how* questions have been the focus of much social movement research, the *when* question should be added, and not just for the mere purpose of periodization. When recognition (Chapter 3), legitimation (Chapter 4), and reincorporation (Chapters 5 and 6) occur is as important as the time span in between each of these stages as well as the characteristics of the movement (Chapter 2). For this reason, the configurative approach of historical institutionalism is crucial because it focuses on how a sequence and temporal ordering of a relational process influences the outcome analyzed. However, I have been as conscious as possible about the fact that "the temporality of history and memory can also collide with each other in a kind of 'non-contemporaneity' or 'time discrepancy' (the *Ungleichzeitigkeit* theorized by Ernst Bloch)" (Traverso 2006: 43, italics in original). The combination of my theoretically guided narration and that voiced by the actors, attempts to partially address this limitation of historical narrations based solely on the actors' memory. The fruitfulness of attempting to bridge the social movement and historical institutionalism literatures will be apparent in the narrative chapters.

CONCLUSION

The conceptualization of the recursive logic of expansion and contraction of the socio-political arena allows us to discern the main struggle of popular movements in Latin America: their quest for (re)incorporation as citizens and wage-earners. The goal of the next chapter will be to

[28] "Analytic narratives – theoretically structured stories about coherent sequences of motivated actions – can contribute to the construction of explanations of why things happened the way they did" (Aminzade 1992: 457–58).

introduce a theoretical perspective to the strategies developed by social movements. This proposal will be illustrated with the *piqueteros*, the main reincorporation movement in Argentina. Then, in the narrative chapters, the theoretical toolkit of Chapters 1 and 2 will be applied to the relational analysis of the second wave of incorporation.

2

Beyond Repertoires of Contention: Conceptualizing Strategy Making in Social Movements

The *piquetero* movement is well known for its repertoire of contention. It is, indeed, this contentious dimension – and specifically its regular use of pickets – that earned this movement its name of *piqueteros* (picketers). A journalist presenting the movement to an English-speaking audience described the main characteristics of the *piqueteros* as follows:

> Very noisy and equally efficient, the *piquetero* movement in Argentina is well organized. They come in hundreds – men, women, and children – to demonstrate. About once a week, sometimes more, and most of the time without any warning, they block off some of Buenos Aires' main streets, causing major traffic obstructions ... and forcing the city to organize itself to avoid total chaos. ... Although some *piquetes* [pickets] are set up to show support for the Kirchner administration, the *piquetero* movement is mainly one of protest against the government.
>
> – "Piquetero Movement – Argentina." YouTube video posted by "Journeyman Pictures," March 23, 2010. 00.00 to 1.12 minutes, www.youtube.com/watch?v=AKE1flrtMR4, accessed October 10, 2012)

This same journalist goes on to explain the steps taken by the movement in a public action directed at the state:

> These *piqueteros* were marching towards Plaza de Mayo, Buenos Aires' main square, in front of the House of Government. They were stopped by the police a few hundred yards before reaching the plaza. They decided to camp out where they were until the president agreed to give them what they wanted: a job. ... And so they did for 35 hours, until the government finally agreed to their demands. The *piquete* has become the most prominent way of protesting nowadays in Argentina – a common method, indeed, and a legal one, at that. But not a popular one.
>
> – "Piquetero Movement – Argentina." 1.13 to 1.49 minutes, www.youtube.com/watch?v=AKE1flrtMR4, accessed October 10, 2012)

In fact, as this narrative illustrates, the repertoire of contention of the *piquetero* movement has been composed predominantly of roadblocks, marches, and encampments.[1] This dimension of politics was the main focus of most of Charles Tilly's (1986, 1995, 2006, 2008) research, leading to his formulation of the extremely useful concept of "repertoire of contention."

However, even this highly contention-prone movement engages in informal collaboration strategies and in bridge building with government officials, and these initiatives cannot be understood through the concept of repertoire of contention. They were the result of strategic decisions to avoid pursuing contentious actions. When an analysis of the history of the *piqueteros* – and any other social movement – is widened beyond contentious and public politics, a double logic of interaction emerges that embraces both public militancy and less public strategic retrenchment. If we were to reduce the analysis to the repertoire of contention, these other strategies would be missed.

In this chapter, I propose two concepts with the aim of contributing to a better understanding of historically rooted and collective processes of strategy making and performing that transcend the overemphasis of the social movement literature on contentious and public action (Goldstone 2003; Abers and Tatagiba 2015). These concepts are *repertoire of strategies* and *stock of legacies*. I propose these concepts in this chapter as a complement to Tilly's "repertoire of contention." The implications of incorporating a focus on strategies are central for social movement studies because they lead us to pay attention to actors and their intentions as well as the interactions among the intentions of a variety of deliberate actors (Jasper 2012: 30). Moreover, with these concepts I aim to recover Machiavelli's analysis of strategies through a historical understanding of the construction of strategies.

The concepts I propose in this chapter are part of the efforts of this book for building a macro-historical analysis without resorting to a structurally determined approach like path-dependency. Originally formulated by Sewell (2005: 100), path-dependency has recently been defined with more precision in order to avoid the risks of conceptual stretching. According to Mahoney (2000: 507) the concept is unambiguously determinist: "path-dependence characterizes specifically those historical sequences in which contingent events set into motion institutional

[1] Between 1997 and 2012, the print media reported 19,811 roadblocks/pickets, the vast majority of them organized by the *piqueteros* (Ichaso 2013).

patterns or event chains that have deterministic properties." For Pierson (2004: 20–21), who proposes a slightly different definition, the main characteristic of path-dependence is the self-reinforcement mechanism that any historical process produces, thereby making it more costly to reverse the course of a sequence of events. It is this consideration for sequencing that prompted some historical institutionalists to pertinently argue that "when a particular event in a sequence occurs will make a big difference" (Pierson 2000: 75, italics removed). However, to acknowledge the importance of sequence and timing in political analysis does not mean that historical processes are determined by an initial moment. Moreover, in path-dependence it is assumed that actors have no guiding principles that might lead them to choose particular courses of action that are not per se the easiest or less costly options within a specific time and space. Consequently, in opposition to what a path-dependent approach would suggest, I propose a historical perspective that is not based on structural determinism or rational choice theory.

Social movement studies is the best-suited literature to mitigate the structuralist limitations of historical institutionalism. Following a relational approach, I argue that macro-processes of transformation such as waves of popular incorporation are a result of poor people's organized struggles for inclusion and participation in the polity and the accumulation of elites' responses to these pressures. These are very contentious dynamics, but when studying the interaction of any social movement with the state, allies, and antagonists, the public performances identified by a "repertoire of contention" approach are just part of the story. There are many other activities performed by social movements that are part of their strategic quest for influencing political decisions that are neither contentious nor public. However, I do not propose as an alternative reducing the analysis to the study of micro tactics or the structural determination of actors' actions. The complete story is built by the multiple and simultaneous strategies that guide and give meaning to each tactical action performed by the collectives that constitute a movement that pushes for and resists social change.

TACTICS, STRATEGIES, AND CONTENTION

Social movement scholars have accorded a great deal of importance to the study of tactics and strategies (Gamson 1975; Piven and Cloward 1979; McAdam 1983; Fantasia 1988; Staggenborg 1991; Ganz 2000). However, until the 2000s, theorizing on this topic was limited, and research was almost exclusively focused on protest events, overlooking other forms of claim making and collective action (Taylor and Van Dyke 2004: 267–68; Smithey 2009; Maney et al. 2012: xiii–xvi).

Even though most of the literature on strategies/tactics does not draw a conceptual distinction between "strategy" and "tactic" (Jasper 2004: 14, n.1; Taylor and Van Dyke 2004), there have been some interesting recent efforts to clarify the differences (Fligstein and McAdam 2011; Maney et al. 2012; Meyer and Staggenborg 2012; Doherty 2013). Nepstad and Vinthagen (2012) have proposed the clearest distinction between tactic and strategy in a "Clausewitz-inspired understanding." In order to avoid any conceptual confusion, I draw on their conceptualization: "we define *tactics* as the means and plan to win a single campaign (one battle) and *strategy* as the plan of how to win the struggle (the war). Thus, tactics involve the small-scale repertoire and subgoals of the movement, while strategy is about how a movement reaches its goals" (Nepstad and Vinthagen 2012: 282, n.1).

A fundamental approach to strategizing is Tilly's concept of "repertoire of contention." His concept has allowed us to study contentious and public events and their slow pace of change as part of what is known as "contentious politics." Tilly (1995: 26–27) defined the repertoire of contention as a limited set of actions based on a relatively deliberate process of choice, in which social relations cluster together in recurrent patterns based on social and cultural capital accumulated through struggle. As he clearly stated: "In stressing open, collective, discontinuous contention, the analysis neglects individual forms of struggle and resistance as well as the routine operation of political parties, labor unions, patron–client networks, and other powerful means of collective action, except when they produce visible contention in the public arena" (Tilly 1995: 32). In other words, his definition is unambiguously limited to disruptive acts performed in the public space (Tilly 1986: 3–4; 2008: 203–4). This focus means that Tilly's definition does not allow for the study of a case of mobilization that did not happen: for example, one that was planned and organized by the members of a movement but never carried out. In this way, the narrative built would neglect to recognize that a public action emerges because several other non-public actions were performed and led to a contentious result. As a result, Tilly's conceptualization alone is unable to explain two crucial aspects of the dynamics of interaction of social movements: first, situations where contention does not emerge, and second, the relationship between the public and contentious events generally described by the media and most narrations and those that were not reported because they were not performed in the public space. The full picture of the strategic dynamics of interaction of social movements with the state, allies, and antagonists emerges if we broaden our scope beyond the contentious and public dimension of social movements only.

In contrast, with the goal of developing an agency-based approach to social movements, Jasper (2004, 2006, 2012) proposes the study of tactical options as a result of concrete dilemmas faced by agents. Jasper (2004: 4) suggests that we need "to understand what happens at the micro level of individuals and their interactions in order to improve our theories at the macro level ... " For this purpose, he proposes a series of "strategic dilemmas/trade-offs" that would allow us to understand the daily decisions of individuals without having recourse to rational choice theory. While this perspective successfully eliminates several limitations of rational choice theory, it still lacks "an understanding of how much dilemmas are interrelated and how their solutions are constrained" (Meyer and Staggenborg 2012: 6). The main issue with the concept of "strategic dilemmas/trade-offs" is that it suggests the universality of micro short-term tactical decisions. An additional problem with this approach is that although sometimes an action seems logical when its effects are retrospectively analyzed, the "social agents have 'strategies' which only rarely have a true strategic intention as a principle" (Bourdieu 1998: 81). It is thus necessary to trace the history of the strategy/tactic that is being performed to provide a contextualized meaning of it.

A crucial difference between Jasper's and Tilly's approaches to the study of tactical/strategic action is the answer they offer to a classic problem posed by Marx (1926 [1852]: 23), in remarkable terms: "Men make their own history, but not just as they please. They do not choose the circumstances for themselves, but have to work upon circumstances as they find them, have to fashion the material handed down by the past. The legacy of the dead generations weighs like an alp upon the brains of the living." While Jasper (2012) disregards the contextual factors as irrelevant, considering that this could take us to a return to structuralism, other authors, such as Bourdieu (1998), Tilly (1986, 2006, 2008), and Meyer and Staggenborg (2012), consider that what limits actors' free choice of strategies is crucial. The question with Jasper's view is that it omits the limitations posed to human agency by historical legacies of past struggles, which provides a meaning to and guides, limits, and enriches each short-term tactic. Whereas how to resolve the relationship between strategies chosen by collective actors and the legacies of past struggles was one of Tilly's main concerns.

In brief, while Jasper (2004, 2006, 2012) has been producing some of the most interesting conceptual ideas on small, short-term, and individually based tactics, Tilly (1986, 1995, 2008) made the most important conceptual contribution to the study of large, long-term, and collectively based repertoires of contention. However, while Jasper offers a universalistic approach to tactics, Tilly's historical approach only focused on public and contentious actions. Thus, there is a clear gap between public collective disruption and small tactical decisions. In order to fill in this gap, I emphasize a historical and collective approach to politics to analyze the background of strategies. Then a conceptualization of collective action that falls outside the realm of public protest needs to be incorporated into the current debates in the literature. In this chapter I propose a conceptual solution to this gap in the literature that would allow us to explain the historically rooted dynamics of *strategic* interaction between social movements and allies and antagonists.

REPERTOIRE OF STRATEGIES

Two questions arise as critical for improving explanations of strategy making and performing by social movements: How can we analyze the interaction of a social movement with the state, allies, and antagonists without reducing the analysis to its public and contentious dimensions only? And how can we put strategy making in historical perspective? The answers to these questions lie in the existence of two types of repertoires being simultaneously performed by the same movement. On the one hand, there is Tilly's repertoire of contention, which is public, militant, and glacially slow to change. This is corroborated by the *piquetero* movement's repertoire, which remained steadfast in its use of roadblocks, marches, and encampments. However, the narrative somewhat changes when the history of the movement is analyzed using an interpretative Weberian approach (*Verstehen*) based on in-depth interviews with movement leaders and state brokers and direct observation of movement activities. If Tilly's sources were supplemented with the ones I suggest in this book, the analysis of the movement would gain access to public, semi-public, and private events that are both contentious and non-contentious. These events broaden the scope of collective action and need to be theorized to help explain what happens in social movements when contentious events are not taking place. I suggest that the concepts "repertoire of strategies" and "stock of legacies" bring into the analysis elements intentionally excluded from the concept of "repertoire of contention." The basic idea is to consider contentious and routine repertoires simultaneously, not limiting the analysis to the in-the-public-space aspects of the movement and achieving a fuller depiction of historical events. Thus, these concepts allow for explaining aspects that the previous concept was ignoring.[2]

By repertoire of strategies I mean a historically constrained set of available options for non-teleological strategic action in public, semi-public (evolving across specific groups), or private arenas. This concept differs from the repertoire of contention in three main ways. First, the repertoire of strategies is more dynamic. Second, it is not solely contentious nor always public. It includes Tilly's forms of public disruption as well as non-contentious private actions such as informal meetings with politicians, audiences with the president, and so on. I use the term "strategy" and not "tactics" because movement actors choose a contentious and public action versus another form of action as part of the movement's long-term goals and a wider understanding of the social reality. Each strategic choice will necessarily include many tactical decisions to achieve the goal. The third difference is that the repertoire of strategies is mostly defined in its relationship to medium- and short-term changes in the political context, while the repertoire of contention is associated with longer-term changes.

Like Bourdieu (2000: 145), I look at action as the product of the accumulation of historical legacies.[3] The inclusion of the actor's socialization and his or her limited capacity to select courses of action places the actor in context. At the same time, the perspective suggested by Bourdieu allows for understanding the *nomos* of each social sphere, thus avoiding the mistaken application of the economic *nomos* to the entire social universe (Bourdieu 1998: 83–84). This latter problem is shared by several scholars of path-dependence due to the increased influence of rational choice in historical institutionalism. Nevertheless, there remains a weakness with Bourdieu's conceptualization of habitus in that it reduces the individual to an automaton within a field, and thus it is unable to explain novel action within a sequence of events that limit innovation.[4]

[2] In other words, what is intentionally excluded from the repertoire of contention definition is what the concept I propose can conceptually explain and connect to Tilly's key concept.

[3] Emirbayer (2010) points out some similarities between Tilly and Bourdieu concerning the contextual constraints for action that are linked to the analysis I am presenting here.

[4] Habitus is defined by Bourdieu (2000: 130) as "a system of dispositions" and thus as "the product of historical acquisition, [being so] what enables the legacy of history to be appropriated" (Bourdieu 2000: 151). The ontology of the definition of habitus is Karl

Though acknowledging the contextual constraints on actors' choices, my approach differs from Bourdieu's in two fundamental ways. First, collective actors, not individual agents, are the ones that perform repertoires of strategies. Second, my definition is rooted in a perspective that is less structuralist than Bourdieu's, allowing for spaces for rupture and dislocation. Conversely, I draw upon one of the attributes of Bourdieu's habitus: that the actor's choices are not necessarily coherent (Bourdieu 2000: 160). Therefore, the definition of repertoire of strategies is sustained by the idea of the restricted nature of the available options perceived as feasible by collective actors.

In other words, while for Bourdieu the individual agent is structurally predisposed to selecting a particular strategy,[5] I emphasize that strategic choice is the result of a historically constrained set of available and concatenated options (which I call the stock of legacies – more on this shortly). To sum up, the accumulation of strategies by a collective actor builds repertoires based on evaluating (whether correctly or not) their (and/or others') past strategies and, thus, opting to emulate, readapt, or reject them in a (socially delimited) conscious and oblivious fashion.

The concept of repertoire of strategies has two specific attributes that differentiate it from that of ideologies. First, it only represents the strategic options chosen and, though modular, is rooted in time and space. Second, it allows for the selection of strategies (contentious or otherwise) to be carried out in public, semi-public, or private arenas and thus offers a tool for improving the analytical connection among multiple types of simultaneous actions pertaining to the same actor. In other words, the repertoire of strategies has a historical origin and tradition that can explain it, but it can, and generally is, redefined by other actors coming from diverse ideological positions and different historical moments. This variety can be clearly seen in **Table 2.1**, which shows the main national *piquetero* SMOs, their diversity of ideologies and repertoire of strategies, and their shared repertoire of contention. In some cases, organizations have similar

Marx's anti-idealist philosophy, which "restores to the agent a generating, unifying, constructing, classifying power, while recalling that this capacity to construct social reality, itself socially constructed, is not that of a transcendental subject but of a socialized body, investing in its practice socially constructed organizing principles that are acquired in the course of a situated and dated social experience" (Bourdieu 2000: 136–37).

[5] Bourdieu (2000: 138–39) argues that the language of strategy implies not a utilitarian calculation but rather that actions oriented toward an end tend to adjust spontaneously to the necessity of the field where they are being produced.

TABLE 2.1 *Main* Piquetero *SMOs, Ideologies, Repertoire of Strategies, and Repertoire of Contention, 1996–2009*

Main Social Movement Organizations	Ideology	Predominant Repertoire of Strategies	Predominant Repertoire of Contention
Classist and Combative Current (CCC)	Maoist	*Basismo* Insurrectional alliance with the right	Encampment March Roadblock
Coordinator of Unemployed Workers (CTD) "Aníbal Verón"	National-populist	Moderate *foquismo* Witnessing	Encampment March Roadblock
"Evita" Movement	Left-wing Peronist	*Basismo* State colonization	Encampment March Roadblock
Independent Movement of the Retired and Unemployed (MIJD)	National-populist	Insurrectional alliance with the right Witnessing	Encampment March Roadblock
Jobless Movement "Teresa Is Alive" (MST "Teresa Vive")	Trotskyist	Morenist entryism Presentialism	Encampment March Roadblock
Neighborhood Organization (OB) "Tupac Amaru"	National-populist and indigenist	*Basismo* Trade unionist State colonization	Encampment March Roadblock
Popular Front "Darío Santillán" (FPDS)	Autonomist	Autonomist-introspective *Basismo*	Encampment March Roadblock
Neighborhoods Standing Up	National-populist	*Basismo* Multi-class popular front State colonization	Encampment March Roadblock

Territorial Liberation Movement (MTL)	Marxist-Leninist	Multi-class popular front Trade unionist	Encampment March Roadblock
Unemployed Workers' Movement "Teresa Rodríguez" (MTR) – Neighborhood Unity Coordinator (CUBa)	Guevarist and Trotskyist	Moderate *foquismo* Trade unionist	Encampment March Roadblock
Unemployed Workers Movement (MTD) "Aníbal Verón"	Guevarist	Moderate *foquismo* Trade unionist	Encampment March Roadblock
Unemployed Workers Movement (MTD) of La Juanita	Social-democratic	NGO-ization	Encampment March Roadblock
Unemployed Workers Movement (MTD) of Solano and allies	Autonomist	Autonomist-introspective *Basismo*	Encampment March Roadblock
Union of Unemployed Workers (UTD) of Mosconi	Syndicalist	Moderate *foquismo* Trade unionist	Encampment March Roadblock
Workers' Federation for Land, Housing and Habitat (FTV)	Liberation Theology and national-populist	*Basismo* Multi-class popular front State colonization Trade unionist	Encampment March Roadblock
Workers' Pole (PO)	Trotskyist	Morenist entryism Presentialism	Encampment March Roadblock

Note: The time period does not imply that the organizations have applied these strategies continuously but rather represents only the period during which the listed repertoires were considered predominant.
Source: Adapted from Rossi (2015c).

ideological traditions, such as Neighborhoods Standing Up (*Barrios de Pie*) and the Independent Movement of the Retired and Unemployed (MIJD), and use a different repertoire of strategies, while in others, organizations with disparate ideological traditions, such as the Unemployed Workers Movement (MTD) "Aníbal Verón" and the Union of Unemployed Workers (UTD) of Mosconi, use the same repertoire of strategies. Also, some strategies are widely used, such as *basismo* (territorially based grassroots assemblies) and trade unionist practices, while other strategies are restricted to one or a few organizations, such as witnessing and NGO-ization. Therefore, there is no straightforward relationship between ideology and repertoire of strategies.

As stated, repertoires of contention and repertoires of strategies are intimately related. **Table 2.1** shows that the use of the same contentious action by several organizations in a movement may result from different repertoires of strategies. Alternatively, the use of different contentious methods may result from the same strategy. In other words, repertoire of contention and repertoire of strategies refer to things happening within the same movement that are related but different. Because of this, to identify the repertoire of predominant strategies used by a social movement during a delimited time period does not entail reducing the complexity of movements as constellations of heterogeneous actors.

THE STOCK OF LEGACIES

The repertoire of strategies represents the predominant set of strategies used by a movement in a specific time period. But what delimits the actors' perception of the availability of strategies in their repertoire? As with the repertoire of contention, there are elements that limit what the repertoire can contain. While the repertoire of contention changes very slowly, linked as it is to macro transformations such as regime changes, the repertoire of strategies is more dynamic, which implies that its demarcation is based on actors' participation in a historical accumulation of events, experiences, and intentional learning processes that build a "stock of legacies." *By stock of legacies I mean the concatenation of past struggles, which, through the sedimentation of what is lived and perceived to be lived as well as what is intentionally learned, produces an accumulation of experience that adds or eliminates specific strategies from the repertoire of strategies as both a self-conscious and oblivious process.*

The concept is inspired by Schutz's (1967) concept of "stock of experience."[6] According to Schutz (1967: 77–78), a "meaningful lived experience" is the reflective product of each individual's flowing stream of experience that builds a stock of knowledge, that which enables each person to guide his or her conduct in the course of their life. In a stock of legacies, the actor opts for actions based on a set of identified available options that are open to innovation. But this process of selection is not that of an entirely free agent, nor is it the result of coherent deliberation. Rather it is limited by socialization, from among (mis)perceived accumulated available options, and within a restricted set of legacies that enrich or impoverish the range of the stock. The stock of legacies offers a complementary explanation to the purely structural limitations to innovations suggested by Tilly (1986: 4, 390–91; 2006: 42–45, 48–49; 2008: 203–4), which tend to make it much easier to explain the stability of repertoires than changes to them.

The stock of legacies materializes as an empirical question when trying to understand, for instance, why the *piquetero* movement only emerged with particular intensity in certain places. An ex-priest and main leader of one of the pioneering *piquetero* SMOs explained this situation to me in the following way:

Q: How do you explain that in Greater Buenos Aires there seems to be three main places where everything emerged ...?

A: The experience of struggle. Despite the crises, which always happen, the lessons of past experience always linger. In other words, you don't go back to zero. You don't go back to the beginning. Situations recur, but with the accumulation of learnt experience. The southern zone [of Greater Buenos Aires] was combative in the 1970s; these were industrial areas, with a relatively high level of industrialization. All this was later dismantled, but the experience of struggle and resistance still lingers, and it re-emerges every now and then – as if going into crisis mode (interview 2007).

[6] In Schutz's own words, "The total content of all my experience, or of all my perceptions of the world in the broadest sense, is, then, brought together and coordinated in the total context of my experience. This total context grows larger with every new lived experience. At every moment there is thus a growing core of accumulated experience. This growing core consists of both *real* and *ideal* objects of experience (*Erfahrungsgegenständlichkeiten*), which of course had once been produced in polysynthetic intentional Acts. But the objects in this reserve supply are always taken for granted" (1967: 76–77, italics in original).

This idea of an "experience of struggle" that "always lingers" was echoed by many others I interviewed. The words of this interlocutor poignantly captures the stock of legacies concept.

The *Piqueteros'* Stock of Legacies

Three main national legacies comprise the overall stock of legacies of the *piquetero* movement. The influence of each legacy varied among the SMOs (see **Table 2.1**), which explains many of the strategic options chosen in concrete historical situations as well as investing them with a sense of Weberian *Verstehen*.

The first element in the movement's stock of legacies is the experience of the armed struggle of the urban guerrillas and the consequences of repression under both democratic and authoritarian regimes between 1975 and 1989. This legacy has a dual basis. On the one hand, it arises out of the trauma produced by the last authoritarian regime and the effect that this had on the perceived strategic alternatives within the left's re-evaluation of democracy (Carr and Ellner 1993; Ollier 2009). This is due to a phenomenon that Roberts (1998: 41–42) also identified in Chile and Peru, what he called the lefts' affirmative and disconfirming experiences of their respective last authoritarian regimes. In Argentina, many of the *piquetero* leaders had disconfirming experiences as guerrilla veterans and now value some aspects of democracy, even if they are divided about its short-, medium-, and long-term value. On the other hand, the legacy of armed struggle is based on attempts by former guerrilla groups and left-wing Peronists to politically reorganize in Greater Buenos Aires between 1981 and 1987. This produced a legacy of organizational and contentious action from former groups of Peronist Montoneros and the Trotskyist Revolutionary Workers' Party – People's Revolutionary Army (PRT-ERP) urban guerrillas within a protracted and self-restrained disruption strategy. Signs of this legacy can be seen in the vanguard organizational models used and the moderate *foquismo* strategy that predominates in the *piquetero* movement in south Greater Buenos Aires and in parts of the province of Salta (this will be defined and expanded on in the next section about the repertoire of strategies).

The second shared legacy is linked to Liberation Theology, and in particular the Christian-based communities' (CBCs) practice of *basista* organization and their urban land occupations between 1979 and 1982 and their re-emergence in the 1990s. As stated by Cerrutti and Grimson (2004) and Merklen (2005), the territorialized mobilization that characterizes the *piquetero* movement is, in part, the historical continuation of the land occupations promoted by the CBCs in the period of democratization. This legacy explains why in some Greater Buenos Aires districts the *piquetero* movement quickly emerged as an organized process (this topic will be analyzed in detail in Chapter 3).

Finally, the third shared legacy is trade unionism, which is the result of the accumulated experience of syndicalist and communist unionism since the late nineteenth century and Peronist unionism since the 1950s. Trade unionism is part of the *piqueteros*' stock of legacies because in Argentina, union density reached Southern European levels, with 50.1 percent at its historical peak, versus a high of 24.3 percent in Brazil, for example (Roberts 2002: 15, table 1). This produced an important accumulation of former factory union delegates, some of whom became main *piquetero* leaders. The Classist and Combative Current (CCC) and the Territorial Liberation Movement (MTL), for instance, define themselves as politico-syndicalist organizations, and one of the two main national leaders of the MTL explains that previous experience "was a very important element for those of us who were trade union delegates and knew how trade unions worked, [because] we transferred all our experiences into the organization of the unemployed movement" (interviewed by Germano 2005: 142). Thus, although trade unionism also owes to the heritage of institutions from the first incorporation process, there is a clear sedimentation of the legacies of union strategies in the *piquetero* movement.

With these new concepts in our toolkit, events similar to the ones described by the journalist quoted at the beginning of this chapter can be reconstructed with the incorporation of additional events that were performed in different arenas but as part of the same set of events that (sometimes) includes contentious politics. In other words, the two repertoires are interrelated, but they bear crucial differences that allow for explaining different phenomena. In addition, each micro and daily tactical trade-off can only be meaningful when viewed as part of a repertoire of strategies and a repertoire of contention, the specific context in which these repertoires are used, and the perspective for the future that they imply.

THE PIQUETERO MOVEMENT'S REPERTOIRE OF PREDOMINANT STRATEGIES

As in any social movement, the *piqueteros* employ a number of strategies. The repertoire of predominant strategies within the *piquetero* movement is quite diverse, and this is summarized in **Table 2.2**. So, what unifies this

TABLE 2.2 *Repertoire of Predominant Strategies of the Main SMOs of the* Piquetero *Movement, 1996–2009*

Repertoire of Strategies	Definition	Stock of Legacies to Which It Is Mainly Related	*Piquetero* Social Movement Organizations
Autonomist-introspective	The use of an assembly as a permanent self-reflective process and tool for transforming society through the collective assemblage of an alternative conception of the state.	Mexican Zapatista Army of National Liberation and assemblies movement of Buenos Aires (2002–3)	MTD of Solano, FPDS
Basismo	A strategy of territorialized organization of the popular sectors for diffusion from below through several nodes of action located in urban and suburban shantytowns.	Christian-based communities and Liberation Theology of the 1980s	FTV, CCC, Neighborhoods Standing Up, FPDS, "Evita" Movement, MTD of Solano, OB "Tupac Amaru"
Insurrectional alliance with the right	To promote a protracted struggle in a multi-sectoral coalition toward a massive insurrectional upsurge based on a long march toward the breakdown of the system while playing within the Peronist structure, interpreted as if the main Peronist party (the Justicialist Party, PJ) is equivalent in structure to the Chinese Kuomintang.	Maoist anti-Japanese front	CCC, MIJD
Moderate *foquismo*	A non-violent strategy conducted with a few vanguardist individuals to produce spaces of permanent contention for the diffusion of disruption within a democratic setting.	Guevarism and the 1970s-redefined strategies of the PRT-ERP	MTR, MTD "Aníbal Verón," UTD of Mosconi
Morenist entryism	The strategy for penetrating other popular organizations with the goal of disputing the hegemony of the labor movement from within and building a vanguard that can guide workers toward a classist unified front.	Nahuel Moreno (Trotskyism) followers in its post-democratization reformulation	PO, MST "Teresa Vive," FOL

(continued)

TABLE 2.2 *(continued)*

Repertoire of Strategies	Definition	Stock of Legacies to Which It Is Mainly Related	*Piquetero* Social Movement Organizations
NGO-ization	Moderation of claims and contentious strategies in a process of collaboration with middle-class foundations and companies for project-focused agendas of action relying on donors.	NGOs from the 1990s onward	MTD of La Juanita
Presentialist	In the quest for their presentation as self-proclaimed vanguards and intransigent fighters, the narration of the movement's past is manipulated for present purposes.	Universal	PO, MST "Teresa Vive"
State colonization	The acceptance of Peronist organizational tools as useful, while simultaneously seeking to access state gatekeeper positions through a "beehive" tactic.	Morenist entryism, Guevarism, and multi-class popular front	Neighborhoods Standing Up, "Evita" Movement, FTV, OB "Tupac Amaru"
Trade unionist	A systematic employment of the mythical disruptive power of the total picket for moderate aims by vertical organizations that seek to enter into negotiations and make use of institutional and rhetorical trade union tools.	Peronist unions (mainly CGT)	FTV, MTL, CCC, PO, MTR, MTD "Aníbal Verón," UTD of Mosconi, CTD "Aníbal Verón" (MPR "Quebracho"), OB "Tupac Amaru"
Witnessing	A way of showing in the mass media the oppression of the political system through portrayals of the personal experience of repression of the leaders of a social movement.	Gandhism and Palestinian Intifada	CTD "Aníbal Verón" (MPR "Quebracho"), MIJD

multiplicity of strategies? The unifying core of the repertoire of predominant strategies in a movement is the "feel for the game." In Bourdieu's (1998: 80–81) terms: "Having the feel for the game is having the game under the skin; it is to master in a practical way the future of the game; it is to have a sense of the history of the game." In other words, the *piqueteros* share an understanding of the contentious and non-contentious game they are playing; they recognize each other as members of the so-called "*piquetero* movement" as well as linking into the legacies of struggles related to other social movements' goals and repertoires. What follows is an overview of the repertoire of predominant strategies of the *piquetero* movement (listed in **Table 2.2**) and its basic characteristics.

Trade Unionist Strategy

Just a few of the strategies are directly related to the repertoire of contention. In the *piquetero* movement, only the "trade unionist" and "moderate *foquismo*" strategies are directly associated with the use of the picket. The trade unionist strategy can be defined as Sorelian. In this strategy, while there is systematic use of radical methods, claims are intentionally moderate.[7] Georges Sorel (1999 [1908]: 118), the key intellectual of syndicalism, talks of the general strike as a *myth* in which major transformation is comprised. The success of the *piqueteros*' strategy is based on another myth, one that has the same power and logic as the general strike: the total picket. In other words, the importance of small protest events, like pickets, is crucial for expanding insurrection based on the idea of wide-ranging economic collapse, as the general strike would imply. The trade unionist strategy can be defined as a systematic use of the mythical disruptive power of the *total picket* for moderate aims by vertical organizations that seek to enter into negotiations and make use of institutional and rhetorical trade unionist tools.[8]

[7] "In order that this system may work properly, a certain moderation in the conduct of the workers is necessary; not only must violence be used with discretion but the demands must not exceed certain limits" (Sorel 1999 [1908]: 201).

[8] In Sorel's (1999 [1908]: 182) words: "It is possible, therefore, to conceive socialism as being perfectly revolutionary, although there may only be conflicts that are short and few in number, provided that these have strength enough to evoke the idea of the general strike: all the events of the conflict will then appear under a magnified form and, the idea of catastrophe being maintained, the cleavage will be perfect. Thus the objection often urged against the revolutionaries may be set aside: there is no danger of civilization succumbing under the consequences of a development of brutality, since the idea of the general strike may foster the notion of class struggle by means of incidents which would appear to bourgeois historians as being of small importance."

The trade unionist strategy is related to the wider influence of trade union logic within the *piquetero* movement. For example, the Workers' Federation for Land, Housing and Habitat (FTV) reproduced the bureaucratic organization of most unions in Argentina in a wholly top-down and personalized organization with power concentrated in its main leader and building a loosely structured network across the country.[9] This organizational characteristic produced a number of internal conflicts and important splits over the FTV's lifetime that will be analyzed in the following chapters (Armelino 2008; Burkart et al. 2008).

At the same time there are particular processes of trade unionism that affect certain SMOs. This happens with what might be called the "enclave logic" that explains the trade unionist strategy that predominates in the UTD of Mosconi, a *piquetero* SMO located in a petroleum extraction enclave near the rural border with Bolivia. As Collier and Collier (1991: 41) state, "The location of many unionized workers in spatially concentrated, large-scale centers of production and/or their strategic position at critical points in the economy or the polity gives them an unusual capacity to disrupt the economic and political system and hence provides incentives for sustained collective action." In the enclaves of Tartagal and Mosconi in the province of Salta, this can be observed through the intense disruption applied by the UTD and the extremely repressive reactions on the part of the state which led to the deaths of several *piqueteros* by the Gendarmerie (military police). The great physical distance from the national government that tends to produce radical union strategies also strengthens a communal building process (Svampa 2003, 2006) while rejecting party organizations. This is a characteristic that defines the UTD of Mosconi, just as it had influenced other cases, such as that of miners in Bolivia during the 1950s (Angell 1998: 106–7).

Moderate *Foquismo* Strategy

There is another strategy that consists of a different use of the picket by the *piqueteros*. Moderate *foquismo* implies the use of radical methods for moderate goals. *Foquismo*, or the *foco* theory of guerrilla warfare, was

9 According to Barker et al. (2001: 20), "Bureaucratic organization involves a hierarchy of offices, with decision-making concentrated at the top, and command following down. Members are either directly excluded from decision-making, or only indirectly consulted through intermittent elections to top offices, occasional conferences, and ballots. Officials are commonly appointed rather than elected. Channels of communication are top-down and monopolized by the leadership."

developed by Ernesto "Che" Guevara as an armed strategy for expanding conflict through a small group of men and women. Its adaptation to non-violent use in a democratic setting for immediate reformist goals is what I call "moderate *foquismo*." This strategy prevails among some SMOs that share a legacy of former guerrilla leadership. It is attached to a vanguardist conception of politics and implies the construction of a site or "*foco*" of conflict and its diffusion by what Guevara called the "beehive effect" (Guevara 1997 [1963]: 389). In Guevara's words:

> Let's consider how a guerrilla *foco* could start . . . Relatively small nuclei of people choose favorable sites for the guerrilla war, be it with the intention of triggering a counterattack or to bide time, and then start to act. The following must be very clearly established: in the early stages, the relative weakness of the guerrilla is such that it must only work on putting down roots, getting to know the environment, making connections with the population and strengthening the places that will eventually become its support bases. (1997 [1963]: 387)

This strategy predominated in the Unemployed Workers' Movement "Teresa Rodríguez" (MTR) and some of its allies. Territorially, they created *focos* of organization with local networks by taking control of *juntas vecinales* (neighborhood associations in poor districts and shantytowns). Later, when the political opportunities were interpreted as favorable due to the increase in unemployment and a lack of access to unions to mobilize workers, the network activated the *focos*, now renamed as MTDs.

Organizationally, moderate *foquismo* is associated with an exclusivist leadership strategy, one which is based on a small group of committed activists where "[s]uch groups seek to *lead* by the indirect method of *heroic example* rather than by the interactivity of persuasion" (Barker et al. 2001: 21, italics in original). Two vanguardist and vertical organizations are the MTR and the Revolutionary Popular Movement (MPR) "Quebracho." But while the MTR applied a purely exclusivist leadership strategy, the MPR "Quebracho" adopted a less exclusivist type of leadership as a participant in the Coordinator of Unemployed Workers (CTD) "Aníbal Verón," accepting internal diversity as well as becoming more flexible in its dogmatic approaches to the political culture of the Argentine popular sectors (Delamata 2004: 58–59). As part of a shared insurrectional perspective, the difference is related to the degree of mass participation present within each SMO.

Contentiously, the MTR, CTD "Aníbal Verón" (MPR "Quebracho") and MTD "Aníbal Verón" focused on systematic pickets at specific locations in Buenos Aires and particularly the Pueyrredón Bridge (the main southern entrance to the city of Buenos Aires) as a moderate *foquismo* strategy.

Autonomist–Introspective Strategy

The autonomist–introspective strategy means the use of the assembly as a permanent process of self-reflection and as a tool for transforming society through the collective building of an alternative conception of the state. Though this alternative conception has not yet been achieved, this strategy has been mainly focused on the promotion of cooperatives, localized protest actions, deliberative public gatherings, and book publications. The autonomist–introspective strategy departs from two main influences: the experience of the Mexican Zapatista Army of National Liberation (EZLN), and particularly John Holloway's (2002) interpretation of it, and the assembly movement of Buenos Aires and its use of horizontal deliberation during the 2002–3 crisis (Rossi 2005a). The Unemployed Workers Movement (MTD) of Solano defines it as follows:

> Autonomy is the project we have chosen to build. We know who we are: we are people capable of transforming reality with constructive work, without the need for exploitation. The space we build is based on new relationships, radically opposed to those of the capitalist system that we don't want. Horizontality is what we practice for our project. Horizontality is not a concept, but rather the practical exercising of a new way of relating to each other. Within a context of terrible poverty we could generate a space for freedom: freedom to think, to put into practice our dreams against a society that represses and frustrates them.
>
> (MTD of Solano website, www.solano.mtd.org.ar/article.php3?id_article=3, accessed September 16, 2008)

This strategy led some sectors to adopt Italian political theorist Toni Negri's idea of counter-power (Hardt and Negri 2000; Negri 2001) and promoting localized actions. An important book edited by promoters of autonomism within the *piquetero* movement includes several strategies for constituting a "counter-power," but the one adopted by the MTD of Solano is the following: "Now it is not a matter of 'conducting' or 'supporting' the struggles but of actively *living in the situation*, supporting, from there, the emergence of a new non-capitalist sociability as an ethical practice towards the political commitment and materialization of counter-power" (Colectivo Situaciones 2001: 37, italics in original).[10]

[10] As the main leader of the non-autonomist "Evita" Movement points out, the limits to this strategy are related to the *piquetero* movement's economic dependence on the state: "There

Basismo Strategy

Another strategy of the territorialized organization of the popular sectors in Argentina is *basismo*. As the name implies, this strategy is meant to build "from below" several territorially based nodes of action sustained on assembly methods located in urban and suburban shantytowns. As Prévôt-Schapira explains, "*Basismo* was forged in activist Christian engagement. In Argentina the 'Church of the Poor' was very much a minority current, and unlike their Brazilian counterparts the Argentinean hierarchy were not at all receptive to the post-Conciliar movement for change. Nevertheless, the Movement of Third World Priests (Movimiento de los Sacerdotes del Tercer Mundo) was, during the 1960s and 1970s, the most visible [expression of this]" (1999: 228, italics in original). In Argentina, the development of *basismo* was linked to the legacy of Peronism and its relationship with "integrist" or ultramontane Catholicism (Prévôt-Schapira 1999: 229). In the 1970s, an important division between Marxist and Peronist Liberation Theology priests emerged that two decades later was also important for the development of the *piqueteros* (cf. Figures A and B in Appendix). As such, *basismo* is one of the main antecedents of territorialized politics, but it was marginal to some sectors of the Christian, Peronist, and Marxist lefts until the 1980s (Merklen 2005: 63, n. 41).

A concurrent change related to this strategy emerged on the left as a response to the traumatic experience of the 1976–83 authoritarian regime. Guerrilla organizations were crushed, leaving the left in disarray. This for many was due not only to the huge disparity in forces but also to the left's vanguardist organizational style, which was considered to be insufficient (Moyano 1992; Ollier 2009). The isolation of the left from most of the popular sectors even led some leftists to engage in violent actions – with no social support – well after the start of the democratization process.[11] The only way to avoid this mistake, according to those

is a sector [of the movement] that had bought into Negri's idea, which says that there is a struggle for counter-power. They say that Greater Buenos Aires shantytowns must become the Lacandón jungle [in Chiapas, Mexico] of Argentina. And they believe in the idea of counter-power, in the organization of the [local] space. However, they all live based on the state as a provider of resources even as they hold this idea of counter-power" (interview 2007).

11 The last armed action carried out by the left was in 1989 in La Tablada. The bloody and swift defeat of the All for the Motherland Movement guerrilla organization was a clear sign of the total failure of this strategy by those left-wing groups that had not yet reformulated their strategies after the traumatic experience of the last authoritarian regime (Hilb 2007).

parties and groups that included *basismo* as part of their repertoire, was to produce massively participatory organizational models. It was this concept that led many former guerrilla members and left-wing party activists to adopt *basismo* as a new way of mobilizing the popular sectors. This was expressed through the CBC-organized massive land occupations in San Francisco Solano (Quilmes) toward the end of the authoritarian regime, a tactic emulated in other districts of Greater Buenos Aires, above all in La Matanza and Florencio Varela (Fara 1985; Merklen 1991; Prévôt-Schapira 1999).

Within the CCC, from 1990 to 2009, these changes on the left were discursively articulated by a rejection of electoral participation as insufficient for the revolutionary purposes of the Maoist Communist Revolutionary Party (PCR), and the organization of the unemployed therefore rested on the vast experience of *basismo* (Svampa and Pereyra 2003: 159–60). As described by the CCC's national coordinator of unemployed workers, in order to avoid vanguardism and political isolation from the popular sectors, the CCC's decision-making process is based on *basismo*:

> Our organization, which corresponds to the unemployed, is organized by territory, by neighborhood. In each neighborhood there are 40, 80, 100 companions [*compañeros*] in some neighborhoods. Each neighborhood holds weekly assemblies where issues are discussed. There [the participants] choose their own leaders. The leaders are revocable – in other words, every three or four months, elections are organized in the neighborhoods, and the companions themselves chose their [delegate] companions by secret vote ... The coordinating group meets once a week for a whole day. Here we meet on Wednesdays ... (National CCC leader, interview 2007)

The neighborhood delegates are selected on a rotating basis, and their mandate is revocable. The deliberative setting is centrally guided by the CCC leaders through the use of "scripts" – a brief guideline for discussion written by them. These scripts determine the agenda of the neighborhood debates, and as a consequence the political decisions of the whole SMO. This organizational strategy is a consequence of the desire of the PCR politburo to control the political agenda of the CCC but mostly stems from an internal struggle for the redefinition of what their leaders call "*la democracia grande*" ("greater democracy")[12] in their quest to politicize

[12] For an evolution of this definition and descriptions of how the CCC is organized, cf. Alderete and Gómez (1999); Delamata (2004: 33–43); Germano (2005: 195, 201); *Política y Teoría* (issue 48, April–June 2002, and issue 51, April–June 2003); and Svampa and Pereyra (2003: 44–49).

the urban poor, through a *basismo* approach, toward a multi-sectoral strategy of insurrectional alliance, as the next section will explain.

Three Types of Multi-sectoral Strategies

Among their several strategies, the *piqueteros* adopted three types of multi-sectoral strategies between 1996 and 2009. By multi-sectoral strategies I mean different versions of a strategy based on the idea that in order to achieve the desired political goals, it is crucial to join forces with diverse segments of society and/or political groupings. Multi-sectoral strategies are not always contentious and involve many not-so-public actions.

A first type of multi-sectoral strategy is the "multi-class popular front," which implies, in the Argentine context, that left-wing parties and organizations should accept alliances with Peronist organizations (PJ, CGT, among others), particularly with their more progressive wings.[13] Before being adopted by the *piqueteros* in relation to Peronist political, social, and labor organizations, this strategy was used in Latin America in the quest to unify the left during the Spanish Civil War (1936–39), where it was mostly successful in Chile. In Argentina, it emerged in the 1950s in the context of the debates about Peronism after the dissolution of the Comintern (Angell 1998: 93–95). The use of this strategy by the *piqueteros* can be noted in their relationship with president Néstor Kirchner's Peronist government (2003–7). While the MTL (linked to the Communist Party of Argentina, PCA) was internally divided as to whether or not to support the government, the FTV and Neighborhoods Standing Up were allies of the government as part of what they conceived as a multi-class popular front (Chapter 6).

A second type of multi-sectoral strategy is the "insurrectional alliance with the right" promoted by the CCC (of the PCR) but also, in a less structured fashion, by the MIJD. Since its beginnings, the PCR has rejected armed struggle as promoted by the guerrilla organizations. At the same time, it has had a long-standing relationship with some sectors of the armed forces.[14] This has been sustained as part of their strategy of

[13] Such alliances include multiple classes from the point of view of the *piquetero* SMOs that enter into them because while they perceive themselves as composed of the working class (or the popular sectors), Peronist organizations reject any classist distinction, and Peronism is characterized by the integration of trade unions, national industrialists, and some middle classes (Rossi 2013a).

[14] This link is not historically exclusive of the PCR, though it is now the left-wing party with the best developed links. The PCA has played this game since – at least – the 1950s, under

building an insurrectional alliance with the right. This strategy seems similar to the popular multi-class front that other *piquetero* organizations promote but differs in some crucial respects: it is electorally abstentionist, and it is inspired by the Maoist 1940 anti-Japanese united front (Mao 1965 [1940]: 422). Thus, until 2009 the CCC promoted a protracted struggle within a multi-sectoral coalition with Peronist organizations, with the expectation that it would lead to a popular insurrection that would bring down the regime.

The multi-sectoral alliance used by the CCC is based on the PCR politburo's interpretation of the Peronist PJ as the equivalent of the Chinese Kuomintang party because of its high level of internal heterogeneity, which opens up the possibility of exploiting the divisions among PJ elites in the same way as Mao Zedong proposed to do with the Kuomintang in 1940.[15] To achieve this goal, it seeks the support of the right-wing factions of the PJ and middle-sized rural producers while establishing long-term personalized contacts with PJ mayors.

A third type of multi-sectoral strategy is what I call "state colonization." Neighborhoods Standing Up adopted this strategy from 2003 to 2008, when it was a member of the governmental coalition. Using a multi-class popular front strategy in combination with Ernesto "Che" Guevara's beehive tactic, Neighborhoods Standing Up encouraged its members and leaders to actively participate in as many electoral, appointed, or technical positions as they could possibly negotiate with the PJ and the other coalition members in the national government while also taking up as many local and provincial posts as possible. In this sense, this strategy implies accepting the Peronist organizations as tools that are useful while simultaneously considering as crucial the access to gatekeeper positions of the state. As a result, in the province of Buenos Aires Neighborhoods Standing Up achieved middle-level positions in the Ministry of Human Development and in several municipalities. They also succeeded in securing several provincial sub-secretariats as well as national ones in the Ministry of International Relations and the Ministry of Social Development and since 2007 have also had a few members

a similar logic. In 1962 it even supported one of the military divisions during the confrontation between "*azules*" and "*colorados*" military factions (Rot 2007: 19).

15 "The Kuomintang is a heterogeneous party which includes diehards, middle elements and progressives; taken as a whole, it must not be equated with the die-hards. ... This point must be clearly recognized if we are to take advantage of the contradictions within the Kuomintang, follow a policy of differentiating between its different sections and do our utmost to unite with its middle and progressive sections" (Mao 1965 [1940]: 427).

elected to the national parliament among other posts. Amid all the *piquetero* organizations, Neighborhoods Standing Up is the one that, until 2008, had achieved the greatest penetration of its members into the state apparatus. This was emulated by the FTV, although with much less success. The FTV suffered from internal indiscipline and co-optation as a consequence of imitating state colonization. Finally, the "Evita" Movement adopted the strategy, with a focus on the province of Buenos Aires, by formally participating in the functional structure of the PJ (cf. Chapter 6).

In brief, the three types of multi-sectoral strategies diverge according to whether they adopt an internal or external relationship with the government or party as well as according to which wing of the PJ or CGT they choose to ally themselves with. By the same token, while the insurrectional alliance implies a non-electoral approach, the CCC, MIJD, and most of the *piqueteros* always play a role, directly or indirectly, during electoral periods (clientelism, protests, boycotts, and so on). This is different from the multi-sectoral coalition with the left-wing sectors of the PJ and state colonization strategies, which involve inclusion in the government coalition and access to parliamentarian and/or other kinds of electoral positions. Lastly, state colonization is focused on penetrating the state rather than the allied organizations.

Morenist Entryism Strategy

Morenist entryism represents a different strategy for penetrating other organizations. A long-standing strategy, it was first developed in 1957 by the Trotskyist party Workers' Word in order to infiltrate and command Peronist unions (Tarcus 1996: 117). The strategy was formulated by the party's leader, Nahuel Moreno, and is an adaptation of Leon Trotsky's Unified Front idea, inspired from Friedrich Engels' proposal for infiltrating the German Social Democratic Party with socialist officials (Tarcus 1996: 326; Castelo 2000). Moreno explained his strategy during a meeting of the International Committee of the Fourth International, as follows:

> The fundamental motivations for the Trotskyist movement in the creation of the strategy of the Revolutionary United Front do not imply that our hands are tied in terms of organizational means or tactics to adopt in developing the tactics of the revolutionary united front in each country. These tactics may be any of the traditional ones, from agreement on very limited and urgent actions with leftist tendencies, to entryism in a wider leftist tendency that might emerge, or in an

already existent center-left party. Any of these variants may be valid if it is the result of a careful study of the national reality ...

(Nahuel Moreno, Tesis sobre el Frente Único Revolucionario, Leeds, 1958)

With this idea as his starting point, after redemocratization, Moreno (1980: 179–84) reformulated parts of his strategy because the context had changed: Peronism was legalized, and many left-wing organizations went into demise with the authoritarian regime of 1976–83. The post-democratization Morenist entryism strategy within the *piquetero* movement can be defined as the pursuit for penetration of other popular organizations with the goal of disputing the hegemony of the labor movement from within its constituent organizations and build a vanguard that can guide the unemployed and employed workers toward a classist united front.[16]

This strategy was mostly used by the Trotskyist Workers' Pole (PO). The PO used Morenist entryism by coordinating seven meetings of the National Assembly of Employed and Unemployed Workers (2001–5) as well as the National Piquetero Block coalition (2002–5, until the PO was expelled). In its redemocratization version, Morenist entryism is used for electoralist goals. According to the national PO leader, those leaders that emerge during the process of struggle later compete for electoral positions through the use of electoral politics as a propaganda tool.

Morenist entryism has also provoked divisions among the *piqueteros* because the other SMOs are aware of this well-known strategy, and thus coordination takes place in an atmosphere of tension. At the same time, there is a tendency for divisions to be produced in the movement's coalitional attempts owing to leadership conflicts among Trotskyist groups.

NGO-ization Strategy

Other strategies that are part of the repertoire of the *piqueteros* do not have a contentious dimension. The "NGO-ization" strategy means the moderation of claims and contentious strategies in a process of collaboration with middle-class foundations and companies for project-focused agendas of action relying on donors. NGO-ization is the strategy that has been used by one small organization only – the MTD of La Juanita, a pioneer in the formation of the *piquetero* movement. After rejecting the claim for unemployment subsidies as a source of clientelism, this SMO initiated a strategy of gradually mutating into an NGO, working under

[16] Morenist entryism is also used outside Argentina because it was widely taken up by Trotskyist groups after Moreno presented his strategic approach in 1958.

the same logic as any post-1990 professionalized NGO. It started to obtain funding from international donors, Avina Foundation supported its main leader, and it became allied with private companies and middle-class parties.

Moreover, when the MTD of La Juanita main leader was elected as the *piquetero* movement's first national parliamentarian, it was done as part of the middle-class and centrist party Civic Coalition – Alliance for a Republic of Equals (CC-ARI), working in a style usual to NGOs. This is atypical of the popular movements' legislative participation in that it is overtly different to the other *piquetero* SMOs with legislators – such as the FTV, Neighborhoods Standing Up, "Evita" Movement, PO, and MIJD – that have maintained leftist territorially based logics.

Witnessing Strategy

The strategy of witnessing is a way of putting on display the oppression of the political system through the personal experiences of the leaders of a social movement. This strategy has been widely used and adapted around the world and has taken many forms, such as Gandhism and the Palestinian Intifada. In the *piquetero* movement, two organizations make systematic use of this strategy, in two variants. The CTD "Aníbal Verón" of the MPR "Quebracho" uses it for insurrectional purposes, while the MIJD uses it for electoral goals. These differences are not ideological, as both these groups can be considered national-populist and anti-imperialist; the repertoire of strategies is what differentiates them. On the one hand, the CTD "Aníbal Verón" (MPR "Quebracho") uses violence against private property, as with the 2007 burning of the conservative Neuquén People's Movement's party office. This protest was not carried out undercover but was openly played out in front of the media, followed by a public declaration at the site of the event by one of its leaders, thereby ensuring fulfillment of his goal: to be immediately sent to jail.

On the other hand, the MIJD has made use of symbolically disruptive tools, such as setting up a popular soup kitchen in the richest neighborhood of Buenos Aires, organizing the participation of one of the MIJD leaders as a contestant on a prime-time television dance show, and protesting in front of McDonald's branches for the supply of 1,000 Happy Meals for the children of MIJD members. Raúl Castells, one of the main leaders of the MIJD, summarizes their strategy: "The Coca-Cola marketing strategists said that a message has to be recurrent and witty ... We want socialism: this is our recurrent message. And we'll make it witty. The traditional left is dead boring. They have 100 years of history and people pay less attention to them than to a flock of sparrows" (*La Nación*, July 29, 2007). During the 2007 election, the MIJD used this accumulated media coverage for electoral purposes by presenting Castells as a presidential candidate under a newly created MIJD ballot, which ended up garnering 54,893 votes (0.3 percent). In 2011, the MIJD was able to improve its electoral results, winning its first seat in the House of Representatives.

The CTD "Aníbal Verón" partially differs from the MIJD because it is abstentionist and thus considers its witnessing strategy as part of an insurrectional path that has the potential to set a revolutionary process into motion, as explained by one of the CTD leaders:

> We still believe in the power of the people, which has to do with a strategy that calls for the need to get the people out in the streets. And additionally we don't believe that "the people" or "people" are closed categories because this would mean denying the [socio-economic and cultural diversity of] Argentina. In other words, the issue with the electorate, with the public opinion polls and these kinds of things, is what they conceal: the existing political proscription. (interview 2008)

Conversely, the MIJD's perspective on witnessing is based on a pragmatic understanding of the mass media, as Castells explains:

> The goal of our political struggle is socialism, but we don't have the economic resources [to promote our ideas] and because of this we use the mass media to spread our ideas. It was one thing to start a social revolution 100 years ago, but it's quite another to do it now, when almost every house has a television and seven million people have Internet access ... For us, the issue is not who are the owners of the media, but who are its consumers. Otherwise, we would not bother with this program because the journalist is tied to the government, or that other one because it's part of an international monopoly that subjugates us. If we saw things this way we would not use any mass media because there are no big TV channels owned by the workers, no cooperative newspapers or influential radio stations that are part of the popular struggle. For us, this [the mass media] is not the interlocutor, but the one who is listening to it or reading it. (*Página/12*, May 20, 2007)

To sum up, in both cases the purpose is to repeatedly access the media in the face of a lack of economic resources to generate their own propaganda. They promote their voice by presenting themselves as witnesses of the oppression of the system. In this way, both organizations hope to increase the number of sympathizers and gain empathy for their organizations and their message by partially relying on the mass media as a vehicle for disseminating their ideas and recruiting activists.

Presentialist Strategy

Among the many strategies, what I call "presentialism" is the one that is used most frequently by Trotskyists in the *piquetero* movement. The presentialist strategy means manipulating the narration of the past for present purposes – thus it implies strategically lying. What is the purpose of lying in politics? Why do these groups make systematic use of the intentional distortion of events? In what way does strategic lying differ from the strategic manipulation and occultation of information that many political actors engage in when talking in public and being interviewed? The difference relies on the specific type of systematic lie performed by some SMOs: it means to claim that you were *present* at each of the main events of the history of a movement and generally playing a key role as the intransigent and revolutionary actor you assert yourself to be. For instance, while the MST "Teresa Vive" claims that its origin in the *piqueteros* can be traced back to its presence at the first protests for employment in the Patagonian towns of Cutral-Có and Plaza Huincul in 1996 and 1997, I have not been able to locate any scholar, journalist, or other actor that could confirm this (Sánchez 1997; Kohan 2002; Auyero 2003; Oviedo 2004; among others).

Another example is that of the PO, which presents itself as if it were in a permanent intransigent relationship with the state as part of the struggle against the state as a class instrument: "We are not an organization that is engaged in the problem of negotiation-administration [with the state] – and this is even less of an issue for the Workers' Pole. We do not share the idea that the problem is how to negotiate with the state. We are sure that to oppose the state what we have to do is to be organized and struggle. Whatever we have obtained was based on this" (national leader, interview 2007). Notwithstanding this discourse, those *piqueteros* that were public officials confirmed to me that the PO is the *piquetero* SMO that has received the most unemployment subsidies from the government of the province of Buenos Aires since 2002 as a result of private and semi-public negotiations.

There may be two major factors in the more systematic use of lying in this sector of the movement. First, the PO and MST "Teresa Vive" were late arrivals to the movement's most dynamic contentious core. Second, a high degree of pragmatism is required in daily negotiations with the authorities to access resources in order to preserve the *piquetero* constituency (something that these small middle-class parties were not used to, thus creating internal problems). As a result, exaggerating intransigence plays a key role in preserving the party's constituency in their drive to legitimate their presentation as the self-proclaimed vanguard and as uncompromising fighters.

EXPLAINING INNOVATION IN THE REPERTOIRES OF STRATEGIES

Some strategies have a long tradition with international roots, such as the three multi-sectoral strategies analyzed. But others are specific to Latin America, like *basismo*, which entails territorial organization of the popular sectors in Argentina. *Basismo* is also an example of a strategy that originated as part of the repertoire of a specific ideological group but has then been widely adopted by others, such as autonomists (Popular Front "Darío Santillán," FPDS; MTD of Solano), Maoists (CCC), national-populists (Neighborhoods Standing Up), and Peronists ("Evita" Movement). Yet, with other strategies included in the *piquetero* repertoire, the opposite happens. One example is Morenist entryism: despite this strategy having been useful for the PO, it did not spread outside the Trotskyist *piquetero* SMOs. How and why some of these strategies have diffused across countries, historical periods, and ideological traditions while others have had more limited take-up is a relevant Tillyian question that, in the case of the repertoire of strategies, has a non-Tillyian answer.

Since the repertoire of strategies is less structurally determined than the repertoire of contention, its transformations happen as a result of debates that are permanently renewed among the *piquetero* leaders as well as the party, union, and intellectual elites related to them.[17] These debates sometimes set into motion modifications that are partially based on experiential learning. In other words, the repertoire of strategies does not evolve through slow and gradual changes at the state and regime levels, but rather through teaching and learning, intergenerational transmission, trial and error, emulation, and so on. In empirical terms, this means that innovation in repertoires of strategies and their diffusion can take place much more quickly and easily than in repertoires of contention.

One way this occurs is through emulation and teaching: situations where strategies are transmitted and created in semi-public or private gatherings. Among the *piqueteros*, the FPDS publishes handbooks for strategizing and organizes regular training gatherings, and the "Evita"

[17] Several examples of the intentional production of strategies by intellectuals in Asia, Africa, and Latin America can be found in Baud and Rutten (2004).

Movement has a house on an island in the delta of Buenos Aires to train young members on ideological and strategic issues. This interest in strategic and ideological training is not unique to the *piqueteros*. In Brazil, the MST has offered courses to its own members and activists from all around the world at the Florestan Fernandes National School, located on the outskirts of São Paulo.

A second way for repertoires to expand is through what I call "resignification" – where the original strategy is taken up by another group with different political goals and inserted within a different set of legacies.[18] One interesting case of this kind of innovation is what I term "*basista* empowerment," that is, the syncretic resignification of *basismo* and World Bank–inspired entrepreneurial social policies of empowerment in the post-neoliberal context by left-wing or national-populist organizations. In the case of the *piqueteros*, it was used by the "Evita" Movement and Neighborhoods Standing Up in particular. This resignification of social policies would be crucial for understanding the last phase of the second wave of incorporation analyzed in Chapter 6.

A third source for enrichment of repertoires of strategies is transnational mutual influence among social movements. Movement leaders and members participate in many gatherings and meetings with other movements, which tends to build a "community of practice" (Wenger 1998). In the case of the *piqueteros*, the community of practice acts as a vehicle for transnational reproduction of patterns and strategies. For instance, the mutual influence and connections between the *piqueteros* in Argentina and the landless peasants' movement in Brazil has produced some commonalities. FTV leaders told me that their urban land occupations in the 1980s were inspired by the CBC experience in Brazil (cf. Isman 2004: 108–9). Brazil's MST has permanent contacts with the MTR and its divisions (the FPDS, mainly), the MTD of Solano, the MTD of La Juanita, and the UTD of Mosconi through the brokerage of the Mothers of the Plaza de Mayo Association. These links led the MST to create its own movement of unemployed workers in Brazil, as was explained to me by national MST leaders in São Paulo. In addition, the CCC has links with

[18] Freedman (2013: 252–53, 400–4) offers a detailed narration of how this process works across diverse ideological traditions (like the contentious strategies borrowed by Engels from Claus von Clausewitz) as well as within more proximate ideological traditions, such as the diffusion of *foquismo* from "Che" Guevara's original formulation to its urban use by sectors of the Black Panther Party in the USA. Freedman's book can be also seen as an illustration of the importance of reading and writing as a conscious process of learning and resignifying strategies as I am conceptualizing it.

the Poor Peasants' League, the Maoist SMO of the Brazilian landless peasants' movement. Finally, the World Social Forum was mentioned several times as a space for mutual learning and connection. However, though these connections all have significant effects, they play only a partial role in the expansion or contraction of the repertoire of strategies.

In brief, experiential accumulation intentionally and unintentionally expands or restricts the repertoire of strategies and thus plays a decisive additional role in comprehending the interactive process of change and continuity. Actors reduce or expand their repertoire of strategies by defining their past actions and how they are linked to their present choice of strategic options. This can empirically take place through a Tillyian logic of repertoire of contention (through slow and gradual changes at the state and regime levels), but also through systematic reading and study (which happens among many philosophically or ideologically minded groups), intentional trans-generational transmission (when the older leaders give courses and informally transmit their experience and knowledge to younger and less experienced members), and so on. In other words, the repertoire of strategies is delimited by non-rationalistic principles as a result of the stock of legacies, as well as the configuration of the political context.

CONCLUSION

The concepts of repertoire of strategies and stock of legacies can be used to identify elements fundamental to a social movement that could not otherwise have been perceived in the tracing of its narrative. First, they allow us to explain what is happening when the repertoire of contention is not deployed, narrating a much more dynamic and rich process of strategic action than is possible through the concept of repertoire of contention alone. Second, they open the door to analyzing the internal complexity of a movement. In other words, even though there are more than fifteen national SMOs within the *piquetero* movement carrying out roadblocks, marches, and encampments, they do not share a common repertoire of strategies and frequently deploy different strategies in the same situation, sometimes learning from one another, but in many other situations developing autonomous strategies that depend on the stock of legacies specific to their SMO. This internal richness could never have been apparent if the analysis had been reduced to the Tillyian approach alone. And third, the conceptualization of strategy making I have proposed helps to close the gap in the social movement literature between an approach that proposes micro analysis of tactical trade-offs and macro analysis of repertoires of contention. Instead, I offer a collective and historically rooted understanding of strategy making.

The concepts of repertoire of strategies and stock of legacies help to bridge the artificial distinction between contentious and routine politics, observing the picture as a dynamic interaction involving the selective use of strategies based on inherited legacies that limit the perception of available options for action. In addition, the configuration of the political context and the innovative capacity of actors to perform actions that – though not always fully logical – are the result of intentionally attempting to produce a public, semi-public, or private event leads to an analysis of strategies that may or may not involve disruption.

The theoretical proposals of this chapter, together with those of the previous one, provide an answer to a crucial problem in historical comparative sociology: the apprehension of the need for bridging the relationship between the pace of long-term historical processes and the expectations of the actors involved in the process, as suggested by Aminzade (1992). The notion of repertoire of strategies links both processes without subsuming either of them to the determinism of the other if combined with a historically rooted analysis.

Moreover, the concepts proposed in this book offer a tool for solving one of the main biases in process-tracing: how to consider negative evidence. This conceptual proposal might allow us to include into the account of a political process an answer to why an event did not happen without resorting to the solutions offered by rational choice (the most cost-effective) or path-dependence (the initial moment of the historical process being studied). Instead, a historical relational analysis could be conceived by considering the restrictive effect of the accumulation of experiences (whether direct or indirect) through its capacity to reduce or increase the perceived alternatives as the interaction dynamically evolves. In order to put this into practice, I suggest an approach that assesses the time-space conditionality of human action without viewing interaction deterministically, as proposed by path-dependence's "relative 'openness' or 'permissiveness' of early stages in a sequence compared with the relatively 'closed' or 'coercive' nature of later stages" (Pierson 2000: 75).

The next four chapters will demonstrate, by studying the story of the *piqueteros*, the utility of retaining Tilly's tradition of contextualized political analysis. Adding in context and the long-term roots of strategies allows us to avoid universalizing what is time-space specific, and pushes us to ask how and why certain strategies enter the predominant repertoire of a movement while others do not. At the same time, and in order to avoid the structuralist trap, I apply this collective and historical understanding of strategy making and performing that lends more weight to actors than does Tilly's repertoire of contention (Krinsky and Mische 2013). In this way, Tilly's approach can be complemented in the analysis of the strategic actions of social movements across time.

PART II

THE SECOND INCORPORATION IN ARGENTINA

3

From the Origin of Unemployed Workers' Protests to Recognition of the "*Piquetero* Question" (1996–99)

This chapter examines the immediate causes that led to the establishment of the unemployed workers' movement in Argentina. The analysis in this chapter suggests that the failure of the state to recognize the "social question" is behind the emergence of the first protests of unemployed people in Argentina. The demonstrations demanding reincorporation grew more and more disruptive and spread across the country because the socioeconomic changes that led to the abrupt increase in unemployment were not followed with social policies to alleviate societal suffering.

However, the emergence of unemployment as a grievance was not the only factor that fed into the rise of the *piquetero* movement. A fuller understanding of the process must, I argue, include analysis of the changes experienced by first incorporation actors, strategic innovation on the part of political actors, and the specific characteristics of the Argentine political regime. On the one hand, the key actors in the first incorporation process disengaged from the popular sectors – the main labor-based party and part of the trade union system. On the other hand, it is very relevant to consider the enrichment in the repertoire of strategies of some left-wing networks, trade unions, and Catholic groups that allowed them to adapt ideas and strategies to the imperative need of politically organizing the unemployed at the neighborhood level. Moreover, I argue that the appearance of the *piquetero* movement was a result of the confluence of previous networks of territorialized actors in the most pluralistic social context of Argentina: the Greater Metropolitan Area of Buenos Aires.

The creation of the *piquetero* movement meant the political organization of the struggle for reincorporation. It was the increased disruptive power of the disincorporated popular sectors – and, in particular, their organization into a movement of unemployed workers – that compelled the national government to do something for the victims of neoliberalism and recognize the existence of a *new* social question – the "*piquetero* question."

THE COLLAPSE OF IMPORT-SUBSTITUTION INDUSTRIALIZATION AND NEOLIBERAL REFORMS

Democratization in Argentina was associated with the expectation of a return to some sort of welfare state. It was expected that this would happen through the relaunching of ISI. However, this ambition was quickly dismissed as the 1980s debt crisis spread across Latin America. Argentina's economy suffered from stagnation with a 7.2 percent contraction from 1983 to 1985, and between 1989 and 1991, a hyperinflation crisis, reaching 3,079.8 percent in 1989 (Smith et al. 1994; Acuña 1995; Saad-Filho et al. 2007). In May 1989, the rate of unemployment had reached 8.1 percent and 47.3 percent of the population was living in poverty. This led to a series of food riots in Rosario, Argentina's third-largest city, and these quickly spread to peri-urban Buenos Aires and other big cities. As a result, the first president since redemocratization, Raúl Alfonsín (Radical Civic Union, UCR), ended his presidency (1983–89) six months in advance, handling power over to Carlos Menem (of the Peronist Justicialist Party, PJ). Although Menem had promised to re-establish the ISI model, the persistence of high levels of inflation (197 percent by July), unemployment (7.1 percent), and poverty (33.7 percent in October 1989) pushed him toward a heterodox neoliberal reform program with the purpose of urgently resolving the crisis (Palermo and Novaro 1996). In August 1989, the Law of State Reform was passed, which allowed for the restructuring and privatization of almost every state-owned company and made the concession of privatizing the administration of public services. In March 1991, the Convertibility Law was introduced, pegging the peso to the US dollar at a one-to-one exchange rate. Even though neoliberal reforms had been applied in Argentina since the initiation of the disincorporation process in the mid 1970s, these two laws combined set off a swift and sweeping process of reform that led to the end of the ISI model and weakened the neocorporatist regime in Argentina.

These reforms were applied in two stages. The first stage was the introduction of stabilization policies aimed at resolving the debt and fiscal crises and the problem of hyperinflation. The focus was on the privatization of state-owned companies and the liberalization of ISI regulations with a neoclassical economic approach (Haggard and Kaufman 1995; Oszlak 2003). The five key policies implemented in Argentina, as in many other Latin American countries, were import liberalization, exchange rate overvaluation, domestic financial liberalization, tax increases and expenditure cuts, and liberalization of the capital account of the balance of payments (Gerchunoff and Torre 1996; Saad-Filho et al. 2007). The second stage of the reform process was focused on the restructuring of the public sector through decentralization and a reformulation of social policies from a universalist approach to a individualist one (Orlansky 1998; Oxhorn 1998; Tokman and O'Donnell 1998).

After the Convertibility Plan, inflation fell dramatically, which generated substantial public support for Menem's reforms (Etchegaray and Elrodi 2001). Menem's government had a parliamentary majority in both chambers thanks to an alliance with small conservative parties from the provinces (Llanos 2002) and a stable pro-reform coalition among some General Labor Confederation (CGT) unions, domestic industrialists, and PJ governors (Levitsky and Murillo 2005). Support from the CGT unions, one of the two main ISI actors, was obtained by agreeing not to reform the corporatist labor legislation and deregulate the health system while allowing unions to participate in the newly privatized companies and retirement funds (Etchemendy 2004, 2005; Murillo 2005). The support of the second main ISI actor, the domestic industrialists, was obtained by compensating them with privileges related to privatizations and protected markets in order to cushion national industrialists from the potential losses of opening up the economy and privatization (Etchemendy 2004, 2005). Finally, the support of PJ governors was obtained by agreeing to postpone and, later, gradually produce adjustments and neoliberal reforms at the provincial level (Gibson and Calvo 2000). This pro-reform coalition allowed Menem to press ahead with further privatizations and neoliberal reforms. This included restrictions on the right to strike and the decentralization of collective bargaining to the firm level in 1990 (McGuire 1997: 224–25).[1]

1 Several wide-ranging reforms affected labor relations and the corporatist mechanism. For a description of these reforms and their limited social policies, cf. Cook (2007: ch. 3); Neffa (2008: 55–64).

THE TRANSFORMATION OF FIRST INCORPORATION ACTORS UNDER NEOLIBERAL DISINCORPORATION

Prior to and leading into the start of Menem's first presidency, the two main organizations of first incorporation underwent deep transformation. First, the PJ, the main labor-based party, experienced a process of de-unionization and reformulation into a machine party, thereby modifying its relationship with the popular sectors, its historical support base. Second, trade unions went through an increased process of pluralization and reformulation of strategies and tactics based on the need to survive and confront disincorporation policies. This reformulation of their relationship with the popular sectors was crucial for the opening of alternative avenues for organizing the poor people in Argentina.

Changes in the Main Labor-Based Party: The Peronist Justicialist Party

As explained in Chapter 1, Peronism is associated with the first incorporation of the Argentine popular sectors in the socio-political arena. Even though the party was an instrument for channeling the claims for incorporation into corporatist institutions, the creation of an autonomous political party was never relevant for Juan Domingo Perón. In 1949 he founded the Peronist Party (later renamed PJ) for the sole purpose of having an electoral label (McGuire 1997: 59–66). After Perón's death in 1975, union leaders largely took control of the party and the Peronist movement included national industrialists and the CGT as well as women's and youth branches (Torre 2004; Rossi 2013a). With the return of a democratic setting and the party's first defeat in a presidential election under free ballot in 1983, the PJ started a process of metamorphosis: a coalition of PJ governors transformed it into a machine party detached from union control (McGuire 1997: 185–215). A faction called Peronist Renovation that intended to emulate the changes enacted by the social-democratic Spanish Socialist Workers Party promoted this conversion. The efforts by Peronist Renovation leaders positioned the main party representatives of the popular sectors as more autonomous from the CGT, while preserving its loosely structured system of organization.

Menem later defeated the Peronist Renovation faction, and the institutionalization of the PJ failed. The result was that in the 1980s and 1990s, the PJ went from being a labor-based party to a patronage-based machine (Levitsky 2003b). Consequently, since the failure of Peronist

Renovation in the 1980s, there are three organizational characteristics that – according to Levitsky (2003b: 86–87) – define the PJ: structural flexibility, bureaucratic flexibility, and the mutual autonomy of higher- and lower-level bodies. That is why "it is perhaps more accurate to describe the PJ as an *informal mass party*. It is a mass party in that it maintains a powerful base-level infrastructure, extensive linkages to working and lower class society, and a large membership and activist base. It is informal in that Peronist sub-units organise themselves, lack a standard organisational structure, and are generally not integrated into (or subject to the discipline of) the party's central bureaucracy" (Levitsky 2001: 35, italics in original). This facilitated the PJ's survival during the neoliberal era, while enacting policies that contradicted its historically predominant commitment to ISI and developmentalist ethos. This process of transformation – which initially meant a grassroots articulation of patronage and clientelistic neighborhood units (in the 1980s) – later led the party to distance itself from the popular sectors (in the 1990s).

The organizational structure of the PJ post-1980s produced an important consequence for its interactions with the organized urban poor. The PJ's deficiencies in the area of coordination, in addition to the flexible networked structure of the party, led to the multiplication of internal factions (called "*agrupaciones*") and a move away from whole-party leadership toward more personalized and territorially based leadership. Therefore, two areas of difficulty arose with respect to coordination among Peronists: first, horizontal tensions between mayors within a province, and nationally between governors; and, second, vertical tensions between mayors, the governor and the presidency, which produces a multi-level space of contention/interaction, especially in Greater Buenos Aires. These two points of tension were key factors in the *piqueteros*' emergence and interactions with the political elites.

The Pluralization of the Trade Union System: Tactics within Austerity

The second area of transformation in the first incorporation actors is the reduction in the power and influence of the CGT after losing the monopoly on labor representation as a result of the pluralization of the union system into a model of segmented corporatism (Etchemendy and Collier 2007). The labor movement has traditionally been strong and well organized by the Peronists in Argentina. However, as a result of the collapse of ISI and its replacement with neoliberalism, the CGT suffered from a decrease in its membership figures in terms of the economically active population, from having by far the highest figures in Latin America, with a 50.1 percent peak between 1970 and 1995 (Roberts 2002: 15, table 1), to representing less than 40 percent of the formal labor force since the 1990s (Etchemendy and Collier 2007: 385). This new context meant that the influence of the CGT on the PJ plummeted during the 1990s. In other words, since the relationship with the CGT was no longer crucial for the electoral success of the PJ, the mobilization and clientelistic capacity of PJ mayors became the key territorial base for this already loosely structured party.

This transformation was attached to the PJ process of de-unionization. According to Levitsky (2003a, 2003b), the de-unionization of the PJ was not a consequence of the party embracing neoliberalism. On the contrary, it had happened prior to this as an unintended consequence of the Peronist Renovation faction's failed project to create non-unionized territorial base units. As a result of this, the whole union system was weakened, with divisions taking place in 1991, 1992, and 1994. These splits were the result of five main tactics adopted within the Peronist union system during this period. The tactics can be distinguished by their degree of detachment from the PJ and their role in the emergence of the *piqueteros*. **Table 3.1** summarizes the main tactics adopted by trade unions during this period.

A first tactic was that of preserving the corporatist link with the state and the PJ. The CGT San Martín, the majoritarian division of the CGT that participated in the 1991 pro-neoliberal reforms coalition, mostly used this tactic. The CGT San Martín was actively involved in the government with Jorge Triaca, who was the Minister of Labor, Employment and Social Security (1989–91). One of the biggest unions, the Metallurgy Workers' Union (UOM), widely implemented a corporatist strategy. Though the UOM under the leadership of Lorenzo Miguel had taken a pragmatic position toward the government by supporting some of its reforms, it was not a member of the pro-reform coalition (Levitsky 2003b).

A second tactic among unions was that of financing and sustaining PJ *agrupaciones* within an electoral strategy to gain places on closed legislative lists (Levitsky 2003b). This tactic did not imply detaching from the PJ but rather that unions emulate the PJ's logic of territorial politics. This tactic had the consequence of intensifying the ongoing fragmentation of the labor movement, while abandoning union representation as the territorial strategy became more relevant (Levitsky 2003a: 24). Among others,

TABLE 3.1 *Main Tactics Employed within the Trade Union System, 1990–99*

Trade Union	Main Tactics	Type of Involvement in the Emergence of the *Piquetero* Movement
Metallurgy Workers' Union (UOM), among others – General Labor Confederation San Martín (CGT, dominant sector)	Preservation of the corporatist link with the state and the PJ. Active participation in the governing coalition with union leaders.	None.
Union of Tourism, Hotels and Gastronomic Workers, among others – CGT San Martín	Financing and support of PJ *agrupaciones* (party factions) within an electoral strategy to gain places on closed legislative lists.	None.
Several CGT San Martín unions	The promotion of "block roundtables" – groups of unions in support of particular candidates, mainly *menemistas*.	None.
Argentine Workers Union (CTA, group of former CGT unions)	Total break with the PJ and participation in the creation of a new party, the Broad Front. Promotion of a multi-sectoral coordinating structure among federations of actors that transcended incorporated workers.	Support for the creation of a federation of unemployed workers that evolved into a few of the *piquetero* SMOs.
Argentine Workers' Movement (MTA, coalition of dissident CGT transport unions)	Partial detachment from the CGT and the PJ. Unsuccessful coordination of a territorial base with student organizations in association with left-wing *agrupaciones* that had abandoned the PJ and were in coalition with other non-Peronist leftist groups.	Failed attempt to emulate CTA strategy.

(*continued*)

TABLE 3.1 (*continued*)

Trade Union	Main Tactics	Type of Involvement in the Emergence of the *Piquetero* Movement
Classist and Combative Current (CCC, the only non-Peronist coalition of grassroots unions)	Attempt to build a territory- and factory-based non-Peronist union supported by left-wing parties, grassroots unions, and groups involved in land occupations. Failure and abandonment of this tactic, becoming an internal faction of the CGT and CTA and one of the main unemployed workers' SMOs.	Reformulation into a *piquetero* SMO.

Sources: Several interviews (2007–13); Ferrer (2005); Levitsky (2003a, 2003b).

it was widely used by union leaders who, in doing so, initiated their own electoral careers, such as the case of Luis Barrionuevo (service sector workers).

A third tactic was that of the promotion of "block roundtables" – groups of unions in support of particular candidates. The expectation was that some union representatives would be included and their interests put on the agenda through electoral conjunctural coalitions, but there was very low post-electoral discipline (Levitsky 2003a). This tactic was widely applied in support of Menem as well as various other PJ governors and leaders who opposed Menem.

These three tactics were for most CGT unions part of a strategy for survival in order to preserve some union privileges within a very unfavorable context. This also implied adopting a less contentious position. Although during the Alfonsín government the CGT had called for thirteen general strikes, the massive job losses resulting from Menem's privatization program led the CGT to call for only two general strikes (in November 1992 and September 1995). This gradually produced the result that as unemployment grew, "compensatory policies biased toward unions and workers who remained in the formal sector cemented a strong insider/outsider divide within the working class" (Etchemendy 2005: 65).

Still, these were not the only tactics used within the union system. Opposing non-contentious strategies was the CGT Azopardo, the smaller division of the CGT led in 1991 by Saúl Ubaldini (brewery workers), Mary Sánchez (teachers), and Víctor de Gennaro (state employees). This group considered Menem to be a traitor to Peronist ideals and pushed for active resistance to his reforms (Godio 2000: 1194–95). In 1990 and 1991 these unions coordinated strikes and uprisings at the local level in Tucumán, Jujuy, Chubut, Santa Cruz, and Chaco provinces that led to the resignation of some governors (Palermo and Novaro 1996: 349). Gradually, the CGT Azopardo lost its power, with Ubaldini deciding to stand as a Peronist non-PJ candidate for the governorship of the province of Buenos Aires in 1991. Ubaldini was defeated by Menem's vice president, Eduardo Duhalde (PJ), receiving just 2 percent of the vote. This result divided the CGT Azopardo even further as electoral success seemed impossible. On the one side were those who supported Ubaldini's attempt to reunify the CGT with the aim of expanding the corporatist strategy. On the other side, several unions promoted an autonomous position in relation to the PJ and political parties while rejecting the reunification of the CGT (Palermo and Novaro 1996: 351, n. 12).

In 1992, the main losers in the neoliberal reforms organized the Congress of Argentine Workers (CTA) to unify state workers, teachers, and people with small- and medium-sized farmers and businesses, among others.[2] Also in 1992, Menem initiated the first Fiscal Pact, an agreement with governors for the reduction of public sector jobs. This was the continuation of a similar policy applied to large urban areas a year earlier (Gibson and Calvo 2000). The CTA was never recognized as a union, and this left it in a weaker position than the CGT, with no access to the income provided by social security contributions (Armelino 2008). At the same time, the CTA promoted the coordination of all those actors who were impoverished by neoliberalism, which meant sponsoring territorialization outside of the PJ. The territorial base of the CTA came from those involved in Christian-based communities' (CBC) land occupations from the 1980s, the cooperative movement of the Communist Party of Argentina (PCA), and small national–populist parties such as Free Homeland.

In 1994 the Transport Workers General Union (UGTT) was created by the twenty-six transport unions of the CGT and coordinated by the *ubaldinistas* Juan Manuel Palacios (bus drivers) and Hugo Moyano

[2] In 1996 the organization became the Argentine Workers Union (CTA).

(truck drivers) (Ferrer 2005: 81–84). These unions rejected the absolute alignment of the CGT with Menem, and particularly the CGT's decision to cancel the call for a general strike in January 1994 (McGuire 1997: 233). This led to another tactic of detachment from the PJ and CGT. The same year, the UGTT created the Argentine Workers' Movement (MTA), a faction of the CGT that actually functioned as an independent union (Ferrer 2005: 93). Though choosing not to work within the PJ and CGT as did the CTA, for the MTA this was a conjunctural option and not the result of perceiving the PJ and CGT as non-modifiable organizations, as was the opinion of the CTA (Ferrer 2005: 146–47). The immediate consequence of the creation of the CTA and the MTA was that the CGT fell completely under the control of the *menemista* sectors (Novaro 2009: 464).

The MTA and the CTA represent two variants of a *fourth* union tactic. Specifically, the territorial tactics of the CTA and MTA constitute one of the points of departure for the *piquetero* movement. Notwithstanding the differences between these unions, both cases show that not all unions failed to resist the recommodification of social relations that neoliberal reforms imposed. While the MTA opted for a partial detachment from the CGT and the PJ, it unsuccessfully tried to organize a territorial base with the student movement of the National University of La Plata, in association with the abstentionist political organization Patriotic Revolutionary Movement (MPR) "Quebracho" – a collaboration of non-Peronist left groups with left-wing *agrupaciones* that abandoned the PJ. The CTA opted for a total break with the PJ and participated in the creation of a new party, the Broad Front (FG), led by dissident PJ parliamentarians who rejected neoliberal reforms and governmental corruption. The CTA partially redefined the repertoire of strategies adopted by Peronist unions by expanding it to territorially based actions. Sustained by the accumulated legacies of the CBC and land occupations rather than factory-based trade union strategies, the CTA promoted multi-sectoral coordination among federations of actors that transcended incorporated workers. This was an important difference compared with the CGT's preservation of the traditional Peronist corporatist repertoire of strategies. Some years later, the MTA attempted to emulate the territorial process enacted by the CTA, but it quickly returned to trade unionist legacies. Beyond their differences, the MTA and CTA cases present a crucial change with the first three tactics adopted by CGT unions: a more active confrontation with neoliberalism and a concern for organizing the unemployed and urban poor with the aim of reincorporating them – but without the aim of influencing the PJ.

The repertoire of contention of Argentina was also expanded during this period. *Puebladas* (town revolts)[3] were introduced to Argentina's repertoire of contention, while traditional protest formats were vigorously revived, such as pickets/roadblocks, soup kitchens, and *escraches* (graffiti protests), also keeping – though in a decreasing number – strikes (Schuster et al. 2006). This was related to the increased coordination among social actors and the collapse of regional economies due to the social impact of the first Fiscal Pact and the application of a second Fiscal Pact in 1994 that expanded reforms to provincial service privatizations and further reduced expenditure. As many of the provincial economies were heavily dependent on public jobs and state expenditure, the required cuts produced an increase in unemployment. In addition, in many provinces the few industries that existed were mostly commodities-based, and as they suffered from the overvaluation of the peso, they were incapable of compensating for job losses. This combination of circumstances led to the failure of several regional economies. In December 1993, Santiago del Estero bankrupted, the first of a series of poor peripheral provinces to do so, provoking wave of *puebladas* and forcing the provincial authorities to resign (Auyero 2003; Farinetti 1999). This was followed that same year by several *puebladas* in Jujuy, which remained unstable until 1995 due to the active resistance of the Union of Municipal Workers and Employees (SEOM), led by Carlos "Perro" Santillán (Rodríguez Blanco 2002; Santillán and Olmedo 1998).

The first main result of the struggles carried out by the CTA, MTA, and SEOM was the organization in 1994 of the first Federal March, a massive national demonstration of resistance to the consequences of neoliberal reforms.[4] This march was intended to give increased visibility in the city of Buenos Aires to the contentious events that were taking place in the rest of Argentina. The CTA and MTA unions, several SMOs from the

[3] The *puebladas* or *estallidos sociales* ("social explosions") bear a series of specific characteristics, defined by Farinetti (1999: 17–18) as follows: 1. The actors are public employees that stopped being paid; 2. The demand is the claim for payment; 3. The mode of expression is the mobilization and the destruction of the symbols of local politics (e.g., the burning of the house of government) and the destruction and looting of politicians' private houses; 4. The scale is local, and protest is never organized into movements; 5. The main target of action is the provincial and local political elite; and 6. The language of the protest is against the local powers and is both moral (e.g., against corruption) and personalized (i.e., targets specific politicians).

[4] Since the only CGT general strike called during this period in 1992, strikes were mostly used at the local level, and only in August 1994 and April 1995 could the CTA and the MTA organize general strikes, albeit restricted to their own unions.

cooperatives, pensioners, farmers, unemployed workers, and all the center-left and left parties marched from around the country to the federal capital. This march also represented the starting point for another union tactic. The only non-Peronist strategy to build a union was developed by a group of Maoist Communist Revolutionary Party (PCR) factory-based internal factions called First of May Classist Groupings. The PCR, in association with some former Movement Towards Socialism (MAS) Trotskyist party members, achieved higher degrees of internal cohesion thanks to the Federal March.

The Federal March led to the creation of the Classist and Combative Current (CCC). As such, the CCC represents a *fifth* union tactic and the second involving a break with the CGT. This group, coordinated by Santillán of the SEOM of Jujuy, had always had a minor role within the CGT, but since the neoliberal state reforms the left-wing party sector of the CGT had tried to build a union based on class struggle and focusing on three areas: employed, unemployed, and retired workers. The CCC's initial aim in 1994 was to be a new union struggling to break the Peronist hegemony, but soon this idea was abandoned and instead it became an internal faction of the CGT and CTA and one of the main unemployed workers SMOs (more about this later). In brief, the fifth union tactic was as contentious as the tactics employed by the CTA and the MTA, while being the most detached union from the PJ and the CGT in terms of its aims. The goal of the CCC was to build a territory- and factory-based non-Peronist union sustained by left-wing parties, grassroots unions, and those involved in land occupations. This idea was unsustainable due to the reduced influence of the left in Argentina and the disparity of resources vis-à-vis the CGT, leading to a dispute of internal positions, and the CCC eventually settled on being a non-Peronist faction inside the CGT.

THE SOCIAL CONSEQUENCES OF NEOLIBERALISM AND THE LACK OF UNEMPLOYMENT POLICIES

In 1994 Menem passed a constitutional reform that allowed him to stand for re-election, and he subsequently won without difficulty in 1995. Menem defeated a newly created center-left coalition called Front for a Country in Solidarity (FREPASO),[5] supported by the CTA, which pushed

[5] FREPASO was a coalition assembled by dissident Peronists who built the FG, the Open Politics for Social Integrity party, the Socialist Party, the left-wing sector of the Christian Democrat Party, and initially also the PCA and other left-wing parties.

the centennial UCR into third position, thereby breaking fifty years of bipartisan majoritarian politics. With most of the core reforms passed during the first term of office, Menem's second mandate faced increasingly high levels of contention. This was the result of a worsening social situation (poverty would affect 27.9 percent of the Buenos Aires peri-urban population in 1996), increased coordination between the CTA, MTA, and CCC, and the emergence of the *piquetero* movement.

The series of *puebladas* (town revolts) represent another point of departure for the *piquetero* movement. With the Santiago del Estero and Jujuy *puebladas*, a diffusion process was set into motion, with *puebladas* taking place in several provincial capitals and forcing many governors to resign. The frequency of *puebladas* grew from the very beginning of Menem's second term to the last days of his mandate. *Puebladas* were the result of resistance by state employees to provincial fiscal austerity policies, with some of the most significant ones those in 1995 in Córdoba (June), San Juan (July), and Río Negro (September and October) and in December 1999 in Corrientes. Owing to the collapse of the economy of some cities in petroleum enclaves, *puebladas* would also emerge in 1996 (June) and 1997 (March) in Cutral-Có and Plaza Huincul (Neuquén) and from 1997 to 1999 in Tartagal and Mosconi (Salta), leading to the creation of the Union of Unemployed Workers (UTD) of Mosconi (Svampa and Pereyra 2003: ch. 3). This issue will be further analyzed in the next chapter.

Despite the magnitude and intensity of the struggle against neoliberal reforms and the consequences of disincorporation, in 1994 the Menem government had not yet recognized the existence of a "social question" regarding unemployment. In 1995 the national rate of unemployment reached 18.5 percent, with only 7.1 percent of the unemployed receiving any kind of economic compensation and just 1.3 percent of the economically active population covered by unemployment benefits (Etchemendy 2004: 282). These figures meant that Argentina had the second-highest rate of unemployment in Latin America, just after Nicaragua (McGuire 1997: 222). To make things even worse, from 1989 to 1992 all the social policies inherited from the Alfonsín government were dismantled and replaced with very limited ones, such as the National Emergency Bond and the Federal Solidarity Program (Repetto 2000: 604–5).

In brief, the Menem government went through two stages regarding the unemployment issue. From 1991 to 1994 the problem was simply denied, arguing that the economic recovery would absorb job losses through privatization and reforms (McGuire 1997: 222). From 1995 onward, some recognition of a "social question" emerged as unrest increased. Nevertheless, the policies applied were focalized measures designed to contain conflict rather than systematic policies that would ease the situation (McGuire 1997: 223; Lodola 2005).

Why were there no unemployment policies? The main reasons were twofold. The first was related to the changes in the PJ-CGT relationship. Though union influence on the PJ had reduced since the 1980s, the Menem government still considered the CGT's participation in the pro-reform coalition as more important than disincorporated workers (Etchemendy 2004). In September 1995, during Menem's first term, the CGT called for the second and final general strike. This strike was in response to the government's decision to lower tax contributions to social security. The outcome of the strike was that "the government and the CGT agreed to keep the tax reductions for all the social security payments except for the one that contributes to the union's health system. The employers' tax that goes to the union's account was reduced only 16 percent, while the business contribution to the unemployment fund was lowered by 52 percent" (Etchemendy 2004: 285). Thus, compensation was focused on protecting the organizational strength of the CGT rather than helping the individual victims of the reforms. This was achieved because some unions agreed to demobilize in exchange (Etchemendy 2004: 287).

The second reason is related to the territorialization of politics, which favored a governability agreement, in place since 1992, between the national government and Duhalde while he was governor of the province of Buenos Aires (1991–99). The agreement led to the creation of the Historical Rebuilding Fund for Greater Buenos Aires, a regular provision of national resources at the discretion of the administration of the province of around US$650 million annually for a decade (Prévôt-Schapira 1996: 90–92; *La Nación* 29/01/1998; Repetto 2000: 606–9). This agreement was the most developed of a generic type of accord that Menem entered into with provincial governors in exchange for their support of his reform policies (Gibson and Calvo 2000). The implications of this agreement were manifold. The first was that Menem agreed not to interfere with any PJ and provincial politics in Buenos Aires after Duhalde won the 1993 internal party election (Levitsky 2001: 62–63; Novaro 2009: 423, n. 17). The second was that Duhalde built a strong clientelistic territorial network in Greater Buenos Aires based on the coordination of a network of local brokers called "*manzaneras*" (block ladies) who administered the distribution of resources across poor districts (Auyero 2000; Repetto

2000). The third was the absence of any national social policy on unemployment in Buenos Aires as a result of this territorial agreement and, instead, the implementation of provincial unemployment subsidies called Plan for Buenos Aires Neighborhoods. Due to this combination of factors, while this agreement was in place (1992–99) the main interlocutor for reincorporation claims in Buenos Aires was the provincial government.

The provincial locus of contention was not limited to Buenos Aires. The "provincialization" of politics and decentralization at the beginning of the neoliberal reforms moved the focus of protest activity to the subnational governments all across the country (Auyero 2002).

THE EMERGENCE OF THE PIQUETERO PROTESTS: FROM THE SITING DECISION TO NATIONAL DIFFUSION

In the Patagonian province of Neuquén the claim for reincorporation emerged as a result of a "siting decision" that annulled what could have been a palliative solution to the economic crisis.[6] This siting decision favored the emergence of protest due to the horizontal political opportunities created by the internal division of the hegemonic provincial party into two factions and the vertical political opportunities produced by the unwillingness of the Menem government to provide economic and political support to Neuquén's governor during the conflict.

In line with much of the literature that follows the political process approach (McAdam 1996; Tarrow 1998), in Argentina division among elites is one of the crucial elements for the emergence of contention too. The only addition that must be made to this generally used dimension of political opportunities is that it is not only *inter*-party division that is relevant but also *intra*-party division, which can offer opportunities for finding allies. This effect is stronger in a hegemonic party system, where the low degree of pluralism becomes a source of internal division among the party elite.

The grievance of unemployment was caused by the bid of the national government to reduce the state's economic deficit through privatization. With this goal in mind, the Menem government decided to downsize the work force of the main state-owned company, the petroleum corporation

6 "By 'siting decision' we mean the announcement by project and government officials of their intention to locate some substantial infrastructure project or facility in a given locale" (McAdam et al. 2008: 325). In this case it is the announcement of the cancellation of a project that sets a contentious dynamic in motion.

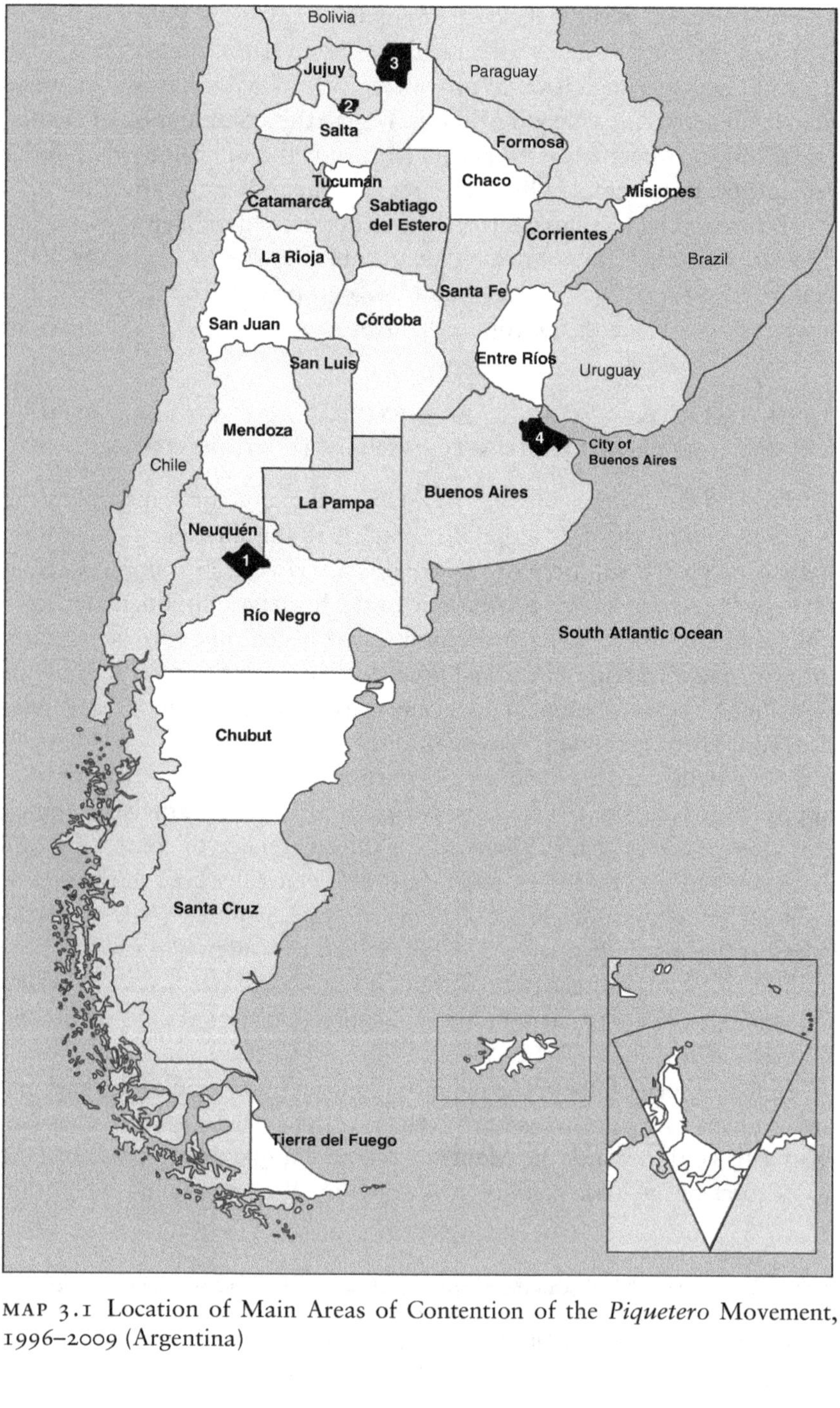

MAP 3.1 Location of Main Areas of Contention of the *Piquetero* Movement, 1996–2009 (Argentina)

Treasury Petroleum Fields (YPF), reducing the number of workers from 51,000 in 1989 to less than 11,000 in 1992. At the same time, YPF transferred or closed petroleum enclaves whose profits were not competitive enough, and in 1992, as part of the agreement for the privatization of YPF, Neuquén province (one of the main petroleum areas) retained control over less profitable oilfields in the Plaza Huincul and Cutral-Có areas (Sánchez 1997; Auyero 2003). This meant that YPF went from suffering a loss of US$570 million in 1990 to recording earnings of US$260 million in 1992 and US$600 million in 1993. With the company more valuable, in 1993 the government made the decision to start a partial privatization process by selling company shares to private investors, provinces with petroleum resources, and even YPF employees. This major decision led to just 20 percent of YPF remaining in the hands of the state (Novaro 2009: 432–33).

In Neuquén, a province dependent to oil extraction and refinement (**Map 3.1**), the downsizing of the YPF work force and the closure of the Plaza Huincul and Cutral-Có branches produced a dramatic social crisis between 1993 and 1995 in these petroleum enclaves. In a desperate move to resolve the crisis, the Neuquén governor Jorge Sobisch ("white" faction of the provincial party Neuquén People's Movement (MPN)) made an agreement with the Canadian company Agrium for the building of a

---

CAPTION FOR MAP 3.1 (cont.)

Key:

1 Cutral-Có and Plaza Huincul districts (YPF petroleum enclave): 1996–97 [pickets, *puebladas*]
2 San Salvador de Jujuy (provincial capital): 1997–98 [strikes, marches, multi-sectoral coalitions including the unemployed]
3 Mosconi and Tartagal districts (YPF petroleum enclave): 1997–99 [pickets, multi-sectoral coalitions including the unemployed, *puebladas*]
4 City of Buenos Aires (national capital), Greater Buenos Aires and city of La Plata (provincial capital): 1996/7–2000 [soup kitchens, pickets, marches, rallies]

Note: The numbering reflects the chronological unfolding of events in terms of the *piqueteros*' process of contention, not the order of emergence of the SMOs. The years indicate the period considered to be when the *piquetero* movement emerged. The repertoire of contention used during this period is between brackets.
Source: Map by Lucas M. Rossi, using a base map from Wikimedia: https://commons.wikimedia.org/wiki/File:Argentina.svg.

fertilizer factory in the area using the enclave's existing infrastructure under provincial control (Sánchez 1997; Auyero 2003). This was offered as a solution to the ruin of the local economy, with 65 percent of the population in Cutral-Có and Plaza Huincul unemployed (Svampa and Pereyra 2003: 33–34). At the same time, as previously remarked, unemployment was increasing at the national level and no systematic policies designed to counteract this had been implemented.

After much negotiation, on June 19, 1996, the new provincial government of Felipe Sapag ("yellow" faction of the MPN) decided to cancel the contract with Agrium because of a shortfall of US$100 million in investment that was required. On June 20 the local radio station aired the news in Cutral-Có and Plaza Huincul that the agreement with Agrium promoted by Sobisch ("white" faction) had been canceled by Sapag ("yellow" faction) (Sánchez 1997). In response, a series of pickets were launched on National Route 22, cutting off traffic as the protestors demanded an explanation and a solution. The "white" faction of the MPN – the internal opposition to the Sapag government – supported these actions (Auyero 2003). The following day, as they had not received a reply, they expanded the pickets to the neighboring highways, National Route 17 and Provincial Route 10, placing the whole area under siege. City Hall (governed by the "yellow" faction), schools, and the electricity cooperative closed in solidarity. Nonetheless, Sapag declared that he would not meet with people who engage in acts of "insubordination" (Sánchez 1997). The following day, the first big rally took place: in a town of 60,000 people, 5,000 met in an open assembly, including the former mayor of Cutral-Có (of the MPN's "white" faction and a supporter of the agreement).

As shown by Sánchez (1997) and Auyero (2003), disputes between the MPN's "white" and "yellow" factions played a crucial role in the emergence of the first *puebladas* and pickets in Cutral-Có and Plaza Huincul. This is because the MPN is an exception to the rule, as other provincial parties tend to lack organizational structure and territorial presence. As De Luca et al. (2002: 427) explain, "The MPN is distinct from the other provincial parties in that it is the only one that possesses an important mass base and strong neighborhood-level presence. Its average percentage of members during the 1983–1999 period (25%) is more than double that of the next largest provincial party, and in 1999 its members represented 36% of Neuquén's registered voters (the closest other provincial party had 10% of its province's voters as members)." This means that the MPN in Neuquén could be considered the equivalent of the PJ in Buenos Aires, the hegemonic actor whose intra-party disputes are more relevant than inter-party competition.[7]

As social unrest continued in Plaza Huincul and Cutral-Có, on June 23, 1996, the Catholic bishop of Neuquén, Agustín Radrizzani, held a public mass for a thousand people at the site of the picket and requested an immediate solution. The bishop was chosen to act as government intermediary, eventually meeting with Sapag in the provincial house of government. Bishops and priests were often called upon during pickets and unemployed workers' protests to act as mediators and supporters. If the diocese was part of the progressive wing of the Catholic Church, a *space for protected contention* was built. By "space for protected contention" I mean a geographical area that, due to its location within the area of influence of a strong allied institution, allows contentious politics to be played out by movements and other actors under conditions that involve less risk than elsewhere. The identification of such spaces introduces another contextual element that might explain where movements can build the networks that allow them to emerge and expand. This happened in Neuquén under the leadership of the previous bishop, Jaime de Nevares (1961–91).[8]

But the Catholic Church is not the only key broker; the CTA was also important during these events. A month earlier, on May 24, as part of the aforementioned attempts to coordinate territorialized action by disincorporated workers, the CTA established a Congress of Unemployed Workers. This congress created the Coordination of Unemployed Workers of CTA Neuquén (Oviedo 2004: 57–60).

As these events were unfolding, rumors of imminent repression by the Gendarmerie (military police) started to circulate. The repression began on June 24. The Gendarmerie arrived in the area by military helicopter to disperse the protesters and open up routes for traffic. Even while informal conversations were taking place with Sapag to arrange a meeting with him in the city of Neuquén, Sapag gave a televised speech justifying the cancellation of the contract and announcing that protestors "must move

7 The Argentine provincialization of the party system and the tendency toward hegemonic provincial parties or the dominance of a PJ or UCR faction in a province was accentuated by the decentralization of health and education during state reforms and the increased subnational redistribution of taxes by the national government (Murillo 1999; Falleti 2010). The series of provincial state reforms of the 1990s enforced this tendency by introducing uninominal representation and authorizing governor re-election, sometimes even on an unlimited basis (Calvo and Escolar 2005).

8 In Jujuy in 1997, as well as in Quilmes (Buenos Aires), the Catholic Church also played a mediating role during the pickets.

immediately away from the highway ... in order to avoid casualties ... because the law must be obeyed" (quoted by Sánchez 1997: 26). The next day, the judge who had ordered the deployment of the Gendarmerie visited the conflict site and told the protesters: "The action that you are taking is a clear demonstration of an uprising against a provincial government. This is a serious offense, that of sedition, and for this reason I publicly declare myself incompetent [to deal with this type of conflict] and I retire from the site of conflict with all the security forces accompanying me" (Margarita Aixa Gudiño, judge, quoted by Sánchez 1997: 14).

As the judge was retiring from the scene, the demonstrators began throwing stones at the Gendarmerie, and the security forces responded with repression. The same day, at a governors' meeting in La Pampa province, president Menem stated that the Neuquén conflict was a "strictly provincial problem," which left governor Sapag with no chance of receiving national support. As the protest evolved, the economic impact of the pickets on oil and merchandise distribution left the governor in too weak a position to ignore this claim for recognition of a new "social question" linked to the disincorporation consequences of neoliberalism. That same afternoon, governor Sapag made the snap decision to travel to Cutral-Có, with no prior notice. He headed to City Hall, where he gave a press conference requesting that the protestors meet him at the local government house. In the evening, he finally went to the highway to negotiate. Just seven days later, on June 26, 1996, a delegation went to the governorship with a list of claims, which the governor fully accepted, prompting the protesters to end the picket (Sánchez 1997: 27–28).

The National Government Responds: Subsidies, Repression, and Judicialization

A growing number of pickets (**Figure 3.1**) that preceded the emergence of the *piquetero* movement gave rise to a threefold state response. In the area of social policies, the first unemployment subsidies were applied on a relatively large scale. To address social unrest, the Gendarmerie's role was reformulated from border guard to a repressive force designed to quell unrest in rural and remote areas. And on the political level, protest was increasingly judicialized, with judges rather than politicians intervening to resolve social conflicts.[9]

[9] By "judicialization" I mean a combination of four processes as defined by Domingo (2004: 110): "First, the process by which there is an increase in the impact of judicial decisions

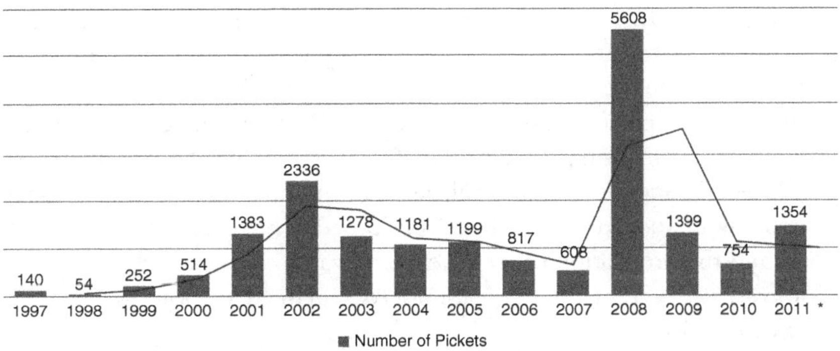

FIGURE 3.1 Annual Number of Pickets in Argentina, 1997–2011
*Until September
Source: Centro de Estudios para la Nueva Mayoría.

Concerning social policy, in 1996 the Menem government created the Work Program (*Plan Trabajar*) as a tool to relieve social unrest and avoid repression. The crucial element to note is that because it was set up late in the game, the Work Program did not appear to stop the mobilization, which had already taken root and was growing; it could only contain it in part (Lodola 2005). The allocation of unemployment subsidies was in response to protests as well as the social and economic needs of the provinces (Weitz-Shapiro 2006; Giraudy 2007), but they were implemented when the structural transformation process was already well advanced, and so "the late government intervention of a compensatory policy did not quiet stop social unrest, nor did it have any effect on the organization of the popular sectors" (Lodola 2005: 516). In other words, unlike the policy that was applied to CGT unions and national industrialists, the Work Program was not a policy designed to compensate the losers of neoliberal reforms in order to avoid mobilization or include them in the pro-reform coalition. It showed up so late that it came across as a desperate solution to increased social unrest. The Work Program was designed by World Bank and Ministry of Labor

upon political and social processes. Second, it refers to the process by which political conflict is increasingly resolved at the level of the courts. Third, at a discursive level, judicialization of politics reflects the degree to which regime legitimacy is increasingly constructed upon the public perception of the state's capacity and credibility in terms of delivering on rule of law, and rights protection. Finally, it refers also to the growing trend by different political actors and groups within society to use law and legal mechanisms to mobilize around specific policies, social and economic interests and demands." On the judicialization and criminalization of *piquetero* protests, cf. CELS (2003a, 2003b), Svampa and Pandolfi (2004), and Artese (2009).

technocrats, and from 1996 to 2001 it covered 20 percent of the unemployed workforce (Lodola 2005: 521). This meant an almost 300 percent increase from the 7.1 percent coverage rate achieved by the limited employment policies in place up until 1995. In 1997 Duhalde replicated the Work Program, implementing the Plan for Buenos Aires Neighborhoods in the province of Buenos Aires. Both policies had a number of aims in addition to controlling of social unrest: clientelism, capacity building among beneficiaries, and the promotion of cooperatives (Svampa and Pereyra 2003: 90). However, 80 percent of the unemployed remained without any kind of social protection.

These social policies were accompanied by a restructuring of the Gendarmerie from its original function as border police to an anti-riot force with specialized training and equipment, following the example of some European police forces (Massetti 2006; Stener Carlson 2006). Also, protest was increasingly judicialized. Even though this process started before the neoliberal reforms of the 1990s, the reformulation of the state's role in conflict resolution initiated by Menem's state reforms reinforced the judicialization of protest due to the dissolution of neocorporativism (Smulovitz 2005). The judicialization of protest became a crucial new element for the state in order to control protests organized by incorporated as much as disincorporated popular sectors (cf. Artese 2009).[10]

The Menem government's approach to the increased social unrest associated with unemployment was put in place before the legitimation of the *piquetero* movement as a political actor. The *piquetero* protests at the time were considered merely a "social question," attributable to the novelty of their claim and the type of actor involved, which were both new developments for Argentina. The gradual recognition of a "social question" began in 1994 when the Menem government created the Secretariat for Social Development, placing it under the direct control of the presidency. As it was not responsible for unemployment policy, it lacked teeth, mainly serving as a vehicle for the discretionary distribution of resources for the purposes of governability (Repetto 2000). This became clearer when new protests emerged, like in the 1997 second *pueblada* at Cutral-Có and Plaza Huincul. To this *pueblada* the national government reacted quickly with unemployment subsidies distributed by the Ministry of Labor.

[10] Permanent cases of judicialization took place in organizations that applied the witness strategy, such as Raúl Castells' MIJP. Castells was in jail from 1999 to 2002 after being convicted of extortion for asking for food at a Walmart supermarket by way of protest (cf. *Página/12*, 04/22–24/1999).

In the same period, Armando Caro Figueroa became Minister of Labor (1994–97), excluding CGT representatives from the Ministry in order to promote a reformulation of corporatist relations for incorporated workers (Godio 2000: 1199).

Diffusion to Public Sector Unions in Jujuy and Petroleum Enclaves in Salta

From 1990 to 1994 the SEOM union, under the Maoist PCR leader Santillán, coordinated the struggle in the northern province of Jujuy against local disincorporation. This struggle forced four governors to resign. The Fiscal Pacts led to a reduction of tax transfers to Jujuy, while public education had already been transferred to the province. At the same time the main areas of sugar production (Ledesma and La Esperanza) and the metallurgical industries (Zapla) were suffering under the effects of economic liberalization and the overvaluation of the peso (Rodríguez Blanco 2002). Despite the increase in contention, there was not yet an organization of unemployed workers; instead, the SEOM was mostly relying on a typical trade unionist strategy (corporatist wage negotiations, strikes, etc.). The coordination of unemployed workers in Jujuy was inspired by the 1996 and 1997 *puebladas* in Neuquén. Over twelve days in May 1997, nineteen simultaneous pickets were organized in Jujuy by a multi-sectoral coalition that included incorporated (CTA, SEOM) and disincorporated unemployed workers (Santillán and Olmedo 1998; Farinetti 1999; Rodríguez Blanco 2002).

This conflict occurred during a period of increased unrest across Argentina. From May 7 to 14, 1997, the petroleum enclaves of Tartagal and Mosconi in Salta emulated the pickets and *puebladas* that had taken place in Cutral-Có and Plaza Huincul. Later that year, a second sequence of disruptive dynamics emerged in Salta, Jujuy, Neuquén, and other provinces within this new repertoire of contention (Barbetta and Lapegna 2001).[11] The emulation mechanism that took pickets from Patagonia to Salta, some 2,450 kilometers north of Neuquén on the

[11] The other main locations where unemployed workers coordinated actions in 1996 and 1997 to claim for recognition and reincorporation were Santa Fe and Rosario (Santa Fe) (Poli 2007: 97–99), Alta Gracia and Cruz del Eje (Córdoba) (Antonello 2004; Oviedo 2004: 86–87; Torres 2006: 71), Belén (Catamarca), Montero (Tucumán) (Farinetti 1999: 21), and Mar del Plata, Florencio Varela, Quilmes, and La Matanza (Buenos Aires) (Svampa and Pereyra 2003).

border with Bolivia (**Map 3.1**), is the same one that had shaped one of the first *piquetero* SMOs in 1996 – the UTD of Mosconi.

As in Neuquén, the mediation activities of bishops were important for containing unrest. The bishop of Orán, Mario Antonio Cargnello, helped with negotiations with the Menem-allied governor of Salta, Juan Carlos Romero (1995–2007). Though Cargnello was not a bishop who supported pickets as a method of protest, increased unrest and the governor's intransigence led to the need for some mediation in order to avoid an imminent repressive response from the state (Svampa and Pereyra 2003: 125–27).

The spread of the picket as part of the former YPF workers' repertoire of contention is attributable to Maoist PCR leader Juan Nievas in Salta emulating Neuquén and non-party-based leader José "Pepino" Fernández's experience of the 1998–99 trade union conflicts in the Comodoro Rivadavia (Chubut) and Santa Cruz Norte (Santa Cruz) petroleum enclaves. The immediate outcomes of these struggles were the obtention of Work Program unemployment subsidies in both Salta and Neuquén and the MTA and CTA forging the agreement for the first Federal March in Jujuy (Santillán and Olmedo 1998: 96–97; Korol 2006: 70; Benclowicz 2011).

In brief, the siting decision favored the emergence of unemployed workers' protests and enriched the repertoire of contention for unions in Jujuy and YPF laborers in Salta. This was a result of what McAdam et al. (2001) call a "diffusion mechanism" of emulation.[12] This is because there is no information about any specific attempts at brokerage in Neuquén and Salta. In other words, the massive process of diffusion through the national media coverage of the pickets in Cutral-Có and Plaza Huincul became a widely acknowledged strategy for contention that (in that initial stage) had shown itself to be mightily effective (cf. Svampa and Pereyra 2003: 33, n. 23 for a list of newspaper articles). The diffusion mechanism does not, however, provoke a scale shift in the locus of conflict. Disincorporation resistance protests grew from a localized reaction to a siting decision, involving a very diverse array of local contexts. Initiated in two enclaves in Neuquén, these protests were emulated by public sector unions in Jujuy, unemployed workers in Cruz del Eje and Alta Gracia (Córdoba) and Rosario and Santa Fe city (Santa Fe) as well as other

[12] "*Diffusion* involves the transfer of information along established lines of interaction while *brokerage* entails the linking of two or more currently unconnected social sites" (McAdam et al. 2001: 333, italics in original).

petroleum-dependent enclaves: Tartagal and Mosconi in Salta. Thus, the conflict up to this stage was still local – though nationally diffused – and uncoordinated, and so we could not yet speak of a *piquetero* movement.

THE CREATION OF THE PIQUETERO MOVEMENT IN BUENOS AIRES

The first pickets in Neuquén were the departure point for a "scale shift" process (McAdam et al. 2001: 332–33), upgrading the scale of action through two related courses that ultimately led to the creation of the *piquetero* movement in Buenos Aires. The first course was the diffusion of the picket as an effective contentious strategy through the national media coverage of the Cutral-Có and Plaza Huincul protests. The second was brokerage with the intention of encouraging the coordination and expansion of protests to suburban Buenos Aires via numerous groups.

This process, however, was not automatic and occurred in two stages. The first stage was emulation and diffusion *without* an upward scale shift, which achieved a higher degree of coordination at the local level. In the immediate aftermath of the success achieved in the petroleum-dependent towns of Neuquén, the people of two equivalent towns in Salta emulated the picket and *pueblada* protests in their claim for employment and recognition from state authorities. A Buenos Aires *piquetero* leader summarized the diffusion of the perception that pickets are successful rather eloquently: "... the *piqueteros*' method has remained in people's blood, people have learned that with this [the picket] things can be achieved" (Oscar Kuperman interviewed by Germano 2005: 128).

The second stage was the level of coordination reached thanks to the brokerage efforts of organizations that brought localized action from the small, remote towns of Neuquén and Salta to the outskirts of the national capital. In 1996 the PCA, former CBC members, and various other informal left-wing groups organized unemployed people in La Matanza in a March against Hunger, Unemployment and Repression. In 1997 another group of unemployed people coordinated by former members of the dissolved PRT-ERP guerrilla organization of Florencio Varela and Mar del Plata led the first pickets in Buenos Aires; in both cases they called themselves Unemployed Workers' Movements (MTD). In some Greater Buenos Aires districts, an emulation mechanism was put in place by networks of left-wing Peronists (Montoneros), ex-Intransigent Party members, and MAS activists that expanded the movement by creating several *piquetero* SMOs, thereby reproducing the strategy of creating an MTD, a process that grew in a sustained fashion from 1999 to 2003.

The process of scale shift by diffusion from the peripheral provinces to the central province of Buenos Aires was also the result of some of the contextual particularities of Greater Buenos Aires. The presence of *piquetero* SMOs in some Buenos Aires districts and not in others is due to the horizontal political opportunities provided by the multiplicity of PJ factions and other parties who compete in this peri-urban area. There are also vertical opportunities produced by the attributes of the regime. Buenos Aires is the national capital in a centralized federal system, and Argentina's population is also largely concentrated there. This means that the federal capital is located in Argentina's main urban area. Buenos Aires city and its suburbs therefore have the particularity of being a site for multi-level competition involving the local, provincial, and national levels. In concrete terms, in La Matanza the PJ was sharply divided into multiple *agrupaciones* not under the leadership of the governor. As a consequence, this electorally crucial district of 1.5 million inhabitants became a highly disputed space in the late 1990s, which allowed *piquetero* SMOs to play on the factional divisions within the PJ through informal agreements. In Quilmes there has been a low rate of mayoral re-election, which produced the uncommon situation of alternation between different parties in power from 1983 to the 2000s. This meant that each new mayor needed to build a support network, which necessarily included the huge urban land occupations from which the *piquetero* SMOs emerged. Finally, Florencio Varela is a district that has been under the total control of mayor Julio Pereyra (PJ) since 1991 – this type of rule is the most common situation in Greater Buenos Aires. In this case the horizontal political opportunities were not as relevant as the vertical ones. In other words, it was not the presence of local-level pluralism that made this district a center of vertical disputes and short-term alliances – as in other cases – but rather the mayor's partial alignment with the governor and the president.

In addition to this configuration of the political context, in most of these districts there was also a strong key ally that provided protection from potentially hostile state and para-state reactions: the local diocese of the Catholic Church. In other words, what the Catholic Church offered in some territories is what I defined as a *space for protected contention*. When the diocese was not sympathetic to the cause, as in La Matanza, a network of unions and parties provided support instead. So, as claimed by the social movement literature, the degree of pluralism within a political context as well as the role of key brokers and allies is important for the emergence of a social movement.

These contextual elements and mechanisms alone, however, cannot explain the quick expansion of the *piquetero* movement to Greater Buenos Aires, its increase in organizational capacity, and the particular format it adopted. The answer to this requires a long-term historical examination of the *piqueteros*' origins, linking the sedimentation of the legacies of past struggles and their impact on the emergence of the *piquetero* movement in particular places. The process of scale shift by national diffusion that brought the struggle against the consequences of neoliberalism and for the recognition of disincorporation from isolated enclaves to the peri-urban areas of Buenos Aires was the result of the brokerage of a collection of networks sustained over a long-term process of reformulation of strategies by both unions and the left.

The historical roots of the *piquetero* movement can be traced to the end of the last authoritarian military junta and are intimately related to how unions have evolved since democratic neoliberal state reforms were applied and how the left and guerrilla organizations have responded to democratization. Figures A and B (Appendix) show how the network that built the *piquetero* movement has two main points of departure: left-wing parties and guerrilla organizations (Figure A) and trade unions (Figure B).

The legacies of past struggles, particularly the land occupations of the 1980s and *basismo*, along with the strategy of territorialization employed by unions and left-wing parties in the 1980s and 1990s, are crucial to an understanding of the paradoxical key difference between the movement in Neuquén and Buenos Aires. It explains why for the former, the movement emerged earlier but did not see the subsequent creation of durable SMOs, whereas for the latter, the delayed emergence of contention was followed by the formation of a multiplicity of SMOs.

There are three main legacies crucial for the emergence of the *piquetero* movement in Buenos Aires (cf. Chapter 2 for a detailed description). The first is the resilience of networks of guerrilla organizations and left-wing parties and their reformulation of their repertoire of strategies as a consequence of the repression they suffered from 1975 to 1989 under both authoritarian and democratic governments. This was mainly experienced through the vanguard organizational models and the moderate *foquismo* strategy that predominated in the *piquetero* movement in southern

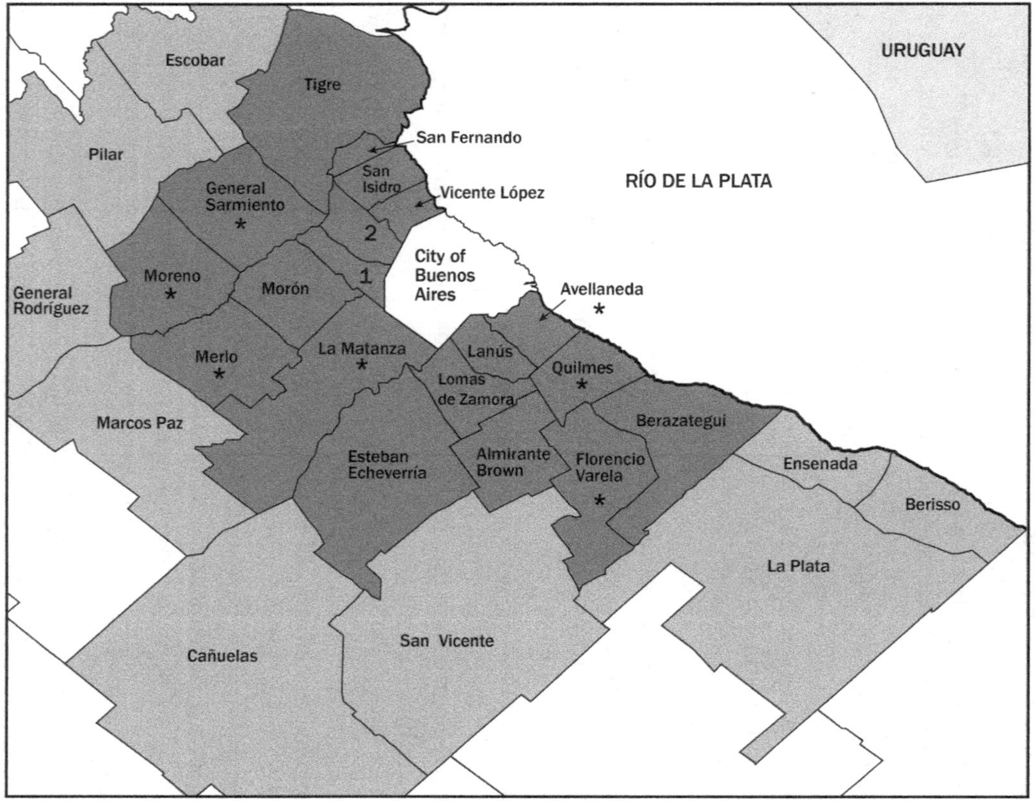

MAP 3.2 Greater Buenos Aires: Location of the Main Land Occupations, 1979–84 (marked by *)

Greater Buenos Aires and in northern Salta (Benclowicz 2011). The second is the CBCs and the land occupations of the 1979–82 period and the reappearance of this struggle during the 1990s. This is observed by comparing the locations of the 1980s land occupations (**Map 3.2**) and the points of emergence of the main *piquetero* SMOs in the 1990s (**Map 3.3**).[13] This has also been noted by scholars such as Merklen (2005) and explains why the *piqueteros* emerged as a movement in the peri-urban Buenos Aires districts of Quilmes, Florencio Varela, and La Matanza. These areas experienced a massive process of CBC-planned land occupations during democratization in the 1980s, starting in San Francisco Solano (Quilmes) and then expanding to other districts (Fara 1985; Merklen 1991).[14] Finally, there has been a strong trade union legacy due to the historical high percentage of unionization under Peronist structures since the 1940s. The experience in Jujuy of the organization of the unemployed that culminated in the creation of the CCC, along with many other processes that I explain later in the book, shows the centrality of the trade unionism legacy in the *piqueteros*. As with any legacy, the repertoire of strategies is enriched with both contentious and non-contentious elements, involving strategies of both types, as well as various organizational models.

The three pioneer *piquetero* SMOs emerged in Greater Buenos Aires as a result of a shared stock of legacies. However, in each case the networks

---

CAPTION FOR MAP 3.2 (cont.)

Key:

White: City of Buenos Aires (national capital, district dependent on the federal government)
Dark gray: Peri-urban Buenos Aires districts
Light gray: Semi-urban Buenos Aires districts and the city of La Plata (capital of the province of Buenos Aires)
1 Tres de Febrero
2 General San Martín

Source: Map by Lucas M. Rossi, using a base map from Wikimedia: http://commons.wikimedia.org/wiki/File:Gran_Buenos_Aires.svg.

[13] For further information on the location of poor and informal neighborhoods in the Greater Metropolitan Area of Buenos Aires, cf. Buzai and Marcos (2012).

[14] In Florencio Varela in particular, the PJ mayor Juan Carpinetti (1983–91) offered his support of the land occupation process (Prévôt-Schapira 1999: 238, n. 16 and 24).

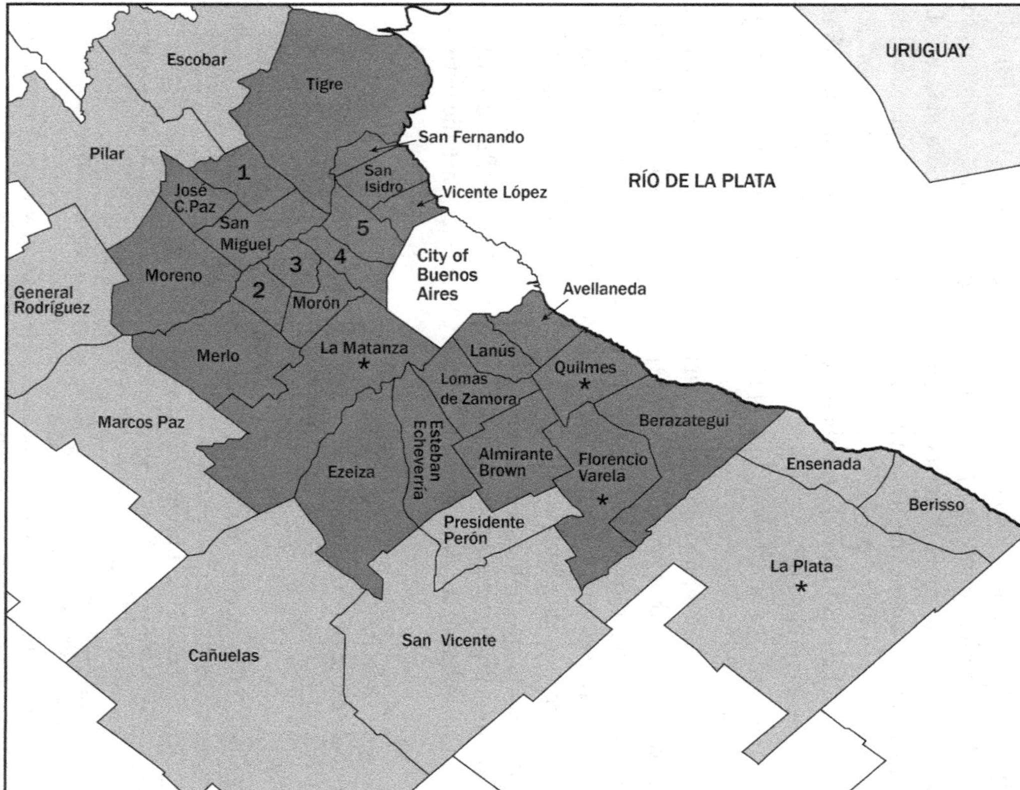

MAP 3.3 Greater Buenos Aires: Location of the Main *Piquetero* SMOs, 1996–99 (marked by *)

involved and the path toward the rise of these strong *piquetero* SMOs were different, thus requiring specific analyses.

The Origins of the Workers' Federation for Land, Housing and Habitat (1994–98)

Neoliberal reforms led to de-industrialization on a massive scale in several regions of Argentina but particularly affected the La Matanza district in Buenos Aires (**Map 3.3**). La Matanza is the most densely populated suburban area of Argentina. Historically an industrial district, from 1990 onward all the major factories began to close – among them those of the automobile industry such as Volkswagen, Chrysler, Borgward, and MAN (Merklen 2005: 54, n. 23) – which meant the loss of many jobs and the decimation of entire communities. One of the main *piquetero* leaders argued that with such a critical situation, they were forced to focus on the subsistence dimension of their community. The pickets were crucial to their strategy:

There was total collapse. There were [very bad] human development indicators and these were made evident to us by the reality on the ground. There were thousands and thousands of people without a job, without food, without medicine. People died and we could not even bury them. One family lay dead for

---

CAPTION FOR MAP 3.3 (cont.)

Key:

White: City of Buenos Aires (national capital, autonomous district)
Dark gray: Peri-urban Buenos Aires districts
Light gray: Semi-urban Buenos Aires districts and the city of La Plata (capital of the province of Buenos Aires)

1 Malvinas Argentinas
2 Ituzaingó
3 Hurlingham
4 Tres de Febrero
5 General San Martín

La Matanza: FTV, CCC, MTD of La Juanita
Quilmes: FTV, MTD of Solano, MTR
Florencio Varela: MTR
La Plata: CTD "Trabajo y Dignidad"

Source: Map by Lucas M. Rossi, using a base map from Wikimedia: http://commons.wikimedia.org/wiki/File:Gran_Buenos_Aires.svg.

four days in their house ... Fathers abandoned their homes and left mothers with the children ... We had entered a process of social decomposition. The massive pickets acted as a self-help group and a site of encounter for people who had lost everything (interview 2007).

Despite these obvious grievances, the scale shift of the *piqueteros*' contentious dynamics did not directly stem from necessity but rather were the consequence of brokerage by a sector of the human rights movement, the CTA, and the CCC, which then led to the movement coalescing.

The origin of one of the largest *piquetero* SMOs, the Liberation Theology–based Workers' Federation for Land, Housing and Habitat (FTV), stems from four processes of political territorialization. The first was the legacies of the CBC land occupations in La Matanza and Quilmes in the 1980s (Merklen 2005). The second was the transfer of activists of the national–populist Free Homeland party from Córdoba to Buenos Aires, in an attempt from the 1980s to adopt a territorialized political strategy following the dismantling of the PRT-ERP between 1975 and 1978. The third was the attempts by the Marxist–Leninist PCA to build a territorial base while participating with Free Homeland in the creation of the CTA.[15] And the fourth was the already mentioned reconfiguration of the relationship between the PJ and the CGT that led to the establishment of the CTA and the partial revision of the tactics adopted by Peronist unions, introducing territorially based collective action (cf. **Table 3.1**).

In relation to the land occupations of the 1980s, the FTV can be traced to two main processes. In 1981–82 the first mass urban land occupations were organized in San Francisco Solano (Quilmes) by CBC activists with the support of Jorge Novak, the bishop of Quilmes (Fara 1985; Woods 2007). This was done via the CBC-related human rights organization Peace and Justice Service (SERPAJ). The process initiated in Quilmes was later diffused by emulation to Ciudad Evita (La Matanza), where the El Tambo settlement emerged in 1986 (Merklen 1991; Grimson 2003).[16] The San Francisco Solano experience was a model for the El

[15] There is also the very small Liberation Revolutionary Party that participated in the creation of the FTV (Kuperman interviewed by Germano 2005: 118).

[16] As referred to by the main leaders of the FTV, the Argentine land occupation dynamics are also part of a regional Latin American process that enriches the local repertoire. The transnational influence of land occupations by the Pastoral Land Commission of Brazil diffused this strategy through gatherings and emulation within the network of Latin American CBCs in the 1980s (Isman 2004: 108–9).

Tambo occupation, which reproduced the model of organizing delegates by neighborhood in La Matanza (Merklen 1991: 124). These two major CBC land occupations, and their later expansion, became the seeds for the future growth of the FTV. As can be seen in **Map 3.2**, the locations of these land occupations and the two original nodes of the FTV overlap. In other words, the same people who occupied land in the 1980s were those who created the FTV as a result of "[t]he policy of the military to encourage the spatial concentration of the poor in the suburbs, combined with that of certain local Mayors who [–] for both ideological and electoral reasons [–] gave their support to land invasions, [leading] to a convergence of the poor in certain municipalities of the outer ring [of Buenos Aires city]" (Prévôt-Schapira 1999: 232).

The left's reconfiguration and adaptation to democracy and territorial politics are parallel and simultaneous processes, and both these processes and the legacy of land occupations were key factors in the creation of the FTV. In addition to the network of urban land occupations, there was also a process of territorialization carried out by Free Homeland and the PCA parties in the post-authoritarian period. The PCA is a historic Marxist–Leninist party that was created in 1918 and that participated in the formation of the FG party in 1994 in an attempt to electorally derail the neoliberal reforms.[17] The PCA also participated in the creation of the CTA with its network of cooperatives while organizing unemployed laborers. Free Homeland was created in 1987 after a split in the national–populist Intransigent Party. Free Homeland – a party that originated in Córdoba and was led by former PRT-ERP leaders – pursued a *foquista* beehive tactic by systematically moving all its key leaders to districts in Greater Buenos Aires. This diffusion tactic, along with its attempts to create a cross-class popular front, led it to function as part of the FTV as of 1999. This was the beginning of the process of territorialization of Free Homeland. After failing to organize already unionized workers within the factory-based affiliates of the CGT, Free Homeland expanded its repertoire by promoting "popular education" in the shantytowns and dormitory districts – inspired by the tradition of *basismo*.

The pluralization of the union system is related to the previously mentioned reformulation of the PJ as a machine party. This process led to a realignment of Peronist and Peronist-friendly left-wing national–populist political groupings. The options for the left-wing factions of the

[17] The PCA was expelled from the FG, along with other left-wing parties, by the leading group of the FG after the FG won its first election (Novaro and Palermo 1998).

PJ (and Peronism in general) were to either continue to participate within the party with the intention of influencing it from the inside or start a process of detachment in view of building an alternative party or movement. Given the organizational structure of the PJ, the chances of influencing the Menem government were almost nil. As one Peronist *piquetero* leader remarked, "Peronism's internal diversity had been destroyed ... There was no possibility of us building a critical mass because we [those opposing *menemismo*] were in the minority" (interview 2008). The metamorphosis of the PJ into a machine party led to the departure of a group of left-Peronist legislators known as the Group of the Eight. This group went on to form the FG and then added more parties by creating the FREPASO coalition (Novaro and Palermo 1998).[18]

These Peronist sectors that split from the PJ and the CGT, working with CBCs and left-wing parties, were those that regrouped to create the FTV in order to represent the mass of disincorporated laborers. In addition, the creation of the CTA and its adoption of a territorially based strategy were crucial for the consolidation of the FTV. In 1994 the CTA held a national congress in Rosario with the intention of unionizing the unemployed. Its secretary general explained the difficulties inherent in such an innovative enterprise:

> So, around 1993 we made our first attempt to generate something that, right from the start, was a contradiction in terms – a union of the unemployed. This attempt ended in failure because the idea of treating unemployed people as if they were in an actual trade union demonstrated inconsistency and, at the same time, a high degree of incoherence in terms of [political] action – because what one expects from a workers' union is that it will struggle for better working conditions. So this first attempt failed (interview 2007).

This initial effort at organizing the unemployed produced the Union of Unemployed Workers (UTD) of Rosario, but the project did not last. One of the main reasons for its failure was that, although the repertoire of strategies was in the process of being enriched in order to integrate unemployed workers within the CTA, it was still based on a traditional understanding of trade unions. However, this effort did have one crucial outcome: the development of a new master frame for the territorialization

[18] This would not be the only split of the PJ. There would be other divisions within sectors related to the Montoneros who were allied with ex-Intransigent Party and ex-MAS members, which led to the establishment of the MPR "Quebracho," Free Homeland, and the Coordinator of Unemployed Workers "Work and Dignity" (CTD "Trabajo y Dignidad"), as will be shown in the next chapter.

of neoliberal politics – "the neighborhood is the new factory." This reconception of the locus for organizing the popular sectors implied expanding the remit of a union's constituency from a traditional Peronist notion of men in a factory[19] to one that encompasses the whole neighborhood and all family members. This new vision also implied enriching the typical trade unionist repertoire of strategies by taking cues from the territorially and family-based ideas of the CBCs. In other words, the 1994 CTA congress produced an initial attempt at unionizing disincorporated workers. Although it failed, it did at least enrich the CTA's repertoire of strategies.

The profile of the FTV began to rise with the creation of the Feeding Network by the El Tambo settlement of La Matanza. The aim was to contest the Duhalde governorship's Life Program and particularly the redistribution of resources based on governorship-sponsored census data (Svampa and Pereyra 2003: 46). After some negotiations with the national government, the result was that the survey of 5,000 needy people carried out by the Feeding Network in response to the official census was accepted as correct by the Secretariat of Social Development and used to calculate resource distribution. The success of this CBC network of settlements in La Matanza led to the expansion of the group, renamed Network of Neighborhoods in 1995. The network grew from the four original settlements of 1993 to include between thirty and thirty-five settlements and popular neighborhoods in 1996 and 100 in 2003 (Calvo 2006: 53).

Unlike the support provided by the Neuquén bishops to the *puebladas*, the San Justo diocese in La Matanza was not at all supportive. Bishop Jorge Meinvielle (1991–2003) initiated a process of "purification" and in 1994 began dismissing priests who were influenced by Liberation Theology. In association with the governorship, one of the priests who promoted the Network of Neighborhoods, Juan José Cantiello, was expelled. These kinds of actions left the Network of Neighborhoods without the shielding umbrella of the Catholic Church and without any space for protected contention. As a result, the network was sustained through the Network of Neighborhoods leaders' work alongside SERPAJ activists and the left-wing sector of the Christian Democrats as well as the

[19] It must be remembered that the Peronist movement was based on four branches: the unionized workers (CGT), the national industrialists (General Economic Confederation, CGE), the youth (Peronist Youth, student movements), and the women's sector (led by Eva Perón). The PJ has been the electoral instrument of the Peronist movement.

State Workers' Association (ATE). Thanks to this alternative network, the FTV was able to receive much-needed support.

In 1996 the Network of Neighborhoods was integrated into the CTA as one of its territorially based members. The Network of Neighborhoods was mainly built in La Matanza under the leadership of Luis D'Elía and in Quilmes under Juan Carlos Sánchez. They had worked together during the land occupations and met again in 1996 for the organization of the FTV. The leadership defined the continuity between the land occupations movement of the 1980s and the *piquetero* movement as follows: " ... the FTV is a movement based around land, housing and habitat that embraced the cause of the unemployed when the tragedy of unemployment affected all of us" (interview 2007).

While D'Elía had a political career within the left-wing sector of the Christian Democrats, Sánchez had been a member of the CGT as part of the Peronist Renovation faction. Later, Sánchez would merge with the Group of Eight and participate in the creation of the CTA in Quilmes. A long-lasting relationship between D'Elía and de Gennaro would later lead them to found the CTA as a national trade union.

New CTA congresses were held in 1996 in Neuquén and in 1997 in La Matanza with the aim of organizing the unemployed. But it was only in 1998 that the CTA finally achieved the creation of a territorial organization with the establishment of the FTV. The founding congress regrouped the urban poor, peasants, indigenous people, homeless, and other territorially based groups from seventeen different provinces. In 1999 the CTA would later widen its repertoire even further by building a structure of federations composed of workers in the petroleum industry, the manufacturing sector, and healthcare and integrating the FTV as the unemployed workers' branch (Calvo 2006: 63–65; Poli 2007: 25–26).

Though the FTV is present through almost the entire country, each of its branches has been autonomously organized through each leader's territorial control, something equivalent to the logic adopted by the PJ. This means that both the PJ and the FTV are loosely structured networks of territorially based leaders that contend for political power both internally and externally. Though the FTV is active in most of the country, it has been hardly distinguishable from the CTA (Svampa and Pereyra 2003: 61). The FTV has two core groups, in La Matanza and Quilmes, and these are the ones that, although with different organizational models (Delamata 2005: 381), share the basic political aims of the FTV. As one leader explains: "One way the FTV differs from other [*piquetero*] groups is that in our case there is an approach [to the popular sectors] that comes from our political understanding, and that is related to the demand for land and habitat" (interview 2007). Different was the conception of the Maoist sector of the *piqueteros*.

The Origins of the Classist and Combative Current (1994–98)

The only non-Peronist strategy to build a union was developed collaboratively by the internal factions of the factory-based Classist Groupings of the Maoist PCR. The PCR, in association with some of the members of the MAS, founded the Classist and Combative Current (CCC), a result of the stronger sense of internal cohesion produced by the Federal March of 1994. The creation of the CCC in 1996 was one of the outcomes of the long process of reconfiguration of the left that had gone on since democratization, and it would eventually become one of the largest *piquetero* SMOs. The Maoist CCC is the result of two processes. The first was the reconfiguration of the PCR in the post-authoritarianism period with the enrichment of its repertoire of strategies by adding a territorialized *basista* repertoire. The second was the aforementioned failed attempt to build a non-Peronist union and the redefinition of a tripartite notion of the "working class" with a focus on disincorporated laborers (cf. **Table 3.1**).

As the PCR was one of the few left-wing parties committed to class struggle without the use of armed conflict and vanguardism, it suffered several splits during the 1960s and 1970s that led to the creation of various guerrilla organizations, such as the Liberation Armed Forces in 1968 (Hilb and Lutzky 1984). The focus of the PCR was rather on trade union organization, which would theoretically lead to a mass-based insurrection. This produced a relatively important network of non-Peronist factory-based unions in Córdoba. With the assassination by the 1976–83 authoritarian regime of several important PCR union leaders the PCR's factory-based groups were disbanded. After the transition to democracy, it took a decade for the PCR to recreate this network (cf. Figure B in Appendix). The effects of repression made renewal difficult, but two main processes emerged. On the one hand, some of the PCR leaders worked during the 1980s on land occupations in La Matanza. On the other hand, in Jujuy trade unionism re-emerged with great impetus due to Santillán's leadership of the SEOM in the 1990s, which was behind the series of aforementioned *puebladas*.

The PCR went through a process of enriching its repertoire of strategies, which was crucial for the success of the SEOM and the creation of the CCC. From 1982 to 1995 the PCR engaged in a predominant strategy of lending support to Peronist candidates while also promoting their own leaders for electoral and propaganda purposes during electoral campaigns. After supporting Menem, with his national–populist discourse, in the 1989 presidential election, the PCR switched to an abstentionist strategy, mirroring the actions of several Maoist parties in the West.[20] These transformations stemmed from both national experience and international dynamics. Nationally, the failure of the non-PJ Peronist candidate Fernando "Pino" Solanas in the 1995 presidential elections demonstrated that electoral politics was insufficient as a strategy for advancing PCR goals. Internationally, the dramatic consequences of the dissolution of the Soviet Union and China's move toward a capitalist economy also affected the PCR's alignments and conceptions of world political economy. The abstentionist strategy was recuperated from the repertoire of strategies from before the 1976 coup and added to the insurrectional mass-based strategy taken from the same period. Though not new, the predominant repertoire of strategies of the PCR during the transition to democracy was limited to electoral and territorial strategies, as the PCR wanted to avoid the destructive consequences of authoritarian repression as well as take a self-restraining approach to democratic transition. Afterward, the repertoire was expanded with the recuperation of strategies from the 1970s in addition to the experience of the land occupations. As social unrest increased after the 1993 *pueblada* of Santiago del Estero, the CCC's strategy for the reincorporation struggle would be to promote an insurrectional alliance with the right. This type of multisectoral strategy meant engaging in a protracted struggle within a multisectoral coalition. This would supposedly lead to an insurrectional upsurge and the eventual breakdown of the system. For this to be achieved it was also considered to be crucial to work within the Peronist organizational structure (cf. Chapter 2; Svampa and Pereyra 2003: 62).

The PCR helped to spread contention from Jujuy to neighboring Salta with the creation of the UTD of Mosconi in 1996 by Juan Nievas, a PCR activist, and a network of former YPF workers (Svampa 2006; Benclowicz 2011). At the same time, another process of reorganization was taking place. In La Matanza, some PCR leaders, such as Juan Carlos Alderete, had been involved in the 1980s land occupations. The PCR occupations were similar to those contemporaneously led by the CBCs that later evolved into the FTV. The María Elena neighborhood was organized by PCR and Peronist leaders using grassroots assembly-based methods

[20] On the PCR's abstentionist strategy, cf. *Política y Teoría* (issue 43, April–July 2000: 78).

inspired by the *basista* repertoire, which in turn enriched the PCR's own repertoire. The outcome was a territorialized approach just like the one taken by the CTA and the FTV.

In 1995 in La Matanza a Commission of the Unemployed was organized and led by Alderete with the participation of the PCR, Workers Party, FREPASO, and the Argentine Confederation of Education Workers (CTERA) – which was affiliated with the CTA – to demand food from the mayor of La Matanza, Héctor Cozzi (PJ) (Svampa and Pereyra 2003: 40). Within the general context of social upheaval, in 1996 Alderete coordinated the María Elena and Villa Unión neighborhoods with part of the Commission of the Unemployed and set up a soup kitchen as a form of protest in front of City Hall to try to obtain what had been achieved in Neuquén: Work Program subsidies and food (Alderete and Gómez 1999: 13; Oviedo 2004: 41).[21] This protest was not preconceived as the most effective strategy but was rather based on the accumulated experience of the popular sectors when faced with the problem of hunger and related basic demands. The CCC's national coordinator of the unemployed and the organizer of this event recalls what happened:

> The first camp we set up in La Matanza was the one on the square [of San Justo, in front of City Hall]. We went with one idea in mind and we returned with another. We went with the idea that the people are supposed to be led by those who know more, that we were the ones that should lead the plan for the struggle. But we came back with another idea because the input of ordinary people was very significant, and what we learned from our comrades is that their experience of activism is actually quite substantial (interview 2007).

In viewing the unemployed as "workers without employment," they reframed the excluded as a potential revolutionary constituency if appropriately guided after basic needs have been satisfied. The type of experience of grassroots organization coming out of suburban land occupations in La Matanza[22] helped the PCR replace its classical Marxist pejorative notion of the unemployed as a lumpenproletariat more rapidly than did the PCA, the Workers Party, the Socialist Workers' Movement, and other classist parties.

[21] In addition, the persecutions and the lack of support from the local bishop Meinvielle pushed the FTV and CCC into an alliance in defense of progressive priests, such as Luis Bicego of El Sagrado Corazón Church in San Justo (La Matanza). The twenty-one-day occupation of this church in 1996 was the start of an alliance between the FTV and CCC that lasted until 2005.

[22] In 1987 and 1988 there were pickets in La Matanza and soup kitchens were organized in the María Elena and Villa Unión neighborhoods.

Due to the embeddedness of the Peronist political culture in the popular sectors, the CCC's identity has a Maoist core overlaid with a national–populist ethos that comes from Peronism. This ideological tolerance permits the inclusion in the CCC of members who are neither PCR activists nor Maoists provided that they do not control the CCC's decision-making process, which is based on a model of democratic centralism. This openness pushed the CCC toward a more flexible identity without achieving a change in political culture. This is a problem common to all the non-Peronist SMOs of the *piquetero* movement. A national CCC coordinator summarizes the CCC's syncretic identity as "Peronist-Maoist [*peronista maoistizado*]," which he considers as made up of a shared practical idea: "The main thing is to struggle against any form of imperialism" (interview 2007).

The identity of the CCC grew out of various historical legacies. Its organizational format is rooted in the sedimentation of the CBC *basista* assemblies and union legacies, such as the use of a points system for the redistribution of assets acquired via struggle and cooperative work. This allowed for the creation of the *piquetero* SMO "CCC – Unemployed Workers Sector" as one of the three sectors of the CCC, conceived as being made up of "[t]he same components that characterize the [working] class: those in work, those who have retired, and the unemployed" (CCC national leader, interview 2007).

Two main networks, each with its own history and stock of legacies, have sustained the CCC. First are the union networks that come out of the reorganized Classist Groupings and CGT Peronist leaders such as Edgardo Quiroga of San Lorenzo (Santa Fe). Second are territorial processes such as the PCR land occupations in La Matanza and the Independent Movement of Retired and Pensioners (MIJP), led by Nina Pelozo and the ex-MAS member Raúl Castells, in Lomas de Zamora, Buenos Aires. This produced a national structure for the CCC that, despite an uneven geographical and functional distribution of power, was almost always sustained by a network of trade unions.

The MIJP followed its own independent trajectory with retired workers and pensioners. This SMO was created in 1993 and integrated into the CCC from 1996 to 2000. It began when Castells, Norma Plá (a local UCR broker from Lomas de Zamora), and members of the PCA of Zárate (Buenos Aires) organized a group of retirees and pensioners, supported by the cooperatives movement, to demand an increase in the state pension. Retired protesters gained notoriety in the mid-1990s. With their hundredth protest in 1995, they were approached by the MTA and the newly created MPR "Quebracho" to form an alliance. This alliance was loosely structured around Plá, and after her death, Castells took control of the process (Svampa and Pereyra 2003: 68). The MIJP can be described as a national–populist anti-imperialist SMO that applies a witness strategy as a way of drawing attention to political oppression through the personal experience of its leaders. Relying on the media as a source for its expansion, this very personalized SMO publicizes oppressive actions taken against its leaders as a means of transmitting its message for both propaganda and electoral purposes (cf. Chapter 2).

The route that led to the CCC creating its unemployed sector in 1996 and adopting a territorialized insurrectional strategy was not straightforward and implied expelling dissidents from the leadership of the CCC. Until 1998 the leader of the CCC was the Ford delegate Miguel Delfino. He rejected the idea of organizing the unemployed because he considered them, within a traditional Marxist interpretation, as the lumpenproletariat and therefore unorganizable. From 1994 to 1996, internal discussions for the constitution of a territorial organization of the unemployed were taking place within the PCR as well as the CTA. In 1998 the PCR politburo decided to create three sectors for the CCC under a redefined conception of the "working class" that included the employed, the unemployed, and the retired. This led to a change in the CCC's leadership, and Delfino was expelled. Amancay Ardura came into the scene as the general coordinator of the employed sector, Alderete of the unemployed sector, and Castells of the retired sector. This restructuring of the CCC as a tripartite organization implied a redefinition of the classical Argentine Marxist frame of political analysis, thus widening the PCR's repertoire of strategies.

From 1999 onward, the La Matanza sector emerged as the most relevant as unemployment grew and the scale shift that nationalized the *piqueteros*' contentious dynamics moved the locus of disruption from Neuquén, Salta, and Jujuy to Buenos Aires. The consequences of the Argentine centralized federal regime affected the CCC in such a way that while the La Matanza chapter emerged as pivotal, the CCC of Jujuy experienced a downgrade in scale shift to the provincial level (Svampa and Pereyra 2003: 60). This dual process of conflict centralization and SMO provincialization was also the fate of other peripheral *piquetero* SMOs, such as the UTD of Mosconi, as the pace of the pattern of interaction was gradually concentrated in Greater Buenos Aires with the CCC, FTV, and a last group of very heterogeneous SMOs.

The Origins of the Unemployed Workers' Movements (1994–97)

The classic explanation for the origin of the Unemployed Workers' Movements (MTDs) of Florencio Varela and San Francisco Solano is that they were a spontaneous imitation of the Plaza Huincul and Cutral-Có *puebladas*. However, if we consider the MTDs as part of longer-term trajectories based on previous networks and sedimented legacies, they can be considered clear cases of diffusion by attribution of similarity.[23] The broker in this process was the radical sector of the human rights movement, the Mothers of the Plaza de Mayo Association. The Mothers connected actors and processes with a common origin in the armed struggle of the 1970s that remained active in the land occupations of the 1980s within the space for protected contention provided by the diocese of Quilmes. In brief, the MTDs are a result of three processes. The first was the adaptation to democracy and territorialized politics of the networks of former guerrilla members who were involved in the PRT-ERP and Montoneros. The second was the barring of access to decision-making positions in the CGT for left-wing classist groups due to Peronist hegemony. And the third was the transnational influence of the Mexican Zapatistas and the theories of Holloway (2002) and Negri (2001) on autonomism and counter-power (cf. Colectivo Situaciones 2001; Chapter 2).

The MTD of Florencio Varela can be traced back to the Guevarist Movement (MG). The MG is sustained by former PRT-ERP members who had reduced their repertoire to a moderate *foquismo* strategy, which means abandoning the armed struggle in the short and medium term. To compensate for this, the MG enriched their repertoire by adding *basismo* to their guerrilla varguardist legacy (*Libro Celeste* – MTR, February 2000; Delamata 2004: 62). The MG created *focos* of organization with local networks through the control of *juntas vecinales* (neighborhood associations in poor districts and shantytowns). Later, the MG network activated the *focos* when the political opportunities were interpreted as favorable with the increase in unemployment and after failing in its attempts to mobilize unionized workers. This was favored by a reconfiguration of the PJ and the Menem government that left several ex-Montoneros sectors outside the party, such as Revolutionary

[23] By "attribution of similarity," I mean "'the mutual identification of actors in different sites as being sufficiently similar to justify common action' … Information alone will not lead someone to adopt a new idea, cultural object, or behavioral practice. This, in turn, depends on at least a minimal identification between innovator and adopter" (McAdam et al. 2001: 334).

Peronism. Revolutionary Peronism was split in 1991 into those who still wanted to attempt to work within the PJ and a new sector that decided to participate in the MG (cf. Figures A and B in Appendix). The latter went on to build the MTD, attributing similarity to the disruptive struggles of Neuquén and Salta for re-organizing the popular sectors in Florencio Varela and Mar del Plata. One of the main leaders recalls:

> What was our inspiration? It was the conflict in Cutral-Có, the assemblies of *piqueteros*, the *fogoneros* [early risers of the first *pueblada* in Neuquén] ... The direct participation in the decision-making process of the workers and their neighbors ... This direct democracy, this way of participating, that was what inspired us. The method – that is, the roadblock by the unemployed workers – was a result of us not being able to halt production with strikes but able instead to halt the distribution of products, affecting in this way the production and the distribution system (interview 2007).

Additionally, the closure of the union system to the non-Peronist left eliminated any chance for the MG to mobilize unionized workers. So, as another of the *piquetero* leaders (and a member of the MG) argued, it was not only the redefinition of the unemployed as an actor with a potential for mobilization that led the MG to create the MTD, but also the closure of the CGT to this same actor: "In fact, we came from a previous experience of trying to organize in factories for several years until 1995, when we came to the conclusion that it wasn't working" (interview 2007). As we have seen, the union system was not closed to everybody, just to some sectors. In 1994 the MG participated in the first of the CTA congresses of unemployed workers but not in the creation of the FTV.

In 1995, thanks to the support of Hebe de Bonafini (the president of the Mothers), the MG and other groups that built the MTDs were able to compensate for the lack of union support. The 1996 and 1997 editions of the Resistance March organized by the Mothers to commemorate the victims of the military dictatorship had speakers who went on to become *piquetero* leaders. The joint work was expanded with the organization of the first protest, the March against Hunger, Unemployment and Repression on September 6, 1996, by a network of activists from the MAS, PCR, and PCA. This march led to Héctor "Toty" Flores creating the MTD of La Juanita in La Matanza and, in Florencio Varela, another MTD being started by Roberto Martino and the priest Alberto Spagnuolo, among others (Flores 2005a: 19).

With the continuing support of the Mothers, in 1997 meetings were organized in Florencio Varela and in La Matanza to set up a unified MTD, but this goal was not achieved. On the one side, the MTD of La Juanita rejected the proposal to demand unemployment subsidies because they were considered to be clientelistic tools (Flores 2005a: 25–28). This decision later led to the isolation of the MTD of La Juanita not only from the other MTDs but also from most of the movement. The MTD of La Juanita focused its efforts instead on creating cooperatives with the support of the Mothers and the cooperativist movement of the PCA (Bergel 2003: 102–4; Flores 2006).

On the other side, the MTD of Florencio Varela accepted unemployment subsides, like the rest of the *piquetero* movement, as a pragmatic short-term goal. After 1997 the MTD of Florencio Varela expanded and changed its name to the Unemployed Workers' Movement "Teresa Rodríguez" (MTR), after the first *piquetero* fatality in Neuquén's second *pueblada*. Based on the MG network, the MTR was then created in Mar del Plata (Buenos Aires).[24] At the same time, another group was created in Hurlingham, and the priest Spagnuolo, who would later be transferred to the church at the San Francisco Solano settlement in Quilmes, would create the MTD of Solano.

The Catholic clergy played multiple and contradictory roles in the formation of the *piquetero* movement. While in Neuquén the Church was supportive, in Jujuy and Salta it was aligned with the governorship. In most areas, and this was particularly true for the province of Buenos Aires, it played diverse roles depending on the particular diocese. In La Matanza the bishop ruthlessly chased leftist priests, while in Quilmes the bishop was supportive even though the La Plata archdiocese did not share his position. In other words, the Catholic Church tends to play three roles: that of mediator for containing social unrest (Jujuy, Salta, and most other cases), that of passive supporter (Quilmes, Neuquén), and that of active supporter (this was never the case for the *piqueteros*, though it was very common elsewhere in Latin America, particularly in Brazil). Each of these roles produces different spaces for contention for social movements. When the Catholic Church was a passive or active supporter, such as during the land occupations of the 1980s, an accumulation of legacies and networks of activists was built up that could re-emerge at a later date even if in the meantime the Church had changed its role, as was the case in La Matanza.

Even in cases – like that of bishop Jorge Novak in Quilmes – where support was available in the 1980s and 1990s, the policy of silencing

[24] The MTR of Mar del Plata would publicly emerge in the national sphere in 1999 with a twenty-one-day occupation of the city's main church (Oviedo 2004: 104).

progressive priests, as advocated by Pope John Paul II, limited the scope for action. Novak was in charge of the Quilmes dioceses (Quilmes, Florencio Varela, and Berazategui) from 1976 to 2001 and was the founder of the Ecumenical Movement for Human Rights during the authoritarian regime. Several Liberation Theology–inspired priests worked within the Quilmes dioceses, such as Raúl Berardo, Luis Farinello, and Antonio Puigjané. In 1983 Novak created the Social Pastoral Vicariate with the purpose of supporting the CBC land occupations (Mignone 2006: 162; Woods 2007).

One tragic event induced Novak to reduce his role from active to passive supporter (Pacheco 2004: 18). On January 23, 1989, the Trotskyist All for the Motherland Movement (MTP) carried out an armed attack on the barracks of the La Tablada army regiment (La Matanza). After suffering a swift defeat by the military and police forces (between twenty-eight and thirty-two militants were killed), the whole guerrilla organization was dismantled (Gorriarán Merlo 2003; Hilb 2007). The MTP was mostly built upon one of two sectors into which the PRT-ERP was divided after the entire leadership was killed off between 1975 and 1979. One MTP sector maintained armed struggle and fought with the Sandinistas in Nicaragua; the other sector started a process of redefinition of its strategies (Hilb 2007: 8–9). While the latter group later dissolved during democratization, the MTP group returned to Argentina and developed a territorial strategy in Quilmes and Florencio Varela with the active participation of the priest Antonio Puigjané (Hilb 2007: 19, n. 4). The immediate consequences of the MTP's defeat in La Tablada were police persecutions, the threat of governmental reprisals, and the devastating effects of demobilization for this network (Svampa and Pereyra 2003: 40).

Almost a decade later, within the same space for protected contention that had been provided by the Quilmes diocese, *piquetero* contention expanded with the creation of the MTDs of Florencio Varela and San Francisco Solano. Soon after the first pickets in 1997, the pro-government archdiocese of La Plata named Gerardo Farrell as co-adjunct bishop in order to limit Novak's power. Bishop Farrell worked until his death in 2000 to counterbalance and control Novak's support of the *piqueteros* (Woods 2007: 80, n. 4). Alberto Spagnuolo, a founding member of the MTD of Solano, was a priest who had been transferred from Florencio Varela. In 1997 and 1998 he coordinated pickets, which ended with governor Duhalde successfully calling for him to be excommunicated from the Catholic Church. Spagnuolo's experience was almost identical to Cantiello's in La Matanza, with the difference that the latter did not have any support from the bishop of San Justo, who demanded his resignation quicker and with less fuss than the former.

In 1997 the MTR received its first Work Programs in response to its protest. In January 1998, as part of the same protest that led to the expulsion of Spagnuolo from the Catholic Church, the MTR was subject to repression as ninety members were sent to jail and the Work Programs they had obtained from the previous protest were subsequently taken away (Svampa and Pereyra 2003: 43; Pacheco 2004: 21).

The MTDs were part of a highly heterogeneous social movement sector. At first, the MTR did not expand its repertoire of strategies with other legacies, and the Guevarist vanguard approach was strongly sustained. However, the vanguardist organizational strategy produced several problems as the SMO quickly expanded from 1996 to 1999 to include more participants coming from outside the Guevarist network who also had little previous political experience or other ideological traditions. At the same time, the MTD of Solano went on to embrace the autonomist–introspective strategy that was transnationally diffused from the Zapatistas through John Holloway's ideas and integrated with Toni Negri's ideas in Argentina by the intellectual group Situations Collective. The autonomist–introspective strategy refers to the permanent internal reflective process of using assemblies as a tool for transforming society through the collective production of an alternative conception of the state (cf. Chapter 2). Finally, the MTD of La Juanita's unwillingness to claim for unemployment subsidies took this SMO on a completely independent trajectory. Notwithstanding these differences – as will be analyzed in the next chapter – the creation of a new SMO by the MPR "Quebracho" led to the formation of a huge coalition built in association with the MTR and MTDs.

RECOGNITION: THE NATIONAL EMERGENCE OF THE "PIQUETERO QUESTION" (1998–99)

The rise of the *piquetero* movement is linked to a claim and a type of actor that were both novel for Argentina's history. This dual novelty generated an initial context that was completely absent in public policy in this area, and in particular the lack of recognition by the state departments of this particular problem, a situation similar to when the first labor and social rights conflicts emerged in the late nineteenth century – what was then called the "social question" (cf. Chapter 1). As a result of this situation, the appearance of the first *piquetero* protests imposed on the second Menem presidency an intra-state dispute for the resolution of the "*piquetero* question."

The rise of the "*piquetero* question" on a national level was sparked by the ending of the informal territorial agreement between the presidency and the governorship of Buenos Aires. This process began when the post of Secretary for Social Development was given to Ramón "Palito" Ortega in 1998.[25] In an attempt to become the PJ's presidential candidate, Ortega fought with Antonio Erman González, the Minister of Labor, over responsibility for dealing with the unemployment issue, the administration of subsidies, and the upgrading of the secretariat into a ministry (*Clarín*, 04/09/1998). The reassigning of these matters were very much resisted by González, who managed to preserve the administration of the Work Programs I and II, even creating a version III under his ministerial responsibility (*Página/12*, 04/14/1998). Ortega would lose his battle with González, the Secretariat for Social Development would remain as such, and Ortega would not gain control over any policy on employment issues until the end of the Menem presidency. However, Ortega did manage to achieve tighter administration of the resources under his control, began his campaign for the PJ presidential candidacy by opposing Duhalde in Buenos Aires, and made inroads with some national social policies in the province (*La Nación*, 08/21/1998 and 09/13/1998). As an unintended consequence, Ortega's presidential ambitions led to the virtual violation of a decade-long informal agreement for the distribution of territorial responsibilities among the national and provincial levels in Buenos Aires.

In 1999 Ortega realized that according to the polls, he would be defeated by Duhalde. This situation led him to agree to run for vice president as Duhalde's running mate, standing down as secretary. Ortega's presence in the Menem government was brief, but it touched off permanent disputes over responsibility for the "*piquetero* question" between the Ministry of Labor and the Secretariat for Social Development in all the subsequent governments.

After the Ortega–González dispute the "unemployment question" became the "*piquetero* question." Even though the *piquetero* movement

[25] Since redemocratization, the Secretariat of Social Action/Development was a subsidiary of the Ministry of Health and Social Action. When Ortega became Secretary, Menem moved the secretariat out from the Ministry of Health and made it part of the House of Government's presidential agencies. Ortega's aim was to upgrade the secretariat to a full ministry.

was not yet accepted as a legitimate actor on a national level, its claim was recognized. In theoretical terms, this was the starting point for the construction of a *piquetero policy domain*. By "policy domain" I mean: "(1) the range of collective actors ... who have gained sufficient legitimacy to speak about or act on a particular issue; and (2) the cultural logics, frameworks, and ideologies those actors bring to bear in constructing and narrating the 'problem' and the appropriate policy responses" (Jenness et al. 2005: 300). In sum, the accumulation of *puebladas* since 1993, the organization in Buenos Aires of the *piquetero* movement, and the intra-governmental dispute for electoral purposes brought the "*piquetero* question" onto the national agenda.

The *Piquetero* Movement's Provincial Level of Interaction

In this period, the *piquetero* movement claimed for recognition but was not yet legitimated because there was no multi-level game involving this reincorporation movement. Until 1999 the *piquetero* movement was a localized issue with national repercussions.[26] This was due to Menem's focalized distribution of unemployment subsidies to the specific sites of conflict but rejection of the presence of a legitimate actor behind them and the Menem–Duhalde agreement that left the main sites of *piquetero* contention under the jurisdiction of the province of Buenos Aires government. The result was that from the movement's origin to its claim for recognition, interaction was "provincialized" in those few cases where SMOs had histories longer than that of the *piquetero* struggle. For this reason, only the FTV, CCC, MIJP, and MTR had links with a few mayors and Duhalde's provincial government.

While Menem never met with any *piquetero* SMO, the Network of Neighborhoods (pre-FTV) had one meeting in 1995 with Eduardo Amadeo, the national Secretary for Social Development at that time. That meeting was prompted by the aforementioned conflict over the census and the Network of Neighborhoods subsequently found out about the territorial agreement between Menem and Duhalde and secretary's inability to grant them unemployment subsidies and food. The broker singled out by Amadeo was Hilda "Chiche" Duhalde, the governor's wife, who was responsible for the province's social policies. All subsequent efforts until 1999 were focused on the provincial level, leading

[26] The national locus of action is based not on the geographical space of contention but rather on its socio-political implications (McAdam et al. 2001: 341).

to an intense territorial dispute between the grassroots networks of the FTV and Duhalde's networks.

The CCC had a similar link with Hilda Duhalde in a territorial dispute for the La Matanza area under the control of the CCC. This dispute even led her to personally enter the neighborhood in an attempt to build an alternative to the CCC network (Alderete and Gómez 1999: 13–18). In 1999 the Duhalde governorship also attempted to co-opt Alderete – the CCC's national leader of the unemployed – by offering him the position of provincial secretary for land regularization issues.

Because the MIJP emerged in Lomas de Zamora, the district where governor Duhalde built his political power base as mayor, its relationship with Duhalde was based on territorial co-existence. This relationship has forged a pragmatic link between the MIJP and Duhalde: governability in exchange for resources. The MTR, for its part, had an alliance with the Florencio Varela mayor, Pereyra (PJ), which allowed them access to resources when the provincial level was closed to them (Oviedo 2004: 97). But this was not the only possible link between a *piquetero* SMO and a mayor. In Lanús, for example, Manuel Quindimil (PJ) had governed from 1973 until the 1976 coup and then again from redemocratization in 1983 to 2007 with a paternalistic total control of the district. This type of leadership was reproduced in his relationship with the MTD of Lanús (a member of the MTR) (Grimson 2003: 55–56).

CONCLUSION

This chapter set out to explain how protests by disincorporated laborers that first emerged in the Patagonian province of Neuquén came to materialize the *piqueteros* – a reincorporation movement – in Greater Buenos Aires. The answer lies in the following argument. The emergence and diffusion of protest from Neuquén to Salta did not produce a scale shift that nationalized and organized the protest in SMOs because the divisions between provincial elites, clientelism, and grievance over a siting decision, while favoring the emergence of local protests, were not sufficient to lead to the organization of a generalized movement. In order to transform protests into movements there are additional contextual and actor-related elements that must be present. The increasing diffusion of local protests of the disincorporated popular sectors and public employees could only coalesce in this period into a movement in some districts of Greater Buenos Aires because these specific areas had certain political configurations favorable for the organization of a reincorporation movement. Argentina's federal centralized regime meant that the national capital was also the most urban and industrialized (and abruptly de-industrialized) area of the country. It also featured a highly pluralist context due to the great level of factionalization within the PJ and the space for protected contention offered by some Catholic Church dioceses, the human rights movement, and the territorial strategy of some unions. The combination of the alliances available, the pluralism, and the high degree of elite fragmentation in Buenos Aires offered a dynamic context of political opportunities and shifts for political organization. However, the contextual elements are not the only ones that are relevant. The emergence of the *piqueteros* in Buenos Aires was due to the incomparably dense network of left-wing activists that were present in peri-urban Buenos Aires, which since redemocratization had expanded its stock of legacies with elements drawn from *basismo* and union struggles.

The organization of the *piquetero* movement in Buenos Aires produced a functional dispute between the Secretariat for Social Development and the Ministry of Labor over the responsibility of dealing with the novel "*piquetero* social question." In other words, the political opportunities were reduced to the horizontal (functional) dimension in this period owing to the territorial agreement between the presidency and the governorship, which impeded intervention by the national government in the province of Buenos Aires. During this stage, vertical (multi-level) disputes were informally resolved, despite Ortega attempting to violate these agreements.

In December 1999 the UCR-FREPASO coalition, with Fernando De la Rúa as president, took office in a climate of increased expectation of changes and social unrest. De la Rúa had beaten Duhalde, while the governor's protégé, Federico Ruckauf, had defeated the UCR-FREPASO Alliance candidate, Graciela Fernández Meijide. Meanwhile, in La Matanza, the FTV and CCC were in conflict with the PJ Menem-allied mayor Cozzi (1991–99). This situation changed in 1999 when Cozzi was expelled from local government over a corruption scandal. This left Menem with no links to this much-disputed district. As will be seen in the next chapter, Alberto Balestrini, the new non-aligned PJ major of La Matanza, entered into a long-lasting alliance with the FTV and CCC during the post-recognition period. In other words, the end of the Menem-Duhalde territorial agreement led to a widening of vertical political opportunities because of a dispute between a non-PJ national government and the governorship, which was still controlled by Duhalde. In addition to this, some non-aligned PJ mayors pushed for a third division – the local – within a multi-level contentious dynamic that grew in intensity. This tense relationship, which will be the focus of the next chapter, takes us from the recognition of the "*piquetero* question" to the legitimation of the *piquetero* movement, a phase defined by a political power game, centralized in Buenos Aires, involving every level of government – local, provincial, and national.

4

From Recognition of the Claim to the Legitimation of the *Piquetero* Movement as a National Actor (1999–2001)

This chapter analyzes the period that led to the national *pueblada* or social explosion of December 2001 that forced president Fernando De la Rúa to step down and legitimized the *piquetero* movement as the reincorporation movement – the interlocutor with the state for the disincorporated popular sectors. This process, though, was not straightforward. A first set of *piquetero* SMOs composed of the FTV, the CCC, and the UTD of Mosconi were legitimated before the rest of the movement did. The first two of these organizations had achieved this by November 2000 and the latter by June 2001 as a result of their increased disruptive power, which put the "*piquetero* social question" on the political agenda. As disruption expanded (**Figure 3.1**), the *piquetero* movement would grow in its power to mobilize, and new SMOs would be created, increasing the movement's effectiveness as a coordinated force, although the FTV and the CCC would also suffer from important splits. The movement as a whole was legitimated in December 2001 during the brief interim presidency of Adolfo Rodríguez Saá (PJ), when some of its main leaders met with the president for the first time. In brief, the period between March 1999 and December 2001 represents the stage when the *piqueteros* went from seeing their claim recognized to the legitimation of the entire movement.

In this chapter I will continue with the theoretical enterprise initiated in the previous chapter. The intertwining of *piquetero* contention with the dynamics of institutional politics will be further studied in order to demonstrate the theoretical fruitfulness of bridging approaches for social movement studies. For this purpose I will analyze how a coalition operating within a presidential form of government produced a party distribution of functions that left the *piquetero* policy domain under dispute among coalition members. I will also examine the emergence of the multi-level game of contentious and institutional politics that led to the collapse of the national government. The territorial alliances between certain mayors and *piquetero* SMOs led to differing outcomes as well as increasing trans-district competition and emulation among mayors. In this way, vertical and horizontal political opportunities will again be dynamically studied. Finally, I will introduce the role of the *political operators*, a crucial informal broker that has generally been overlooked by other studies of Argentine politics. With the inclusion of the political operators I aim to direct scholars' attention to the role of the main state actor that has built informal links of trust between SMOs and the state.

This chapter also offers the possibility of showing, with much more clarity than in the previous chapter, the heuristic power of my proposal of a repertoire of strategies because the *piquetero* movement grew, diversified, and achieved legitimacy as a political actor during this period. A dynamic analysis of the predominant repertoire of strategies of the *piquetero* movement will show how this repertoire changed over time. As will be seen, the repertoire of strategies mutated more rapidly than did the repertoire of contention during the struggle for legitimacy. However, it will be also made evident that the predominant repertoire of strategies preserves a limited range that is not directly related to junctural shifts.

THE NEW GOVERNMENT AND THE CORRIENTES PUEBLADA OF 1999

As Menem was coming to the end of his decade in government and the new president Fernando De la Rúa was taking power, a *pueblada* in the province of Corrientes was taking place. The *pueblada* in Corrientes was a central contentious event for the new government because this conflict represented a first direct confrontation with some of its coalition members and an indicator of how the national government would abruptly end two years later. However, the Corrientes *pueblada* was just the first of six town revolts the new government would need to confront while they continued to spread across the country.[1]

[1] The Corrientes *pueblada* happened at the same time as a second *pueblada* in Tartagal and Mosconi (the first having been in 1997), but due to the magnitude of the Corrientes conflicts, the latter attracted no media coverage and was resolved by the governorship without direct intervention on the part of the national government.

Although inflation was no longer an issue, the economic recession, coupled with de-industrialization and mass privatization, had maintained high levels of unemployment (15.6 percent) and increased the number of those living below the poverty line (27.1 percent) (May 1999). Within this context many provinces – by now immersed in socioeconomic crises – were trying to operate with fiscal restraint.

The Corrientes *pueblada* started in March 1999 when teachers and public sector employees began a strike to obtain payment of their salaries, which had not been paid in three months. This was followed in June by a demonstration of 35,000 people led by the CTA. Then multiple roadblocks emerged across the main provincial highways and bridges, while police started their own protest by refusing to leave their barracks. This series of events led the governor to step down, and a coalition agreement was achieved by the PJ, the UCR, and the main provincial party. In the meantime, protestors set up of tents in front of the governorship to claim their salaries and call for the resignation of the entire provincial political elite.

In October the Argentine presidential elections were held and the UCR-FREPASO Alliance for Work, Justice and Education (Alliance, thereafter) beat the PJ candidate. On December 10, the new president, Fernando De la Rúa, started his mandate, and on the same day the protests in Corrientes were intensified with the hope of inciting the national government to fulfill its promise to solve the crisis in the province by committing US$120 million and implementing a federal intervention that would lead to the removal of the governing political elite. The main access road to the provincial capital was cut in an attempt to radicalize contention on the part of teachers, judiciary workers, and other public sector employees. After six days, the national government ordered the Gendarmerie to clear the protestors by force in order to reopen transit routes. This action resulted in the death of two civilians and the expansion of contention, the population expressing its anger with the political elites by shouting "All must leave!" Finally, the federal government also intervened at the level of provincial leadership, with De la Rúa installing an interim governor (Sánchez 2000).

THE MULTI-LEVEL GAME FOR MOVEMENT EXPANSION: HORIZONTAL AND VERTICAL POLITICAL OPPORTUNITIES

The Alliance government (December 1999–December 2001) was defined by a very contentious context – that included several *puebladas* and a growing *piquetero* movement – and two key divisions: first, an intra-government horizontal division between the UCR and FREPASO coalition members; and, second, a trans-government vertical division between the national, provincial, and local governments in the Greater Metropolitan Area of Buenos Aires.

The electoral success of the UCR-FREPASO Alliance coalition headed by De la Rúa over the PJ candidate Eduardo Duhalde was not total. While nationally Duhalde was defeated, in the crucial province of Buenos Aires the PJ beat the Alliance. This situation created a scenario that introduced a multi-level division between the national and provincial governments in addition to the traditional division between the government and the opposition. Furthermore, as the Alliance was a multi-party coalition, the government was divided between two clusters of ministries that each responded to either the UCR or FREPASO leadership.

These two key divisions provided the main *piquetero* SMOs with allies both inside the national government (FREPASO) and outside it (mainly the PJ mayors of La Matanza and Florencio Varela in suburban Buenos Aires). The mutations in the vertical and horizontal political opportunities from the struggle for recognition to the struggle for legitimation are schematically compared in **Table 4.1**.

The Horizontal Political Opportunities: The Uneven Formation of a National Coalition

The Alliance government was constituted by two very different parties. On the one hand was the UCR, a century-old catchall party that included several governorships and thousands of local governments and was sustained through highly developed internal discipline. On the other hand was the FREPASO coalition of small center-left parties, less than a decade old and with no executive posts. FREPASO was mainly sustained by the Broad Front (FG), a party with a low degree of internal institutionalization, built upon the personalized leadership of the Alliance vice president, Carlos “Chacho” Álvarez, and a few other individuals (Abal Medina 2009). The FG and FREPASO were allied with the CTA, but as they had no territorial networks, their electoral success was dependent on the mass-media presence of their leaders. This huge disparity between the UCR and FG was even evident when the percentage of the electorate that was a member of these parties was taken into account. While the PJ had a national membership of 14 percent of the electorate and the UCR 10

TABLE 4.1 *Schematic Comparison of the Shifts in Political Opportunities in Greater Buenos Aires, 1996–2001*

Political Opportunities	**Struggle for Recognition (1996–99)**	**Struggle for Legitimation (1999–2001)**	**Moment of Legitimation (December 23–30, 2001)**
Horizontal (functional)	Dominance of the Ministry of Labor until the emergence of the dispute over responsibility for the *piquetero* policy domain with the Secretariat for Social Development.	Division and dispute for influence over the *piquetero* policy domain among FREPASO and UCR/allies coalition members. Upgrading of the Secretariat for Social Development to ministerial status.	No policy definition, just distribution of subsidies. First ad hoc participation of a *piquetero* SMO (CCC) in the *piquetero* policy domain.
Vertical (multi-level)	Territorial agreement of non-intervention between the presidency (*menemista* PJ) and the governorship (*duhaldista* PJ). The governor has nearly hegemonic control over peri-urban politics.	End of the territorial agreement and development of a multi-level dispute between the presidency (UCR-Alliance), the governorship (*duhaldista* PJ) and peri-urban mayors (non-*duhaldista* PJ).	Total support of the national government by the governorship of Buenos Aires (*duhaldista* PJ), though not of the rest of the governors.

Note: Political opportunities are dynamic by definition (cf. Chapter 1, **Table 1.4**). This schematic presentation is intended to capture the most representative synthetic shifts in political opportunities from one stage to the other in the struggle for reincorporation.

percent, the FG only exceeded 1.5 percent in the provinces of Buenos Aires and Mendoza (Abal Medina 2009: 362, table 3 and n. 6).

FREPASO saw the Buenos Aires provincial election as its golden opportunity to build a paired relationship with the UCR. However, Graciela Fernández Meijide's defeat by Duhalde's protégé Federico Ruckauf (PJ) for the post of governor of Buenos Aires left FREPASO with no governorships. The unequal power relationship between FREPASO and UCR became more evident as the UCR went on to win or retain seven provinces.[2] With FREPASO's poor showing in the crucial elections for the governorship of Buenos Aires, the executive cabinet was almost completely made up of UCR members. Of the ten ministries, only the Ministry of Labor and the newly created Ministry of Social Development were given to FREPASO members as well as only eight secretariats (out of a total of 42) and four sub-secretariats (out of a total of 58) (Ollier 2001: 159).

For the *piquetero* movement, FREPASO represented the only actor allied to any CTA and FTV claims. It was strategically in charge of the Ministry of Labor and also controlled the Secretariat of Employment, which was responsible for unemployment subsidies. FREPASO was also in charge of the Ministry of Social Development, which was created to expand and develop social policies. FREPASO's entry into these ministries, crucial for the *piqueteros*' claims, and its weakness vis-à-vis the UCR gave the movement – and particularly the FTV, the CCC and the UTD of Mosconi – a very limited ally.

In the case of the FTV, its national leader, Luis D'Elía, was elected as a city councilor for La Matanza under the FG umbrella. Despite this, when asked about his priorities, D'Elía cited his own organization – the FTV – and not the Alliance with which he was allied. As a part of the sedimentation of union legacies onto the *piquetero* movement, the FTV's prioritization of its own SMO over the FG/Alliance reproduces the traditional centrality given to social organizations over party structures within the Peronist movement.[3]

[2] In the 1999 elections the UCR won the following governorships (under a nominal alliance with FREPASO in all cases except the first): Catamarca, San Juan, Río Negro, Chaco, Chubut, Entre Ríos, and Mendoza. In 2000 FREPASO achieved its only electoral success in the city of Buenos Aires (Ollier 2001: 128–29).

[3] Historically, this has happened before with the CGT's relationship vis-à-vis the PJ – something that was particularly evident during the conflict between CGT leader Augusto Vandor and Juan Domingo Perón in the 1960s (Collier and Collier 1991: 493–96; McGuire 1997). As shown by Levitsky (2003b), during the Peronist Renovation

In the case of the CCC, the relationship with the FG was a result of the alliance between the FTV and the CCC since 1998. The MTA-CTA-CCC collaboration that allowed for the organization of the two Federal Marches during the Menem government ended over the different electoral positions of these organizations. However, the FTV and the unemployed workers' sector of the CCC maintained an alliance in La Matanza based on a shared grievance, though with different strategies in mind. This alliance would produce several coordinated contentious events and exploit informal and non-disruptive links with the government. For instance, in 1999, immediately after De la Rúa had won the elections, a secret meeting to define the cabinet was organized. As the FG was going to receive very few posts and because the FTV could not directly promote a protest against a newly elected government in which it was involved, a FTV member told a CCC leader where this meeting was to take place so the CCC could protest there and encourage the formation of a cabinet that was more "socially minded." This protest did not actually alter power relationships within the cabinet, but it is an example of the type of links the CCC produced as an outsider with the Alliance parties during this period.

In the case of the UTD of Mosconi, the relationship emerged in November 2000, but a political approach to this SMO was only adopted at the very end of the government's tenure in 2001 when Juan Pablo Cafiero became Minister of Social Development. He legitimized the UTD of Mosconi and facilitated some meetings for them with the few remaining FREPASO members in government.

The Vertical Political Opportunities: The End of the Territorial Agreement

Duhalde's defeat at the national level but success with Ruckauf at the provincial level put an end to the territorial agreement that had sustained most social policy through the Menem years. The end of this agreement also had several important effects on the reconfiguration of the political arena that allowed for the *piqueteros*' legitimation. The new scenario produced a vertical division between the national Alliance government and the PJ governorship of Buenos Aires. The vertical political opportunities, in addition to the horizontal ones, favored the movement's capacity

reforms and the Menem governments, this same strategy was sustained by the CGT as part of its strategy for survival.

to strategically manipulate these elite divisions through short- and medium-term alliances.

In addition, Duhalde's partial defeat did not allow him to take up the PJ presidency and replace Menem as party chair, and this led to the division of the PJ into two contested camps disputing control over the party. The PJ's lack of national cohesiveness produced an increased territorialization of politics where "[p]rovincial bosses are not linked together horizontally or vertically integrated into a central hierarchy, but rather tend to remain entrenched in their own fiefdoms" (Levitsky 2001: 49). Thus, the PJ governors were subsequently divided in their negotiations with the national government for resources in Buenos Aires, Córdoba, and Santa Fe as well as in the smaller provinces that had worked in coalition (Novaro 2009: 571–72). Additionally, in Buenos Aires a series of non-*duhaldista* PJ mayors began to challenge Duhalde's iron grip over the province.

Finally, the UCR's weaker territorial penetration compared with the PJ pushed the De la Rúa government to actively dispute the PJ networks in peri-urban Buenos Aires. This was done by bypassing the PJ mayors in the implementation of social policies in the province. The Work Program III, launched near the end of Menem's tenure, constituted the main unemployment policy under De la Rúa's mandate. Though this program, designed and financed by the World Bank, had already been implemented in its first and second versions in cooperation with governorships and municipalities, this third version included NGOs as possible beneficiaries (World Bank 2000). This modification to the Work Program was not implemented during Menem's tenure but rather under De la Rúa. This policy was first implemented in the allied municipality of Rosario (Santa Fe), with relative success, and then was expanded to Greater Buenos Aires. In the first months of De la Rúa's government, *piquetero* SMOs that had created or recycled already registered NGOs began requesting subsidies from the Ministry of Labor without municipal mediation, while PJ-governed municipalities received a lower percentage of these resources (Gómez 2006).

The decision to enforce the application of the NGO requirement for the Work Program III, however, produced some unintended consequences. For the *piquetero* movement, those SMOs that did not depend on unions or party alliances, such as the MTR, could survive and even grow (Svampa and Pereyra 2003: 96), while the FTV and the CCC could become national actors and increase their disruptive capacity. For the state, the Buenos Aires municipalities with PJ mayors were affected by the lack of resources and the increased deterioration of social conditions, which promoted increased *piquetero* protests. Therefore, the logic that dominated the distribution of unemployment subsidies under Menem was inverted: through the year 2000 local governments were granted fewer subsides even though the number of pickets grew (Gómez 2006: 99, graph 1).[4]

Taken together, these vertical disputes turned municipalities into crucial areas of conflict. In the few cases where mayors were allied with the *piqueteros*, conflicts included direct confrontation with the national and provincial governments. In theoretical terms, the Work Program III set into motion a "feedback effect" where "once a set of institutions is in place, actors adapt their strategies in ways that reflect but also reinforce the 'logic' of the system" (Thelen 1999: 392).[5] In other words, the unintended consequence of De la Rúa's decision was that, rather than reducing levels of *piquetero* contention and PJ power, it did exactly the opposite. De la Rúa's decision put the *piqueteros* in the situation where they would need to become allied with mayors against the national government to then share the spoils of their gains. As contentious dynamics developed, a pattern of exchange was set into motion that was based on the threat of disruption on the part of *piqueteros*/mayors and the provision of resources to secure informal agreements of governability that the national government was later powerless to stop from reproducing.

In brief, within a context of increased social unrest and movement growth, the combined horizontal and vertical political opportunities defined the struggle for reincorporation as a relational multi-level process. As I will show in the rest of this chapter, this process moved from the appearance of the "*piquetero* social question" to the ultimate recognition of the *piquetero* movement and its legitimation.

THE EMERGENCE OF A MULTI-LEVEL GAME (DECEMBER 1999–NOVEMBER 2000)

The multi-level game materialized as a consequence of a combination of contentious events and disputes among the UCR and FREPASO members

[4] Another difference from the Menem government, but in the opposite sense, was that while Menem had given increased subsidies to provinces allied with his government, De la Rúa did not do this. According to Lodola (2005), Weitz-Shapiro (2006), and Giraudy (2007), this differing logic of provincial distribution of unemployment subsidies can be inferred to be a result of the lack of a majority in the Senate and the need to secure support to pass austerity laws to deal with the recession combined with the huge number of protests across the country.

[5] It is important to note that the concept of "feedback effect" does not imply a deterministic analysis. The Work Program III pushed forward a logic of interaction but did not determine this logic, nor is it the only – and, even less so, the main – relevant element in the pattern of interaction.

of the government. The main division was generated by a lack of agreement on how to respond to the growing number of *puebladas* and the claims for reincorporation by the *piqueteros*.

The Corrientes, Mosconi, and Tartagal *puebladas* of 1999 were not the last. A third *pueblada* was organized by the UTD of Mosconi, in cooperation with the whole community, which lasted more than ten days in May 2000, ending in a strong crackdown by the authorities (*Clarín* 05/12-13/2000).[6] Parallel with this conflict, on May 5 the Dissident CGT (ex-MTA)[7] called for the first national strike against De la Rúa to resist the approval of a new labor law that would bring in more flexible working conditions. Despite social unrest and union resistance, on May 29 the government decided on a 13 percent decrease in pensions and the salaries of public sector employees. On June 9 the unions responded with another general strike, but this time the Dissident CGT was also joined by the Alliance-allied sector of the CTA. A 300-kilometer march from Rosario to Buenos Aires, which took place between July 16 and August 10, was organized by the CTA in cooperation with the Dissident CGT and many other organizations to demand a universal unemployment subsidy and a monthly allowance for any poor family with dependents under the age of eighteen. The march culminated in the presentation to the president of a petition containing 450,000 signatures. De la Rúa claimed that he supported the idea but that it simply was not feasible (*El Cronista Comercial* 08/10/2000). Although it did not produce any governmental policy change, this march had the same effect as the Federal Marches against Menem in that it led to increased coordination and cooperation between various groups. This march would later evolve into the National Front against Poverty (FRENAPO), a popular front strategy campaigning for a universal citizenship right to an income.

[6] This repressive strategy was followed by the continued judicialization of protest, which was particularly effective for those who applied the witness strategy. In addition to Castells of the MIJP, who was already in jail in Buenos Aires, Emilio Alí was added to this list in June 2000. A Mar del Plata CTA activist, he organized the claim for food at a Tía Supermarket and was, like Castells, convicted of extortion. Alí and Castells would remain in jail until 2002 despite the efforts of the *piqueteros*, the CTA, the Dissident CGT (ex-MTA), and human rights organizations (cf. Paid-for Announcement "Freedom for Emilio Alí and Raúl Castells Who Struggle against Hunger," *Página/12* 11/27/2000).

[7] After 1996 the MTA increased its power within the CGT, but as it could not achieve an internal agreement to expel the *menemista* Secretary-General Rodolfo Daer, it continued to work independently, and in 2000 was renamed the Dissident CGT while struggling for control of the Official CGT (Godio 2000: 1212–13).

The Same Protest in Five Provinces

REPORT. Correspondents

The roadblocks due to social protests in the interior are as follows:

Neuquén. A group of unemployed people has been claiming for subsidies since Monday and has blocked national route 22 in Plottier, 20 kilometers from the capital of Neuquén. The demonstrators – among whom are women who are heads of families – receive 150 pesos per month through the municipal employment plan and are demanding an increase of 50 pesos in subsidies, as well as food.

Salta. Around 300 policemen departed yesterday afternoon for Tartagal, where 200 unemployed people from the national communal vegetable garden program and Work Programs blocked route 34, stopping vehicles from crossing the Bolivian border. The protest started on Monday with more than 100 people picketing in Cuña Muerta. Yesterday, the number of people doubled as another picket was set up, this time over the Bailey bridge in Zanja Honda.

Jujuy. Using roadblocks and the occupation of the local ministerial offices on the border [with Bolivia], school teachers in the interior protested yesterday over a delay in their pay and expressed their dissatisfaction with governor Eduardo Fellner – who they accused of discriminating against them with the pay schedule. Teachers and professors in La Quiaca occupied the Region I branch of the Ministry of Education, threatening to block the traffic on route 9 and the international bridge, while their colleagues from Libertador General San Martín blocked national route 34. The protests were triggered when it was discovered that – besides the delay in the teachers' September pay – teachers in the provincial capital had already been paid.

Catamarca. Around 80 unemployed people in western Catamarca – mainly from Belén – blocked national route 40 in protest at the delay in the payment of Work Programs.

In Chaco, 500 unemployed people cut national route 11 in the morning at the entrance to Resistencia demanding the reinstatement of 170 Work Programs and the distribution of 500 more. Additionally, they requested a 20-kilogram bag of food for each family. The protest was cancelled in the afternoon due to a storm.

FIGURE 4.1 *Clarín* Newspaper Article: "The Same Protest in Five Provinces" (11/02/2000)

The year 2000 was marked by the systematic use of pickets, by far the most commonly used form of protest (Schuster et al. 2006: 49, table 15). Due to the enormous quantity of pickets (**Figure 3.1**), newspapers adopted a new way of presenting them in the form of a list of routine disruptive events across the country, as illustrated in a *Clarín* article (**Figure 4.1**).

The De Facto End of the Alliance Coalition

To the already difficult relationship between the UCR and FREPASO was added in 2000 a corruption scandal that severely affected the UCR ministries and legislators involved in approving a controversial new labor law. Once more, the response of the Alliance members to the situation was divided, making of the horizontal divisions an insurmountable problem. While FREPASO leader and vice president Álvarez pushed for an investigation, president De la Rúa was against this. At the same time, increased social unrest and the inability and unwillingness to divert from the neoliberal path also affected CTA-sector relationships within the Alliance. This unsustainable situation forced De la Rúa into a major cabinet reshuffle on September 29, without consulting Álvarez. This further weakened FREPASO's already marginal position in the government and resulted in Álvarez's resignation one week later. As a result, a major crisis erupted within the Alliance, and almost all the FREPASO members in government ended up resigning, signaling the de facto end of the coalition. The ones who remained in office were in the areas that were most relevant to the *piqueteros*' claims: the Secretariat of Employment and the Ministry of Social Development.

The vice president's stance touched off FREPASO's quick dissolution and increased the autonomy of the party members within government (Abal Medina 2009). De la Rúa would later continue to pursue a governmental path that would even divide his own party. According to De Luca (2008: 208–9), De la Rúa's decisions are "explained by a combination of circumstances: the fractious and conflictive rather than homogeneous coalition he led, his lack of leadership skills, and the severe economic and political crisis over which he presided that eroded his initial support." For the *piquetero* movement, and part of the PJ, this represented a moment of particular governmental weakness that rendered self-evident the need to push for further change.

The Multi-level Interaction in Buenos Aires: The Locus of National *Piquetero* Contention

While the horizontal divisions inside the Alliance government were diluting the government's internal cohesion, a policy decision of De la Rúa increased the vertical divisions with subnational governments. The national government's decision to bypass PJ mayors for the distribution of Work Programs and promote NGOs in order to demobilize the *piquetero* movement had the unintended consequence of creating alliances between PJ mayors and *piquetero* leaders in some districts. In addition, some governors, such as Duhalde's protégé Ruckauf, reduced the provision of provincial subsidies to a minimum in the hope of pushing the conflict in the direction of the national government and relieving pressure on the collapsed provincial economy. This strategy also came with the expectation of even further deterioration of the weak Alliance government. The goal was to pave the way for Duhalde at the next presidential election. However, some mayors – such as those of La Matanza, Florencio Varela, Almirante Brown and Avellaneda – did not share this goal, and thus did not support efforts to coordinate the distribution of provincial subsidies.

Some mayors, such as Alberto Balestrini (La Matanza, PJ) and Julio Pereyra (Florencio Varela, PJ), supported *piquetero* protests, with varying degrees of success. While for both mayors the goal was to increase the resources transferred to their districts, for Balestrini it was also a way of disputing Duhalde's hegemony in the province. At the same time, Pereyra represented the most successful emulation of Balestrini in the intra-PJ dispute for power among mayors.

The *piqueteros*' quest for subsidies only partially responded to the urgent need for some source of subsistence for their constituency, the unemployed urban poor. For the FTV, the claim for subsidies was part of a strategy for building a multi-class popular front in the hope of pushing the government to abandon its neoliberal policies. For the CCC, the claim was part of a strategy for the insurrectional collapse of the government that would lead toward a whole new system. While for the MTR, the subsidies were tools for feeding their members as well as representing the diffusion of insurrectional *focos* in a beehive tactic toward revolution. These strategies coexisted until increased levels of movement coordination in 2001 led to a series of confrontations over how to exit from De la Rúa's government and avoid socioeconomic collapse. To achieve their goals, the *piqueteros* exploited the political opportunities presented by the horizontal divisions within the coalition between UCR and FREPASO officials and the vertical conflicts between state levels that were produced by the situation.

The centralization of the *piquetero* dynamic at the political core of the country and the combination of the strategies of *piqueteros*, mayors, and governors resulted in a multi-level, non-staggered process of interaction based on the disruptive effect of pickets, embedded within the logic of electoral accumulation. This process was mostly focused on the districts of La Matanza and Florencio Varela, each representing opposite paths due to movement and governmental differences.

LOCAL CORPORATIST INCORPORATION AND THE ROLE OF POLITICAL OPERATORS: LA MATANZA AND FLORENCIO VARELA

The experiences of the districts of La Matanza and Florencio Varela present two crucial relational features that would later become a model for the reincorporation of the *piquetero* movement at the national level. The first aspect was the local corporatist incorporation through multi-sectoral councils, developed with more success in La Matanza than Florencio Varela.[8] These councils were emulated by the national government after the *Matanzazo* picket, reproducing them as national policy in other municipalities (*Página/12* 11/08/2000), although this would never be applied at the provincial level.

The second aspect is that there were always public officials placed in charge of informal negotiations and agreements with the *piqueteros*, even though this did not fall within their formal functions. This increased personalization of the state's links with the *piquetero* movement would be carried out by individuals in charge of dissimilar areas. While in La Matanza it was the secretary of employment, in Florencio Varela it was the secretary of government. These areas of the *piquetero* policy domain that were not strictly defined would mean that the links were sustained by the figures of political operators, informal brokers in charge of the daily negotiations with the movement.

[8] In 2001 the local council of La Matanza would administer 120,000 Work Programs obtained from the national government as a result of pickets during 2001, while nothing equivalent to this happened in Florencio Varela.

The Crucial Role of Informal State Brokers: Political Operators

There is a crucial brokerage role played by a semi-public actor in the establishing of the pattern of interaction between the *piqueteros* and state institutions: political operators. In more general terms, what I propose by including the role played by the political operator is to understand how processes and institutions work in a way that transcends merely contention-focused and institutionally focused perspectives to political dynamics. For this, what we need to see is the way "[i]nformal rules shape how democratic institutions work" (Helmke and Levitsky 2006: 2). The sedimentation of ad hoc practices that constitutes the second wave of incorporation is a relational dynamic sustained by informal trust ties between political operators and SMO leaders. The accumulation of precedents as to what can be obtained, how, and through which channel/person carves out a routine that increasingly formalizes this process. Before these practices were formalized at the national level after reincorporation (more about this in Chapter 6), the pattern was overwhelmingly sustained by the figure of the political operator. A *piquetero* leader defined "[t]he political operator [as] someone that works somewhere, and he works as a consultant in whatever secretariat, or maybe he could be the vice-minister of another ministry, but he actually works as the person that enacts a series of political informal actions everywhere (not only with us) and he is the one the state sends you to for an initial softening of positions" (interview 2007).

In other words, a political operator can be defined as a person who works for a party within the state structure whose duties are not regulated by any formalized code. The political operator works following orders in a discretionary fashion for various brokerage objectives and disruptive or anti-disruptive actions, specializing in a particular type of actor or conflict. The actions carried out could be patronage; clientelism; distribution of resources for disruption control or promotion; gate-keeping of mayors, governors, or ministries; and electoral mobilization or demobilization, among others. What political operators are not usually responsible for are repressive and espionage activities. Generally they are middle-range politicians with a very low or non-existent public profile but are well known by those routinely involved with these types of conflict. The political operators have no technical knowledge about the area in which they are formally inserted within the state structure.

Political operators are a result of the personalization of political relationships in Argentina due to the increased territorialization of politics caused by the weakening of corporatist arrangements and the Peronist informal way of working. In addition, they are a symptom of a dispute over who is to be responsible for the "*piquetero* question," a dispute that could only be resolved with time, since – as with any historical process – practices in institutions and state functions need time to become formalized and structured. While on the *piquetero* side this process encouraged the personalization of power within the movement, on the state side there were a large number of political operators, and who they were was constantly evolving. Hence, in order to grasp the informality intrinsic to the pattern of interaction, the role of political operators is a determinant element in the modeling of a personalized relationship that became increasingly routinized.

The FTV-CCC Territorial Agreement with the Mayor of La Matanza

Since democratization La Matanza has been governed by the PJ, but the district was never under the total control of any sector. Until 1991, mayor Federico Russo governed in an alliance with the CGT and a right-wing faction of the PJ. In 1991 Russo was defeated in the local internal party elections by Alberto Pierri, an outsider who built a relationship first with Duhalde and later Menem. Pierri's success allowed him to impose Héctor Cozzi as mayor. Under Cozzi, the influence of the CGT in local government was severely diminished, and the clientelistic network of territorial brokers was expanded, financing 480 base units (Levitsky 2003b: 127–28). With the support of the diocese of San Justo, Cozzi's government was also characterized by a highly conflictual relationship with SMOs and progressive priests. For instance, dialogue was blocked to such an extent that the CCC once entered the municipal building with Molotov cocktails to try to force the secretary of employment to distribute resources such as food outside of the mayor's clientelistic networks.

Cozzi governed from 1991 to 1999, when a major corruption scandal around vote-rigging for his re-election led to his impeachment. This scandal was discovered by the president of the city council, an FG member from an *agrupación* that included D'Elía and had the support of the national deputy Alberto Balestrini. The 1999 local elections were won by Balestrini, a non-aligned PJ candidate. La Matanza district remained under a PJ government, but as of then, it was under neither Duhalde's nor Menem's leadership. Due to this, an electorally crucial district became a highly disputed space in the 1999–2001 period, which allowed the *piquetero* SMOs to exploit these factional divisions within the PJ through informal agreements.

Balestrini had two main limitations that affected his tenure. First, he emerged as a result of a political crisis and was governing the largest local district during its worst ever economic crisis. Second, he was not allied to Menem or Duhalde and hoped to weaken the influence of the latter in La Matanza and – if possible – in the province as a whole. The political conflict with the province was such that the provincial Secretariat of Labor stopped sending Plan for Buenos Aires Neighborhoods unemployment subsidies to La Matanza. To this was added the national government's policy of bypassing certain municipalities in the distribution of subsidies. These two limitations rendered ineffective the efforts made by Daniel Barrera, the local secretary of employment (1999–2003), to promote a collegial administration of the resources provided to the district under municipal responsibility.

As a result, it was crucial for mayor Balestrini to find some allies. Even though, since Cozzi, unions were no longer crucial allies for governing, Balestrini needed to build a territorial base to dismantle that of his rivals and secure minimum levels of governability. In addition to these problems, since the 1990s the CBC and left-wing parties had been going through the most disruptive process of their recent local history by organizing the *piquetero* movement. In short, it was Balestrini's quest to rebuild a territorial base and secure the support of the movement for his mandate that led the mayor to offer the FTV and the CCC a role in municipal government. Although the CCC did not accept the offer and the FTV already had its main leader serving as a city councilor for another party, both SMOs participated actively in the informal definition of local social policies.

In May 2000 the municipality declared a local economic and social emergency in La Matanza. To face this critical situation, the first trial of reincorporation through a corporatist format was modeled with the creation of the Council for Social Emergency (CES) – which came out of D'Elía's proposal as city councilor (*Página/12* 05/13/2000). The CES was inspired by two legacies: first, the councils that had organized at the local level during the 1989–91 hyperinflationary crisis to stop lootings and secure food provision, and second – with the goal of stimulating citizen participation at the municipal level – the example of participatory budgeting in Porto Alegre, Brazil. Even though the CES never came near the participatory budget model, it was, as it had been in 1989, a very effective tool for the distribution of resources and coordination of the main local actors through a corporatist logic. The CES was under the responsibility of the municipal Secretariat of Employment, and it involved the city council, the bishop of San Justo, local Rotary Clubs, the local CGT, the FTV, the CCC, and other organizations in La Matanza. The structure was decentralized into fifteen grassroots offices for the administration of 7,000 Plan for Buenos Aires Neighborhoods that the provincial government agreed to deliver after much bargaining.

It was in 2000, as social unrest grew, that the FTV and CCC initiated the so-called "*Matanzazo*." The *Matanzazo* was the inaugural contentious action of the FTV-CCC alliance, and it was truly national in its scope. The *Matanzazo*, the first massive picket carried out in Greater Buenos Aires, consisted of a roadblock set up by 3,000 members of the FTV and the CCC. It lasted from October 31 to November 4. Their claim was for the national government's participation in an agreement between the provincial and local governments.[9] It had the support of the CTA, the Dissident CGT, part of FREPASO, the mayor, and the governorship. In a clear supportive gesture, mayor Balestrini went to the picket and declared to the media: "These requests are entirely just. If anyone even thinks about sending in the police, both the vice-governor and I will act as human shields to prevent this from happening" (quoted by *Página/12* 11/01/2000). This declaration closed the door to any form of repression while for the first time aligning the mayor and part of the governorship against the presidency.[10] This reshuffling of vertical political opportunities was particularly unfortunate for the reluctant new national minister of labor, Patricia Bullrich (Alliance-allied party). Eventually, the CTA and the Dissident CGT threatened to call for a new national strike if the agreement with the *piqueteros* was not signed. Evidently there was no other way out for the national government than to finally provide the FTV and CCC with legitimacy as national political actors, something that was done by the rest of the political spectrum during the *Matanzazo* protest. However, although the national government did participate in the negotiations that led to this first agreement, in the end, the presidency did not sign it (Svampa and Pereyra 2003: 98; Calvo 2006: 122–23).

As one national leader of the FTV later recognized, the crucial difference with La Matanza's mayor compared to others was that: "This guy

[9] The *Matanzazo* was carried out to request the provision of 4,500 subsidies, an increased allowance of twenty tons of food per month, the improvement of local public health services, the rebuilding of five public schools, and the provision of US$5 million to the municipal government for social spending, among many other demands (*Página/12* 11/01/2000).

[10] The day after the mayor's declaration of support, governor Ruckauf said he would not send in provincial police to repress the roadblock (*Página/12* 11/02/2000).

was crafty enough to make those running the conflict his allies instead of his enemies," and the presence of such an ally was crucial because: "We expanded the pickets because the guy supported us" (interview 2007). In other words, Balestrini was able to convert the municipal government into the key articulator between social conflict and the provincial and national governments in this crucial electoral district. This allowed him to push for the resolution of the municipal crisis by the provincial and national governments. In exchange, for the FTV and the CCC this represented a turning point that allowed for the legitimation of these two SMOs.

The MTR's Failed Emulation of the Territorial Agreement with the Mayor of Florencio Varela

Some other mayors followed Balestrini's lead. The most relevant case was in Florencio Varela due to the importance of the *piquetero* movement in the district and the electoral relevance of this municipality. Unlike in La Matanza, though, the results of this experience were less than satisfactory.

In January 2000 the first government-led march against unemployment was organized by the mayor of Florencio Varela. The reason for this was the cancellation of 2,500 unemployment subsidies without prior notice. According to a territorialized logic of control of governability/disruption, this march was explained by the mayor as follows: "The social pressure was so strong, so tough, that I myself decided to lead the mobilization. I led it for two reasons. One, so that there was a political containment [of the mobilization] and there would be no damage [of property]. And another reason was because the claim was valid ... [and thus,] ... I expelled the protest from the municipality and took it to the federal capital" (Julio Pereyra, interview 2008). This march to Buenos Aires, organized in cooperation with Mariano West (PJ mayor of Moreno) but not with *piquetero* SMOs, led to a meeting with the minister of labor and then with vice president Álvarez.

The relationship between mayors and *piqueteros* was never coordinated across districts but rather was the result of individual decisions in each municipality. Balestrini in La Matanza never promoted or coordinated his decisions with Julio Pereyra (PJ) in Florencio Varela and only made specific requests to mayors West and Hugo Curto (Tres de Febrero, PJ) at the behest of the CCC to help reduce local persecution by these mayors' clientelistic networks. At the same time, the relationship with Quilmes mayor Fernando Geronés (Alliance) was of competition for resources and spaces to mobilize and with Manuel Quindimil (PJ) in

Lanús oscillating between a paternalistic and a repressive relationship (Cerrutti and Grimson 2004). In most of the suburbs relations were highly conflictual, such as those with Merlo mayor Raúl Othacehé (PJ) and San Vicente mayor Antonio Arcuri (PJ), among many others.

Within this context Pereyra was an exception. Although originally part of the *duhaldista* group while interim mayor (1991–93), after his initial election in 1993 he developed a non-aligned position that led him to a quest for needs fulfillment similar to Balestrini's. On the one hand, in a very poor district with a strong legacy of land occupations, he needed to secure local governability by controlling disruption or directing it outside his district, as shown at the beginning of this section. On the other hand, Pereyra saw the example of the *piquetero*-mayor alliance that elevated Balestrini to national prominence as a very attractive strategy for promoting himself and not losing political space within the landscape of horizontal competition among PJ mayors in Buenos Aires.

As far as the *piquetero* movement was concerned, the situation was less favorable for the MTR than it was for the FTV and the CCC in La Matanza. In terms of the movement's evolution, the type of relationship enjoyed with the local government was crucial. Even though the MTR was quite strong in Florencio Varela and Quilmes, the latter district was less favorable to alliances than the former because its mayor was from the president's party and was totally aligned with his policies. It must also be noted that Quilmes is a highly disputed district, in close proximity to the core *duhaldista* territories, and in which the provincial secretary of labor Aníbal Fernández built his own political career as mayor. This situation also very much affected the evolution of the FTV of San Francisco Solano (Quilmes), maintaining it in a secondary role.

Emulating the actions of the CCC in La Matanza, in 1998 the MTR occupied the municipal building in an attempt to modify the closed distribution of resources, confined to the mayor's own network. This situation led to intervention on the part of a person who would become the political operator of the relationship at the local level with the *piquetero* SMOs – Carlos Kunkel, the municipal secretary of government (1991–2003) of Florencio Varela, who had been a Montoneros deputy in the 1970s.

In Florencio Varela a CES was also created, emulating the one in La Matanza and involving the same type of actors: the Catholic Church, the CGT, and *piqueteros*, among others. The CES also included the MTR, which was less predisposed to negotiation than the FTV and the CCC. The MTR developed an intransigent position of confrontation with the municipality as a means of achieving an autonomous position vis-à-vis the state institutions. In addition to this, the MTR introduced global claims that were irrelevant to the local context, such as political declarations about not paying the national external debt – areas in which the CES and municipal government had no jurisdiction. The MTR's position regarding the municipal government was mostly sustained by one of its leaders in particular. In 2000, after the MTR saw itself excluded from subsidy distribution, other sectors began promoting a more conciliatory position.

Even though, like in La Matanza, the local government had a person in charge of the relationship with the *piqueteros*, the MTR was less predisposed to dialogue than the FTV and the CCC. This opened up opportunities for other groups that took more pragmatic approaches toward the municipal government. The main division was produced by a strategic cleavage of the Guevarist Movement (MG), which, under the leadership of Juan Cruz Daffunchio, organized a picket with the participation of the mayor in 2000. This picket represented a double emulation dynamic, with the mayor going in with the hope of performing a mediating role like Balestrini and the MTR of Florencio Varela emulating the FTV and CCC strategy of using the mayor's support to force the hand of the governorship or national government to distribute subsidies in an agreement for the sharing of the spoils.

The results were as expected, and the provincial secretary of employment and political operator for *piquetero* issues Héctor Metón went to the municipality to negotiate, helping the MTR receive unemployment subsidies in Florencio Varela, Quilmes, and Lanús. But, unlike what happened in La Matanza, where initial success led to increased coordination among *piquetero* SMOs, in Florencio Varela the MTR of Solano rejected this approach toward the municipality. The conflict between the sectors that made up the MTR was the result of disagreement over a repertoire of strategies that was not shared by all concerned. While the MTR sector of Florencio Varela was mostly in favor of a vanguardist moderate *foquismo* approach, the MTR of Solano was evolving toward an autonomist–introspective strategy that rejected any type of embedded relationship with the state. Finally, differences emerged within the MTR of Florencio Varela regarding the intensity of confrontation that ought to be used at the local and provincial levels, although all shared the idea that confrontation on a national scale was necessary. The end result was that the MTR did not obtain the same public exposure, resources and legitimation that were achieved by the FTV and CCC, and the mayor failed to generate an SMO ally to propel his political career to the national level as he had desired.

FROM MULTI-LEVEL DISPUTE TO CRISIS (NOVEMBER 2000–SEPTEMBER 2001)

The sustained conflicts placed the strategy for resolving the "*piquetero* question" high on the agenda of governmental priorities. The Alliance government dispute revolved around the struggle to define the political or social character of the *piqueteros*' policy domain and for control of this policy domain. These conflicts implied the continuation, within a new context, of the struggle for this policy domain that had taken place during the end of the Menem presidency. Throughout De la Rúa's period in office, as under Menem, resolution of the *piqueteros*' claims would continue to fall under the jurisdiction of the Ministry of Labor, with a secondary role for the Ministry of Social Development. Under De la Rúa, the latter ministry would become a more active contender in the drive to achieve a level of participation in the *piquetero* policy domain.

Contention increased also outside Greater Buenos Aires. In Mosconi and Tartagal a fourth *pueblada* was happening while in La Matanza the FTV and the CCC achieved legitimacy, and in Florencio Varela the MTR failed to emulate them. This *pueblada* ended on November 14, 2000, after fifteen days of pickets thanks to mediation on the part of the Catholic Church and strong repression on the part of the Gendarmerie (Svampa and Pereyra 2003: 130–31). As was the case in La Matanza, it was the first time national officials were sent to negotiate with the *piquetero* SMO in Mosconi (*Clarín* 10/07/2000 and 10/12-14/2000).[11] In order to calm social unrest the authorities had to enter into semi-public negotiations with the UTD of Mosconi leaders, José "Pepino" Fernández and Juan Carlos "Jipi" Fernández. Each and every agreement achieved in the private negotiations was presented to the SMO members demonstrating on the road, who deliberated over them in an assembly format to reach a final decision (*Clarín* 10/15/2000). Another result was increased coordination, although short-lived, between the UTD of Mosconi, the CCC, and the Workers Party of Salta, with the organization in December 2000 of the first Unemployed Workers' Congress for northern Salta, although it failed

[11] Some of the main national political operators for *piquetero* conflicts were sent to Mosconi: Lautaro García Batallán (formally the secretary of institutional issues for the Ministry of the Interior), the secretary of employment Horacio Viqueira (FREPASO), and a few low-ranking government officials, such as César Mastucci (subsecretary of the interior), Walter Ceballos (secretary for the relationship with the provinces), and Eduardo Bustelo (secretary of social policy) (Svampa and Pereyra 2003: 131, n. 45).

due to disputes over leadership and was never organized again (Oviedo 2004: 171–74 and 222).

In addition to increased *piquetero* contention, the first year in government for the Alliance ended with another national strike on November 23 and 24. Coordinated by the CTA and Dissident CGT, it included, for the first time, the active participation of the FTV, the CCC, and the MIJP (*Clarín* 11/24/2000). In reaction, in December the government issued an unsuccessful call for a "social dialogue" toward building a multi-sectoral agreement (*Clarín* 04/12/2000).

The Alliance's Strategic Division Regarding How to Approach the *Piqueteros* in La Matanza

Weakened by the *Matanzazo*, Fernández Meijide resigned as minister of social development and another FREPASO leader was nominated as her replacement. The arrival of Juan Pablo Cafiero to the ministry marked the beginning of a direct dispute with Bullrich, the minister of labor, regarding how to deal with the *piquetero* movement. Cafiero's confrontation with Bullrich was not part of a coordinated FREPASO policy but rather his personal decision. This was possible because the near dissolution of FREPASO left the few FREPASO members in government with high levels of independence.[12]

The division between the minister of labor and the minister of social development was made public in *Clarín* (05/21/2001) during a seventeen-day picket coordinated by the FTV and CCC (May 7–23, 2001) in La Matanza. This publicized debate was the synthesis of two disparate positions that were dominating the government. One stance, represented by the Ministry of Labor and the Ministry of the Interior, was in favor of a policy of political exhaustion of the movement by not responding to any claim and the simultaneous judicialization of the conflict by legally persecuting the *piquetero* SMOs, who were accused of the clientelistic use of subsidies and the employment of extortion for mobilization (*Clarín* 03/12/2001; Svampa and Pereyra 2003: 77). This position was countered by another stance, represented by the Ministry of Social Development as well as the secretary of the presidency, Leonardo Aiello, in favor of solving

[12] As a result of Bullrich's position of pursuing the *piqueteros*, a couple of months later the FREPASO Secretary of Employment resigned from this key area related to the *piqueteros* policy domain (*Página/12* 08/20/2001). This left Cafiero as the last relevant figure from FREPASO in the government.

each situation through dialogue and recognizing social unrest as legitimate due to the critical economic situation of the mobilized people (Federico Storani interviewed by Germano 2005: 264). Acting somewhere in between, De la Rúa proved either unwilling or incapable of imposing a unified position on the cabinet. As one minister said: "De la Rúa left everything to flow ... flow, flow, that was his thesis, flow. Everybody float, float!" (interview 2008).[13]

At the same time, in the province of Buenos Aires the governor and vice governor were also divided as to how they should approach this second massive picket. While governor Ruckauf favored a passive attitude in the hope of destabilizing the Alliance government, vice-governor Felipe Solá favored active intervention in order to resolve it in a manner similar to what Cafiero had achieved with his approach (*Clarín* 05/20/2001).

In the end, with the continued support of mayor Balestrini, the provincial secretary of labor, the national minister of labor, and the secretary of the presidency went to La Matanza to negotiate directly with the *piqueteros*. Just as in Mosconi, the authorities were obliged to negotiate in a semi-public context. Each agreement reached in private negotiations would be taken to the picket for the demonstrators to deliberate over and come to a decision. This negotiation strategy was employed by several *piquetero* SMOs as part of the *basista* strategy that predominated in the movement. However, it disgusted the provincial Secretary of Labor Aníbal Fernández so much that he pulled out of the negotiations.

The *basista* decision-making strategy and the practice of rotating the *piquetero* interlocutor applied by some autonomist SMOs were recalled by *piqueteros* and government officials as permanent sources of conflict. The reason is that these practices alter the personalized relational logic that political operators require in order to sustain informal agreements through valid interlocutors that can offer the state the capacity to easily determine who they need to deal with to control disruption provoked by the *piqueteros*.

Finally, as a result of this second round of pickets, in 2001 a private meeting between Balestrini, Bullrich, D'Elía (FTV), and Juan Carlos Alderete (CCC) was organized to move forward with the delivery of the promised resources. At the same time, but uncoordinated with these events, in Florencio Varela a twelve-day protest was organized with partial mayoral support (Pereyra did not intervene personally like

[13] The president's passivity was also recognized by Federico Storani, UCR-Alliance minister of the interior (interviewed by Germano 2005: 264).

Balestrini, but the protest was allowed to proceed with no police crackdown). Unlike with the FTV and the CCC, this MTR protest failed in its goal to obtain increased subsidies and media attention (Gabriel interviewed by Germano 2005: 165).

Innovation in the Policing of Protest and the Legitimation of the UTD of Mosconi

In June 2001 a fifth *pueblada* was organized in Mosconi. This contentious action had important consequences for the movement and the government. On the *piquetero* side it meant the legitimation of the UTD of Mosconi as a political actor and the consolidation of autonomy from any party. On the government side it meant crucial changes in the policing of protest and the ratcheting up of the dispute among sectors of the Alliance over how to resolve the "*piquetero* question."

The UTD of Mosconi – like the *piqueteros* in Buenos Aires – reflects resilience of the left in the face of repression during the 1970s. It was founded in 1996 by Juan Nievas (PCR) and José Barraza (Workers Party), later joined by José "Pepino" Fernández and some ex-YPF workers, along with other political groups (Benclowicz 2013). In 1999 a feud for the control of the SMO emerged among these groups. The dispute was finally won by Fernández, who proceeded to expel political parties from the UTD in 2000. Through this "filtering" of its membership, the UTD defined a communal non-partisan approach toward "recreating a scenario of working life that had been lost since the privatization of YPF through the transformation of unemployment subsidies into productive projects" (Svampa 2006: 153). These projects were developed for the first time by the UTD in cooperation with the national secretary for small and medium-sized businesses thanks to contacts made with technocrats of De la Rúa's government.

Juan Carlos Romero (PJ Menem-allied governor of Salta from 1995 until 2007) had such firm control over his province that the national government could not easily intervene. This type of zealous territorial control over the province was equivalent to that exercised by Duhalde in Buenos Aires and is practiced by many other governors. Romero was committed to cracking down heavily on the *piqueteros* once the federal judge for Salta had declared the *pueblada* in Mosconi an act of "sedition." Two demonstrators were killed and another 200 were seriously injured as a result of repressive actions carried out by the Gendarmerie. To try to curb this escalation of violence, several personalities traveled to the site of contention, including Hebe de Bonafini of the Mothers, Roberto Martino of the MTR, and laborers from the worker-managed factory Zanón (Neuquén). From the national government, Minister Cafiero, without informing the president or governor, also traveled to Mosconi to negotiate a solution, and once there he declared: "There are more delinquents in the House of Government than in this square of humble workers."

The fifth *pueblada* of Mosconi was characterized by a particular innovation in the way state repression is carried out. It was the first disruptive event in which the Gendarmerie intervened within the framework of the recently reformed Procedural Penal Code. In 2001, Law 24,434 revised articles 184 and 186 and added article 230*bis* to the Procedural Penal Code, increasing the responsibilities of the federal police, the Naval Prefecture, and the Gendarmerie. In practice, this law expanded the responsibilities of the Gendarmerie to include social conflicts. Showing the recursive logic of incorporation dynamics, the redefinition of repressive institutions during the *piqueteros*' struggle for legitimation reproduced part of the tactics applied by the elite against the struggles of anarchists, syndicalists, and socialists for the first legitimation of workers in the late nineteenth and early twentieth centuries (Chapter 1; Isuani 1985; Suriano 1988, 2000).

These changes to the policing of protest were applied for the first time on June 20, 2001, in Mosconi by the federal judge for Salta, Abel Cornejo (*Página/12* 06/21/2001). Even though the Gendarmerie had been involved in *piquetero* conflicts in rural and enclave areas since the first *puebladas* in Cutral-Có and Plaza Huincul, in those cases this military police had intervened within a different legal framework. The Gendarmerie's role from redemocratization to the emergence of the *puebladas* and *piqueteros* was as a border and national highways guard. Thus, when the *piqueteros* blocked a national route, it was the Gendarmerie that was in charge of applying the right to free transit. However, after 2001, the Gendarmerie turned into an anti-riot force, mainly operating in peripheral, enclave, and rural areas. Condemned by human rights organizations as an abuse of state power (*Página/12* 06/21/2001; CELS 2003b), this innovation in the policing of protest rested on the increasing role played by judges in the resolution of socio-political conflicts strengthening the judicialization of contentious politics (Artese 2009).

Another result of this *pueblada* was that the mayor of Mosconi was dismissed. As part of the second incorporation process, and after repression was again proved to be ineffective, the national government proposed that the UTD present one of its leaders as a mayoral candidate for the municipality of Mosconi (*Clarín* 07/01/2001). This would imply a possible "political solution" to the conflict, as claimed by Cafiero after visiting the town. Although this offer was rejected by part of the UTD, the offer saw the SMO as a whole gain legitimacy as a political actor. For the national government, this conflict revealed De la Rúa's total lack of authority and the insurmountable divisions within the national government.

MOVEMENT GROWTH, INCREASED COORDINATION, AND DIVISIONS

The period of multi-level disputes opened by the multiplication of *puebladas* and the *piqueteros*' increased disruption would eventually lead to the legitimation of the whole movement. But first, the movement went through a process of growth and diversification (synthesized in **Table 4.2**).

New SMOs were created and unprecedented levels of coordination within the movement were achieved since the pioneering experience of the CTA in Neuquén in 1996 and the brief period of cooperation in Salta in 2000. In 2001 the first and second National Piquetero Assemblies involved almost all the SMOs and led to the coordination of the main *piquetero* campaign against the national government. Each Assembly would be characterized by strategic confrontations among the social movement sectors. After this experience, several other coordinating bodies were created (the main ones are presented in **Table 4.3**). Finally, the internal disputes of some of the SMOs and long-lasting strategic disputes produced splits within the MTR, FTV, and CCC, the movement's older SMOs (**Table 4.2**).

TABLE 4.2 *Diversification of the* Piquetero *Movement: Main SMO Divisions, 1996–2001*

From 1996–99 ●——→	To 1999–2001
FTV	MTL, CUBa, Neighborhoods Standing Up, FTV
CCC	MIJD, CCC
MTDs-MTR	CTD "Aníbal Verón" (MTDs and CTD "Trabajo y Dignidad"), MTR
UTD of Mosconi	UTD of Mosconi
None	PO, MST "Teresa Vive," and other smaller SMOs

TABLE 4.3 *Most Stable or Relevant Coordinating Bodies of the* Piquetero *Movement, 1996–2009*

Period	Coordinating Body	Main Participants
1994–97	Federal Marches I and II	SEOM of Jujuy (pre-CCC), CTA, MTA
1996	Congress of the Unemployed of Neuquén (one meeting)	CTA and allied organizations
1996–97	Informal group linked by the Mothers of the Plaza de Mayo (Hebe de Bonafini sector)	MG (pre-MTR of Florencio Varela and Mar del Plata), ex-YPF workers of Salta (José "Pepino" Fernández), Héctor "Toty" Flores of La Matanza
1998–2005	FTV-CCC alliance	FTV of La Matanza, CCC of La Matanza
2000	Congress of the Unemployed of northern Salta (one meeting)	UTD of Mosconi, CTD of Tartagal, PO, CCC
2001	South Coordinator	MTR, CTD of La Plata, CTD of Almirante Brown, CTD of Lanús, MTD of Solano
2001	I and II National Piquetero Assemblies	FTV, CCC, UTD of Mosconi, Neighborhoods Standing Up, South Coordinator
2001–3	Coordinator of Unemployed Workers' (CTD) "Aníbal Verón"	MTD of Solano, MTD of Lanús, MTD of Almirante Brown, MTD of Guernica, MTD of Allen (Río Negro), CTD "Trabajo y Dignidad"
2002–7	National Piquetero Block	PO, MST "Teresa Vive," Neighborhoods Standing Up, MTL, CUBa, FOL
2002–5	National Assembly of Employed and Unemployed Workers	MTR, PO, MTL, MST "Teresa Vive," CUBa
2004–5	Popular Organizations Front	FTV, Neighborhoods Standing Up, "Evita" Movement, National and Popular Transversal Front
2004–8	Piquetero Unity	MST, MIJD, FOL, PO, CCC, MTD "Aníbal Verón," CTD "Aníbal Verón," CUBa
2008–	Popular Movements Union	FTV, Octobers, MTD "Aníbal Verón," "October 8" Movement, "July 26" Movement, "July 9" Popular Patriotic Movement, Second Centenary

Note: Figures A and B (Appendix) show the coordinating bodies in the context of the movement's general development.

Sources: Several interviews (2007–13); Ferrer (2005); Oviedo (2000, 2004); Svampa and Pereyra (2003); Poli (2007).

The Origins of the Workers' Pole (1999–2001) and the Trotskyist Party-Family Emulation

Even though the Workers' Pole emerged in late 1999, we need to go back to the mid-1990s to trace the origins of the main Trotskyist *piquetero* SMO. The Trotskyist Workers Party participated in the 1995 soup kitchen protest of unemployed people organized by the PCR in La Matanza. However, due to the ideological rigidity of the Argentine Trotskyist party-family, the Workers Party got involved in the *piquetero* movement much later than did the Maoist PCR or the FTV (inspired by Liberation Theology). Trotskyist participation was highly debated. On the one hand, the Workers Party in 1999 and the Socialist Workers' Movement party in 2001 redefined their understanding of the unemployed and stopped considering them as part of the lumpenproletariat. On the other hand, the PTS and the MAS totally opposed the organization of the *piquetero* SMOs (Natalucci 2008b: 208).[14] This process toward expanding their repertoire of strategies allowed the Workers Party to be the first Trotskyist group to create a *piquetero* SMO.

In 1999 the Workers Party created the Workers' Pole (PO), a *piquetero* SMO with the aim of mobilizing unemployed people, mainly in Greater Buenos Aires and Salta. There is a subsidiary relationship between the Workers Party and the PO, with the latter the territorial branch of the party, as explained by its national coordinator: "the Workers' Pole is the territorial and neighborhood organization through which the Workers Party program is expressed" (interview 2007). In other words, the party guides the movement through its programmatic definitions, which are then translated to the unemployed grassroots in a "pedagogical link" for the building of political consciousness (Delamata 2004: 78–79; Natalucci 2008b: 213). The first public action of the PO was its participation in the first National Piquetero Assembly (July 2001), after which the organization grew exponentially.

The PO combines three predominant strategies in its repertoire: trade unionism, Morenist entryism, and presentialism (Chapter 2). Regarding the trade unionist strategy, on several occasions the PO presented to parliament, the Supreme Court, and the national Ministry of Labor claims for the establishment of a law mandating for corporatist-fashioned negotiations for the unemployed.

[14] The PTS started organizing unemployed people in 2003 and in 2004 had some sporadic contact with the MIJD.

Concerning Morenist entryism, the PO has increased its participation in Salta through the UTD of Mosconi and the Coordinator of Unemployed Workers' (CTD) of Tartagal. While in Mosconi Fernández's non-partisan group expelled them, as it did with the PCR, in Tartagal the PO achieved control of the CTD of Tartagal (Oviedo 2004: 134). This strategy led to the Workers Party's first important electoral success in its history in Salta's legislative and local elections, managing to get a few provincial deputies and city councilors elected since 2001 (Oviedo 2004: 217). This strategy has also been used in the promotion and control of coordinating bodies, such as the National Piquetero Block (**Table 4.3**).

While the presentialist strategy is not exclusive to the PO, its members have exploited it heavily in their desire to present themselves as intransigent revolutionaries that never surrender their principles to the government. Though such a discourse did not characterize their actual approach toward state institutions, it arose from the novelty of a historically small, middle-class, and university-based party controlling a massive territorial grassroots organization of poor people.

The PO was emulated by two Trotskyist parties, the Socialist Workers' Movement and the MAS. Respectively, these parties created in 2002 the Jobless Movement "Teresa Is Alive" (MST "Teresa Vive") and the Combative Workers' Front (2002–3).[15] Both are very small SMOs with no relevant national presence and with some limited mobilization capacity restricted to the city of Buenos Aires.

In the case of the MST "Teresa Vive" the relationship between party and SMO was reproduced by emulating the PO. This did not mean that the whole party was linked to the MST "Teresa Vive": indeed, the party was composed of two main factions before it split in 2006. Only the majoritarian faction under the leadership of legislator Vilma Ibarra was the one related to Gustavo Giménez, the coordinator for the MST "Teresa Vive."[16] Finally, as in the PO, the Morenist entryism and presentialist strategies are predominant in the MST "Teresa Vive." This is a permanent source of rupture and dispute with the PO and FOL as a result of the parties competing in elections for the same small Trotskyist constituency.

15 As of 2006, the MAS would organize the very small Front for Organizations Engaged in Struggle (FOL).

16 The other faction was led by Rubén Sobrero, a middle-range union leader of La Fraternidad (the train workers' union, CGT) who in 2006 became the main figure of the new Trotskyist party Socialist Left.

The Origins of the Coordinator of Unemployed Workers' "Work and Dignity" (1994–2000)

The creation in 2000 of one of the main *piquetero* SMOs in the southern part of Greater Buenos Aires, the Coordinator of Unemployed Workers' "Work and Dignity" (CTD "Trabajo y Dignidad"), arose out of three processes that can be traced back to the early 1990s. The first was the student movement in La Plata's cooperation with former PRT-ERP, Montoneros, and the Intransigent Party groups reorganized in the post-democratization context. The second was the decision by leftist Peronists to embrace a "collectivist alternative" to the clientelistic transformation of the PJ machine party (Levitsky 2003b: 213–15). The third was the Dissident CGT's (ex-MTA) failed attempt at territorialization to emulate the CTA (Chapter 3).

In 1994 the student organization Popular Unity Movement (MPU) "Quebracho" engaged in its first public political action at the 100th demonstration of pensioners and retirees. Following this protest, the MPU "Quebracho" went on to develop a relationship with the MTA and the pensioners' group. In 1996, the MPU joined a collection of Peronist, Intransigent Party, and PRT-ERP groups to form the national–populist anti-imperialist group Patriotic Revolutionary Movement (MPR) "Quebracho."

This process of reorganization of left-wing networks in the post-democratization context was related to the former PRT-ERP reducing its repertoire of strategies by eliminating armed struggle as an available strategy in the short and medium term.[17] It also involved the reaction of left-wing Peronists to the PJ's metamorphosis into a patronage machine party. Some *agrupaciones* left the PJ and participated in the creation of the FG-FREPASO, others got involved in the CTA-FTV process, and a small number of them created the MPR "Quebracho." The participation of some Peronist *agrupaciones* from within and outside of the PJ and the reorganization of former guerrillas to suit a democratic context were very relevant for the resistance to disincorporation and the constitution of the *piquetero* movement.

In 1996 the MPR "Quebracho," in a short-lived effort, got involved in the territorial organization of unemployed workers in La Plata, and the

[17] Since the 1980s the Popular Group "July 9" and the All for the Motherland Movement (MTP) were involved in the San Francisco Solano land occupations. The MTP (a division of the PRT-ERP) did not participate in the creation of the MPR "Quebracho" because it opted for the preservation of the PRT-ERP repertoire of strategies (Chapter 2).

same year in Alta Gracia (in the province of Córdoba) it participated in a picket. After these initiatives, in 1998 the MPR "Quebracho" created a *piquetero* SMO in Buenos Aires, located in La Matanza (based on a small land occupation), the La Plata suburbs, Monte Chingolo (Lanús), and the borders between Quilmes, Lanús, and Avellaneda (Torres 2006: 71–72).

In 2000 the MPR "Quebracho" requested the support of the MTA for the growth of the *piquetero* SMO. The MTA agreed to support the establishment of the CTD "Trabajo y Dignidad" emulating the CTA's territorial strategy (Chapter 3). However, the MTA could not use the CTD "Trabajo y Dignidad" as its territorial SMO in the same fashion as the FTV was for the CTA. Nevertheless, from 1996 to 2001 a tactical agreement was preserved between the MPR "Quebracho"/CTD "Trabajo y Dignidad" and the MTA/Dissident CGT (Hugo Moyano interviewed by Germano 2005: 249; Rubio and Del Grossi 2005: 167–68). In addition to this, the relationship between the political organization MPR "Quebracho" and the *piquetero* SMO CTD "Trabajo y Dignidad" was different from the one adopted by the Trotskyist social movement sector. While the CTD and the MPR "Quebracho" were very much interrelated, they had a relationship of what could be described as "functional autonomy" – both organizations' tactical decisions were in sync, though this was not determined by the MPR "Quebracho" (Delamata 2004: 73).

In 2001 the CTD "Trabajo y Dignidad" joined a coalition with the MTR of Florencio Varela and the MTDs in order to counterbalance the FTV-CCC alliance. The aim was to coordinate a protest in support of the UTD of Mosconi's fifth *pueblada* and then to ensure a common strategy for the first Coordinator of Unemployed Workers (Burkart and Vázquez 2007: 7). This coalition, called South Coordinator, was short-lived but was an important first step toward the subsequent establishment of the Coordinator of Unemployed Workers' (CTD) "Aníbal Verón" (**Table 4.3**).

The First National Piquetero Assembly: Disputes over the Extent and Goals of the *Piquetero* Struggle

The Alliance government was faced with a *piquetero* movement that achieved an unprecedented degree of coordination with the two National Piquetero Assemblies. In the church of El Sagrado Corazón in San Justo (La Matanza), around 2,000 *piqueteros* participated in the first National Piquetero Assembly (July 24, 2001), convened and organized by the FTV and the CCC (Pacheco 2004: 55).

The Assembly engaged in two main strategic debates. The first discussion was about the extent of the *piquetero* struggle: for the MTR the conflict was both national and provincial, while for the FTV and CCC it was only national. This first dispute located the territorialization of Argentine politics at the heart of the *piquetero* struggle.

The second debate was related to the coalition's goals. This discussion was expressed in a threefold fashion. First, the degree to which the coalition should extend beyond the *piquetero* movement was discussed. The MTDs, MTR, and PO wanted the coalition restricted to the *piqueteros*, some left-wing parties, and the CTA. For the FTV and the CCC, it should include the Dissident CGT and as many political actors as possible, reproducing what had been achieved during the Federal Marches under Menem. This issue came to the fore when Dissident CGT secretary general Hugo Moyano and some of the PJ legislators tried to participate and were booed by the PO and MTR members. This dispute placed under intense scrutiny the relationship of the movement to actors that were useful for the movement's immediate goals but did not share its ideology.

The second point of contention in relation to the coalition's goals was whether an alliance with other actors would mean having to moderate some of their methods, such as agreeing to carry out only partial roadblocks, no longer covering their faces, and abandoning the use of self-defense strategies (Burkart and Vázquez 2007: 8).

There was also a third issue that was not agreed upon. The CTA and FTV had been attempting to build a coalition to call for an unofficial national referendum to force the government to apply the right to a universal income. They hoped to consolidate this coalition, but the referendum proposal was not considered relevant by the other *piquetero* SMOs and was dismissed, thus failing to make it onto the *piquetero* agenda (Svampa and Pereyra 2003: 81).

The movement finally agreed on a protest plan that would escalate levels of disruption. There would be a partial national roadblock that would progress in stages: a first protest on July 31 for 24 hours, another one week later for 48 hours, and another for 72 hours in the last week. The protests went according to plan and even led government officials to publicly recognize that this was a controlled disruptive action carried out by an actor that is the "representative of a sector – the unemployed – that till now had no voice" (a public official quoted by *Página/12* 08/01/2001).

The only event that diverted from the plan was organized by the MTR. During the South Coordinator picket in Florencio Varela, the MTR entered the local branch of the state-owned provincial bank with the goal of forcing a confrontation at the Buenos Aires level, albeit without the agreement of the FTV and the CCC – nor, indeed, the rest of the South Coordinator members. This vanguardist style of action taken by the MTR was rejected by the groups that, like the MTD of Solano, were looking for a grassroots assembly organization influenced by autonomist ideas (MTD de Solano and Colectivo Situaciones 2002: 63).

In addition to this, and as a clear sign of disagreement with the decision made by Martino (MTR), Alderete (CCC) urged "the comrades to return to the picket at [Florencio] Varela and leave those who want to occupy the bank isolated." At the same time, D'Elía (FTV) discredited the MTR by saying: "I wouldn't like to think that Martino was possibly acting in conjunction with the SIDE [State Intelligence Service] or some other government agency" (both phrases quoted by *Crónica* 08/01/2001).

This dispute within the *piquetero* movement represented not just an internal division but also the expression of informal agreements between elites and SMOs for territorialized governability. The issue was that the MTR was intentionally violating an informal agreement between the FTV and CCC and the Buenos Aires government to focus contention on the De la Rúa government only. This multi-level political game opened up vertical divisions at the state levels and allowed the FTV and the CCC to ally themselves with La Matanza's mayor and garner the support of the vice governor against the national government.

The MTR continued insisting on the expansion of contention to the provincial level with no support from the rest of the movement. Five days later it coordinated the occupation of the provincial Secretariat of Labor to demand the reinstatement of 200 unemployment subsidies and the introduction of 180 new ones (Pacheco 2004: 58). The plan was to secretly wait inside the ministry's building in order to put more immediate pressure on the authorities. The action was effective because there were no police waiting for them, and after the minister was caught by surprise, he was compelled to agree to the payment of the 380 subsidies. The MTR had apparently won. Shortly after Martino's declaration affirming the minister's goodwill, the police arrived and 55 MTR members were thrown into jail. The majority of the South Coordinator, on the street to support this action, left soon after the occupation to avoid conflict. Only the MTD of Solano and the human rights organization H.I.J.O.S. remained to support the MTR.[18]

[18] The MTR also suffered due to the judicialization of social conflict, with Martino accused of extortion by Secretary Fernández after this protest (*La Nación* 08/07/2001).

The Origins of the Coordinator of Unemployed Workers' (CTD) "Aníbal Verón" (2001–2)

In 2001 all the South Coordinator SMOs joined the CTD "Aníbal Verón," with the exception of the MTR of Florencio Varela.[19] The creation of the CTD "Aníbal Verón" launched a process of atomization and demobilization of the MTR. The marginalization of the MTR of Florencio Varela (the core of the MG) arose from conflicts that were internal to this social movement sector and dynamics that were external to it. Regarding the internal factors, the MTDs that built the MTR and later the South Coordinator did not have a stock of legacies in common that could produce, as in the case of the FTV and the CCC, a common repertoire of strategies rising above ideological differences. The adoption of a moderate *foquismo* vanguardist strategy by the MTR produced constant tensions within this social movement sector. Things finally boiled over after the MTR organized the two disruptive actions mentioned previously without discussing it with the rest of the *piquetero* movement.

In theoretical terms, the MTR had applied an "exclusivist leadership" strategy, one that is based upon a small group of committed activists who seek to lead by heroic example (Barker et al. 2001: 21). This was an important point of difference for the MPR "Quebracho," an SMO very similar to the MTR. The MPR "Quebracho" is a vanguardist and vertical organization, like the MG. However, the former developed a less exclusivist type of leadership than the latter, allowing it to participate in the CTD "Aníbal Verón" (Delamata 2004: 58–59).

In terms of the external dynamics, the territory within which the MTDs and CTDs had emerged and expanded was much less favorable than that of La Matanza. This was due to the fact that it was situated within the core of the *duhaldista* group of municipalities, which even included Quilmes – the provincial secretary of labor's original territorial power base. Thus, for the MTR and MTDs, the confrontation with the governor was as relevant as the national dispute.

The clash for territorial penetration between the *duhaldista* sector of the PJ and the MTR and MTDs was not equally relevant for the FTV-CCC alliance. This explains why the two strongest SMOs never supported

[19] The SMOs were: CTDs "Trabajo y Dignidad" (La Plata and Lanús), MTD of Solano, MTD of Florencio Varela, MTD of Lanús, and the smaller SMOs: MTD of Almirante Brown, MTD of Quilmes, MTD of Esteban Echeverría, MTD of José C. Paz, MTD of Guernica, MTD of Lugano, and the only one not located in Buenos Aires: the MTD of Allen, Río Negro (Torres 2006: 73).

including the provincial level in the conflict. It was the internal disputes within the CTD "Aníbal Verón," together with the lack of support from the FTV-CCC, that left the MTR isolated, making it much easier for the governorship to repress and atomize the MTR.

The provincial secretary of labor Aníbal Fernández played two roles in the isolation of the MTR. First, after the occupation of the secretary, the MTR came under heavy pressure and several members were put in jail, including its main leader, Martino. He was behind bars for more than twenty days until the liberation of the MTR members was negotiated in exchange for information about unemployment subsidies. Second, Héctor Metón, the political operator of the Ministry of Labor, acted disloyally as a broker by encouraging internal divisions in the South Coordinator. He did this through the personalized distribution of unemployment subsidies in uneven quantities to each MTD of the South Coordinator, a move designed to foster internal tensions and the loss of mutual trust.

In short, as one of its main leaders recalls, the CTD "Aníbal Verón" "emerges as a desperate attempt to coordinate diverse districts that had territorial difficulties, or that had – as in the case of [Florencio] Varela – more or less managed to resolve things at the territorial level, but we needed to bring together several districts to reach the provincial or national governments" (interview 2007). Detachment from the MTR reduced internal diversity within this social movement sector, but dispute over how to define a common repertoire of strategies persisted and would produce further division in 2002.

The "Filtering" of Members by the CCC: The Expulsion of the Independent Movement of Retired and Pensioners

The CCC continued to expel dissidents from the SMO's leadership for strategic and internal reasons. First, at the CCC's 2001 national congress, it was decided to pursue an insurrectional clash with the De la Rúa government (*Página/12* 07/09/2001). This decision was not supported by the CCC's employed workers' and national coordinator Carlos "Perro" Santillán. As a result of this, Santillán was not as involved in the first National Piquetero Assembly as he had been in the Federal Marches of the 1990s. Eventually, Santillán was replaced by Amancay Ardura as general coordinator of the CCC.

Second, there was a conflict between the Independent Movement of Retired and Pensioners (MIJP) and the CCC's unemployed sector over the dominance of the CCC. Since 2000, retired sector leader Raúl Castells and unemployed sector leader Alderete were competing for control of the unemployed group. While Castells was in jail, the CCC leadership tried to dismantle the MIJP in order to effectively turn it into a division of the CCC, focusing its work on the retired and transferring the support of all the unemployed members to the CCC sector under Alderete's leadership. The tripartite composition of the CCC encompassing the employed, unemployed and retired worker sectors was in place between 1996 and 2000 in an alliance with the MIJP, an SMO with its own autonomous history (cf. Chapter 3). This issue generated a heated dispute that ended with the expulsion of the MIJP from the CCC in 2001 and its re-founding as the Independent Movement of the Retired and Unemployed (MIJD). The CCC's sector for retirees and pensioners was then created, and Mariano Sánchez was nominated as its leader.

From then the MIJD quickly grew from Villa Albertina (Lomas de Zamora) to Berazategui, La Matanza, and José C. Paz in Buenos Aires and to the provinces of Salta, Chaco, and Tucumán. The source of the MIJD's rapid development was the charismatic leaderships of Castells and Pelozo, the use of a witness strategy, and the provision of social services. Emulating the social security logic employed by unions and adopting a territorial logic, the MIJD reported having 1,500 soup kitchens, basic health services, and cooperative enterprises for its members. Everything was sustained by a monthly membership fee and access to state resources through state social programs and political agreements.

The End of the FTV as a Federation: The Splitting Off of the Territorial Liberation Movement and Neighborhoods Standing Up

In parallel with the CCC process, the FTV would also experience two important splits[20] as a result of its redefinition as an organization instead of a federation of organizations. The FTV was created as an umbrella organization for the unemployed in the CTA union. As a federation, it included the Network of Neighborhoods, CBC-related land occupation cooperatives, and other SMOs as well as several parties, such as Free

[20] There was a third split, though it was not particularly relevant in light of the magnitude of this SMO. In 2000 the Liberation Revolutionary Party left the FTV and created the Neighborhood Unity Coordinator (CUBa) in La Matanza. Later it participated in several coordinating bodies, merging in 2004 with the MTR (Oscar Kuperman, interviewed by Germano 2005: 117–30).

Homeland and the PCA. However, the de facto organizational structure of the FTV has been absolutely top-down and personalized, consisting of a small group of leaders around Luis D'Elía in a loosely structured network across the country. This produced several internal conflicts within the FTV as even minimal levels of internal democracy were not present, and with the FTV controlled by D'Elía's group, the PCA and Free Homeland could not achieve leadership posts within the organization (Armelino 2008; Burkart et al. 2008).

The PCA participated in the foundation of the FG and its trade union branch, the Politico-Syndical Liberation Movement (MPSL), which was one of the first members of the CTA. At the very beginning of the FG, the PCA was expelled from the party, and the MPSL then created an unemployed workers' SMO, the Territorial Liberation Movement (MTL), which joined the FTV in 1998 (Alcañiz and Scheier 2007). The MTL left the FTV in June 2001[21] and participated as an independent organization in the first National Piquetero Assembly. Detached from the FTV, at the CTA's 2002 national congress the MTL lost its affiliation to this union as a SMO, deciding to exit the CTA as a result of this (Poli 2007: 57–58).[22]

The MTL is self-defined as a territorial organization that struggles for employment and housing. It focuses on the city of Buenos Aires.[23] Like the FTV, the issue of housing is central for the MTL. In the case of the MTL, the issue is approached through the organization of occupations of abandoned buildings to force the city government into expropriating them (Poli 2007: 65–66). This predominant strategy owes much to a CBC legacy adapted to a district with no rural or semi-urban areas.

The restriction of the MTL to the city of Buenos Aires only was due to contextual factors. The MTL shares with the FTV the same perspective, goals, repertoires of contention, and strategies and applied these to the city of Buenos Aires because, according to its national leader, there was "a vacant niche" (Alberto Ibarra, quoted by Poli 2007: 87). On the one hand, the majority of the *piquetero* SMOs and the stronger PJ networks are located outside the city – in Greater Buenos Aires, an area with too much competition for a latecomer. On the other hand, the city of Buenos Aires offered a context very favorable for the PCA to build a *piquetero* SMO

[21] The MTD of La Juanita participated in the MTL's founding meeting, but the MTD leadership decided not to become part of the MTL.

[22] The MTL would return to the CTA due to new changes in 2006 regarding the FTV-CTA relationship, analyzed in Chapter 6.

[23] The MTL also developed a mining cooperative in Jujuy with the support of the Credicoop bank (Alcañiz and Scheier 2007).

due to the weakness of the PJ networks[24] and the support available from city mayor Aníbal Ibarra (FREPASO, 2000–6), a former member of the PCA's student movement. This strategy permitted the MTL to start a very successful housing project that was supported by credit given to the SMO by the PCA-related bank Credicoop and the local government state-owned bank (Epstein 2009).

The relationship between party and SMO in the case of the PCA-MTL is not a subsidiary one, as envisioned by the Trotskyist party-family. Rather, the model is that established by the PCR-CCC relationship. This means that while the MTL leadership is affiliated with, and intimately related to, the party elite, it has greater room for maneuver in the definition of its policies on topics that do not imply a confrontation with the PCA's electoral goals.

The case of Neighborhoods Standing Up, the second main division of the FTV, is different. The party behind this SMO, Free Homeland, was sustained by former PRT-ERP leaders from Córdoba province. Though its origins are in the geographic center of the country, the leaders made the strategic decision of pursuing a beehive tactic from the mid-1980s by systematically moving all of their key leaders to Greater Buenos Aires. This beehive tactic, along with a multi-class popular front strategy, led them to participate within the FTV from 1999 onward with their first *piquetero* SMO, CTA of the Neighborhoods. In 2001 CTA of the Neighborhoods was renamed Neighborhoods Standing Up, and in December it was expelled from the FTV because it did not recognize the validity of the internal elections for the FTV leadership that re-elected D'Elía and his sector (Svampa and Pereyra 2003: 66–67; Jorge Ceballos interviewed by Germano 2005: 213).

Neighborhoods Standing Up had no long-standing relationships with any government because in the 1990s the Free Homeland party had applied a direct-action insurrectional repertoire very similar to the one of the MPR "Quebracho" (without the latter's use of a witness strategy). At the same time, Free Homeland had transferred key party figures to La Matanza while still working in Alta Gracia and Cruz del Eje in Córdoba province (Antonello 2004). Unlike the MTL, Neighborhoods Standing Up

[24] The PJ was very strong in the city of Buenos Aires during the Carlos Grosso, Saúl Bouer, and Jorge Domínguez governments (1992–96), all *menemista* PJ politicians. They built up a patronage system that collapsed in 1996 after the PJ was defeated by the UCR in the local election (Levitsky 2003b). Since then, this district has become the one with the weakest Peronist electoral clout.

directly competed with the FTV for constituency and territory, although it shared some of its goals and ideological perspectives.

The Free Homeland-Neighborhoods Standing Up relationship resembles that of the Trotskyist party-family due to Free Homeland's middle-class composition as well as the sedimentation of *basismo* legacies within a model of democratic centralism. As is the case with the PO and MST "Teresa Vive," Neighborhoods Standing Up is based on a party that was built on the student movement.

The Second National Piquetero Assembly: The Dispute about the Radicalization of the Process

The second National Piquetero Assembly (September 4, 2001) represented the crystallization of the *piquetero* movement's diversification during the period of struggle for the movement's legitimation (**Table 4.2**). The FTV and the CCC called for the continuation of this coordinating body, but actual participation was much different. First, it involved the CTA, MTL, CUBa, UTD of Mosconi, "July 17" MTD (Chaco), PO, and MST "Teresa Vive" but also the Mothers and the Dissident CGT (*Página/12* 09/05/2001; Pacheco 2004: 64–65). Second, the CTD "Aníbal Verón" did not participate because it rejected the FTV-CCC leadership, instead organizing a smaller parallel meeting (Pacheco 2004: 65–66). Third, although the MTR was not invited, it managed to participate all the same.

The main dispute at the second Assembly revolved around the type of confrontational strategy needed to force an exit from the political and socioeconomic crises. There were two main positions on this: an electoral multi-class popular front (FTV and CTA) and an insurrectional, vanguardist (MTR) or multi-class front (CCC). A third position that was not represented at the second Assembly implied a combination of moderate *foquismo* and autonomist strategies, a position that would coalesce within the CTD "Anibal Verón" from 2002.[25]

The FTV and the CTA insisted on supporting FRENAPO, a proposal that was dismissed at the first Assembly but approved at the second. FRENAPO was part of a multi-sectoral popular front strategy to influence the government with the aim of channeling social unrest toward an

[25] Although this position was a weaker one and did not influence the core debates at the second Assembly, it was also the electoral solution to the crisis promoted by the PO, a newly created and still very small SMO. The MST "Teresa Vive" was still in the process of being set up.

electoral resolution of the crisis. One sector represented by the CTA had not defined how to approach the Alliance, which it had previously supported. Another sector, which included the FTV, FREPASO groups, CBC-related sectors, and the Dissident CGT, promoted an electoral coalition called Social Pole for the October legislative polls. This election led to D'Elía being chosen as a provincial deputy, thereby becoming the first *piquetero* legislator.

The CCC and the MTR represented two different types of insurrectional strategies to defeat the government. Though the MTR, in coalition with the MTL, PO, CUBa, UTD of Mosconi, and "July 17" MTD, managed to participate in the second Assembly, all its proposals were rejected (Svampa and Pereyra 2003: 82–83). The CCC opted to preserve the FTV alliance during the second Assembly and avoided confrontation, but this did not mean lending support to the FTV proposals. The CCC would not participate in the Social Pole and FRENAPO.

During the first Assembly in July, a journalist asked the CCC leader Alderete, "What are you proposing the De la Rúa government should do?" He replied: "We don't want them to do anything, not even quit. What we want is to expel them – it is that clear? [We want to] Expel them, [we do] not want them to just leave the National Congress, and then for Duhalde and Alfonsín to agree on common government solution and install another guy that is the same [as the actual president]. We want people to take to the streets and expel them once and for all" (quoted by *Crónica* 07/22/2001). This statement came out of a strategic resolution taken in July at the CCC's national congress, when it decided to call for an insurrectional end to De la Rúa's government by proposing a national *pueblada* or "*Argentinazo* that would lead to a national unity government" (*Página/12* 07/09/2001). This strategy implied enriching the repertoire of strategies by reviving the insurrectional alliance with the right that had been in place prior to the 1976–83 authoritarian regime (Chapter 2). To achieve its insurrectional goal, the CCC sought the support of the right-wing sector of the PJ and middle-sized rural producers. The CCC called for a picket and a march on December 20, which the PO, FTV, and MTR accepted.

Even though many *piquetero* SMOs were willing to come together at a third Assembly, it was not organized because the CTA and the FTV wished to quell disruptive escalation on the part of the other SMOs to avoid what they perceived as the risk of helping a right-wing coup (Oviedo 2004: 222–23).

THE MOUNTING OF THE CRISIS AND THE LEGITIMATION OF THE PIQUETERO MOVEMENT (OCTOBER–DECEMBER 2001)

The multi-level game of disputes grew at the pace of five *puebladas*, two national strikes, a diversified but tactically unified *piquetero* movement, and a totally divided government. In addition, October was a very bad month for the government in political and economic terms. Economically, unemployment reached 19 percent (plus 16.2 percent underemployment), and levels of poverty were at 35.4 percent in the Greater Metropolitan Area of Buenos Aires. This was the consequence of an annual decrease of 4.4 percent of the GDP and an accumulated rate of deflation of 20.5 percent since 1995 (Novaro 2009: 595).

Politically, the government lost the legislative mid-term elections and thus the majority in both chambers. This eliminated any possibility for De la Rúa to propose policies without PJ agreement. As a result, part of the PJ stuck to a stance of "semi-loyal opposition"[26] that was favorable to the president's early resignation (*Página/12* 12/07/2001). What the PJ could not foresee with its semi-loyal opposition was that the PJ could not be seen as the clear winner in this election (19.3 percent). The only majority was that of abstention and blank votes. In a country that never had less than 75 percent electoral turnout, this election saw, for the first time, more non-voters (27.2 percent) and negative voters (15.7 percent) than votes for any single party (Calvo and Escolar 2005: 213). The effect of this election was the deterioration of the legitimacy of the entire political elite and not only that of the government.

To make things even worse, on November 29 there was a run on the banks. The government tried to control the situation by imposing the *corralito* ("little farmyard"), a measure severely limiting the amount of cash allowed to be withdrawn weekly from bank accounts. The *corralito* drove desperate clients into systematic protests in front of central bank offices.

The National *Pueblada*: Lootings, *Cacerolazos*, the Semi-loyal PJ, and *Piquetero* Demobilization

The process of diffusion of *puebladas* that started in 1993 went from the periphery in Santiago del Estero to the core of Argentina in the federal

[26] The term "semi-loyal opposition" is used following Linz's (1978: 32–33) classic definition.

TABLE 4.4 *Comparison of Strategies Pre-crisis and during the National* Pueblada, *by* Piquetero *SMO, 1999–2001*

Piquetero SMO	Pre-crisis Strategy (December 1999–December 2001)	National *Pueblada* Strategy (December 14–22, 2001)
CCC	Multi-class insurrectional front	Pre-coup demobilization
CTD "Aníbal Verón"	Internal dispute between moderate *foquismo* and autonomist-introspective strategies	Pre-coup demobilization and continued internal disputes
FTV	Multi-class electoral popular front	FRENAPO and pre-coup demobilization
MIJD	Witness strategy	None (main leader in jail)
MST "Teresa Vive"	SMO emergence process	None (not yet consolidated as an SMO)
MTL	Multi-class electoral front	FRENAPO and pre-coup demobilization
MTR	Vanguard insurrectional	Pre-coup demobilization
PO	Classist electoral front	Support of the *cacerolazo* mobilization
Neighborhoods Standing Up	SMO emergence process	FRENAPO
UTD of Mosconi	Enclave syndicalism	None

Source: Several interviews (2007–13).

capital in 2001. From December 14 to 22, PJ territorial brokers organized 261 lootings in Buenos Aires, Rosario, Neuquén, Tucumán, and several other cities (Auyero 2007: 78, map 3). The mobilized middle classes, the semi-loyal PJ factions – but not the *piquetero* movement – were the key figures in the sixth (and national) *pueblada* against De la Rúa. As can be seen in the comparison in **Table 4.4**, the *piquetero* movement had different strategies before and after the national *pueblada* started. However, in most cases, after lootings began most *piquetero* SMOs decided to demobilize.

Governor Ruckauf is mentioned most often as a promoter of the destabilization of the De la Rúa government through the coordinated lootings in Greater Buenos Aires (Bonasso 2002; Auyero 2007; Novaro 2009: 612, n. 48).[27] While a coup was not the governor's aim, what the

[27] According to provincial secretary Aníbal Fernández, the provincial government tried to quell the situation without repression by proposing an agreement with large supermarkets

duhaldista PJ factions wanted was to provoke early elections through the use of disruption. Auyero (2007) shows with particular skill how the police and PJ territorial brokers encouraged and controlled lootings during this period. His analysis presents evidence supporting my own arguments about increased territorialism in Argentine politics. For instance, while Greater Buenos Aires as a whole saw many lootings, in Florencio Varela there were none (Auyero 2007: 75). This is explained by the role played by mayor Pereyra and the territorial brokers' capacity to control disruption as well as the *piqueteros*' relationship with the mayor during that period.

The sector of the *piquetero* movement that agreed to promote the FRENAPO was very busy with this activity during the crisis and later decided to demobilize. From December 14 to 17, the CTA, FTV, MTL, Neighborhoods Standing Up, and other organizations were organizing the FRENAPO referendum. Though it only had the support of the governor of Santa Cruz, Néstor Kirchner (PJ), FRENAPO collected 3,083,191 votes in favor of a universal right to income for citizens.

To prevent lootings from multiplying, president De la Rúa declared a state of siege on December 19. The general populace's initial reaction to his speech was massive defiance. The urban middle classes spontaneously initiated a *cacerolazo* (saucepan banging) in the main squares of the city of Buenos Aires and in some other big cities. Later that night thousands went to the Plaza de Mayo (in front of the House of Government) to demand the resignation of the government but also all the judges of the Supreme Court as well as each and every one of the governors, deputies, senators, and union leaders. The people in the square shouted – as in Corrientes in 1999 – "All of them out, not a single one must remain!," considering all the political elites responsible for the critical situation.[28]

Within this context, the CTA's national secretariat, perceiving the risk of an imminent coup, called on its members to demobilize and wait inside the CTA branches. As D'Elía had said a few months earlier in a TV interview, the goal was an electoral solution to the crisis:

for food distribution, which the supermarkets refused, and later by organizing a mobilization in Buenos Aires with the mayors of Moreno and Quilmes, which was later canceled (Fernández interviewed by Germano 2005: 278–80).

[28] The use of *cacerolazos* had been part of the repertoire of contention of the middle classes in Buenos Aires since at least 1997, when FREPASO organized this type of protest against Menem (Rossi 2005b).

This can only be changed with people on the streets, with people voting on the streets, because the financial district gambles our vote away every day ... Our only chance of voting is to be out on the streets ... And I sincerely hope that once a critical point has been reached, it is resolved in a democratic fashion. In other words, that we go to the Argentine people and ask them what they want (documentary film "¿Piqueteros? Sí ... Piqueteros" directed by Pablo Navarro Espejo: FTV and Adoquín Videos, 2001. 38.09 to 38.47 minutes).

For some of the SMOs that were in favor of an insurrectional solution during the second Assembly, territorial agreements and the perception of the crisis as a pre-coup led to their demobilization. Even though the second Assembly had decided to organize pickets for December 20, the CCC also decided to demobilize. According to the interviewees, the CCC's decision to avoid mobilization was in reaction to a phone call they received from a Buenos Aires political operator informing them that police would crack down on them strongly and this might lead to potential fatalities. This led the CCC to opt for a local mobilization in La Matanza. The CCC's strategy of forming an alliance with the right-wing sector of the PJ for an insurrectional solution weakened its commitment to increasing disruption, fearing that it would violate the territorial agreement with the municipal and provincial governments, which could also lead to the resignations of mayors and governors. In the few cases where *piquetero* SMOs encouraged mobilizations during this period, they were for organized claims for food from large supermarket chains, which represented just twenty-eight events out of 289 (Auyero and Moran 2007: 1346). This was the case of the CTD "Aníbal Verón," among others (MTD de Solano and Colectivo Situaciones 2002: 142–43; Pacheco 2004: 78–80).

As a result of the lootings and *cacerolazos*, on December 20 the national cabinet resigned as a means of facilitating the formation of a government of national unity with the PJ. Protests and lootings continued for the rest of the day and led to the resignation of the president as well as the deaths of twenty-five people, with 400 more seriously injured. The following day, Senate vice president Rodolfo Puerta (PJ) was named as provisional president. There was no agreement among the elites as to whether the best option was to immediately call for new elections or to wait until the official end of De la Rúa's mandate in December 2003 (Rossi 2005a). Finally, on December 23 the governor of San Luis, Adolfo Rodríguez Saá (PJ), was named as interim president for 90 days.

It is intriguing that even though the *piquetero* movement was a key actor in the weakening of the national government and the construction of the crisis, it was not a relevant actor during the social explosion of lootings, *cacerolazos*, massive protests, and the presidential resignation. The explanation for this can be discerned by understanding what had led some to perceive this national *pueblada* as a pre-coup scenario. In other words, while the crisis unfolded as a democratizing demonstration of popular defiance against elite incapacity or refusal to solve the crisis (Rossi 2005a), several *piquetero* leaders perceived it as a right-wing pre-coup (**Table 4.4**). This interpretation of the overall contentious dynamics can be traced back to the trauma produced by the left's experience of repression during the last authoritarian regime. This dramatic period led to the elimination of armed insurrections and coups from their repertoire of strategies. While this favored the revalorization of democracy in the short and medium term, it also highlighted the need for promoting self-retrained strategies. In other words, the *piqueteros* detached themselves from the national *pueblada* of December 14 to 22 because they perceived the risk of a coup, and this led them to adopt demobilization as a tactic to avoid repeating historical mistakes.[29]

Even though the idea came to be commonly accepted, it is erroneous to claim that the PJ and the *piqueteros* had coordinated their actions in order to cause the collapse of the national government. As I showed in this chapter, the government's end was the result of a multi-level, non-staggered game generated as an unintended consequence of the presidential inability to divide *piquetero* and PJ claims by selectively promoting demands. The feedback effect of this multi-level game set into motion a dynamic that favored, in some districts, alliances between mayors and *piqueteros*. This series of specific pacts coalesced haphazardly for the end of the Alliance government.

The Moment of Legitimation: The Meetings with the President

During his inaugural ceremony on December 23, the new president Adolfo Rodríguez Saá declared that the country had defaulted on the national external debt and promised to create a new currency and one million jobs during his ninety-day mandate. In spite of these declarations,

[29] The redefinition of the value of democracy among left-wing political actors is a process that started in the 1980s in Argentina, as it did in almost all of Latin America (Barros 1986; Castañeda 1993; Roberts 1998; Ollier 2009). The *piquetero* movement's strategy during the December 2001 *pueblada* put into action this change in the Argentine left's repertoire of strategies.

during the Rodríguez Saá government no substantial public policy decisions were made in the *piquetero* policy domain. Nevertheless, this period represents the moment of legitimation at the national scale for the whole movement. From December 23 to 27 the president met with the main social actors that had resisted disincorporation: the CTA, the CGT, the pensioner and retiree groups, the human rights movement, and the *piquetero* movement.

The CCC was the *piquetero* movement's link with the government. A few months before the crisis exploded, the PJ governors took part in secret meetings to negotiate possible solutions to the crisis. These meetings included representatives of the CCC and the FTV on at least one occasion. During that meeting the CCC developed a relationship with the San Luis governor Rodríguez Saá and the FTV with the Santa Cruz governor Kirchner. The FTV, CCC, and PO were able to meet with Rodríguez Saá on December 26 and 27. Other meetings were planned with the rest of the movement and the FRENAPO committee, but the abrupt end of the government prevented these from taking place. These meetings culminated in 3,000 subsidies being distributed among the FTV, CCC, and PO (*Prensa Obrera* 21/27/2001).[30]

The process of legitimation of the *piqueteros* as the reincorporation movement took a non-staggered path from the early-riser SMOs to the rest of the movement. The FTV and the CCC gained national legitimacy in November 2000 and the UTD of Mosconi in June 2001 when they got to divide the elites, receiving the support of some authorities, but the movement as a whole was only legitimized during the Rodríguez Saá presidency. This is because it was the first time the *piquetero* leaders met with a president. The consequences of this meeting were manifold: first, it meant an enlargement in the number of legitimate actors in unemployment policies by including the *piquetero* movement as a core actor in this policy domain, and, second, since that moment, meeting with the president became a common practice for the movement, beginning a process of increased state incorporation.

In the attempt to compensate for his lack of electoral legitimacy, Rodríguez Saá received in just a few days the support of the CCC, CGT (Dissident and Official), former president Menem, and some of the governors, such as Ruckauf and Ángel Rozas (Chaco, UCR). On December 27 government officials declared their interest in continuing beyond the

[30] Rodríguez Saá distributed 116,060 subsidies to provincial and municipal governments, except for the 3,000 of them that went to the FTV, CCC, and PO (*Clarín* 12/26/2001).

agreed ninety-day mandate. In the meantime, politicians could not circulate publicly in the streets because when recognized they were attacked by non-organized citizens. On December 28, a new protest for the renewal of the Supreme Court was coordinated by the Labor-Law Lawyers Association of the CTA (Kohan 2002: 101). That night, a third spontaneous *cacerolazo* in the Plaza de Mayo emerged. "We got through Christmas Eve, we got through Christmas Day, we expelled De la Rúa, and now we will expel all the rest!" was one of the major new chants that emerged that night expressing the claim for a total democratic renewal of the political elite. That night, repressive actions were initiated. After a few people failed in their attempts to enter the House of Government, some others entered the National Congress, the door having been opened from the inside, and set alight some of the furniture – with no police presence to stop the continued *pueblada*. On December 30 a weakened president summoned governors to a meeting in support of his mandate, but just five out of twenty-four governors attended. The same day Rodríguez Saá resigned. The causes were the violation of the agreement with the governors and sustained contention on the streets (Rossi 2005a). Again, the *piquetero* movement was not a relevant actor in this contentious dynamic.

CONCLUSION

This chapter attempted to provide a relational answer to the problem of the building of the national *pueblada* of 2001 and the concurrent legitimation of the *piquetero* movement as the main political interlocutor for the disincorporated popular sectors.

During this period, due to Argentina's centralized federal regime, the territorialized nature of the struggle for legitimation preserved its locus in Greater Buenos Aires. The consequences of the end of the territorial agreement revitalized the vertical political opportunities, producing a multi-level routine and contentious political game crucial to an understanding of the struggle for legitimation. The vertical disputes were by and large between the UCR-FREPASO Alliance national government, the PJ *duhaldista* Buenos Aires governorship, and the most relevant municipalities under non-*duhaldista* PJ control.

In conjunction, the presidential form of government emerged as a relevant feature in the institutional politics explanation for the legitimation of the *piquetero* movement. The dispute between the FREPASO and the UCR and the former's control over the main state areas within the *piquetero* policy domain were crucial elements in the *piquetero* movement's capacity to manipulate the horizontal divisions within the elite. Simultaneously, the role of the political operators for *piquetero* issues saw them emerge as relevant informal actors in the building of the state institutions' day-to-day relationship with the movement. The role of the political operators would also prove to be quite relevant during the ensuing stage of reincorporation.

The national *pueblada* of December 2001 poses a historical puzzle that I also intended to answer in this chapter. While the *piquetero* movement was the main contentious actor that pushed for the national *pueblada*, at the peak of social explosion the movement was in fact an irrelevant political actor. The emergence of new SMOs and the increasing divisions enriched the repertoire of strategies by adding strategies that were novel to the movement. However, this enrichment produced difficulties in terms of adopting a common strategy that could transcend short-lived tactical agreements. As the movement grew and diversified, the difficulties of sharing a common repertoire intensified.

In the cases where territorial agreements did not lead to demobilization, it was the perception of an imminent right-wing coup what led part of the *piquetero* movement to demobilize. In other words, the *piqueteros*' crucial mobilization prior to, and demobilization during the national *pueblada* were a result of an enriched repertoire of strategies produced by the movement's diversification along with a self-restrained approach due to a positive valorization of democracy. The *piquetero* movement shows that a predominant repertoire of strategies changes dynamically over time more quickly than the repertoire of contention, with these being related parallel processes. However, the 2001 national *pueblada* shows that even though the repertoire of strategies is fluid, this is not directly related to junctural shifts.

The moment of legitimation ended with Rodríguez Saá's resignation. Two days later, the year 2002 started with a new interim president. Duhalde, the main PJ leader, was chosen by parliament to finish De la Rúa's presidential mandate. Duhalde started the partial reincorporation of the popular sectors, a process that was continued by Kirchner after 2003. The following chapter takes us from movement legitimation to the first (failed) attempt for incorporation: state territorial reincorporation. Chapter 5 will also show the beginning of the redefinition of the *piquetero* policy domain as well as some of the movement's new main political divisions and predominant strategies.

5

From Movement Legitimation to Failed State Reincorporation in the Socio-political Arena (2002–3)

This chapter examines the first attempts to reincorporate the popular sectors and demobilize the *piquetero* movement during Eduardo Duhalde's interim presidency (January 2002–May 2003). During this period, the *piqueteros* were the main contentious actor and were crucial for the failure of this first reincorporation effort.

The stage of the second incorporation is the longest of the whole process and is analytically divided into two chapters. The first stage is studied in this chapter and regards the initial attempts made by the elites for *state* incorporation (and its subsequent failure) during 2002 and 2003. The focus of the following chapter is the continuation and expansion of the reincorporation process, this time taking the form of *party* incorporation, from 2003 to 2009. Collier and Collier (1991: 162–68) define two types of incorporation based on the goals of the elites, whether the principal political agent is involved during the incorporation stage, and the mode and scope of incorporation. While "state incorporation" is defined by the state's demobilization goals, promoted for the purpose of depoliticizing popular movements, "party incorporation" is defined by mobilization goals for the electoral purposes of a movement or party – whether these are pre-existing or need to be created during the incorporation process.

The chapter will also show the multiplicity of strategic debates inside the *piquetero* movement. While the two main SMOs will negotiate from inside government, the rest of the movement will radicalize and promote insurrectional strategies.

THE PIQUETEROS' MULTI-SECTORAL STRATEGIES (JANUARY–JUNE 2002)

The whole of 2002 was very contentious. Even though lootings were mostly controlled, the *piquetero* movement continued to expand and increase the number of protests. There was also improved organization between other protesting groups. The *cacerolazos* were brought together by the assembly movement – a new middle-class urban movement that turned out to be a short-term ally for the *piqueteros*. Savings account holders increasingly coordinated their protests around a UCR leader, and factory occupations grew from one in 1998 to almost 200 in 2002, organizing themselves into the movement of worker-managed factories (Ruggeri 2010). Simultaneously, levels of poverty (54.3 percent in October) and unemployment (21.5 percent plus 18.6 percent underemployment in May) reached their highest peak in Argentina's contemporary history.

In this setting, Duhalde's first days in government were as complex as the rest of his short term. Governor Ruckauf, who had initially quit the same day as interim president Rodríguez Saá, later joined Duhalde's cabinet. However, Duhalde did not receive the support of the main PJ governors who had electoral ambitions.[1]

In terms of the *piquetero* policy domain, on January 7 D'Elía and Alderete met the new president to secure the continuity of the subsidies distributed by his predecessor as well as campaign for their expansion. Immediately afterward, the government decided to increase the number of subsidies under a new system called Unemployed Heads of Household Program (PJJHD), which became part of a redefinition of the state's approach to the legitimated *piquetero* movement and its claim for the reincorporation of the popular sectors. This decision implied expanding the restricted *piquetero* policy domain to a general policy constituency when unemployment policies reached almost two million individuals and when distribution was no longer under the exclusive control of mayors and governors.

On January 11 Duhalde declared a 29 percent devaluation of the peso, and it quickly reached a depreciation of 400 percent. On January 14 Duhalde called for a social-Christian approach to the resolution of social conflicts through the massive expansion of the PJJHD and the constitution of a space for negotiation and articulation inspired by the Moncloa Pact. This space, the Argentine Dialogue Board, would be the responsibility of

[1] Those governors were Carlos Reutemann (Santa Fe), José Manuel De la Sota (Córdoba), Néstor Kirchner (Santa Cruz), and Adolfo Rodríguez Saá (San Luis).

the Catholic Church and the United Nations Development Program (UNDP) for Argentina. Along with all parties[2] and unions, the FTV, CCC, and MIJD all went on to participate in it, while the rest of the *piquetero* movement refused to join it.

On January 25, another *cacerolazo* was organized, but this time a new movement drove it. The recently created assembly movement decided to continue using the anti-elite slogan "All of them out, not a single one must remain!" that had emerged in December. The assembly movement appeared as the merging of two different – but connected – framing processes, one coming from the networks of left-wing activists who interpreted the situation as pre-revolutionary and the other the product of a perception among the general population of deep political crisis (Rossi 2005a). As a result, in 2002 in Buenos Aires there were 113 self-organized assemblies of 70 to 150 people each, meeting once a week on the streets to deliberate how, when, and for what purpose the movement's goal of total elite renewal should be pursued (Rossi 2005b: 204, graph 1).

While the urban middle classes were increasingly organizing through the assembly movement, the *piqueteros* were preparing a unified march, which the assemblies supported. On January 28, around 40,000 people from the FTV and the CCC marched to the Plaza de Mayo, crossing the entire city of Buenos Aires. They were joined in the square by the PO and MTR. Throughout the day the assemblies backed the *piqueteros* with water, food, and a new slogan: "Picketing and saucepan-banging, there is but one struggle!" This slogan effectively summarized the multi-sectoral strategy promoted by the *piquetero* movement. The government understood the potential of such a multi-sectoral coalition, and Duhalde replied to this protest by saying: "People protest with good reasons. My responsibility lies elsewhere. If I were not the president, maybe I would be in a picket or with a saucepan" (*Radio Nacional* 01/29/2002).

Nonetheless, this coalition would be short-lived. On the one side, the assembly movement was divided into two different strategic positions, one sector supporting unified activities with the *piqueteros* and the other preferring to focus on neighborhood-based actions (Rossi 2005a). On the other side, for the *piquetero* movement, the goal of promoting a multi-sectoral coalition to make the most of the political opportunities that the crisis had opened up was shared, but this goal took four different forms, contested by the FTV, CCC, PO, and MTR.

[2] The parties that participated were those with parliamentary representation. Thus, most of the parties related to the *piquetero* movement did not participate.

From Inside: The FTV and the CCC's Governability Pact with the Government

The FTV and the CCC preserved their alliance during the Duhalde government because both SMOs considered the period of crisis initiated by the end of the De la Rúa presidency as the ideal setting for the launching of a multi-sectoral strategy that included the government.

While this basic strategy was held in common by these two organizations in terms of their governability pact with the government (*Página/12* 02/20/2002), in other strategic approaches toward Duhalde their styles were quite different. The FTV promoted a multi-class popular front strategy with the PJ and the center-left parties for the building of an electoral alternative to neoliberalism. In this regard, the FTV maintained its strategy from the De la Rúa period, which had justified its participation in the Alliance coalition.

In 2002, however, the FTV actively promoted a governability pact because there was an actual governability problem that was sparked by increased contentious defiance toward the political elites as a result of the insurrectional and electoral alternatives promoted by part of the assembly movement and the remainder of the *piqueteros*. A member of the FTV's national committee explained this strategy: "[W]e felt that Duhalde did not represent anything related to us. However, it was necessary to somehow bring order to the country because if not we were heading for civil war. Thus, governability agreements were drawn up in order to hold things together" (interview 2008).

As part of the governability pact, Duhalde offered D'Elía the post of director of the Rootings Program, in charge of legally regulating land occupations. D'Elía refused to personally participate in this, but the FTV's lawyer and notary entered into the second and third ranks of the Rootings Program. This was the first time that a *piquetero* SMO had become part of the national state structure. The FTV also participated with the CTA in the Argentine Dialogue Board and its Consultative Councils with the goal of influencing state policies. At the same time, Free Homeland officially left the FTV to create Neighborhoods Standing Up.

The CCC promoted a multi-class popular front strategy with center-right PJ factions and other Peronist parties, the lowest ranks of the military, and medium-sized rural landowners for the promotion of a national unity government to build an alternative to capitalism. This strategy stemmed from the PCR politburo's interpretation of the applicability, within the Argentine context, of Mao's strategies of multi-class fronts.[3] In this regard, the CCC changed its strategy as of the beginning of Rodríguez Saá's short presidency (of the PJ's conservative sector). As the CCC's alliance with the right implied using the PJ conservative sectors of government as allies, they continued during Duhalde's presidency with this strategy. For the CCC, this strategy meant neither pushing for the collapse of the Duhalde government nor integrating into the governmental coalition itself. The CCC's strategic support of the government was based on the building of personalized links of trust with PJ leaders, such as the one developed with La Matanza mayor Balestrini, for a long-term revolutionary goal as if under a protracted war. In the short term, the CCC participated in the Argentine Dialogue Board and its Councils and mobilized under a strategy of restraint while at the same time expanding the resources for the satisfaction of the CCC constituency's immediate demands.

This strategy led to a final "filtering" of the CCC leadership. To the dissidence of Jujuy's sector under Santillán with the CCC's decision to adopt an insurrectional approach against De la Rúa was added the complications produced by a series of internal conflicts within the CCC of Jujuy, which diluted Santillán's power. These internal disputes led to the dissolution of the CCC of Jujuy, making room for the emergence of other independent provincial SMOs. In its competition with Santillán, the CTA of Jujuy contributed to the creation of the Neighborhood Organization (OB) "Tupac Amaru," an indigenist and national–populist SMO (Russo 2010: 45–56). The OB "Tupac Amaru" emerged in 2002 and was part of the FTV until 2006. This gave the OB "Tupac Amaru" access to the first PJJHD subsidies, which allowed for the SMO's quick and exponential growth at the provincial level (Battezzati 2012). Emulating this strategy, but without much success, Santillán would later create the "Tupaj Katari" Movement. Finally, after Castells was freed, the MIJP's expulsion from the CCC was made official.

Even though access to subsidies was important for the FTV and the CCC, it was not the key factor in their decisions as to whether to participate in state departments offered by the Duhalde government. The multi-sectoral strategies of FTV and the CCC entailed not demobilization but

[3] In Mao's (1965 [1940]: 423) own words: "Winning over the middle forces means winning over the middle bourgeoisie, the enlightened gentry and the regional power groups. ... The middle bourgeoisie constitutes the national bourgeoisie ... Then there are the enlightened gentry who are the left-wing of the landlord class, that is, the section with a bourgeois coloration, whose political attitude is roughly the same as that of the middle bourgeoisie."

rather action for purposes different to the rest of the *piquetero* movement. Among the many marches, pickets, and rallies organized by this social movement sector, the first national strike against Duhalde was called for May 29 by the CTA. This strike had the partial support of the CGT, and the FTV, CCC, and Neighborhoods Standing Up organized more than a thousand pickets across the country (*Página/12* 05/30/2002). The focus of contention was not to bring down the government but rather to achieve influence over specific government decisions while building a multi-sectoral coalition. As Alderete stated during a protest coordinated by the CTA, FTV, and CCC against a visit by International Monetary Fund (IMF) officials to Argentina: "We will defeat the IMF when we can unite to build together a popular unity government" (*Página/12* 06/21/2002).

From Outside: The National Piquetero Block Coalition with the Mobilized Actors

The national government also invited the CTD "Aníbal Verón," PO, and MTR to the Argentine Dialogue Board. But since they rejected any form of state incorporation, none of them agreed to participate.

These SMOs also rejected the multi-sectoral types of strategies promoted by the FTV and the CCC. As Néstor Pitrola, the national leader of the PO at the time, said: "We reinforce our call [for the CCC and the FTV] to break off their involvement in the Government" (quoted by *La Nación* 04/22/2002). The cleavage within the movement that had originally emerged in the first and second Piquetero Assemblies evolved into a clear inside/outside dichotomy during this period. The PO, MTL, MTR, FTC, and CUBa organized the National Piquetero Block (BPN) in December 2001 as a coalition of the SMOs that were in favor of pushing for the escalation of the national *pueblada* of December as a means of achieving an immediate end to the Duhalde government. The BPN also worked in alliance with the CTD "Aníbal Verón," the MIJD, the MST "Teresa Vive," and Neighborhoods Standing Up (Burkart et al. 2008: 37–38).

After a coordinated series of pickets, on February 16 to 17 the BPN and the CTD "Aníbal Verón" organized the National Assembly of Employed and Unemployed Workers (ANTOD), which defined allying with the assembly movement as a priority (*Página/12* 02/17–18/2002). The SMOs that participated in the ANTOD considered the period of crisis begun at the end of the De la Rúa presidency as the right setting for promoting a multi-sectoral strategy with other mobilized actors. While this was the basic shared strategy that unified them at the ANTOD, there was no agreement about exactly what type of crisis Argentina was experiencing. While for the PO, MST "Teresa Vive," and FTC it was a pre-revolutionary moment, the others did not see it that way. As summarized by the national coordinator of Neighborhoods Standing Up, these SMOs all came together at the ANTOD "because there was a tactical agreement among us . . . Now, we didn't share the Trotskyist vision of forming a left-wing front rather than a national [i.e., multi-sectoral] front, or their interpretation of the role of workers [in this front] . . . [Also] they argued that the participation in the assembly movement of the middle strata represented a pre-revolutionary situation . . . We didn't see it like that . . . " (interview 2007). In addition to this, there was a major strategic dispute: did a multi-sectoral strategy mean a multi-class popular front for electoral or insurrectional purposes? While for the PO, MST "Teresa Vive," and MIJD the answer was the former,[4] for the MTR and CTD "Aníbal Verón" the aim was clearly insurrectional.

Finally, the predominance of vanguardist Morenist entryism strategies meant that the relationship between the BPN members became unsustainable. The PO carried out this strategy by gradually coming to dominate the seven editions of the ANTOD (2001–5) as well as the BPN coalition (2002–5). For the Trotskyist party-family, these two strategies led to rivalry between the PO and MST "Teresa Vive" that culminated in the PO's domination of the BPN until its expulsion in 2005. Additionally, within the assembly movement the respective parties unsuccessfully disputed the control over the movement, thereby leading to a deterioration of the relationship between the assemblies (Rossi 2005a). In the end, as the Morenist entryism strategy is a well-known feature of the PO and MST "Teresa Vive" among the community of activists, those other SMOs that also opted for confrontation with the government gradually exited the BPN and came together as allies.

The case of the MIJD was very different. It was expelled from the BPN because it negotiated an alliance with the CGT (Burkart et al. 2008: 44–45). The relationship between left-wing parties and the Peronist CGT had been a constant problem since the first Piquetero Assembly and was always an impediment for this sector of the social movement's multi-sectoral strategy. It would not, however, prevent the BPN from organizing several protests with the MIJD.

[4] According to this strategy, the leaders they would set up during the process would be later used to compete for electoral positions as part of the aim to use electoral politics as a propaganda tool.

In spite of all these differences, the immediate goal of expelling Duhalde from power was compelling enough to unify these forces for the organization of several protests. The government reacted to this defiance by refusing to meet with this social movement sector, even though the ANTOD called several protests and negotiations to try to obtain a meeting (*La Nación* 07/23/2002). This governmental response was part of a wider tactic to demobilize the *piquetero* movement.

MORE HORIZONTAL THAN VERTICAL POLITICAL OPPORTUNITIES

The government was also divided over how to demobilize the *piquetero* movement, which made the authorities' situation even more difficult. Duhalde, a president elected not by the citizens but by a discredited elite agreement, was in urgent need of obtaining governability and legitimacy. In the meanwhile, he was the target of the *piqueteros* and the assembly movement mobilized for a total renewal of the elite, be it by insurrectional or electoral means.

In addition, the vertical political opportunities that became available during the De la Rúa presidency were not totally closed off during the Duhalde government. Even though the three levels of government in Buenos Aires province from 2002 to the end of the period under research were governed by the PJ, vertical coordination between the provincial and national governments was lacking because of the way the party was structured. For instance, in December 2002 the political elites were concerned about the possible resurgence of lootings, but there was no multilevel coordination over how to approach this issue in Greater Buenos Aires. While the cause of this lack of coordination during the Menem government was the territorial agreement with governor Duhalde, and during the De la Rúa government the confrontation with Ruckauf and PJ mayors as opposition parties, during the Duhalde presidency it was a result of governor Felipe Solá's (PJ, non-aligned) dispute with the *duhaldista* factions.

Horizontal political opportunities were more important than vertical ones during this period. The divisions over how to contest the *piqueteros*' strategies were based on disagreements among clusters of ministers representing individual positions toward the issue rather than among various PJ factions (the Duhalde government was almost entirely composed of the *duhaldista* faction). These personal divisions within the government went through several stages. In **Table 5.1**, the dynamic mutations in the vertical

TABLE 5.1 *Schematic Comparison of the Shifts in Political Opportunities in Greater Buenos Aires, 2001–8*

	Struggle for Reincorporation Period (January 2002–December 2008)		
Political Opportunities	**Beginning and Failure of State Territorial Reincorporation (January 2002–May 2003)**	**Expansion as Party Territorial Reincorporation (May 2003–October 2004)**	**Consolidation and Stagnation of Party Territorial Reincorporation (October 2004–December 2008)**
Horizontal (functional)	Generalization of the policy domain through the continued dominance of the Ministry of Labor. Addition of some corporatist arrangements (Consultative Councils). Increased role of the Ministry of the Interior (political operators). First official participation of a *piquetero* SMO (FTV) in the national government.	Increased role of the Ministry of Social Development in areas related to the *piquetero* policy domain. Incorporation of some *piquetero* SMOs in Social Development, though not through the Ministry of Labor (controlled by the PJ and unions). Decreased role of the Ministry of the Interior, replaced by the Secretariat-General of the Presidency (the *piqueteros'* collegiate body).	Definition of the responsibilities of the Ministry of Labor (subsidies and employment) and the Ministry of Social Development (social issues related to the consequences of unemployment) in the *piquetero* policy domain. No relevant role for the *piquetero* SMOs. Consolidated role of the Secretariat-General of the Presidency.
Vertical (multi-level)	Multi-level dispute between the presidency (*duhaldista* PJ), the governorship (non-aligned PJ) and, less so, with peri-urban mayors (*duhaldista* and non-*duhaldista* PJ).	Multi-level alliance between the presidency (non-PJ Peronist) and the governorship (non-aligned PJ), but dispute with peri-urban mayors (*duhaldista* and non-*duhaldista* PJ). Territorial and ministerial clash between PJ mayors, CGT and *piquetero* SMOs in the governing coalition.	Multi-level alliance between the presidency (non-PJ Peronist), the governorship (non-aligned PJ), and most mayors (non-*duhaldista* PJ, UCR, and local parties). Continued clash between PJ mayors, CGT and *piquetero* SMOs in the governing coalition.

Note: This table is a continuation of Table 4.1.

and horizontal political opportunities during the period of the struggle for reincorporation that favored this process are schematically compared with those of the beginning of the incorporation period and – what will be the analyzed in Chapter 6 – its final consolidation and stagnation phase (this table is a continuation of **Table 4.1**).

The Threefold Governmental Strategy for Restoring Governability and Legitimacy

The core of the governmental logic toward the *piquetero* movement was the promotion of governability agreements with some of the SMOs and the demobilization of the social movement sector that was embracing an insurrectional path. To achieve this, the Duhalde cabinet adopted three simultaneous strategies: first, the expansion of the unemployment policy domain from a restricted to a general constituency; second, the rebuilding of the state's capacity for governability; and third, the selective distribution of resources and the use of repression aimed at weakening the insurrectional stance within the *piquetero* movement.

The *first strategy* was the expansion of the unemployment policy domain from a restricted to a general constituency. The Duhalde government initially opted to expand pre-existing policies: the Labor Emergency Program (PEL) of the De la Rúa mandate reached 287,079 people in November 2002 and later quickly extended without much control (CELS 2003b: 35–43; Neffa 2008: 78). In a parallel measure, on January 31, 2003, the FRENAPO committee finally met with the president to present the results of its popular consultation and claim for a universal income. Though the president initially replied in the same way as De la Rúa had – i.e., that this policy was impossible for the state to finance – in April the government launched the PJJHD, therefore acquiescing to FRENAPO's claim. The PJJHD was a reproduction of the cash transfer logic for social policies promoted by the Inter-American Development Bank (IADB) and applied by the programs School Scholarship in Brazil and Opportunities in Mexico (*Clarín* 02/01/2002; Barrientos and Santibáñez 2009; Colina et al. 2009). This social policy was the most far-reaching unemployment program ever applied in Latin America and was carried out through the distribution of almost two million unemployment subsidies[5] to governors, mayors, the

[5] In May 2003 the number of PJJHD subsidies reached its maximum, with 1,990,735 subsidies (Reports and Statistics section of the Ministry of Labor, Employment and Social Security: www.trabajo.gov.ar/jefes/infostats/index.asp, visited June 5, 2010).

CGT, the CTA, the two main religious charity organizations,[6] and the *piquetero* movement (Neffa 2008).

The *second strategy* was the rebuilding of the state's capacity for governability. This strategy implied reconstructing the PJ's territorial network and avoiding confrontation with the widest possible range of religious, social, and political (electoral and contentious) actors. This strategy also involved returning the administration of unemployment subsidies to the municipalities, which included the creation of several local Councils, emulating the La Matanza experience. This decentralization process was done in order to re-establish the role of the municipalities in controlling social unrest and aimed at rebuilding the PJ's clientelistic networks.

Additionally, this second strategy included the creation of a vehicle for political articulation, the Argentine Dialogue Board, and integrated into it the broadest political spectrum. As the non-declared goal of the Board was the containment of social and political pressures – as opposed to providing a means of participation in the decision-making process for governmental policies – the majority of the *piqueteros* declined to participate in these spaces for articulation. The BPN elaborated a joint declaration against the Board and the Councils as mechanisms for co-opting the movement and rebuilding the PJ's clientelistic and patronage networks (*Rosario/12* 03/29/2002). The lack of government interest and a boycott by most of the contentious actors led to the failure of the Board and its dissolution on February 28, immediately after delivering to the president a series of policy recommendations.

The main effect that these policies and the application of a generalized subsidy had on the reincorporation process was to build a vertical relationship between the state's executive branch and the *piquetero* movement. The type of *piquetero*–state institutions relationship built was similar to the trade unionist relational pattern that had emerged during first incorporation period but with a difference: that it is territorialized. Many *piquetero* conflicts were resolved within this new, redefined framework of trade unionist institutions that added disincorporated workers to those who were incorporated. One example of this is that of what was called the "*paritaria social*" by the CTA.[7] The *paritaria social* is a modified wage negotiation system that includes claims for housing,

[6] These organizations were Caritas (of the Catholic Church) and the Delegation of Argentine Israelite Associations.

[7] A *paritaria* is a corporatist salary negotiation called by the government and carried out between unions and companies with state mediation.

living conditions, health provision, and education along with the traditional salary negotiations for a constituency that is conceived as the whole community and not only the workers.[8]

And, finally, this second strategy involved the backing of an informal governability agreement with the two main SMOs – the FTV and CCC. During Duhalde's tenure, informality predominated. This meant that even though the Argentine Dialogue Board and the Councils were created for the distribution and control of the PJJHD, subsidies were mainly distributed as a result of clientelism and patronage and as a response to protests (Giraudy 2007). For those subsides that were prompted by *piquetero* protests, the role of Héctor Metón, as the political operator, was crucial. Metón was formally in charge of the Rooting Program, the office for land tenure legalizations within the structure of the Ministry of the Interior. Despite this formal role, his real job as political operator was to informally negotiate the resolution of *piquetero* conflicts under the authority of Aníbal Fernández, secretary-general of the presidency. He had been tasked with carrying out this role in the province of Buenos Aires, work that allowed him to build personalized relationships and trust with established *piquetero* leaders, which cemented his role as a key broker from then on. A *piquetero* leader explains the logic behind Metón's role:

> The window Metón offered was for the pariahs, that's why it was a secret window in the shadows. But they knew that somehow we could generate more conflict or contain the same conflict, and that's why there was a window ... And what he had been doing was negotiate ... let's call them "governability agreements", or "agreements to preserve social peace" with the different organizations. And he was administering some resources within this scheme [as the Rooting Program and the PJJHD] ... Basically, that's what his job was. But he was not an official of the Ministry of the Interior, so he did not have any authority to repress or to give orders (interview 2008).

The *third strategy* was the state's selective distribution of resources and the use of repression in order to weaken the insurrectional component of the *piquetero* movement. This final strategy was intimately related to Metón's role and implemented by favoring for subsidies the sector that promoted an electoral strategy (FTV, MIJD, PO, CCC) and snubbing the sector that promoted insurrectional means (CTD "Aníbal Verón," MTR,

[8] The claim for a *paritaria social* was not limited to the CTA. The PO was also claiming for one in the BPN, and on August 12, 2012, 350 CTA, FTV, and CCC activists began a 100-kilometer march that ended four days later in the provincial capital of La Plata with 20,000 activists demanding a *paritaria social* at the Buenos Aires level.

Neighborhoods Standing Up, UTD of Mosconi). This strategy meant ignoring the assembly movement's claim for total elite renewal and focusing only on the economic claims of those affected by the *corralito* (freezing of bank accounts).

Even though all the *piquetero* SMOs received PJJHD as a tactic to demobilize the movement's insurrectional sector – the much bigger MTR and CTD "Aníbal Verón" received significantly fewer subsidies than the small PO. The authorities had correctly predicted that the PO's legacy of non-violent struggle in the 1960s to 1980s would lead it toward an electoral strategy during the 2002 crisis. This was in contrast to the MTR and CTD "Aníbal Verón," which, being made up of former PRT-ERP and Montoneros guerrilla leaders, could potentially go for non-electoral strategies. In addition to this, the MTR and CTD "Aníbal Verón" had a decade-long history of territorial disputes in the area of Duhalde's core power base and had built an antagonistic relationship with his faction of the PJ (as shown in the two previous chapters). Duhalde's demobilization strategies were, however, not effective with this sector. During his time in office, the *piqueteros* carried out their most contentious actions, and his government was also responsible for the most drastic repressive responses. The killing of two *piqueteros* during the roadblock on Pueyrredón Bridge in Buenos Aires would have crucial consequences for both the government and this sector of the *piquetero* movement.

BUILDING A SCENARIO TO END THE INTERIM PRESIDENCY (JUNE 2002–MAY 2003)

On June 22 and 23, the second ANTOD met to radicalize the struggle against the government. The plan was to start a series of pickets along the main highways and avenues that connect the city of Buenos Aires to its suburbs, occupy public buildings, and finally set up an indefinite encampment on the main public squares (Burkart et al. 2008: 46). The aim of the BPN, MIJD, CTD "Aníbal Verón," and Neighborhoods Standing Up was to push the government over the edge: "The economic model was failing and we needed to try to force them to retire [from power] in the most disorderly way possible ... [which] meant that Duhalde must not be allowed to participate in the transition [to the next government]" (interview with *piquetero* leader 2007). These *piquetero* SMOs wanted to apply a *foquista* strategy to ensure that the process of diffusion of contention would be so wide-reaching that it would lead to the eventual collapse of the regime.

Duhalde noted this strategy of defiance, and members of the cabinet responded on several occasions to the ANTOD action plan by stating that the state would not allow these pickets to go ahead and that the government "will make use of all the necessary mechanisms to ensure the rule of law is respected" (quoted by *Clarín* 06/26/2002). Through a mixture of fortuitous and planned economic and political results, Duhalde had achieved the much-needed legitimacy to start thinking of running as a presidential candidate in 2003. The demobilization of the *piqueteros* was one of the crucial unresolved issues. In addition to this, Duhalde was facing numerous contenders for his electoral project. First, there were the electoral ambitions of other PJ leaders, in particular Menem. Second, the president was embroiled in a provincial dispute with the non-*duhaldista* Buenos Aires governor Solá, who expected to be elected in 2003 in spite of Duhalde's opposition to his candidacy. Finally, the extremely corrupt provincial police force was in conflict with governor Solá, who was gradually attempting to impose some civil control over a police force that had been autonomously self-regulating since Ruckauf's tenure (1999–2001) (Sain 2006).

On June 26, the first step in the *piqueteros*' plan to upscale the level of contention was carried out with the organization of a massive picket on Pueyrredón Bridge, the main southern entrance to the city of Buenos Aires. The SMOs were prepared for a response that would involve repression as the authorities had announced publicly that this would be the case. What the *piqueteros* were not expecting was the severity of this repression: the Pueyrredón Bridge picket led to the killing of two young *piqueteros* by the police.

This outcome was a result of the intertwining of multiple simultaneous electoral and contentious political disputes (Sain 2006: 51–53). However, the Pueyrredón Bridge incident and its aftermath were also part of a relational pattern that had involved the repression of the most intransigent sector of the *piquetero* movement since 1996. This episode, like many others, highlights that reincorporation is a contentious and selective process. While in Buenos Aires this event would signal the end of the governmental strategy of direct repression of the *piquetero* movement, in rural areas and the petroleum enclaves repression continued under the auspices of the Gendarmerie and the provincial police within the framework of the Procedural Penal Code, modified in 2001.

What none of the actors who were involved in this contentious event expected was the level of media coverage of the repression and the detailed reconstruction of events carried out by a group of journalists from the main national newspaper (*Clarín* 06/26–29/2002). *Clarín*'s massive media coverage and the swift international and national outcry in favor of the *piqueteros* (Burkart et al. 2008: 48) led to an unintended consequence. The next day the *piqueteros* united with the assembly movement, human rights organizations, political parties, and the CTA in a massive multi-sectoral march in support of the victims.[9]

The *foquista* strategy of scenario-building led to bloodshed that was not anticipated by the *piqueteros*, but it did produce the desired consequences. State reincorporation failed, and Duhalde was forced to give up on his electoral ambitions, end his tenure early, and call for elections. The authorities also finally agreed to meet with this social movement sector, being first received by governor Solá and then by the national Ministry of Labor (*Página/12* 07/12/2002; *La Nación* 08/02/2002). After that the PJJHD would grow exponentially to reach the massive scale that was promised by Duhalde (Gómez 2006: 108, graph 3). What the *piqueteros* did not see coming was that the repression would kick-start a process of internal struggle within the CTD "Aníbal Verón" that would eventually lead to its dissolution.

Unintended Consequences: The Dissolution of the CTD "Aníbal Verón" (2002)

The bloody consequences of the Pueyrredón Bridge protest underscored internal diversity within the CTD "Aníbal Verón." The CTD was working within an agreement that had not provided for a shared repertoire of strategies. The only thing that unified it was the short-term tactical desire to bring an end to the Duhalde government.

A series of cleavages that would continue into 2003 were set in motion by two issues. The first issue revolved around tactics. The sector of CTDs (Lanús, Quilmes, and La Plata) under MPR "Quebracho" leadership maintained the need to continue using methods of protest characterized by self-defense (such as covered faces and the use of slings and sticks). The MTD of Florencio Varela, in opposition, was in favor of abandoning these methods to foster the participation of the CTD "Aníbal Verón" in the multi-sectoral popular front promoted by the CTA. This divergence

[9] The only SMO that did not participate was the FTV. This was because D'Elía had previously been involved in a public confrontation with the BPN and CTD "Aníbal Verón" leaders over his disagreement with the *foquista* insurrectional strategy and its goals (*Clarín* 06/28/2002).

pointed to two different visions of the new correlation of forces between the movement and the government and, thus, a divergence in terms of the necessity of continuing or abandoning the insurrectional path that had led to the Pueyrredón Bridge events.

The second issue, intimately related to the first, was in connection with the repertoire of strategies. The CTDs wanted to continue to pursue an insurrectional resolution to the crisis, the MTD of Florencio Varela was in favor of a multi-sectoral strategy, while the remaining MTDs (Solano, Lanús, Almirante Brown, Guernica, Allen, Cipolletti) were in favor of demobilizing in order to redefine their strategies and goals. This last group was undergoing a process of enrichment of their stock of legacies thanks to the influence of the assembly movement, the Zapatistas, and the MST of Brazil. This process had led to the integration of an autonomist-introspective strategy permeated by *basismo*. This last group of MTDs, then, opted to focus on rebuilding social relations rather than ratcheting up levels of contention (Burkart and Vázquez 2007).

These two issues came to a head, leading to a split in the CTD into one group that would continue with the insurrectional path and keep the name CTD "Aníbal Verón" (MPR "Quebracho") and another group that would adhere to the autonomist-introspective path and call itself the MTD "Aníbal Verón." Only the CTD "Aníbal Verón" (MPR "Quebracho") would maintain its alliance with the BPN.

ELECTORAL VERSUS ABSTENTIONIST STRATEGIES

The Pueyrredón Bridge events pushed forward the date for the elections, originally scheduled for October 2003, to April, with no clear favorite for president. This situation drove electoral and contentious actors to intensify their political bargaining. The PJ, the UCR, and the majoritarian parties started negotiating candidacies and electoral alliances. Simultaneously, the *piqueteros*, assemblies, and left-wing parties initiated a discussion about the best electoral tactic. Their diverse strategies and tactics, summarized in **Table 5.2**, can be grouped into two main debates.

The first debate was between the actors that were in favor of an electoral solution. The choice was between promoting an electoral popular front and calling for a constituent assembly to redefine the entire political regime.[10] On July 9, 2002, the assemblies, the BPN, the MST

[10] The idea of calling for a constituent assembly to redefine the whole system might be interpreted as a recovery of Nahuel Moreno's strategy from 1982 during the transition to

TABLE 5.2 *Comparison of Pre-electoral Strategies with Electoral Tactics, by* Piquetero *SMO, 2002–3*

Social Movement Organization (Election Day April 27, 2003)	Pre-election Strategies (2002–3)	Presidential Election Tactics
CCC	Call for electoral abstention	Tacit support for Rodríguez Saá
CTD "Aníbal Verón"	Insurrectional collapse of the regime	Electoral boycott
FTV	Electoral popular-front	Open support for Kirchner
MIJD	Call for a constituent assembly	Tacit support for Rodríguez Saá
MST "Teresa Vive"	Call for a constituent assembly	Presidential ticket
MTD "Aníbal Verón"	Autonomist long-term cultural change	Electoral boycott
MTL	Call for a constituent assembly	Presidential ticket
MTR	Insurrectional collapse of the regime	Failed presidential ticket/passive abstentionist
PO	Electoral call for a constituent assembly	Presidential ticket
Neighborhoods Standing Up	Insurrectional collapse of the regime	Failed presidential ticket/passive abstentionist

Source: Several interviews (2007–13).

"Teresa Vive," the CTD "Aníbal Verón" (MPR "Quebracho"), and some of the MTDs organized a march with the slogan "So that everybody leaves!" following a resolution taken by the coordination assembly of the assembly movement. The ARI party also participated in the protest in the form of its presidential candidate Elisa Carrió (*La Nación* 07/10/2002).

After intense negotiations, a call for a joint action was issued that would bring the aims of the slogan to fruition. This led to a collective effort at the end of August to propose a candidate to represent the

democracy (*1982: Comienza la Revolución*, available at www.nahuelmoreno.org/pdf/1982.pdf, accessed July 6, 2010, especially page 13).

assembly movement, CTA, ARI, MIJD, BPN, FTV, CCC, and several left-wing parties, but there was no final agreement on a common electoral strategy (*Página/12* 08/16/2002; Burkart et el. 2008: 54–55). The MIJD, PO, CTD "Aníbal Verón" (MPR "Quebracho"), and half of the assemblies were in favor of a constitutional assembly to redefine the regime, while the FTV, CCC, and CTA were in favor of an electoral popular front to present an alternative presidential formula that would increase their chances of winning.

In the end, no agreement was achieved as to which presidential formula to support. In April 2003, the PCR-CCC publicly abstained from supporting a particular candidate but quietly supported Rodríguez Saá, preserving its alliance with La Matanza mayor Balestrini and its multi-sectoral alliance with the right-wing sector of the PJ. Meanwhile, the PO presented its own candidate as part of the Workers Party, and the MST "Teresa Vive" (MST party) and MTL (PCA) created their own electoral alliance (United Left) and put forward their presidential candidate. Lastly, the FTV publicly backed Duhalde's candidate Néstor Kirchner.

The second debate was among those actors that were in favor of a non-electoral resolution of the crisis. The debate in this case was between actively boycotting the elections and promoting alternative autonomist or neighborhood-based types of social relationships toward a cultural transformation in society without the taking of state power. The June 2002 repression drove the MTDs to detach themselves from active participation in contentious actions, though they subsequently became intimately involved with the assembly movement. This led to a debate among the CTD "Aníbal Verón" (MPR "Quebracho"), the MTR, and the MTD "Aníbal Verón" over how to approach the elections.

The MIJD, PO, CTD "Aníbal Verón" (MPR "Quebracho"), and many assemblies were in favor of ending all mandates and calling for a constitutional assembly that would restructure the entire political system. Yet despite this stance, the MIJD supported Rodríguez Saá behind the scenes.[11] The CTD "Aníbal Verón" (MPR "Quebracho"), some of the autonomist MTDs, and some of the assemblies organized an active electoral boycott under the slogan "Against the electoral trap!" The electoral boycott failed, with voter turnout no lower than usual. The assembly movement would largely demobilize in the months after the elections, and the assemblies that survived did so by integrating the CTA or by

[11] This was negotiated at a meeting between Rodríguez Saá and the MIJD leader, Castells, on August 12, 2002 (*La Nación* 08/13/2002).

reconverting into cooperatives or neighborhood-based organizations (Mauro and Rossi 2015).

Finally, the MTR and Neighborhoods Standing Up, two organizations previously in favor of an insurrectional solution, redefined their strategy toward achieving a presidential outcome. The MTR, Neighborhoods Standing Up, and the UTD of Mosconi tried to build a presidential ticket. The project failed, and this sector played only a passive role during the elections.

In the meanwhile, the government continued the pattern of responding repressively to the radical segment of actors struggling for the reincorporation of the popular sectors. In November 2002, the CTA, FTV, and CCC organized, in concert with the worker-managed factories movement, a protest to modify bankruptcy law and favor the expropriation of factories by the state; this protest attracted no repression (*Clarín* 11/20/2002; *Página/12* 11/21/2002). However, in April 2003, the support given by left-wing parties and the radical sector of the *piqueteros* to the occupied Brukman factory was answered with the most repressive intervention of the final part of Duhalde's presidency. While this action suggested that the transition toward a democratically elected government was already under way, this did not prevent people from protesting.

The Electoral Results: An Unexpected President

Duhalde's interim presidency and the state reincorporation attempt ended abruptly over the killings of the two *piquetero* activists at Pueyrredón Bridge. This situation opened the door for new presidential elections, which some of the movements had been claiming for. Néstor Kirchner (center-left Peronist Front for Victory, FpV) won the election with 22.2 percent of the vote. Kirchner actually came in second in the first round but won by default when Menem (24.3 percent, center-right Peronist) decided not to run in the ballotage.

This election revealed the effects of the 2001–2 crisis on party politics. It atomized the party system and diluted the UCR's electoral power at the national level but reinforced the tendency toward electoral hegemony of Peronists. There were in fact three Peronist presidential candidates, with the conservative PJ candidate Rodríguez Saá (14.1 percent) competing along with Kirchner and Menem. There were also three Radical candidates: center-right Ricardo López Murphy (16.3 percent), center Elisa Carrió (14 percent), and, with the UCR ballot, center-left Leopoldo Moreau (2.3 percent). This election represented the worst historical result for the UCR since its foundation. However, only these establishment candidates obtained substantial electoral support. According to Levitsky and Murillo (2003: 160–61), several factors explain the success of the traditional candidates: the electoral resilience of the Peronist sector, the importance of subnational territorial politics with the associated patronage networks, and the relative economic success of Duhalde.

In terms of contentious politics, these electoral results can be seen as a product of the division and partial demobilization of the most radical sector of the *piquetero* movement as well as the lack of a shared repertoire of strategies among the left, the assemblies, and the *piqueteros* that made it impossible to propose any unified electoral or contentious alternative (**Table 5.2**). The electoral path failed as no respectable electoral coalition could be built beyond the unsuccessful attempts of the candidates of the Workers Party (0.7 percent) and United Left (1.7 percent). The left-wing parties that were in favor of an electoral resolution to the crisis maintained their historically poor voting results.

The contentious path also failed because the campaign against the elections was only able to garner limited acceptance on the part of the other *piqueteros* and assemblies. In fact, despite the arduous struggle for total elite renewal and the election boycott, the atomization of the party system was not followed by a massive rejection of electoral politics. Turnout at the 2003 elections was 78.2 percent, thus restoring historically high rates of voting participation.

CONCLUSION

This chapter studied the beginning of the territorial reincorporation phase. The reincorporation period went through two attempts, the first being the focus of this chapter. From January to June 2002 Duhalde attempted a model of *state reincorporation*, which failed in achieving to demobilize the *piquetero* movement. However, in this same period, a crucial policy was formed to respond to the claims for reincorporation: the PJJHD – the most massive unemployment subsidy of Latin America.

Regarding the *piqueteros*, state reincorporation divided the movement in two sectors. The two main SMOs playing from inside government (CCC and FTV) and all the rest of the movement from outside (CTD "Aníbal Verón," CUBa, FTC, MST "Teresa Vive," MIJD, MTR, PO, and Neighborhoods Standing Up). This division in two social movement sectors also will characterize the second attempt of reincorporation. In any case, the whole *piquetero* movement played with a wide array of strategies as part of a predominant repertoire of strategies that went from promoting electoral coalitions to *foquista* insurrections.

The subsequent mode of reincorporation derived from the consequences for the elites and *piqueteros* of the repression of Pueyrredón Bridge. Once Néstor Kirchner entered into power, his government tried to incorporate the organized popular sectors with a different approach that demonstrated itself to be more effective: *party territorial reincorporation*. Almost half of the *piquetero* movement entered as secondary actors in the state, mostly in areas related to their claims for reincorporation. As I will show in the next chapter, this same process was associated with an increased formalization of the interactions between state institutions and the movement.

6

Party Territorial Reincorporation in the Socio-political Arena (2003–9)

This chapter examines the period of *party territorial reincorporation* that took place from 2003 to 2009. With the advanced end of Duhalde's interim presidency what essentially failed was the first trial of reincorporation for demobilization purposes: state territorial reincorporation. This obliged the new government of Néstor Kirchner to explore with a different mode of reincorporation that proved more successful because it could channel mobilization in favor of the government: party territorial reincorporation.

As will be analyzed in this chapter, this period is divided between a phase of expansion (May 2003 to October 2004) and another of consolidation and stagnation of party territorial reincorporation (October 2004 to December 2008). In this period, horizontal opportunities were related to the dispute for the definition of the responsibilities for the *piquetero* policy domain between the Ministries of Labor and Social Development.

Vertical opportunities were associated with a multi-level alliance between a presidency, governorships, and mayors that were mainly Peronists. To this was added the clash between first incorporation (CGT) and second incorporation (*piqueteros*) actors for the same constituency of popular sectors. And since the nature of second incorporation is territorial instead of corporatist, the emergence of disincorporated workers as an organized force implied a challenge to mayors' source of power (all this is synthesized in **Table 5.1**).

The stage of reincorporation is defined by a dynamic but clear division of the movement into two sectors, according to two clusters of SMOs: those that were positioned within the government coalition and those that were not. While the sector within government was incorporated into diverse ministries, this was always in secondary roles. Those that remained in opposition aligned and realigned multiple times and sometimes even innovated on the *piqueteros*' predominant repertoire of contention as they tried to reverse the increasingly unfavorable correlation of forces vis-à-vis the government. These alliances pointed to the difficulties this sector encountered in its attempts to maintain cohesiveness once contentious dynamics re-emerged under the initiative of other actors, such as the 2004 middle-class security protests and the 2008 rural lockout.

The end of the second wave of incorporation in Argentina was marked by a breaking point as strong in political and economic terms as coups had been for closing the first incorporation. The impact in political and economic terms of the unprecedented rural lockout against export taxes was an insurmountable blow in terms of the capacity of the state to finance the long-term sustainability of the second incorporation in the context of the global financial crisis that started in 2008. It was during a specific period in Cristina Fernández de Kirchner's first mandate (March–July 2008) that this juncture was reached, leading to the stagnation of the reincorporation process and the winding down of this historical period through 2009.

This chapter completes my analysis of the second wave of incorporation of the popular sectors in Argentina – a process of both contentious and routine politics that involved the use of a repertoire of contention and a repertoire of strategies. As shall be seen, both repertoires changed differently over time and at a dissimilar pace owing to their related but diverse natures. While the repertoire of contention was not substantially altered during reincorporation, the repertoire of strategies was enriched as the *piquetero* movement grew and diversified. However, the modifications to the predominant repertoire of strategies proved not to be a direct byproduct of junctural shifts.

PARTY TERRITORIAL REINCORPORATION (MAY 2003–DECEMBER 2008)

Néstor Kirchner was a weak president – he had received fewer votes than the combined number of unemployed and underemployed people (34.4 percent of the population in May). In addition, Kirchner won as a protégé of Duhalde, and they had a joint governing agreement, keeping in place an almost identical ministerial cabinet. To make things even worse for Kirchner, in Congress he did not have a majority as the *menemista* and *saadista* PJ factions had received the most votes (Calvo and

Escolar 2005: 32, n. 14). The new government was faced with a highly conflictual political setting and an already legitimated *piquetero* movement. Kirchner's government would decrease the repression of protests and promote the territorialized incorporation of the *piquetero* movement as part of the mobilization base of the Peronist FpV coalition, but it would also maintain the judicialization of social conflicts.[1]

Among the first acts carried out by the new government was the decision to meet with the most active contentious actor. These meetings were divided by social movement sector and never included the entire *piquetero* movement at the same time. The purpose was to provide each sector with specific resources as a vehicle for incorporating, co-opting, or demobilizing the SMOs.

After these meetings, the FTV, Neighborhoods Standing Up, and the newly created "Evita" Movement joined the governmental coalition. In 2004, the CCC ended its alliance with the government, and the OB "Tupac Amaru" and part of the MTL would participate in the coalition as external allies. In 2007 part of the MTD "Aníbal Verón" of Florencio Varela joined the social movement sector of the *piquetero* movement that was supportive of the government. The SMOs that agreed to participate in government would do so based on differing conceptions of the movement's role in office. The *piqueteros* went on to occupy several posts within the executive branches of the state at the national, provincial, and municipal levels but only had a secondary role in the decision-making process in the *piquetero* policy domain. Additionally, this stage of reincorporation would be related to the *piqueteros*' initial entry into the provincial and national parliaments, though not always as part of the governmental coalition.

Almost half of the *piquetero* movement either joined or supported the government. The remainder did not accept the government's invitation and continued to pursue contentious strategies. Those SMOs that did not agree to join the governmental coalition or support the Kirchner

[1] The highly controversial "Anti-terrorist" Law 26,268 (approved in 2007 and modified in 2011) includes articles that were rejected by the human rights movement because they could imply a criminalization of protest. This law had the potential to further increase the judicialization of social conflicts in Argentina, which had already been steadily increasing – and leading to the virtual criminalization of certain movements – before this law was approved. However, Law 26,268 should not be regarded as part of the vernacular process of judicialization. It was rather the result of lobby exerted by the Financial Action Task Force on Money Laundering on Argentina as part of its efforts to combat money laundering and the financing of terrorism.

presidency regrouped in order to confront it. Nonetheless, the movement in Buenos Aires experienced a gradual demobilization from 2003 to 2006, and it was not until 2008 that the confrontational approach yielded some positive results (**Figure 3.1**).

Moreover, the 2006 protest data shows that picket events upheld the Buenos Aires–centric nature of contentious politics with 49 percent of the total number of pickets in that metropolitan area, followed by Jujuy (10 percent), Salta and Santa Fe (5 percent each), and Tucumán and Córdoba (4 percent each).[2] In addition to this, the distribution by actor of the picket data reveals the inclusion of roadblocks in the Argentine repertoire of contention as well as the demobilization of the *piquetero* movement. For instance, the *piqueteros* were the promoters of just 9.1 percent of the total number of roadblocks in 2006 and less than 1 percent of the massive roadblocks in 2008 (more on this later).[3]

Meanwhile, in Jujuy and Salta contention continued at the provincial level. While the OB "Tupac Amaru" grew systematically through cooperative housing construction projects supported by the national government (Battezzati 2012), the UTD of Mosconi followed an enclave-based trade unionist path. The main disruptive action of the UTD of Mosconi during the Kirchner mandate was the burning of the local branch of the petroleum company Tecpetrol on November 20, 2003. The claim was trade unionist in its nature: the payment of severance pay to former YPF workers that had been promised and never delivered and new jobs in the local petroleum industry. This protest led to an initial meeting between president Kirchner and the UTD on November 23 and the charging of the UTD leader Fernández with the offense of "abetting crime" (*Clarín* 11/26/2003).

Finally, the formation of the Kirchner government also led to an attempt by Peronists to rebuild their territorial base. This would involve already incorporated (unions) as well as reincorporated (*piqueteros*) popular sectors. As a result, the 2003–8 period would see the consolidation of a dynamic but clear division of the movement into two sectors according to the positioning of the *piquetero* SMOs as either within or outside of the government coalition. As a by-product of reincorporation, the *piqueteros*

[2] According to Herrera (2008: 183, table 11), between 1991 and 2002 the main sites of *piquetero* contention were Buenos Aires, Salta, Santa Fe, Neuquén, and Río Negro.

[3] The breakdown of data by actor and province is not shown in Figure 3.1, but the data is taken from the same sources and based on the same number of roadblocks presented in this figure.

would compete with the CGT for the constituency of the popular sectors and expand their territorial dispute with the PJ into the electoral arena.

THE RELATIONAL CONSTRUCTION OF THE MODE OF REINCORPORATION

The reincorporation stage initiated by Duhalde and expanded by Kirchner implied – as during the first incorporation – the institutionalization of socio-political conflicts and the development of spaces for their resolution. Due to the territorialized nature of the second incorporation, the state departments that had played a crucial role in the first incorporation – such as the Ministry of Labor – were not those in charge of reincorporation. Instead, the main spaces for the second incorporation were two newly created ministries, the Ministry of Social Development and the Ministry of Federal Planning, and the redefinition of the role of the Secretariat-General of the Presidency, an executive agency that since democratization was in charge of informal arrangements.

During the Duhalde presidency a new predominant relationship began that can be defined as "agreements for the sustainability of governability." After 2003, president Kirchner reinforced the mechanism and added a new requisite: government participation. This created a new boundary between the SMOs that participated in government and those that stayed in the opposition. This went hand in hand with Kirchner's need to build a territorial base for the governmental coalition. The relational construction of the mode of incorporation went through a process of formalization for which three phases can be identified.

First Phase: The *Piqueteros* as External to the Government and the Bridging Role of Political Operators

The first phase was from May 2003 to June 2004, during which the relationship between the government and the *piqueteros* was based on the latter being treated as external to the coalition. This was also a period of transition within the Kirchner-Duhalde co-government agreement. During this period, political operators were in control of informal links with the movement as part of the process of developing a space for *piquetero* participation in government. This was also related to the fact that the sector of the *piqueteros* that had decided to remain outside the coalition still had a strong capacity for mobilization.

There were four main political operators in charge of bridging the *piquetero* movement with the state and developing a routinized relationship. Because as a social policy the PJJHD had stringent regulations for awarding them, the continued discretionary distribution of PEL subsidies[4] and funds for emergency and critical social situations was the main asset under the control of these political operators. The purpose was to solve specific *piquetero* demands in a manner governed by the logic of exchange of resources for governability.

One political operator was Carlos Kunkel, the subsecretary-general of the presidency from 2003 to 2005. Kunkel had been responsible for relations with the *piqueteros* in the municipality of Florencio Varela. After Kirchner came to power, he was placed in charge of creating a *piquetero* collegiate body within the Secretariat-General of the Presidency (more about this later).[5]

Two more political operators were Rafael Follonier and Héctor Metón, who continued in their roles established during the Duhalde presidency under the leadership of the minister of the interior Aníbal Fernández. Follonier was vice minister of the interior (2003–7) until he was moved to the protocol area of the House of Government. Metón was in charge of the Rooting Program (2003–5), located within the Ministry of the Interior.[6] When formal state departments replaced their duties, Follonier maintained a limited level of power while Metón gradually lost his.[7]

Finally, there was the political operator Sergio Berni, who was in charge of social and natural emergencies within the Ministry of Social Development. Berni was a former military doctor who had worked as a political operator for the governorship of Santa Cruz under Kirchner. Berni maintained his ministry role as he moved to the policing of protest matters. However, interactions with the *piqueteros* were

[4] The Community Employment Program (PEC) gradually replaced the PEL after July 2003, under a similar logic of discretionary distribution (Neffa 2008: 78).

[5] After this was achieved in 2004, Kunkel resigned as subsecretary-general to become a member of the National Congress in 2005.

[6] Metón had worked under Aníbal Fernández since he had been mayor of Quilmes. When Fernández went to the provincial Secretariat of Labor, Metón became the political operator for *piquetero* issues there too.

[7] First, the Ministry of the Interior delegated informal links with the *piqueteros* to the Secretariat-General of the Presidency. Second, the FTV took over the Rooting Program in an expanded version of this land issues portfolio. As a result, from 2005 onward, Metón tried to deal with the movement of worker-managed factories, but he was not able to achieve the same results he had enjoyed with the *piqueteros*. Thus, he returned to Buenos Aires as the main provincial political operator for *piquetero* issues.

increasingly formalized in those ministries working on issues that concerned the *piquetero* policy domain: the Ministry of Social Development, the Ministry of Federal Planning (in charge of Keynesian-style policies such as building social housing) and – to a lesser degree – the Ministry of Labor.

The Dispute for the Ministry of Labor between Trade Unions and the *Piqueteros*

Even though the Secretariat of Employment (Ministry of Labor) had always been the state body in charge of the administration of unemployment subsidies since the emergence of the *piquetero* movement, the Secretariat and the Ministry were never opened up to *piquetero* participation. Although there was at least one attempt to participate in the Secretariat of Employment by the "Evita" Movement, the only organizations that participated within the ministry were trade unions.

On October 23, 2003, the Ministry of Labor was occupied by a series of small SMOs that had splintered from the CTD "Aníbal Verón" and the MTR. This group of *piqueteros* remained within the ministry building for eight hours with the minister, Carlos Tomada, trapped inside (*La Nación* 10/28/2003). The event was a reproduction of the MTR's occupation of the provincial Secretariat of Labor in 2001 (recounted in Chapter 4). However, this time the government's response was different, avoiding the use of repressive means and even refraining from expelling the SMOs from the building. Instead, after the SMO leaders left from exhaustion, a judicial case was launched against them (*La Nación* 10/28/2003, 12/30/2003). The judicialization of *piquetero* protests went hand in hand with the decrease in the use of repressive methods to quell them.

The second incorporation process produced a conflict for the constituency of the popular sectors between the organizations of those who were already incorporated and those who had been disincorporated. With the 2003 occupation of the ministry, *piquetero* SMOs attempted to put pressure on Minister Tomada (a CGT labor relations lawyer), while the ministry actually supported the mobilization of trade unions in order to provide a counterbalance to the growth and influence of the *piqueteros*. As Tomada privately told a group of unions, "I think it is very good that you mobilize. It is very positive, do not allow the *piqueteros* to win over the streets" (quoted by *Clarín* 10/25/2003). Though the CTA continued to support the *piqueteros*, the Dissident and Official CGT, with government support, initiated a process of reunification under the leadership of pro-government Dissident CGT Hugo Moyano that ended with a single CGT in July 2004 (*Clarín* 12/09/2003, 07/16/2004; *Página/12* 07/17/2004).

The second incorporation process also implied continuity with PJ de-unionization. Though the CGT and CTA were allied with the government, the electoral coalition and the PJ did not increase the number of union leaders on electoral ballots. In contrast, the union system would "display more autonomy than in the pre-neoliberal period from both the state and the increasingly fragmented party system" (Etchemendy and Collier 2007: 395). In other words, the second incorporation implied the end of the hegemonic role of the PJ and the CGT as interlocutors for popular sector claims. When the union system was liberalized the CGT lost the exclusive representation of incorporated workers. The *piquetero* movement also disputed the PJ's almost complete territorial hegemony in Greater Buenos Aires and in a few other provinces. The results were twofold. For incorporated workers second incorporation changed the union system to a moderately pluralist model that increased its autonomy from the PJ. For reincorporated workers second incorporation implied opening up a non-corporatist path in newly created institutions for territorial politics.

Second Phase: Judicialization and Selective Inclusion/Exclusion

The second phase in the formalization of the relationship between the *piqueteros* and the government was from June 2004 to September 2005. In this period, the government was able to build a coalition with the support of some *piquetero* SMOs and demobilize the rest of the movement through the selective distribution of resources and the non-repressive judicialization of protest.

This period was characterized by increased tension in the Duhalde-Kirchner co-government agreement. This cohabitation included a division of labor between the *duhaldista* and *kirchnerista* factions.[8]

In the meanwhile, the *piquetero* movement was divided between adopting an insider or outsider position. This tension became evident on the second anniversary of the 2001 national *pueblada*. Three main protests took place in the Plaza de Mayo. The SMOs that had made up the

[8] For example, while the Ministry of the Interior was aligned with Duhalde, the Ministry of Social Development was under the president's sister Alicia Kirchner. There she was in charge of developing, in association with part of the *piquetero* movement, a territorial network that could dispute the power of Duhalde and his allied mayors in Greater Buenos Aires. These efforts were rewarded when a series of electoral results changed the balance of power in favor of the *kirchnerista* faction.

CTD "Aníbal Verón," part of the assemblies, and the radical sector of the human rights movement organized the first march. The CCC mobilized independently, and the BPN, MST "Teresa Vive," and MIJD prepared the third event of the day in the square (*Clarín* 12/21/2003). Finally, the FTV did not mobilize, organizing a rally at a football stadium instead (Delamata 2005: 372). These divisions within the *piquetero* movement stood in contrast to the process of reunification of the CGT.

Unlike what happened when the *piqueteros* were struggling for recognition and legitimation, during the reincorporation stage the government applied a tactic of non-repressive exhaustion, while most claims received no official response. What's more, the *piquetero* social movement sector that was outside government was defeated on several occasions, making things even more difficult for the SMOs that were still mobilized. The first important unsuccessful protest happened on May 27 and 28, 2004, when the BPN, MTR, MIJD, MST "Teresa Vive," and CCC coordinated a forty-eight-hour series of 144 pickets throughout the country to claim for the reduction in public services fees for the popular sectors (*Clarín* 05/13/2004). The second was on November 2, 2004, when the MIJD and MST "Teresa Vive" occupied the national Ministry of Labor for five days.

In addition to the dividing of the *piquetero* movement, the human rights movement was also breaking up. Part of this movement became an ally of the government since Kirchner had decided to overturn the amnesty laws regarding human rights violations carried out by the military during the last authoritarian regime. He also favored a very active process of bringing military criminals to justice and remembering the victims of the authoritarian regime, both long-standing claims of the human rights movement. The divisions within the human rights movement particularly affected the group of MTDs, which since their very beginnings had relied on some of the human rights SMOs as their main allies.

The *piquetero* movement within government tried to devise a common strategy in office. Its first achievement in coordination was the National Assembly of Popular Organizations, held June 21, 2004, and organized by the FTV, Neighborhoods Standing Up, the "Evita" Movement, and the *kirchnerista* faction of the CTA, the National and Popular Transversal Front (FTNyP). Ministers Tomada and Alicia Kirchner and Secretary-General Parrilli also participated in this event. The result was the existence, between December 2004 and October 2005, of the Popular Organizations Front (FOP) as the first achievement of coordination of the social movement sector in government. Due to internal differences, the

FOP was only capable of building a short-lived electoral alliance for the 2005 legislative elections without managing to present a list of *piquetero* candidates.

The CCC maintained its governability agreement with Kirchner until 2004, when the president initiated a process of detachment from Duhalde, completed in 2005, along with the end of the Kirchner-Duhalde cohabitation. Though the CCC had not campaigned for Kirchner, the support given to the Duhalde coalition was not suspended as the CCC still considered itself to be participating under a government of national unity. This decision of the PCR-CCC politburo was not reflected in posts in the government because of the PCR-CCC's tactic of acting as an external ally. However, the CCC was gradually demobilized over the time it continued with the Duhalde agreement. The first mobilization of the CCC against Kirchner, in alliance with the ANTOD, took place in March 2004 (*Página/12* 03/04/2004).

In Jujuy, the OB "Tupac Amaru" became the biggest SMO in the north of Argentina thanks to the very pragmatic bond it established with the national government. This helped the OB "Tupac Amaru" quickly expand its provision of benefits to local communities with an indigenist ethos (Russo 2010: 113–20; Battezzati 2012). Organized into cooperatives for housing construction and providing social infrastructure, schools, hospitals, and swimming pools, the OB "Tupac Amaru" resembled the welfare organizations created by European immigrants in the pre-incorporation period in the early twentieth century (cf. Belmartino 2005: 32–36).

The last crucial defeat for the *piqueteros* outside government during the Kirchner presidency was in August 2005. No state repression was involved; in fact, there was no official response at all to the four-day encampment protest in the Plaza de Mayo. The demand was for the reactivation and expansion of the PJJHD to all the *piqueteros* in opposition, who referred to themselves as "Piquetero Unity" (*La Nación* 08/20/2005; Torres 2006: 50; Table 4.3).

The Secretariat-General of the Presidency: The Institutional Space for the Articulation of Territorial Reincorporation

In 2004, an important institutional innovation led to the redefinition of the role of the Secretariat-General of the Presidency as the unit in charge of the articulation of the *piqueteros* within the state apparatus. *Piquetero* members, along with PJ political operators, occupied this office with the aim of offering an institutional space for the articulation of reincorporation claims of a territorial nature. This process was highly informal and evolved over time, but always within a space where debates on public policy elaboration did not take place. The Secretariat-General was rather the environment where *piqueteros* could participate in the daily resolution of political and social conflicts. The collegiate body of *piqueteros* within the Secretariat-General was relatively stable for the entire Kirchner mandate.[9] Only the FTV would eventually suffer from the cooptation of its representative in 2005, after which D'Elía intervened personally.

The role of this collegiate body changed over time. From 2004 to 2005, its main aim was to restore governability. As one *piquetero* member in the Secretariat-General said, the goal was to incorporate or demobilize the movement: "Our duty was to rebuild the social fabric destroyed by the 2001 crisis ... in fact the goal of the government was at best to incorporate, and at the very least to draw the movement away from social conflict, to channel social conflict ... " (interview 2008). After the incorporation of part of the movement, the most conflictive environment was the province of Buenos Aires with the smallest new groups that resulted from the dissolution of the CTD "Aníbal Verón" and in Salta with the UTD of Mosconi. This was the focus of the efforts of the Secretariat-General group of *piqueteros* until the political agenda changed their role. From the 2005 legislative elections campaign to the 2007 presidential elections, the main work of the *piqueteros* in this area was to build the coalition's territorial electoral base. The purpose was to counter the *duhaldista* and PJ mayors in order to win the elections without the support of Duhalde and the core of the PJ. After this strategy succeeded, their duty from 2007 to 2008 was the routinization of the relationship with the *piqueteros* and other contentious actors, which implied the return of governability through informal negotiations to resolve specific disruptive events in the most troubled provinces.

The role of the *piqueteros* in the Secretariat-General was not the coordination of policies as officially stated; in fact, no public policies ever came out of this collegiate body. The actual purpose was to build a routinized relationship equivalent to the corporatist one, but for actors and conflicts of a territorial nature. According to one *piquetero* member in the Secretariat-General, the PJ could make up for its horizontally and vertically uncoordinated nature by exploiting the vertical cohesion of

[9] Its members were Carlos López (FTV), Santiago Martorelli ("Evita" Movement), Néstor Moccia (Neighborhoods Standing Up), and Víctor Gómez (FTNyP).

some of the *piquetero* SMOs for communication and coordination between different levels of the state. This coordination capacity was limited, however, to specific contentious or electoral events and did not work very well for the elaboration of public policies. According to another *piquetero* member in the Secretariat-General, coordination was "rickety" and mostly done with the technocratic sectors of the Ministries of Education, Labor, Social Development, and Federal Planning. The reasons for this were twofold: first, many policies and decisions were still channeled through political operators such as Berni and Follonier; and second, the relationship between the ministries and *piquetero* leaders were based less on shared public policy domains and more on the territory under dispute.

Third Phase: The *Piqueteros* as the Territorial Allied Sector of the Government

The third phase in the formalization of the relationship between the *piqueteros* and the government went from September 2005 to December 2007. During this period, the effects of the accumulation of positive subnational electoral results produced a reconfiguration of the balance of power in favor of Kirchner. The mid-term national legislative elections in October 2005 signaled the death knell for Duhalde in his former stronghold as the Kirchner FpV triumphed in the province of Buenos Aires with strong backing from the *piqueteros* (coordinated within the Secretariat-General) but little support from PJ mayors. These electoral results gave the government the legitimacy and the territorial network it needed. The main effect was the rearrangement of the Kirchner cabinet, with the *duhaldista* faction ministers either leaving or switching their allegiance (*Página/12* 12/02/2005).

The reconfiguration of government internal relations meant the expansion and consolidation of the second incorporation redefined as a dynamic of party territorial reincorporation (**Table 5.1**). In this third stage, the *piquetero* movement started being considered as part of the territorial allied sector of the government. Specifically, the redefinition of this relationship meant the incorporation of the main leaders of the FTV, Neighborhoods Standing Up, and the "Evita" Movement into executive posts. As already noted, in this phase the Secretariat-General was in charge of generating the territorial support of the government and routinizing the relationship with contentious actors. This second phase kept the trend of selective inclusion/exclusion, with the *piquetero* sector within government expanding its role in secondary state positions and the group outside government increasingly marginalized from state resources.

For the *piqueteros* who were working with the government, this phase of incorporation exposed the limits of the process itself. The role given to the *piqueteros* and the impossibility of transcending the PJ's structure of horizontally and vertically uncoordinated informal, individualized, and territorialized links meant that the *piqueteros* were secondary actors with a reduced capacity to influence the public policy process. For the *piqueteros* who were external to the government, this process did not imply having other *piqueteros* within the government as allies who could help in the provision of resources or for the coordination of political actions. Instead, it represented increased competition for resources among the "insider" and "outsider" *piqueteros*, which reduced the opportunities for mobilization for those groups that had not joined the governing coalition.

FROM WITHIN: THE PIQUETEROS' PARTICIPATION IN GOVERNMENT

The partial incorporation of the *piquetero* movement divided it into two main social movement sectors according to stance toward the government, either inside it and supporting it or outside and in opposition. As part of this relational process, a predominant repertoire of strategies can be identified for this stage of the second wave of incorporation (**Table 6.1**). This section will analyze the specific path taken by each SMO inside or outside government.

The FTV in Government: A Multi-class Electoral Popular Front

The FTV joined the coalition by viewing the Kirchner period as "a government under dispute" between the traditional PJ and the new forces coming from social movements. The role of the FTV in government was to push the coalition – as it had also attempted as part of the Alliance – toward a more progressive position within a multi-class electoral popular front. This specific strategy was intimately related to the central purpose of the FTV according to its leadership, which stated that: "The main goal of the FTV is to build an organized popular power base that is able to sustain a popular government. I think that a popular government does not exist without a strong popular power base in the streets" (quoted by Delamata 2004: 42, n. 19).

TABLE 6.1 *Predominant Repertoire of Strategies for the Main* Piquetero *SMOs, 2003–9*

Social Movement Organization	Allied with or in Government	In Opposition
CCC	National unity government (2003–4)	Insurrectional alliance with the right (2004–)
CTD "Aníbal Verón" (MPR "Quebracho")		Insurrectional witness strategy
"Evita" Movement	PJ and state colonization	
FTV	Multi-class electoral popular front	
MIJD		Electoral witness strategy
MST "Teresa Vive"		Classist electoral front/ Morenist entryism
MTD "Aníbal Verón"	Territorial survival/ cooptation (2007–)	*Basismo foquista* (2003–7)
MTD of La Juanita		NGO-ization
MTD of Solano and allies		Autonomist-introspective strategy
MTL (divided into two sectors)	Multi-class electoral popular front (as an external ally)	Multi-class popular front/*basista* cooperativism
MTR-CUBa		Substantial citizenship rights and judicial claims/*basismo foquista*
OB "Tupac Amaru"	Territorial diffusion/ clientelism	
PO		Classist electoral front/ Morenist entryism
Popular Front "Darío Santillán" (FPDS)		Multi-sectoral *basista* and autonomist-introspective strategy
Neighborhoods Standing Up	State colonization (2003–8)	Multi-sectoral electoral front (2008–)
UTD of Mosconi		Enclave syndicalism

Within the multi-class electoral popular front strategy, the FTV followed a variety of stages in its interaction with the government. From 2003 to 2005 personalized links with governmental officials predominated and the FTV could be considered as an ally that was external to the government.

With the Kirchner government realigning its correlation of power with Duhalde and ending the joint government agreement, the FTV also redefined its relationship with the government. From 2005 to 2006, the FTV emulated a strategy that Neighborhoods Standing Up had adopted since the beginning: colonizing the state (Chapter 2 for the definition of this). This led to the creation of the Subsecretariat of Land for Social Habitat under the new Ministry of Federal Planning. The creation of the subsecretariat meant closing the Rooting Program as the subsecretariat was given control over all land issues. The subsecretariat was charged with legalizing urban land occupations and was under the direct responsibility of Luis D'Elía.[10] This decision represented the second direct involvement of the FTV in the national public policy domain. In this subsecretariat – as in all the other departments of the Ministry of Federal Planning – there was no participation of any other *piquetero* SMOs.

However, not all the FTV leaders shared the state colonization strategy. The San Francisco Solano branch (Quilmes district) participated in the subsecretariat with another model of incorporation in mind. According to the FTV leader for Solano, his role was as a "bridge" that shortened the distance between the state institutions and the FTV. For him, there was a permanent tension between being within and outside the government: "[with the ministry] we conduct a complete diagnosis of the property situation [of the land], [then] we turn our attention to the administrative management [of property regularization], but we need the organized neighborhood to put pressure on us. We need this pressure on ourselves so that we can pressurize other officials who do not have the same conception as us" (interview 2007).

The state colonization strategy failed for the FTV due to two main reasons. The first was the lack of any budget for the application of land reform and regularization policies. Due to intense conflicts with the Ministry of Federal Planning stemming from the lack of funds for land expropriations, in 2007 D'Elía was replaced in the post by Rubén Pascolini, a second-ranking FTV leader. D'Elía's exit from office was the result of a political scandal provoked by him as part of the FTV's tactic of pressurizing to obtain political answers or resources.

The second reason for the failure of the state colonization strategy was the cooptation of one of the FTV's main leaders after he entered the

[10] Unlike the other *piquetero* leaders, for D'Elía this was not his first experience of executive office. He had been a member of the province of Buenos Aires' Schools Directorate and a school councilor from 1988 to 1992. The subsecretariat was his first national post.

Secretariat-General of the Presidency. Because of this, from 2005 to 2008 the FTV returned to its initial strategy of forging individual links with the state. Though state cooptation of social movement leaders is a common practice, this did not happen with the two other large *piquetero* SMOs in government, only with very small groups. The FTV had suffered from the cooptation of some of its leaders due to its low degree of internal cohesion. As a territorial organization with no political party backing and increasingly detached from the CTA, it depended almost completely on a small group of leaders, but mostly on D'Elía. In addition to this, since the 1980s the FTV had developed long-standing personalized relationships with various PJ faction leaders that it could now profit from. These long-lasting links and the organization's low level of internal cohesion had allowed the FTV to preserve a national territorialized structure that was fluid and decentralized as well as being weakly vertically coordinated.[11] In this sense, the FTV's organizational structure is very similar to that of the de-unionized PJ, which favors the personalization of links.

For the FTV, participating in the governmental coalition was not a means of demobilizing the SMO. On the contrary, it meant the production and control of disruption as a source of negotiation for resources, a strategy that was already in use before entering into government. The repertoire of strategies was enriched with discursive/symbolic disruption to obtain resources, political posts, and influence in the multi-class electoral popular front that Kirchner's "government under dispute" represented for the FTV. The March 2006 issue of the FTV newspaper synthesizes this strategy on its front page: "Neither Opposition nor Indifference. The FTV and the Kirchner Government: Support and Participation without Losing Autonomy."

The FTV's support and participation in the governmental coalition led to a conflict with the CTA. This tension was in addition to the process of mutation that was going on within the FTV, which since 2001 had gone from being a federation to an organization. This conflict increased from 2003 onward and ended with the FTV leaving the CTA in 2006.[12]

[11] In this period, the FTV was represented in every province except for La Pampa and Santa Cruz. However, this presence was through SMOs that only loosely identified themselves with the FTV as an umbrella organization or – until 2006 – as the territorial sector of the CTA.

[12] Though the FTV was officially part of the structure of federations within the CTA, it had never functioned as such, being more of an independent SMO that worked in coordination with the CTA. As analyzed in the previous chapter, intense disputes that had emerged within the FTV in 2001 between the two principal internal minority factions had led Free

The CTA then created the Coordinator of Neighborhood Organizations, giving more power to the previously marginalized SMOs. This last decision produced the return to the CTA of the MTL in 2006 and Neighborhoods Standing Up in 2008. From 2006 to 2008, Milagro Sala, the main leader of the OB "Tupac Amaru" (Jujuy), and Daniel Barragán, the main leader of the small Buenos Aires Neighborhoods Movement, led the Coordination of Neighborhood Organizations.

Neighborhoods Standing Up in Government: State Colonization

After some internal debate about which position to take, Neighborhoods Standing Up entered government as an external ally with the goal of colonizing the state.[13] Even though it had adopted a different strategy from that of the FTV, it shared the latter's interpretation of the Kirchner presidency as a government under dispute. The main leader of the party Southerners' Freedom Movement (ex-Free Homeland), which controls Neighborhoods Standing Up, explains that "this is not our government, it is an alliance government ... It is a heterogeneous government with various interests that in some cases are counter-interests ... This is neither a reactionary nor a revolutionary government" (interview 2007). This characterization of the government led Neighborhoods Standing Up to adopt the strategy of occupying as many elective or appointed state posts as possible to push policies in a leftist direction. This gained it places within the Ministry of International Relations (as members of the Social Organizations Committee), Women's National Council, National Youth Directorate, Secretariat-General of the Presidency, and, mainly, the Ministry of Social Development within the following departments: the National Directorate of Critical Assistance, the Subsecretariat for

Homeland (Neighborhoods Standing Up) and PCA (MTL) to leave the FTV in 2001 as well as the CTA in 2002. After 2003, these conflicts were followed by part of the CTA deciding not to support the Kirchner government (headed by Víctor de Gennaro's group, the ATE). In the 2006 elections, the tension between the CTA and the FTV was such that the latter decided for the first time not to present candidates to be part of the governing body of the union.

[13] The pro-government position was a local decision made by Neighborhoods Standing Up as well as a consequence of a shared strategy on the part of SMOs participating in the Bolivarian Circles, a network of Latin American SMOs in support of progressive governments. This network grew out of the attempt by Hugo Chávez's government in Venezuela to produce a left-wing regional alliance. As part of the same transnational community of practice, the MST of Brazil participated in the Bolivarian Circles and supported the Luiz Inácio Lula da Silva government (Chapter 8 for more about the MST).

Training and Popular Organization, and the voluntary programs for literacy and university students (Decree 904/2004; *Página/12* 12/05/2005).[14]

In a similar vein to what happened with the FTV, an area was created to give to Neighborhoods Standing Up to manage. The Subsecretariat of Training and Popular Organization was formed specifically for the incorporation of Neighborhoods Standing Up and was the responsibility of the SMO's national coordinator (first Jorge Ceballos, then Roberto Baigorria) between 2005 and 2008.[15]

The Subsecretariat had a dual role in the second incorporation process. For the government it was part of the apparatus erected in order to develop a territorial network in the province of Buenos Aires to compete with Duhalde (*La Nación* 09/04/2006). This was done through the creation of the Community Integration Centers (CIC), the local offices of the Ministry of Social Development (Perelmiter 2012), one of the few ministries free of *duhaldista* influence from the start of the government. For Neighborhoods Standing Up this represented the chance to access resources to strengthen and expand its organization from Buenos Aires and Córdoba to the national level. Within the Subsecretariat, the *kirchnerista* faction together with Neighborhoods Standing Up built the network of Territorial Promoters for Social Change, local brokers for the dispute of territorial spaces with PJ factions and other Peronist groups.

One of the main difficulties experienced by Neighborhoods Standing Up in government was the permanent rivalry with the technocratic and PJ-controlled areas within the same ministries, secretariats, and subsecretariats. Like the FTV and "Evita" Movement, Neighborhoods Standing Up was faced with duplicate social policy administration that was in competition with the movement. All the *piqueteros* in charge of social areas who were interviewed referred to non-coordinated work with other actors within the same state agency. The *piqueteros* promoted a *basista* conception of social policies, in contrast to the technocratic apolitical vision of some public officials and the clientelistic and paternalistic modus operandi

[14] At the provincial level, Neighborhoods Standing Up occupied subsecretariats in Corrientes, Tucumán, Río Negro, La Rioja, and the city of Buenos Aires. Massetti (2009) offers a detailed analysis of Neighborhoods Standing Up participation in the city of Buenos Aires' Ministry of Human and Social Rights.

[15] When Ceballos left the National Directorate of Critical Assistance in order to take the position of subsecretary, the political operator Berni was designated to replace him at the National Directorate. The National Directorate was responsible for the discretionary distribution of resources for crisis situations. Political operators have generally occupied secondary posts where there is a relatively large amount of money available for distribution under limited bureaucratic control.

of the PJ and other Peronist groups. In some ways, this was a result of the typical accumulation of state officials that patronage produces. However, this specific duplication of actors in the same area with different public policy ethos was a result of the second wave of incorporation itself, which inserted new actors with different claims and visions into already functioning institutions.

Unlike the FTV, for Neighborhoods Standing Up its participation in government implied demobilization.[16] This strategic decision was made to achieve access to resources and political gains through non-contentious involvement in the public policy process and the political distribution of posts within the coalition. The national coordinator of Neighborhoods Standing Up explained it as follows: "[W]e characterize our participation in government as the result of a shift in stage. We had passed from a stage of resistance – fundamentally of resistance – to a stage for the construction of a new country, becoming part of a government that is building a new country. Thus, this implies a certain degree of demobilization in some areas" (interview 2007).

Only when internal channels were exhausted did Neighborhoods Standing Up turn to protest measures. While part of the governmental coalition, this happened only once, in 2006 against the Ministry of Federal Planning to push for the approval of subsidies for the Neighborhoods Standing Up housing construction cooperatives (*Perfil* 07/06–07/2006). Neighborhoods Standing Up needed to use protest because none of its members was participating in this ministry, as the FTV was more dominant. Finally, in the province of Buenos Aires, Neighborhoods Standing Up could not develop its state colonization strategy because the "Evita" Movement was already occupying all the main areas with a similar strategy. Until 2008, the three main SMOs in government had divided their roles within the state without competing for spaces, although they did not coordinate their efforts for social policies.

The Origins of the "Evita" Movement and Its Participation in Government: The PJ and State Colonization

The "Evita" Movement was created in 2005 from above and from below. The development of this SMO is one of the outcomes of the second wave

[16] The demobilization of Neighborhoods Standing Up was not on the pro-government agenda, as it actively participated in events supported by the government, such as the People's Summit of Mar del Plata in November 2005 (Bidaseca and Rossi 2008).

of incorporation of the popular sectors in Argentina, a process that took place according to a territorialized logic instead of a corporatist one. The "Evita" Movement was the product of Kirchner's goal of building a territorial organization and coordination among non-PJ left-wing Peronists. This decision led to struggles between this Peronist newcomer and the traditional Peronist organizations – mainly the PJ. Concretely, the origins of the "Evita" Movement reach back to 2002, when a sector of the CTD "Aníbal Verón" that was part of the MPR "Quebracho" created the MTD "Evita" in La Plata. The MTD "Evita" expanded its scope toward becoming a multi-sectoral organization when it joined the governmental coalition in 2004 and then formed the "Evita" Movement in 2005.[17]

The strategy of the "Evita" Movement was to become a Peronist *agrupación*. This strategy had two stages: from 2004 to 2007 the SMO participated from outside the PJ and from 2007 to 2008 it did so as a PJ *agrupación*. The decision to become a PJ *agrupación* was related to Kirchner's decision to become head of the PJ and abandon the goal of building a non-PJ center-left Peronist party. Neighborhoods Standing Up and the FTV rejected this decision on the part of Kirchner, and the former ended up leaving the coalition a year later. However, the "Evita" Movement opted to join the party's national council, and its national leader, Emilio Pérsico, was named Secretary of Social Organizations of the PJ.

Its participation in government rested on its interpretation of the post-2001 crisis as the end of the stage of "resistance to neoliberalism," when Kirchner started the "popular revolutionary counteroffensive." For this SMO, the transformation of Argentina until 2003 was terminologically defined within the left-wing Peronist ideological ethos and discourse, which differ from the Marxist left. This interpretation of the period 1991–2003 represents a discursive reproduction of Peronist struggles during the period 1945–76 (cf. James 1988; Baschetti 1997).

The "Evita" Movement also reproduces on a smaller scale the Peronist movement before the de-unionization of the PJ. It is composed of the Women's Movement "Evita," Peronist Youth "Evita," "Jauretche" Movement of Professionals and Businesspeople, the small Union Front, the underdeveloped Agrarian Leagues, and, at the core, the unemployed workers' "Evita" Movement for Jobs and Dignity.

17 The "Evita" Movement includes several other small Peronist MTDs, such as the MTD "Resistir y Vencer" and the Patriotic Movement "December 20," together with some members of the human rights SMO H.I.J.O.S. (Natalucci 2008a: 122).

The emulation of symbols, the rhetoric, and the structure of the "Evita" Movement all find their origins in the stock of legacies of the Peronist movement prior to the PJ de-unionization of the 1990s. The leadership of this SMO had its origins in the lower ranks of the Peronist revolutionary left: a combination of Montoneros from the pre-1976 coup and leaders from the period of democratic reorganization who left the PJ in 1991 (Figure A in Appendix). This is why the "Evita" Movement saw the Kirchner mandate as the third historical stage of Peronism. To its members, the first stage was the emergence of the Peronist movement in 1945, the second was the attempt by left-wing Peronist organizations to gain power in 1973, and the third began in 2003 with Kirchner's reincorporation policies. According to the national coordinator, this new stage would mean that "[t]oday we have the opportunity of allowing new social sectors to enter into politics and advancing toward the transformation of politics" (interview 2007).

The "Evita" Movement focused its strategy of participation in government on the province of Buenos Aires from 2003 to 2007. The national government's aim was to expand the weak *kirchnerista* networks in this province while the SMO's focus was on colonizing the governorship of the province of Buenos Aires. These two goals together led to an agreement with governor Solá that as of 2003 made Pérsico vice chief of Cabinet. With his re-election in 2003, for governor Solá the incorporation of the "Evita" Movement meant the chance to build a territorial base to compete with the provincial PJ power base of Duhalde. For the "Evita" Movement it implied the possibility of building the network it needed and of accessing resources in order to expand the SMO, just as Neighborhoods Standing Up was doing at the national level.

Pérsico was not the only "Evita" Movement representative to participate in the governorship. Using a strategy of state colonization as demonstrated by Neighborhoods Standing Up, the "Evita" Movement occupied as many areas as possible: the Secretariat of Human Rights, Subsecretariat of Socio-Educational Policies, Subsecretariat of Youth, and several other provincial departments in areas related to infrastructure, housing, and employment. Finally, until 2007 the "Evita" Movement presided over the provincial bloc of members of Congress of the *kirchnerista* FpV. Even though the "Evita" Movement occupied the most central position a *piquetero* SMO had ever reached in any governmental office, Pérsico's role in the definition of social policies worked in parallel to what was carried out by the PJ-related and bureaucratic-technocratic officials. This dual command system was similar to what happened with Neighborhoods

Standing Up at the national level. The main difference regarding social policies between the experience of the "Evita" Movement and the FTV and Neighborhoods Standing Up was that Pérsico created a space for autonomous public-policy decision-making. The Council for Social Integration was created within the executive structure of the governorship and coordinated by Pérsico along with the provincial *piquetero* legislators.[18] This council developed social policies within a *basista* approach that led to the application of policies in parallel with those enacted by the Ministry of Human Development and the Ministry of Labor.[19]

Finally, the "Evita" Movement suffered from problems similar to the FTV associated with the relationship with the PJ due to the SMO's lack of a solid organizational structure (a consequence of the novelty of the "Evita" Movement). This also led to some cooptation of members – but not leaders – and a number of internal problems resulting from the sudden integration of several diverse groups into an SMO that grew very quickly (Natalucci 2008a: 135).

FROM OUTSIDE: THE PIQUETEROS' CONTINUED CONTENTION

The SMOs in the *piquetero* movement that remained outside of government followed three different paths. The first path was that taken by the SMOs that adopted their own individual strategies. The MIJD expanded with relative success its witness strategy, combining it with electoral ambitions. The MTR tried, without success, to enrich its repertoire of strategies by including the judicial claim for "substantial citizenship" – understood as social and economic rights. The second path was the redefinition of post-electoral strategies among the SMOs that had opted to put forward a presidential candidate in 2003. While the PO, MST "Teresa Vive," and MTL continued to pursue a multi-sectoral strategy as they had during the Duhalde mandate, important differences emerged among some of them regarding the type of multi-sectoral

[18] The council was made up of the provincial deputies Cristina Álvarez Rodríguez (PJ government- and *piquetero*-allied), Juan José Cantiello (FTV), Laura Berardo (Neighborhoods Standing Up), and the provincial senators Hugo Gómez (FTNyP) and Adela Segarra ("Evita" Movement).

[19] Cf. *Las Organizaciones Sociales y el Estado. Balances y Proyecciones*, document presented by the Council for Social Integration and the vice chief of Cabinet at the governorship of the province of Buenos Aires, October 4, 2007, La Plata.

coalition that was being proposed. The third path was the dissolution process of the CTD "Aníbal Verón." As this process continued, it saw the consolidation of the autonomist-introspective strategy into two different versions and the recovery of a moderate *foquismo* strategy in another SMO.

The Individual Goals of the MTR and MIJD: Judicial Claims for a Substantial Citizenship and Electoral Witness Strategies

The MTR was invited to participate in the governmental coalition through a political operator that had been a PRT-ERP militant and personally knew the MTR *piquetero* leaders (some of them former PRT-ERP too). However, this was not enough for the MTR to accept the invitation. Instead, between 2003 and 2007 the MTR enriched its repertoire of strategies by adopting a strategy of presenting citizenship claims through the judicial system. This was totally new for the *piquetero* movement. This strategy was pursued by presenting a petition to the Supreme Court, in association with the UTD of Mosconi, for the application of universal rights for substantive citizenship. The purpose was to dispute the discourse on reincorporation as presented by the Kirchner government. Because the citizenship rights strategy did not bear fruit, from 2007 onward the MTR returned to its original insurrectional vanguardist repertoire of *basistas focos*. It then merged with CUBa to become MTR-CUBa and continued mobilizing within the BPN and in coalition with several other SMOs until Roberto Martino was jailed in a new case of judicialization against the radical flank of the movement.

The MIJD was also invited to participate in government, and due to its decade-long experience of working with pensioners and retirees it was offered a position in the agency for the administration of retirement funds. The MIJD rejected this invitation and continued with its witness strategy, but also created a political party with electoral ambitions. The MIJD's witness strategy during the Kirchner period entailed the judicialization of protest but was never repressed. The MIJD participated in trade unionist-style protests such as blocking ticket offices at train stations and opening toll barriers on highways (*Página/12* 06/14/2004). The MIJD continued with its witness strategy and gained media attention, which Castells and Pelozo have tried to exploit for electoral purposes since 2007.

The Redefinition of Post-electoral Strategies by the MTL, PO, and MST "Teresa Vive": Multi-sectoral Strategies

Of the SMOs that had challenged Kirchner with their own presidential candidate, only the MTL changed its position vis-à-vis the government. On the one side, the MTL suffered a split into two sectors according to the position toward the Kirchner government. On the other side, the PO and MST "Teresa Vive" maintained their classist electoral front strategy within the BPN and ANTOD.

The split within the MTL happened when a sector of the PCA that later created the Communist Party – Extraordinary Congress (PC-CE) opted for a multi-class popular front strategy as an external ally to the government. The MTL was divided over which position to take, and after a meeting with the president in July 2003 it broke up, just as the PCA did. While the faction under Alberto Ibarra's leadership shared the decision made by the PC-CE, the faction under Carlos "Chile" Huerta was against this decision and shared the view of the rest of the PCA (Ibarra interviewed by Germano 2005: 154; Poli 2007). Ever since, two MTL SMOs have been in existence, sharing some work in the joint cooperatives but not coordinating political actions. The presence in the city of Buenos Aires of a sympathetic government during the tenure of Aníbal Ibarra (FG) (2000–6) and Jorge Telerman (2006–7) would help the MTL to grow in the city (Alcañiz and Scheier 2007).

Unlike the other SMOs, the PO and MST "Teresa Vive" were never invited to participate in government. This is because the political operators knew that the Trotskyist party-family adopts a strategy of electoral participation only in working-class popular fronts. However, the moderate and electoralist tradition of the parties behind these SMOs made informal agreements regarding protest self-restraint and other accords much easier to achieve than with the rest of the *piquetero* movement.

The PO and MST "Teresa Vive" revived their idea of a classist electoral front of employed and unemployed workers. While the MST "Teresa Vive" never grew significantly, the PO was able to build an important territorial grassroots network. The rapid development of the PO during 2002 meant that the post-electoral context implied two things for this SMO. First, after rejecting the claim for unemployment subsidies in 2001, from 2002 onward the PO enriched its repertoire by adding a trade unionist strategy. This meant adding demands for recognition and reincorporation (i.e., the universalization of and increase in subsidies; access to housing, water, and gas; food provision), thus expanding the previously solely political claims of the middle class–based Workers Party. This trade unionist strategy was the result of the integration of the urban poor into the Workers Party through the PO.

Second, the PO continued with its classist electoral front of employed and unemployed laborers with the BPN and ANTOD. While the BPN continued to coordinate protests, the PO's strategy of Morenist entryism led to several confrontations that ended with the expulsion of the PO from the BPN in 2005 and, eventually, the dissolution of the BPN in 2007. The expulsion of the PO was a consequence of three conflicts that highlighted the lack of a common strategy for the reincorporation stage. The first conflict was the result of the PO's non-consultative actions and attempt to push the rest to follow them in a vanguardist model. For example, the PO participated in the middle-class security protests that were organized in 2004 by a coalition of right-wing parties and organizations against the will of their allies in the BPN (Poli 2007: 55). The second conflict emerged as tension increased among some BPN SMOs when the PO attempted to merge the BPN into the ANTOD in order to build a classist popular front. This conflicted with the MTL's decision to return to the CTA in a multi-sectoral popular front. One of the MTL's main leaders refused the classist front because he believed that it introduced the " ... risk of reducing the struggle to a trade unionism of the excluded ... " (Huerta quoted by *Clarín* 07/22/2004). Since that moment, the ANTOD became a PO process that met regularly with no participation from other *piquetero* SMOs. The result was the constitution of a new coordinating body solely for the purpose of mobilization. This alliance, known as the "Piquetero Unity," functioned between 2005 and 2007 and involved almost all the SMOs outside government while also avoiding the PO's quest to dominate this space (**Table 4.3**).

The Dissolution of the CTD "Aníbal Verón": The Consolidation of Autonomism and the Routinization of Moderate *Foquismo*

The CTD "Aníbal Verón" was also invited to join the governmental coalition, but talks with the government failed due to increased divisions among its members, which led to the final dissolution of the CTD "Aníbal Verón." The first meeting with president Kirchner involved all the MTDs who demanded justice for the two killings on Pueyrredón Bridge in 2002. The killers were condemned to life sentences by the courts, but the issue was never resolved politically.

A new division emerged among the MTDs over how to approach the Kirchner mandate. A dispute for control over the MTD sector struck up between the MTDs of Lanús and Florencio Valera after the MPR "Quebracho" decided to create its own CTD. The dispute was over the establishment of a new coordinating body with a centralized organizational model to create a common strategy. The clash signaled the end of the coalition as it prompted the MTDs of Solano, Guernica, Almirante Brown, Allen, and Cipolletti to leave.

In addition to this situation, trust was lost among the MTDs when it was discovered that one of its sectors was conducting negotiations with the government without consulting the rest. To make things even worse, the Ministry of Social Development gave the MTDs funds to use for social programs. This plunged the MTDs into an intense internal struggle over the distribution of the money with no organizational structure to enable the resolution of the dispute or strong institutionalized allies that could channel these resources. The result was the departure of the MTD of Florencio Varela, later renamed MTD "Aníbal Verón."

Compared to the increased access to resources obtained by the *piquetero* social movement sector that was in government, the MTDs were in a less favorable position because their two main allies were not as supportive as they had previously been. Since the death of Bishop Novak, the diocese of Quilmes was less active in its support of the *piqueteros*, and in 2004, the Mothers became an ally of the government and also stopped backing this *piquetero* sector.

The dissolution process of the CTD "Aníbal Verón" showed the effects of the lack of an internal routinized mechanism for coordination when no group, leader, or ideological or strategic perspective dominates due to the multiplicity of legacies. In addition, the absence of a strong and organic external ally – such as a union or party – that could force agreements meant that any decision was always exposed to intense internal disputes. The relative parity of power among the CTD "Aníbal Verón" members meant that each MTD tried to impose on the others its own perspective until trust was totally lost.

This process of atomization of the CTDs and MTDs was reflected in a 2004 report of the Ministry of Human Development of the province of Buenos Aires that identified an annual growth rate of 442.85 percent in the number of *piquetero* SMOs (from 14 to 62) (*La Nación* 03/14/2004). This situation forced governor Solá to expand the distribution of Plan for Buenos Aires Neighborhoods to contain competition for resources among SMOs. As part of this process of division, the CTD "Aníbal Verón" (MPR

"Quebracho") experienced a significant reduction in its territorial diffusion. In 2006, it was present in the city of Buenos Aires and thirteen districts of Greater Buenos Aires.[20] By 2008, it was only present in La Plata and Lanús. This sharp decrease was the consequence of the dissolution of the CTD "Aníbal Verón" but also of the loss of several members who moved to the "Evita" Movement or joined municipal governments.

In parallel with this development, another division emerged among the autonomist MTDs within the CTD "Aníbal Verón." The core dispute was over how to understand autonomism (defined in Chapter 2). The autonomist strategy is rooted in two main influences: the practices of the Zapatistas – and particularly John Holloway's interpretation of Zapatismo – and the assembly movement's experience of horizontal deliberation in Buenos Aires. In its quest for an autonomist strategy, the MTD of Solano left the CTD "Aníbal Verón" in September 2003. The allied MTDs of Guernica (Presidente Perón, Buenos Aires province), Cipolletti, and Allen (Río Negro) followed it. This led them to work with Toni Negri's idea of counter-power and to promote localized actions. For instance, thanks to the brokerage of the Mothers, during 2003–4 the MTDs of Solano, Lanús, and Almirante Brown cultivated four hectares of land for the self-provision of food (Vommaro 2008: 347).

One important new SMO emerged through the reconfiguration process of the autonomist sector of the *piqueteros*. The Popular Front "Darío Santillán" (FPDS) arose in 2004 as a coalition established by the MTD of Lanús with other MTDs, some assemblies of Quilmes, cooperatives, the human rights SMO H.I.J.O.S., and some anarchist groups (Svampa 2005: 232; Poli 2007: 120, n. 19). Though presenting themselves as autonomists, the FPDS had a critical view of the classic left as well as of the Holloway-Negri-inspired autonomist perspective adopted by the MTD of Solano. Like the MTD of Solano, the FPDS favored highly introspective reflective processes, publishing several books, but aimed at a more-than-local approach to the revolutionary transformation of the Argentine state by promoting the transformation of daily social relations.

As argued by Fornillo et al. (2008: 386–87), for the FPDS "the confrontation with the state is expressed both in the struggle *against* the state's unfulfilled promise of the provision of citizenship rights, as well

[20] The districts in Greater Buenos Aires were Florencio Varela, Berazategui, Quilmes, Esteban Echeverría, Ezeiza, Lanús, Malvinas Argentinas, José C. Paz, General Sarmiento, Tigre, Moreno, Almirante Brown, and Lomas de Zamora (Torres 2006: 75).

as the struggle *for* a new type or conception of the state" (italics in original). This project was carried out using a multi-sectoral *basista* strategy. Unlike the MTD of Solano, the FPDS tried to establish links with as many actors as possible and participated in the Inter-union Classist Movement (MIC), an attempt to build a new union.

Finally, the moderate *foquismo* strategy that led to substantial political outcomes during the legitimation stage and the struggles for an insurrectional exit to the 2002 crisis was less effective during Kirchner's government. The MTD "Aníbal Verón" of Florencio Varela, in coordination with the FPDS, would organize a monthly picket on Pueyrredón Bridge to demand justice for the June 2002 killings. This protest evolved from the *foquista* strategy of Pueyrredón Bridge that effectively led to the end of the Duhalde mandate to the development of a routinized action. From September 2002 to September 2004, there was an average of almost three roadblocks on Pueyrredón Bridge per month (my calculation based on *Clarín* 09/20/2004) with no repression neither media attention. The commemorations on the 26th continued, but coordination among former CTD "Aníbal Verón" SMOs was reduced to a minimum. The second wave of incorporation implied a routinization associated with a reduction in the intensity of disruption promoted by protest events related to the struggle for reincorporation. This had historically happened with the labor movement and after 2004 began to happen with the *piquetero* movement.

SOCIAL POLICIES: THE DEFINITION OF MINISTERIAL RESPONSIBILITIES AND THE EMERGENCE OF A PIQUETERO POLICY STRATEGY (MAY 2003–DECEMBER 2007)

With Kirchner's accession to power, the responsibilities between the ministries were again redistributed. However, this was not done according to the predominant logic followed by the previous governments: that of the resolution of a social issue versus the resolution of a political conflict. Instead, during this period it was done on two bases: first, according to the specific claim presented by each SMO (for example, whether it is in the area of housing, land, food, employment, etc.); and, second, according to an inside/outside the government coalition rationale. For the second wave of incorporation this would imply the *piqueteros*' participation in the decision-making process for general social policy. Consequently, this would simultaneously mean the end of the national dispute over responsibility for the *piquetero* policy domain.

In this period, the Kirchner government ended the distribution of PJJHD subsidies and defined institutional tasks related to the "*piquetero* question." Even though responsibility for all unemployment programs and subsidies continued to remain with the Secretariat of Employment, following the sanctioning of Decree 1506 in 2004, an innovation was introduced into the *piquetero* policy domain. For the first time ever since the emergence of the "*piquetero* question," this decree established a clear distribution of roles for this policy domain between the Ministry of Labor and the Ministry of Social Development. This would confirm the Ministry of Labor's responsibility over the distribution of subsidies as exclusive. In addition, the Ministry of Social Development was assigned responsibility for the remaining social policies related to the *piquetero* policy domain (the territorial claims for access to water, health, etc.), except for the subsidies to help unemployed people needing training to re-enter the labor market. Only a third ministry, the new, Keynesian-style Ministry of Federal Planning, would be directly involved in the *piquetero* policy domain, and this was mainly for housing construction and legalizing occupied land. In historical terms, the gradual institutionalization of the new "social question" that emerged during the recognition stage of this dispute over responsibility for the *piquetero* policy domain was concluded with the sanctioning of Decree 1506, which formalized territorial reincorporation.

The Kirchner government simultaneously took two predominant approaches to the distribution of unemployment subsidies: first, the informal distribution of subsidies and resources by political operators as instruments for political negotiation and for the resolution of concrete conflictual situations; and second, the distribution of increasingly formalized PEC subsidies by the Secretariat of Employment to individuals during periods of unemployment.

Territorial reincorporation would not take place in an equal manner at the national and subnational levels. At the national level the process would mean an increase in participation in official spaces for the allied *piquetero* social movement sector and the simplification of bureaucratic procedures for access to subsidies for the whole movement. On the other hand, in the province of Buenos Aires the pre-reincorporation logic would be preserved. This meant funds from the Plan for Buenos Aires Neighborhoods were mostly allocated on a discretionary basis as a response to disruptive acts carried out by the *piqueteros*. The distribution of Plan for Buenos Aires Neighborhoods would therefore follow an opposing logic to that of the national distribution of PEC subsidies.

While nationally there would be an increase in subsidies to allied SMOs to the detriment of the SMOs in opposition, in Buenos Aires the distribution would favor those in opposition, and in particular the PO, followed by the MTD "Aníbal Verón," the FPDS, the CCC, MST "Teresa Vive," and the MTR-CUBa. This was due to both intra-movement dynamics and favorable vertical political opportunities. First, sustained mobilization of the *piqueteros* at the provincial level was ensured by the atomization and competition among small SMOs that resulted from the internal divisions in the CTD "Aníbal Verón" and MTR. Second, the multi-level division among PJ factions between Kirchner and Solá in the province of Buenos Aires increased the governor's urgency for responding to protests. In addition, in 2003 the Solá governorship would upgrade the Secretariat of Labor to a ministry, and a year later, the province would emulate the national executive and create a Ministry of Human Development (Torres 2006: 125, n. 2).

In other words, between the national and provincial governments there was a vertically unsynchronized process of reincorporation. While there was increased institutionalization and routinization at the national level, at the provincial level an informal pattern was preserved. Under the guidance of Metón, the political operators maintained control over the Ministry of Human Development's daily interactions with the *piqueteros*. Moreover, in contrast to the national level, in the province of Buenos Aires unemployment subsidies were the responsibility of the Ministry of Human Development.

In the city of Buenos Aires the situation was different. Though Ibarra was not a Peronist politician, he was allied with Kirchner because Ibarra's government was based on the ill-fated FG. For the MTL, the city of Buenos Aires presented a very positive environment as the presence of an allied government allowed for the local consolidation of this group. No other SMO would benefit as much as the MTL, although the leaders of the Southerners' Freedom Movement and Neighborhoods Standing Up became, respectively, the subsecretary of public administration (Humberto Tumini) and the director of social economy (Alberto Vivanco) within the city government in 2007 (*La Nación* 03/07/2007; Massetti 2009).

At the municipal level, each district followed its own path, but the crucial municipalities emulated the national level. In La Matanza, the FTV and Neighborhoods Standing Up became part of the local government. While the CCC and the FTV maintained their alliance with the municipal government, Neighborhoods Standing Up reproduced its state colonization strategy and participated in the Secretariat of Youth until 2007. In Florencio Varela, reincorporation was expressed as the other side of the coin: after the failure of the local Councils, the intransigent MTR and its allies would be increasingly marginalized from processes for resource allocation.

As part of the Kirchner government's pursuit of a territorial base independent from Duhalde, social policies on *piquetero* issues were directly channeled to the *piquetero* SMOs without municipal participation. Until 2008, all the Greater Buenos Aires municipalities lost the role they had enjoyed with the PJJHD as the main centers for the distribution of resources. The most emblematic case in this regard was the housing construction program Plan for Local Development and Social Economy "Let's Get to Work" (*Manos a la Obra*) that led to the creation of *piquetero* cooperatives for the self-construction of housing by the unemployed within their own *piquetero* SMO (*Página/12* 08/14/2003). This program promoted a massive Keynesian-style housing construction policy that engaged almost all the movement (mainly Neighborhoods Standing Up, PO, MTL, FTV, CCC, MIJD, MTR, and MTD "Aníbal Verón"). Of all the *piqueteros*, the most emblematic case is that of the OB "Tupac Amaru" in Jujuy, which built even more houses than did the province (Battezzati 2012).

Public Policy Resignification: *Basista* Empowerment

The second incorporation implies the expansion of the actors and views involved in the production of social policies. The *piquetero* movement's access to the ministries crucial for the development of reincorporation policies produced a resignification of certain social policies. The "Evita" Movement and Neighborhoods Standing Up applied at the provincial and national state levels what I term a "*basista* empowerment" strategy to reincorporation policies. *Basista* empowerment means the syncretic resignification of *basismo* and World Bank and IADB–inspired entrepreneurial social policies of empowerment in the post-neoliberal context by left-wing and national-populist SMOs.[21] In the words of the general secretary of the

[21] Regarding the World Bank and IADB idea of "empowerment" and its limitations, Casaburi and Tussie (2000: 25–28) have argued that: "While in the level of the ideas the discourse rests on concepts of popular participation and 'empowerment,' the practice would seem to be more related to the search of the satisfaction of the client like a private company" (cf. also Rabotnikof et al. 2000: 53–54).

youth branch of the "Evita" Movement, who was also the subsecretary of youth within the provincial government of Buenos Aires (2003–7):

> The popular organization determines the possibility for participants' appropriation of public policy decisions and of the allocation of resources. And this generates a much more solid relationship of public policy [with the beneficiaries] that makes this process more difficult to reverse. When a person in a cooperative builds fifty houses, how can you tell him that he no longer has his job? On the other hand, when the houses are built by a company, the company just submits another tender to the state. This does not produce a relationship of power in which the active participants are the people. We call this social policy as Evita [Perón] called it: "the organized popular force," "the popular power" (interview 2007).

In this statement we can see how a *piquetero* public official understands a policy that the World Bank had adapted from *basismo* in the early 1990s to explain the actor's present social policy aim of the territorial reorganization of the popular sectors. Repertoires of strategies are not ideologies; they are flexible tools for action that get enriched from multiple sources that modify their content and meaning as they are used and learned from. Thus, the diffusion of strategies can also be a result of a process of resignification – where the original strategy is taken up by another group with different political goals and inserted within a different set of legacies.

In other words, resignification meant that a policy originally formulated in the 1970s and 1980s by the Latin American *basista* left as a source of territorial organization of the popular sectors was incorporated in the 1990s into the language of an actor that was the *basista* left's ideological opposite (for historical analyses: Orlansky 1998; Prévôt-Schapira 1999). The World Bank and IADB had redefined this policy in a technocratic sense as a justification for the formulation of decentralized local policies to encourage entrepreneurship among the popular sectors. In the 2000s this policy strategy was retaken up by the *basista* actors and resignified using a juxtaposition of both the 1970s–80s and 1990s approaches under a new context characterized by decentralization and neoliberal reforms. *Basista* empowerment is thus a combination of the original *basista* conception of territorial organization of the popular sectors with the addition of the locally focused technocratic entrepreneurship approach of the World Bank and IADB.[22]

[22] Tussie (2000), Barrientos and Santibáñez (2009), and Colina et al. (2009) offer excellent analyses of the application of the empowerment ethos by the World Bank and IADB to Argentina, Brazil, Chile, Colombia, Mexico, and Peru as well as the related social policies and their partnership relations with social organizations in the period analyzed in this book.

The incorporation of the *piqueteros* meant competition between contradictory public policy goals. As a result, there was rivalry between *basistas* and technocrats in Greater Buenos Aires municipalities, just as Prévôt-Schapira (1999) showed had happened in the 1980s–90s. In the Ministry of Social Development, Neighborhoods Standing Up confronted what Perelmiter (2012) calls the "territorial knowledge" of the SMO volunteers within the ministry clashing with the bureaucrats' understanding of public policies. This was a problem common to the entire movement working within the state, as other *piqueteros* and public officials also confirmed this to me. As pointed out in previous sections, the SMOs in government promoted policies in parallel and often in contradiction with policy developments endorsed by the PJ brokers and state technocrats.

Finally, *basista* empowerment is related to a territorial conception of political representation. For the SMOs not implicated in the governmental public policy process, the idea of territorialism was related to building power for the struggle for social rights at the level that is needed according to the type of claim. One of the national leaders of the MTL explains this: "Popular power means that people have the capacity to know what their rights are, to get organized and be strong enough to tear resources away from the state – at the municipal, provincial or national level – whatever corresponds to them" (interview 2007). However, for those SMOs that were involved in policymaking, territorialism meant representing disincorporated workers: "Our strength is not our state administration capacity. In other words, I believe in the political vision that one represents a social sector, that one really represents someone. Thus, our strength lies in our capacity for representation" ("Evita" Movement national leader interview 2007).

In practice, the in-government *basista* empowerment policy was related to the reuse of the movement's territorial brokers but was guided by a different ethos. This means that for the "Evita" Movement and Neighborhoods Standing Up, a territorial broker that empowers is one that builds the territorial organization of the popular sectors when public policies are applied. Emilio Pérsico, the provincial vice chief of Cabinet and main leader of the "Evita" Movement, explains it as follows:

> What should the difference be between a "neoliberal broker" – from the left or the right – and a "revolutionary broker"? The difference is that the "revolutionary broker" has to attempt to empower the people. This means giving power to the popular sectors. What does it mean to give them power? It means giving them power as Perón said: to give them power here [touches his stomach], in their house, in their pocket ... money in their pocket. This is a process of political accumulation ... (interview 2007).

The "Evita" Movement attempted this strategy at the provincial level with the Council for Social Integration.

For Neighborhoods Standing Up the empowering of territorial brokers was not justified within a Peronist ideology but as part of a national-populist ideology inspired by Hugo Chávez owing to their continental participation within the Bolivarian Circles. Neighborhoods Standing Up tried it through its direct involvement in the CICs, the territorial offices of the Ministry of Social Development (Perelmiter 2012).

In brief, the *basista* empowerment strategy for policymaking is related to the neoliberal redefinition of citizenship that is a revival of one of the traditional liberal conceptions of citizenship and other novel ideas coming from *basismo*. As Dagnino (2003: 8) argues concerning neoliberal citizenship: "First, they reduce the collective meaning of the social movements' redefinition of citizenship to a strictly individualistic understanding of it. Second, they establish an attractive connection between citizenship and the market. Being a citizen comes to mean individual integration into the market as a consumer and as a producer." All these legacies together compound the logic underlying the predominant social policies of the second wave of incorporation: to encourage the entrepreneurship of organized popular sectors in social programs for their reincorporation into wage-earning society.

THE 2007 ELECTIONS: THE CRUCIAL DISPUTE BETWEEN THE PJ AND THE PIQUETEROS

Néstor Kirchner ended his mandate with an unemployment rate of 8.5 percent (October 2007), just one national strike in April 2007 (which was not related to wage demands),[23] and an increasingly demobilized *piquetero* movement. After the setbacks of 2004–5, the social movement sector in opposition was unable to organize another relevant protest until the end of Kirchner's presidency (*Página/12* 12/11/2005; **Figure 3.1**).

Cristina Fernández de Kirchner won the elections with 45.29 percent of the vote, putting her government in a much better position than her husband's previous mandate. This was not expressed through more posts for the *piqueteros* – indeed, their number remained roughly the same. Simultaneously, Néstor Kirchner became the PJ party president and increased his reliance on the PJ mayors' territorial network. This

[23] The 2007 strike was to denounce the assassination of a schoolteacher by the provincial police during a strike in Neuquén.

decision redefined Neighborhoods Standing Up interpretation of the political context. While the FTV continued to characterize the Fernández de Kirchner mandate as a "government under dispute," Neighborhoods Standing Up believed it had been defeated by the PJ in the internal struggle. Between September 2007 and December 2008 Neighborhoods Standing Up progressively abandoned the coalition.[24] The "Evita" Movement and the FTNyP quickly filled the positions left vacant by Neighborhoods Standing Up. Moreover, the "Evita" Movement in particular opted for a strategy opposite to that of Neighborhoods Standing Up: it became a PJ *agrupación* and Pérsico joined the national council of the PJ after Kirchner became the party's president.

At the same time, the FTV expanded its control over executive posts with Alicia Sánchez heading up the Commission for Nursery Schools, part of the Secretariat of Childhood, Adolescence and Family (Ministry of Social Development), while it kept the Subsecretariat of Lands for Social Habitat (Pascolini).

Cristina Fernández de Kirchner maintained the Secretariat-General of the Presidency as the *piquetero* collegiate body but with a different membership. The representatives for the FTV (D'Elía), FTNyP (Oscar Torres), "Evita" Movement (Diego Lovera), and Neighborhoods Standing Up (Néstor Moccia until December 2008) continued to participate. To them were added representatives from the youth and student organization La Cámpora (Rogelio Iparraguirre) and the student and *piquetero* SMO Movement for Popular Unity (MUP) "May 29" (Juan Carlos Cibelli). This arrangement worked until the March–July 2008 rural lockout that would undermine the government's power and alter the configuration of the *piquetero* movement.

At the level of the province of Buenos Aires, the 2007 election to the governorship of former Kirchner vice president Daniel Scioli (FpV–PJ) reduced *piquetero* participation to a minimum. The differences between the Kirchners and Scioli meant that the multi-level dispute among various PJ factions continued. While Scioli tried to establish a clean break from *kirchnerismo*, Kirchner was able to impose Balestrini as vice governor and controlled two ministries in alliance with some "Evita" Movement and

[24] To track this gradual change in Neighborhoods Standing Up's interpretation of the Kirchner mandate one can look at the differences between two of Humberto Tumini's editorials in their newspaper *Patria Grande* (issues 10, 11/18/2006, and 23, 02/17/2008).

ex-FTV members.[25] As a counterbalance, Scioli did not renew Pérsico's role and dissolved the Council for Social Integration created by the "Evita" Movement leader. The province maintained a less formalized relationship with the *piquetero* movement and reinstated the role of political operators such as Metón (officially as director of regions) and an ex-FTV member who was placed in charge of the distribution of Plan for Buenos Aires Neighborhoods. Finally, the "Evita" Movement was able to maintain some influence, albeit limited, over the provincial government through Cristina Álvarez Rodríguez, the Minister of Infrastructure.

Municipally, some contradictory results emerged. In La Matanza, Balestrini maintained his control of the territory as the PJ's provincial president and elected vice governor. This meant that *piqueteros* Ceballos and D'Elía could not get Kirchner's support to stand as mayoral candidates in La Matanza. Simultaneously, some positive results were obtained for the *piqueteros* with the election of Francisco Gutiérrez as mayor of Quilmes (Social Pole–FpV) – an ally of the FTV.

The First *Piqueteros* in the National Congress

The 2007 legislative elections were crucial for the second incorporation with its expansion of the number of legitimate actors in the electoral arena. It led to the election of the first *piquetero* representatives to the National Congress and increased the number of provincial and local legislative posts occupied by figures from the movement. Neighborhoods Standing Up was the SMO in government that gained the most from the legislative election. It built two different alliances: one with Kirchner and the Grandmothers of the Plaza de Mayo in order to obtain a member of Congress representing Buenos Aires and another representing Córdoba with Luis Juez, the mayor of Córdoba city who was in opposition to Kirchner. The FTV did not manage to elect national legislators, but it did gain four Buenos Aires provincial senators and a provincial deputy.

The *piqueteros*' access to legislative seats was not limited to members of the coalition in government; it was also achieved by *piqueteros* in the

[25] As part of the Kirchner-Scioli multi-level dispute, there was a two-day occupation of the provincial Ministry of Human Development in the first weeks of the Scioli governorship. This action was carried out by the small MUP "May 29" and was interpreted by some *piqueteros* and journalists as an attempt by Kirchner to limit Scioli's independence (*Clarín* 12/19–20/2007).

opposition. The MIJD, as part of a coalition of the assembly movement, some Evangelical Church ministers, and informal street workers, presented its main leaders as candidates. The *piquetero* SMOs linked to the two main Trotskyist parties addressed the elections in contrasting ways. While the national leader of the PO was the main candidate of the Workers Party, the MST "Teresa Vive" supported a ticket with no *piquetero* representatives in the Socialist Workers Movement (MST) party. However, these parties all had similar outcomes: the national electoral results were disappointing (MIJD: 0.26 percent; Workers Party: 0.56 percent; MST: 0.64 percent). Still, the PO achieved a relatively good result in Salta and elected some provincial legislators there. Finally, the MTD of La Juanita allied itself with the centrist party CC-ARI and managed to elect its main leader Héctor "Toty" Flores as a member of Congress.

THE END OF THE SECOND WAVE OF INCORPORATION: THE RURAL LOCKOUT (MARCH–JULY 2008)

Just one year after the start of Fernández de Kirchner's mandate, a decision made by the government to finance second incorporation placed at risk the whole process as such. A five-month rural lockout against increased taxation on soy and sunflower exports temporarily undermined the government's power and strongly altered the relationship among sectors of the *piquetero* movement. The importance of the rural lockout for the second incorporation process stems from the economic centrality of agriculture exports for Argentina's balance of trade.[26] The possibility of transferring a larger proportion of the revenues produced by this economic sector to social policies was crucial for the long-term sustainability of the second wave of incorporation.

The immediate radicalization of the conflict was a clear signal of the structural importance of the massive transfer of resources that this tax modification would mean if enforced. On March 11, 2008, the new Minister of the Economy launched a redesign of the taxation system on commodities exports in order to increase state revenues and control food inflation (Ministerial Resolution 125/08). Rural associations contested this decision, as it would mean a huge decrease in their exorbitant profits

[26] In 2008, eight out of the ten main exporting goods of Argentina were agriculture-based, followed by the automobile industry, oil, and gas (ECLAC, http://estadisticas.cepal.org/sisgen/ConsultaIntegrada.asp?idIndicador=1941&idioma=e, viewed October 17, 2015).

in a period of worldwide growth in the price of commodities. A coalition of all the rural associations[27] called for a lockout of agricultural production on March 13, which twelve days later expanded to an undetermined length of time. The radicalization of the lockout, which began to result in the scarcity of certain products in supermarkets, prompted president Fernández de Kirchner to give a televised speech on March 25 rejecting the protest and the coalition's demands. The response to this speech came that very evening, with *cacerolazos* in small and mid-sized cities that were dependent on agribusiness production and in the traditional upper-middle-class neighborhoods of the cities of Córdoba, Buenos Aires, Tucumán, and Santa Fe (*Crítica de la Argentina* 03/26/2008). These events involved the participation of the center-right party Republican Proposal (PRO) and the centrist CC-ARI, which was allied with the MTD of La Juanita. That same evening, after the *cacerolazos* arrived at the Plaza de Mayo, FTV, "Evita" Movement, Neighborhoods Standing Up, and FTNyP leaders gathered in the same square with a clear purpose: "Tonight we mobilize to confront the pro-coup sector that is seeking to overthrow the popular government led by president Cristina Kirchner" (FTV communiqué quoted by *La Nación* 03/26/2008). While the sectors promoting the lockout were accused of attempting to destabilize the government, those supporting the government were accused of being authoritarian.

On March 27 the president organized a rally for her supporters and gave a speech in which she stood by the tax resolution as a source of income distribution. The same day more *cacerolazos* took place in upper-middle-class districts of Buenos Aires in repudiation of her speech. On March 28 the PO, MST "Teresa Vive," CCC, CTD "Aníbal Verón" (MPR "Quebracho"), MTD "Aníbal Verón," FPDS, and some of the left-wing parties organized a march rejecting the rural lockout as well as the governmental tax resolution (*Clarín* 03/29/2008).

The movement was divided into three strategic positions during the lockout protests. While the CCC, MIJD, MTD of La Juanita, and MST "Teresa Vive" supported the rural lockout, the FTV, "Evita" Movement, MTL (PCA sector), and Neighborhoods Standing Up (to a lesser extent) supported the government. The third stance was taken by the PO, MTR-CUBa, MTD "Aníbal Verón," CTD "Aníbal Verón" (MPR "Quebracho"),

[27] The coalition was composed of the organizations for the traditional large landowners, the medium-sized producers, and the rural cooperatives as well as the CTA-affiliated small landowners' federation.

and FPDS, whose position was against both the rural associations and the government.

The cycle of increased mobilization continued. In the city of Buenos Aires a massive pro-government demonstration was organized on April 1 by PJ mayors, the CGT, the CTA, the entire human rights movement, and the in-government *piquetero* movement sector, among others (*Página/12* 04/02/2008). On April 2 in Gualeguaychú (Entre Ríos, a large producer of crops) an assembly of rural associations agreed to temporarily halt the lockout for a month in an attempt to re-open negotiations with the government. On April 23 the Minister of the Economy resigned as a result of this conflict. Nevertheless, on May 7 the lockout was restarted because the agribusiness organizations rejected the reform measures of Resolution 125/08 that decreased taxes for small and medium producers but retained the proposed increase in taxation for the rest (*Clarín* 05/08/2008). During May, Neighborhoods Standing Up, the FTV, and the "Evita" Movement organized pickets and marches against supermarkets, shopping centers, and large food distributors to call for an end to inflationary speculation on commodities (*Clarín* 05/08/2008). Soon after, part of the MTL increased its active support for the government.

The *piqueteros* in government scarcely coordinated their actions during the lockout conflict. The Secretariat-General of the Presidency barely managed to plan common actions among its members. Contentious actions were organized in the heat of the moment, with the FTV being the most active. With its gradual departure from government, Neighborhoods Standing Up supported these actions without enthusiasm. The decision made by Kirchner to become the PJ president had changed Neighborhoods Standing Up's strategic position vis-à-vis the Fernández de Kirchner mandate.

The pro-government demonstrations reopened the decade-long struggle between *piqueteros* and PJ mayors over territory. During the April 1 march, mayors and *piqueteros* clashed over the use of space in the Plaza de Mayo – a reduced-scale representation of their fight to be recognized as the coalition's territorial source of power. Since the nature of the second incorporation is territorial instead of corporatist, the emergence of disincorporated workers as an organized force implied a permanent challenge to the PJ's source of power.

On May 20 the second lockout ended, but negotiations failed again, and on May 25 in Rosario (Santa Fe, the largest city in the Pampas) around 250,000 people participated in a protest in support of the lockout (*La Nación* 05/26/2008), which then was restarted. The government again reformed the tax resolution, and on June 6 the lockout ended again, only for it to restart just nine days later. In La Matanza the CCC, MTD of La Juanita, and MIJD separately organized protests in favor of the lockout (*NCO* 06/13/2008), and pickets on national highways were coordinated by rural organizations (*Crítica de la Argentina* 06/15/2008). Contention was so intense during the lockout that the rural associations produced the highest number of pickets since 1996 (**Figure 3.1**).

In the province of Entre Ríos, one of the epicenters of the lockout, the CCC and the CTA-related Argentine Agrarian Federation (FAA) had built strong links during the environmental protests of 2005. For several years local politicians, the CCC, the FAA, and quite a few other organizations had coordinated a recurring picket on one of the main international bridges that connects Argentina with Uruguay. The increased use of pickets by the FAA and rural organizations were a result of the modularity of this type of protest, which has been incorporated into the standard Argentine repertoire of contention. The specific diffusion of pickets from the *piqueteros* to the FAA was also a result of the CCC providing capacity-building to the leaders of the FAA of Entre Ríos. This did not mean that the CCC was a crucial actor in the rural lockout, but through its role as a secondary mobilizing actor, it had enriched the repertoire of strategies of the FAA. The strategic explanation for this choice by the CCC is that since the end of its participation in the Duhalde-Kirchner agreement, this SMO returned to its 2001 insurrectional multi-class front strategy with the right. Since that time, the CCC had aimed to create a new national *pueblada*, as illustrated by the headline in its April 2008 newspaper: "In the Agrarian Pickets Is Brewing the *Argentinazo*."

The president decided, in a last desperate move, to send to parliament a bill legitimizing the tax resolution. Rural organizations claimed a different law in the name of federalism and the respect for regional economies. The MIJD and the CCC each independently set up encampments in the square in front of the National Congress to reject the proposed bill. The MIJD continued with its electoral witness strategy, deploying the encampment and other protest actions as a way of profiting from the conflict in terms of self-promotion. Finally, the Mothers also set up an encampment but in support of the law.

In an extremely polarized situation that mirrored the Peronist versus anti-Peronist divisions of the period 1945–73, two massive protests were organized on July 15 to separately press for the approval or rejection of

Tras el masivo acto de los partidarios de las retenciones móviles en Congreso, el oficialismo confía en conseguir la aprobación de la ley. En la plaza confluyeron sindicatos, movimientos sociales, intendentes del conurbano con sectores ciudadanos independientes

TODOS UNIDOS TRIUNFAREMOS

2 Manifestaciones, por J. M. Pasquini Durán

3 Los dos actos, por Mario Wainfeld

4 El acto de los invisibles, por Luis Bruschtein

17 La ventana. Escriben: Analía Eliades y Roberto Follari

Página/12

40 Pantallas, por Rodrigo Fresán

10 Dos marchas, dos vidas, por Alejandra Dandan

8 Del otro lado del Zoológico, por Marta Dillon

PRECIOS

TODOS UNIDOS TRIUNFAREMOS

Tras el masivo acto de los enemigos de las retenciones en Palermo, los empresarios del campo confían en que el Senado rechace la ley. En Avenida del Libertador confluyeron los ruralistas y casi toda la oposición, incluidos los gremialistas de Barrionuevo, con vecinos de la ciudad, sobre todo de ese barrio

FIGURE 6.1 Front Page of the National Newspaper *Página/12*: "United We Shall Triumph" (07/16/2008)

the law. While the coalition favoring the lockout held a massive rally in front of the headquarters of the traditional large landowners' organization, the Argentina Rural Society (SRA), the pro-government coalition held an important but less impressive rally in front of parliament (both shown in **Figure 6.1**). At the pro-government protest the same organizations that participated in the April 1 protest could be found. However, the lockout coalition grew with the participation of the *duhaldista, saadista*, and *menemista* factions of the PJ, the non-*kirchnerista* CGT sector, CC-ARI Coalition, PRO, MST "Teresa Vive," MTD of La Juanita, MIJD, and the CCC (*Clarín* 07/16/2008). After an extended parliamentary debate and a vote that was tied, the vice president, in clear disagreement with the president's position, rejected the law with his deciding vote. The next day the tax resolution was annulled, and this severely undermined the possibilities of sustaining in the long term the expansion of the second incorporation.

CONCLUSION

This chapter studied the expansion, consolidation, and end of the territorial reincorporation phase. The reincorporation period went through two attempts. The first was Duhalde's government *state reincorporation* analyzed in Chapter 5. The second attempt during Kirchner's mandate demonstrated itself to be more effective: *party territorial reincorporation.*

Party territorial reincorporation was associated with an increased formalization of the interactions between state institutions and SMOs. It was also achieved a clear definition of ministerial responsibilities for the *piquetero* policy domain, ending a dispute between the social development and labor agencies that had begun in 1998. An outcome of the incorporation of new actors and perspectives to the state was that social policies were reformulated, producing syncretism and tensions between competing policymaking ethoses amid technocrats, traditional Peronists, and *piqueteros*.

The reincorporation stage featured very high levels of contention during 2002. These later gradually decreased, though this did not mean that the movement had become passive. The repertoire of strategies was substantially altered as a result of the partial incorporation of the *piquetero* movement in the governing coalition. This change did not produce a reformulation of the predominant repertoire of contention – it continued to be the same as it had since the inclusion of pickets/roadblocks in 1996. However, the repertoire of strategies was expanded with multiple strategies for intervening inside the state. This chapter concentrated on the different strategies adopted by the SMOs that were incorporated into the governing coalition in comparison with those that had rejected this option.

The rural lockout of 2008 represented a breakpoint for the second wave of incorporation in Argentina. Even though the Fernández de Kirchner government continued and was even re-elected in 2011, the second incorporation phase entered into financial difficulties since the lockout. As we could see, the second incorporation was a period of crucial transformations for Argentina, and the *piquetero* movement was a central actor on some of these changes. The next chapter will evaluate the aftermath of second incorporation and the outcomes of the struggle of the *piqueteros* for reincorporation.

7

The Aftermath of Second Incorporation: Between Continuity and Change (2009–15)

> "So, politically, what happened? The *piquetero* organizations started to be considered as a political player within the political arena. Until that moment we were not a political subject: we were just *piquetero* organizations that made a mess."
>
> – former FTV leader and state broker in the Ministry of Human Development, province of Buenos Aires (interview 2008)

The 2008 rural lockout had major consequences for the second incorporation in Argentina. Due to the enormous political and economic costs for the government of its defeat, the process reached a stalemate that signaled the end of the second wave of incorporation. However, several changes took place in Argentina with the struggle for reincorporation. The *piqueteros*, in their bid to reduce the distance between the popular sectors and the state and wage-earning society, pushed for transformations in the political economy and political culture of Argentina. In this chapter, I evaluate the institutional changes produced, which claims were eventually translated into policies, and the impact of the *piquetero* movement on the political culture of Argentina.

THE RELATIONSHIP BETWEEN THE STATE AND THE POPULAR SECTORS

At the core of reincorporation is the redefinition of the relationships between state institutions and the organized popular sectors, creating new channels and logics for political participation. The period of reincorporation went hand in hand with an increasing formalization of the interaction between state institutions and SMOs. Since 2009, the activities of the collegiate body of *piqueteros* in the Secretariat-General of the Presidency came to an end. The reasons given were the marginal results achieved and the increased power conferred to the PJ sector of the coalition to the detriment of the *piquetero* SMOs. As part of a process of augmented institutionalization, this informal arrangement within the Secretariat-General was replaced in March 2009 with the Subsecretariat of Relationships with Civil Society under Edgardo Depetri (FTNyP).[1]

However, as this formalization was never total, the bond between state institutions and the *piquetero* movement was forged through formal and informal channels. The pattern of interaction rested upon a foundation that was aptly described in the following way by one of the informal state brokers in the General-Secretariat: "The root of the problem always lies in the harmonization of the network of vested interests; there is a relationship based on interests" (interview 2008). Whether formal or informal, this relationship operated through personal agreements and divisions that more often than not were of an unofficial nature and applicable only to localized areas or districts, something characterized by this same state broker as "a nonpublic institutionality that exists." The concept of repertoire of strategies and its applicability to public, semipublic, and private arenas proved very useful for analyzing the relational characteristics of the bond between the *piquetero* movement and state institutions.

During the struggle for reincorporation, a double logic was dynamically built into the relationship between the state and the *piqueteros*. First, the evolution of public policy on the issue of unemployment was significant. When relations between the movement and the state revolved around a claim for an issue that is subject to a precise public policy domain (such as housing construction or food provision), the link was through the state department responsible for that policy. The second element was the tension around territorial governability-disruption. When relations between the movement and the state grew out of a dispute for territorial control and/or tension between governability and disruption, the link was through certain PJ factions or the FREPASO party during the De la Rúa government or the divisions among the municipal, provincial, and national governments.

[1] In October 2010, this Subsecretariat would be dissolved after Néstor Kirchner suddenly passed away and Depetri needed to replace him as national deputy because he was the substitute legislator.

In theoretical terms, the first element is that of the constitution, as a result of *piquetero* protests, of a new *piquetero* policy domain according to specific formal divisions and procedures of the state. The second element is based on the territorialization of politics and the tension between the organized disruption instigated by social movements and the state's attempts to control that disruption.

For the first element, divisions within the state apparatus, such as disputes between ministries, have been crucial. For the second element, there have been two possible types of elite divisions: within the same scale of action (for example, among party members within the same governmental coalition) and through multiple scales of action (for example, between mayors and the governor in a province). In analyzing this, as I showed, we should consider political opportunities as consisting of a horizontal component (intra-scalar elite divisions) and a vertical component (inter-scalar elite divisions).

THE CREATION OF A NEW POLICY DOMAIN

The emergence of the *piquetero* movement marked a new claim and a new type of actor in Argentina's history. This dual novelty made very apparent the total lack of public policies regarding unemployment and, in particular, that there were no state agencies with responsibility for the issue. This had also been evident in the first labor and social rights conflicts related to the so-called "social question" in the late nineteenth century. As a result of this, during Menem's second presidency the emergence of the first *piquetero* protests prompted a dispute between different ministries over responsibility for the "*piquetero* social question" that was only to be resolved during Kirchner's mandate. This process is synthesized in **Table 7.1**.

During the period of 2009–14, in the aftermath of reincorporation, there was sustained conflict for the distribution of resources under the Program for Social Income with Work "Argentina Works" (*Argentina Trabaja*) of the Ministry of Social Development because it favored PJ mayors to the detriment of the entire *piquetero* movement (*La Nación* 02/11/2014). The "Argentina Works" program meant that the policy domain was partially returned to the network of PJ mayors for the first time since 2003. As such, the "Argentina Works" was a reversal of the "Let's Get to Work" (*Manos a la Obra*) policy predominantly developed alongside the *piquetero* movement. In any case, the relationship between movement and government was less organic – preserving the movement's secondary role as well

TABLE 7.1 *Evolution of the* Piquetero *Policy Domain, 1999–2009*

Period	Main Changes
April 1998–December 1999	Diffusion of the *piquetero* movement causing the definition of the "unemployment question" as a national policy domain with no clear state and society interlocutors.
December 1999–December 2001	Struggle for the definition of the political or social character of the policy domain and the state department responsible for the policy domain between the Ministries of Labor and Social Development.
December 2001	Enlargement of the number of legitimate actors dealing with unemployment policies when Rodríguez Saá becomes the first president to meet with the *piqueteros* to define social policies.
January 2002–May 2003	Expansion of the restricted policy domain to a general policy constituency when unemployment policies reach almost two million persons and when the distribution of subsidies is no longer under the exclusive control of mayors and governors.
May 2003–December 2009	Participation in/exclusion from the decision-making process for the general social policy with the incorporation of half of the *piquetero* movement in the Ministries of Social Development and Federal Planning, but not in the Ministry of Labor.

Source: Reproduced from Rossi (2015a).

as a higher degree of autonomy – than the one achieved by trade unions during the first incorporation (cf. Collier and Collier 1991: 331–50).

THE NEO-DEVELOPMENTAL MODEL

We still need to ask whether reincorporation is associated with greater welfare. While every process of incorporation is related to the identification of a new "social question" and the production of social policies to respond to the most mobilized actors' claims, it is not necessarily associated with an increase in the welfare of the popular sectors. However, the (re)incorporation of the popular sectors into the socio-political arena should mean a redefinition of some of the dimensions of the previous order. In this sense, the aftermath of second incorporation featured the application of a neo-developmental model, meaning heterodox economic policies that mixed neoclassical principles with statist ones in pragmatic and selective interventions in the market economy, policies that replaced the neoliberal approach that previously had dominated (Levitsky and Roberts 2011: 21; Cornia 2014).

Although incorporation does not necessarily bring about an increase in welfare, in Argentina certain socioeconomic figures improved during this second wave. Unemployment fell to 6.3 percent in 2015, and a considerable number of new social policies were enacted, covering 1,990,735 unemployed people in 2003. The economy was partially reindustrialized (the value added by the manufacturing sectors represented 24.08 percent of the GDP in 2004) (Tables 7.2 and 7.3 and Figure 7.1). New institutions, such as the Ministry of Social Development and the Ministry of Federal Planning, were created to make Keynesian-style policies more robust.

There was also a growth in public expenditure for social policies. Between 1997 and 2008 (that is, the emergence of the movement and the end of the partial incorporation of the *piqueteros*) it can be seen that public expenditure was expanded in a gradual, but sustained, fashion (**Table 7.2**). An even greater increase is seen in the same table between the beginning of neoliberal reforms in 1990 and 2008 at the end of the reincorporation period. Overall, social policies reached unprecedentedly high levels of coverage from 2002 (Barrientos 2014; Keifman and Maurizio 2014). Even though in **Table 7.2** there is no differentiated information about the *piquetero* policy domain, this increase in state social expenditure can be interpreted as an imperfect quantitative proxy for the recognition and legitimation of the "social question" (cf. also **Table 7.1**).

TABLE 7.2 *State Expenditure on Social Policies as a Percentage of the GDP, 1990–2008*

State Level	1990/1991	1997/1998	2000/2001	2007/2008
National	11.3%	10.6%	11.0%	11.8%
All levels	17.9%	18.5%	20.2%	21.9%
Excluding financial state departments	19.1%	20.0%	21.8%	23.6%

Source: Based on data from ECLAC (2010).

TABLE 7.3 *The* Piquetero *Movement Goals and Achievements, 1996–2015*

Degree	Goals (Verbalized or Practiced)	Achievements (Intentional or Unintentional)	Social Movement Organization
General (sought by the whole movement)	Reincorporation of popular sectors into wage-earning society.	• Reduction of unemployment from 18.4 percent in 1995 to 6.3 percent in 2015. • Application of far-reaching social policies on unemployment (reaching 1,990,735 unemployed people in 2003). • Reindustrialization of the economy (manufacturing as value added of the GDP reached 24.08 percent in 2004 and 21.2 percent in 2009).* • Creation of the Ministry of Social Development for the application of inclusive social policies, and the Ministry of Federal Planning for Keynesian-style policies. • Incorporation of *piquetero* SMOs in the governing coalition (2002–15). • Election to the national and some provincial parliaments of *piquetero* representatives as of 2007.	All

(continued)

TABLE 7.3 *(continued)*

Degree	Goals (Verbalized or Practiced)	Achievements (Intentional or Unintentional)	Social Movement Organization
		• Participation of *piquetero* SMOs in hundreds of municipal governments (as mayors, city councilors, and non-elected public officials), mainly in Buenos Aires, Córdoba, Santa Fe, Salta, and Tucumán.	
	End of neoliberalism or capitalism.	Major reformulation of neoliberalism between 2002 and 2015.	All
	Ideological transformation of the popular sectors' political culture.	Resilience of the Peronist popular sectors' political culture. Ideological flexibility of the non-Peronist left.	All, except for "Evita" Movement
	Creation of an alternative to the PJ and CGT territorial network within the popular sectors in Greater Buenos Aires.	Effective dispute of most of the main territorial spaces in urban and suburban politics.	All
	End of PJ clientelism in Greater Buenos Aires.	Continuity with clientelism, though not completely dominated by the PJ in Greater Buenos Aires.	All

(continued)

TABLE 7.3 *(continued)*

Degree	Goals (Verbalized or Practiced)	Achievements (Intentional or Unintentional)	Social Movement Organization
Specific (sought by some SMOs only)	Winning the presidential elections.	Winning of legislative posts as of 2007 and/or participation in the governing coalition as of 2002.	FTV, MST "Teresa Vive," MIJD, MTL, PO, Neighborhoods Standing Up
	Application of a universal basic income.	• From 2002 to 2004, the application of the largest unemployment subsidy program in Latin America (PJJHD). • Since 2010, the distribution of 3,670,000 subsidies to poor people below 18 years of age, covering 70 percent of the underage population living in poverty (Universal Child Allowance for Social Protection).	FTV, MTL, Neighborhoods Standing Up
	Payment of severance pay owing to former YPF workers and jobs in the local petroleum industry.	Implementation of Law 27,133 providing 10 percent of YPF as a participatory propriety program for ex-YPF employees as a severance payment benefit (2015).	UTD of Mosconi

(continued)

TABLE 7.3 *(continued)*

Degree	Goals (Verbalized or Practiced)	Achievements (Intentional or Unintentional)	Social Movement Organization
	Revolutionary or insurrectional regime change.	Deep crisis internal to the regime from 2001 to 2003 and changes in government due to disruptive events in 2001 and 2003.	CCC, CTD "Aníbal Verón" (both), MTR-CUBa, Neighborhoods Standing Up
	Development of an autonomist ideology.	Creation of autonomist projects at the local level.	FPDS, MTD of Solano

* *Note*: Although manufacturing recovered from a level of 16.96 percent in 2001, Argentina was never again to reach the pre-1990 percentages following a regional pattern on deindustrialization (World Bank Database – World Development Indicators and Global Development Finance – 2010).

Sources: several interviews (2007–13); INDEC data 1974–2003: www.indec.gob.ar/nuevaweb/cuadros/4/shempleo1.xls (viewed August 15, 2010); INDEC data 2010: www.indec.mecon.gov.ar/ (viewed June 20, 2011); Reports and Statistics section of the Ministry of Labor, Employment and Social Security: www.trabajo.gov.ar/jefes/infostats/index.asp (viewed June 5, 2010); Report for 2007–9 of the Ministry of Social Development: www.desarrollosocial.gob.ar/Uploads/i1/1.%20Rendimos%20Cuentas.pdf (viewed June 20, 2011); World Bank Database – World Development Indicators and Global Development Finance – 2010: http://data.worldbank.org/indicator/NV.IND.TOTL.ZS/countries/1 W-AR-ZJ?display=graph (viewed June 20, 2011); Neffa (2008); Barrientos and Santibañez (2009); Colina et al. (2009); and Gasparini and Cruces (2010).

In addition, the analysis of the data on inequality shows that the exclusionary pattern that characterized the neoliberal period had changed, indicating the achievement of some degree of socioeconomic inclusion for the popular sectors in Argentina. While in 1999 the Gini index was 0.539, by 2012 it had decreased to 0.475, according to the Economic Commission for Latin America and the Caribbean (ECLAC 2014: 124, table II.A.2).[2] According to the UNDP, Argentina's Human Development Index rose

[2] Other index formulas also show clear reductions in inequality in Argentina when comparing 1999 with 2012: the Theil index shows a change of 0.667 to 0.457 and the Atkinson index ($\varepsilon = 1.5$) one of 0.530 to 0.454 (ECLAC 2014: 124, table II.A.2).

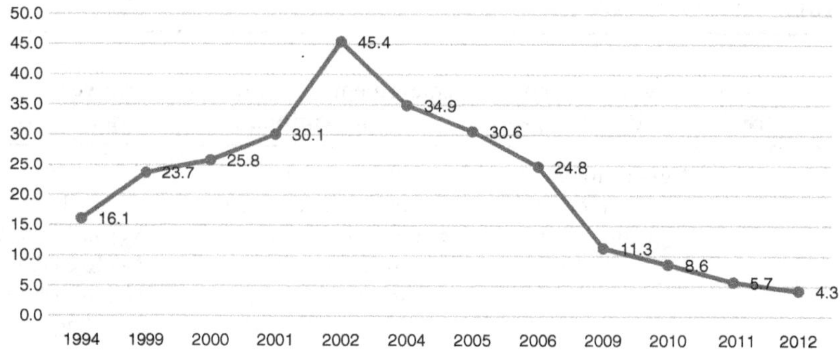

FIGURE 7.1 Changes in Poverty Levels in Buenos Aires Urban and Suburban Areas, 1994–2012
Source: ECLAC – Statistics Division (www.eclac.org, 2015).

from 0.705 in 1990 to 0.836 in 2007 (UNDP 2015: 210, table 2). The fall in inequality was, according to Colina et al. (2009) and Lustig et al. (2012), mostly a result of the application of social policies from 2002, while for Gasparini and Cruces it is the result of a mix of factors: "the recovery from the crisis of 2001–02; realignments after the devaluation of the peso; strong expansion of employment; productive changes after new relative prices; slower technical upgrading; stronger labor institutions and labor policies; and a more extensive safety net" (2010: 127–28).

In **Figure 7.1** the improvement in social conditions can also be measured through changes in the percentage of poor people in urban and suburban areas of Buenos Aires (forming the core of the *piquetero* movement). While almost 20 percent of the population was poor when the first unemployed workers' protest took place in 1996, after a 2002 peak in poverty rates owing to the economic crisis and a 400 percent devaluation of the currency, poverty consistently decreased to 4.3 percent in 2012, its lowest percentage since the beginning of state reforms in the 1990s.

In short, there seems to have emerged after 2003 a combination of factors that began to change the neoliberal socioeconomic structure of the country into a neo-developmental model *without* corporatism. However, there was not enough time for this new model to develop to the point of being able to bring about a reformulation of the production matrix. Among the economic reasons was the world financial crisis that started in 2008, the same year as the rural lockout, making it impossible to increase the taxation of agriculture exports. This led to a trap that has historically been the bane of Argentine growth, whereby the bulk of the resources for (re)incorporation came from commodity exports in a period of decreasing crop prices.

To what degree did the *piquetero* movement contribute to these changes? Obviously, while the movement was not the only factor in producing these transformations, it is evident that they would not have been possible without the *piqueteros*' struggle for reincorporation. A recurrent point that this book has made is that the agency of actors conditions the way history develops. In other words: if the *piqueteros* would not have existed, the political, socioeconomic, and cultural changes that Argentina experienced since the 1990s would not have been the ones here described.

During incorporation periods, the project of an elite does not usually coincide with that of the mobilized actors from below. In the same way as unions during the first incorporation did not always share the elites' aims and procedures, the *piqueteros* had a set of goals that were not necessarily linked to those of the elites. Even though to distinguish between what a movement aims to achieve and what it has actually achieved is always a difficult task (Giugni 1998b; Bosi et al. 2016), it is clear that the *piqueteros* did have a set of goals that were partially reached by 2015. Reincorporation was the *piquetero* movement's most important aim; however, it was not the only one. The schematization of its goals, in **Table 7.3**, shows that all the goals that were general to the movement have been realized, except for one – the end of capitalism (although neoliberalism was greatly reformulated). However, only some of the specific goals of the SMOs were achieved.

THE PIQUETEROS' REORGANIZATION INSIDE AND OUTSIDE THE STATE

Has the *piquetero* movement disappeared as a result of its increasing demobilization? Not at all; rather, the sector of the *piquetero* movement that had entered into the governing coalition adopted a non-contentious repertoire of strategies as a result of its incorporation. The rest of the movement, remaining in an outsider position, adopted an electoral strategy or entered into a phase of introspective reevaluation that is typical of social movements after intensive cycles of protest (Melucci 1989; Tarrow

1989). However, demobilization was never total, with pickets intermittently reemerging since 2009.[3]

For the *piquetero* movement there were some important conjunctural changes in its alliances as a result of the 2008 lockout and Kirchner's decision to become PJ president. In December 2008, Neighborhoods Standing Up made its departure from the Fernández de Kirchner coalition official (*Página/12* 12/06/2008). The abandonment of the Neighborhoods Standing Up state colonization strategy meant that the "Evita" Movement and the FTNyP stepped into most of the national and provincial positions Neighborhoods Standing Up had vacated.

The majoritarian sector of the MTD "Aníbal Verón," under Juan Cruz Daffunchio's leadership, made its support of the government official in 2007. Even though no MTD "Aníbal Verón" leader occupied a national state position, an immediate consequence of this decision was the split between the original SMO and the MTD "Aníbal Verón" New Space rejecting Daffunchio's decision. The support of the MTD "Aníbal Verón" for the government did not represent an ideological change but rather a desperate act of survival on the part of an SMO under increased risk of dissolution. In 2012, the Daffunchio sector of the MTD "Aníbal Verón" integrated into the Fernández de Kirchner coalition in full with the election of its leader as city councilor in Florencio Varela.

The remainder of the CTD "Aníbal Verón" reduced mobilization but participated in a multi-sectoral coordination effort under the CTA's leadership. The CTD "Aníbal Verón" (MPR "Quebracho"), MTR-CUBa, MTD "Aníbal Verón" New Space, FPDS, MST "Teresa Vive," "Tupaj Katari" Movement, and MTL all participated in the Social Constituent (*Crítica de la Argentina* 08/30/2008). This was a project led by the CTA sector opposed to the national government to constitute a center-left party-movement emulating the left in Brazil.[4] Later, the CCC, Neighborhoods Standing Up, the MST "Teresa Vive," and the FPDS

[3] c.f. Figure 3.1 and data from the *Centro de Estudios para la Nueva Mayoría* updated until 2015.

[4] The Social Constituent gathered around 30,000 people in Jujuy on October 24 and 25, 2008. For its main documents and a detailed description of the process, cf. *Agencia de Noticias CTA*: www.agenciacta.org.ar/article9583.html, www.ctaenmovimiento.org.ar/spip.php?article242, and *CTA en Movimiento*: www.ctaenmovimiento.org.ar/spip.php?article242 (both 2008 websites viewed January 15, 2009).

continued their alliance with this anti-government CTA sector, organizing strikes, mobilizations, and pickets in March, June, October, and November 2012.

The FTV maintained its detachment from the CTA and created the Popular Movements Union with a series of small *piqueteros* and student SMOs (Octobers, Second Centenary, Popular Movement "October 8" and Popular Movement "July 26"), allied with the MTD "Aníbal Verón" and with the support of a part of the national cabinet (*Perfil* 12/20/2008). These efforts finally led to the creation in 2011 of a small party-movement called Latin American Integration for Social Expression Movement (MILES).

In Salta, the UTD of Mosconi continued with its provincial-enclave trade-unionist path. In Jujuy the CCC's detachment from its former leader Santillán widened as he expressed his disagreement with the CCC's support of the rural lockout (*Veintitrés* 05/28/2008). Within these processes of provincialization, the OB "Tupac Amaru" grew systematically as the CTA and the national government backed it.

Finally, the PO and the FPDS each suffered a small group splintering off in support of Fernández de Kirchner with the creation – respectively – of the Revolutionary Piquetero Tendency and the FPDS National Current.

In subsequent legislative elections, the *piqueteros* increased their presence in the Chamber of Deputies. This expansion included some in-government *piqueteros* but mostly favored those in the opposition. In 2011, the MTD of La Juanita lost the CC-ARI's internal election and could not stand for re-election. However, the MIJD achieved its first national representative with its own Socialists of the MIJD party in a very pragmatic alliance with Rodríguez Saá. Finally, Neighborhoods Standing Up exited the coalition in government but was still able to re-elect one of its members. In 2013, the number of *piqueteros* in parliament grew once again with the election of two members of the government-allied "Evita" Movement. The main leader of the PO was also elected as national legislator in a coalition of Trotskyist parties. For the Workers Party, this election was a great success, electing subnational legislators in several provinces and even becoming the second largest party in Salta (19.1 percent). Although all these results gradually expanded the number of *piqueteros* in the Chamber of Deputies, they have never become relevant actors within the National Congress.

TERRITORIAL CLASH WITHOUT POLITICAL CULTURE CHANGE

The second incorporation involved the first massive mobilization of the poor by non-Peronist political organizations since 1945. However, the factionalization of the movement, together with the resilience of Peronist popular culture, prevented the *piquetero* movement from producing a change in political culture among the popular sectors.

The emergence of the *piquetero* movement was partially enabled by a reduction in the capacity of PJ territorial brokers to provide the popular sectors with basic resources for survival. This left some leeway for those groups with previous *basista* experience to encourage the organization of the disincorporated popular sectors. However, territorial reincorporation had its limits. The predominant Peronist popular culture proved itself more resistant to authoritarian regimes, neoliberal reforms, and PJ and CGT transformations than any other Peronist entity. This is why even though most of the grassroots members of the *piqueteros* have cut or weakened their ties with the PJ and the CGT, the majority still consider themselves Peronists. As a leader of the MTR argues, the Peronist " ... sentimental identity, that is that issue of struggle for dignity, exploded in 2000–2001. [As a result,] There was an important group ... of Peronist territorial brokers that broke away and came over to us. [But] doesn't mean that they adopted our ideology. What they adopted was our politics" (interview 2007). In other words, while the first wave of incorporation was associated to the emergence of Peronist ideology and popular culture, the second wave represented the first instance of massive left-wing defiance of Peronist hegemony in the daily lives of the popular sectors.

The second incorporation process signaled the end of the hegemonic role of the PJ and CGT as interlocutors for the demands of the popular sectors. The union system was liberalized and the *piqueteros* emerged as the main actor challenging the PJ's near-total hegemony through the territory. The effects of reincorporation on both the disincorporated and the incorporated workers were equally significant: for the incorporated workers, the union system became moderately pluralist and more autonomous from the PJ; for the reincorporated workers, a non-corporatist path materialized in the newly created institutions. As can be seen in the whole process of struggle for reincorporation, a greater plurality in the number of organizations disputing the territory produced competition for constituencies and resources between PJ mayors and *piquetero* SMOs.

The seventeen national *piquetero* SMOs are a response to the multiplicity of PJ factions governing locally with different styles and links to the movement, which has reinforced the left's historical tendency to factionalize. However, the fragmentation of the movement means not that there has been more than one reincorporation process, but rather that the process of second incorporation has followed a fragmented, territorial logic, as distinct from the corporatist, centralized logic of first incorporation.

At the same time, *piqueteros* suffered once more from the institutional limitations put in place by the actors of the first incorporation. Despite all the efforts of the "Evita" Movement, there was no access to the Ministry of Labor for disincorporated workers' organizations as unions retained the control of this department. Instead of obtaining the post he requested within the Ministry of Labor, in 2008 Pérsico was appointed Subsecretary for the Commercialization of the Social Economy within the Ministry of Social Development, which was more open to the *piqueteros* (Decree 2286/08).[5] In other words, the *piquetero* movement could never transcend the secondary role that was offered to it; nor could it overcome the informal, territorialized, individualized, and horizontally and vertically uncoordinated interactive logic of the PJ and traditional Peronists that has predominated.

Therefore, even though there was no ideological conversion of the popular sectors during the struggle for reincorporation, many have reorganized outside of the Peronist group of organizations. What the process of struggle for reincorporation shows is that the Argentine Maoists, Trotskyists, and Marxist-Leninists, in becoming more flexible with their stock of legacies and adopting syncretic visions of social transformation, gave them the capacity to mobilize as never before. Overall, the second incorporation had less to do with a novel ideological conversion of a social segment than with innovation in the group that has been mobilizing the popular sectors. In part this explains why even though *piquetero* leaders have adopted a revolutionary discourse, their struggle has been focused on the reincorporation of the popular sectors into wage-earning society.

[5] In 2009 Pérsico had to resign from the Subsecretariat due to a legal scandal involving his son (*La Nación* 10/21/2009).

CONCLUSION

In the aftermath of second incorporation, data shows an improvement in the social conditions of the popular sectors. The increased investment in social policies was gradual but steady until it reached a stalemate in 2009. From a long-term historical perspective, the stalling of this process was the first sign of the end of the second incorporation of the popular sectors in the socio-political arena in Argentina.

The struggle for reincorporation from below was crucial for many of these achievements. The elite's reaction to the *piqueteros*' "social question" through gradual transformations is what reincorporated the popular sectors and produced a policy domain to deal with this new actor and claim for Argentina. However, no substantial change was produced in the political culture of the mostly Peronist constituency mobilized by the *piqueteros*.

In terms of the political economy of second incorporation, the process was carried out through the institution of a neo-developmental model. However, the impossibility of transferring to the internal market an increased share of the revenues produced by agriculture led to a fundamental trap for Argentine growth: much of the resource base for reincorporation came from commodity exports. That is why the defeat of the government in the rural lockout of 2008 was a turning point for second incorporation in Argentina.

PART III

COMPARISONS AND CONCLUSIONS

8

Social Movements and the Struggle to Reshape the Socio-political Arena in Bolivia and Brazil

The second wave of incorporation is not a process that is unique to Argentina. Latin America went through a cycle of continental mobilization against neoliberal disincorporation from the mid-1990s to the first decade of the 2000s (Schefner et al. 2006; Almeida 2007; Silva 2009). These mobilizations were not limited to resistance struggles, as the reshaped socio-political arenas in several countries following the reincorporation of urban or rural popular sectors show. Although this book has focused on Argentina, arguments concerning struggles for reincorporation are equally valid elsewhere. Therefore, this book poses a critical question for comparative research: has the shift from corporatist to territorial incorporation appeared in other Latin American countries that have also experienced neoliberal reforms? This chapter aims to show that the conceptualization of the second wave of incorporation, reincorporation movements, and struggles could be applied to other countries, like Bolivia, Brazil, Ecuador, and Venezuela (while necessarily bearing in mind each country's specificities).[1]

In those countries where reincorporation has taken place, we can expect considerable variation in the path taken and the pace of change. Concerning the territorialization of second incorporation, four main sources of variation can be identified. The first is the degree in which the locus of politics was reshaped during the last authoritarian military regime in each country, whereby democratization was carried out from the local to the national level or just at the national level. The second is the effect

[1] A collective comparative effort following the approach of this book is presented in Silva and Rossi (forthcoming).

wrought by neoliberalism on the mainstream parties claiming to represent the popular sectors. The third is the ways in which the trade union system was modeled by the corporatist period and remodeled by neoliberalism. The fourth is how the first incorporation of the popular sectors (urban or rural) was produced and how its achievements were eroded by military regimes and neoliberalism.

Affecting all these variations cross-nationally is the timing of each particular process. Second incorporation may be a relatively quick process, as it was in urban Argentina after 2002; a long process, brought on by several regime breakdowns, as in Bolivia and Ecuador; or even the result of gradual change over the course of a protracted struggle, as in Brazil. Moreover, reincorporation processes generally involve the remobilization of popular sectors in struggles that are not merely defensive, but this does not necessarily imply the ideological transformation of the popular sectors' political culture. In Argentina, Peronism has continued to supply the main political ethos of the popular sectors, while Katarism has emerged as relevant for Bolivian coca growers' movements (Yashar 2005: 24–25; Lucero 2008: 81–88).

However, all these cases share certain traits. Each of these struggles against disincorporation was contentious and included a reincorporation movement (e.g., indigenous and coca growers in Bolivia, indigenous people in Ecuador, landless peasants in Brazil). The second incorporation was conducted in territorial terms, with the emergence of institutions such as the citizenship territories in Brazil (Delgado and Leite 2011), the missions in Venezuela (Ellner 2008), and the partly formalized articulation of movement claims through the General-Secretariat of the Presidency in Bolivia and Brazil. Also, new institutions, such as social councils, were created to deal with multiple non-corporatist claims in Brazil (Doctor 2007), and even constitutional reforms in Bolivia, Ecuador, and Venezuela were implemented to deal with the new "social question" (Lupien 2011).

In this chapter I examine the different paths to second incorporation of Bolivia and Brazil.[2] While Brazil was characterized by gradual metamorphosis, Bolivia's sharper rupture and change defined it. In Brazil second

[2] While for the Bolivian case I use secondary sources, for Brazil I rely on information gathered during three-month fieldwork in 2008 in Brasília, Goiânia, Presidente Prudente, and São Paulo, where I conducted my own forty-five in-depth interviews (with national ministries, national and subnational parliamentarians, union leaders, bishops and priests, informal party and state brokers, and human rights activists) and analyzed around 1,000 alternative and mass-media articles.

incorporation featured a mix of neo-corporatist and territorial features, and in Bolivia it was mostly territorial. Beyond their differences, these countries are introduced in this chapter because indigenous and coca growers' movements in Bolivia and the movement of landless peasants in Brazil represented the other main reincorporation movements of Latin America.

BOLIVIA'S FIRST INCORPORATION OF THE POPULAR SECTORS

In Bolivia, a territorial-ethnic cleavage emerged with the territorialization of politics that followed the collapse of ISI and its corporatist arrangements (Yashar 2005: ch. 3; Lucero 2008: 8–13). During the ISI era in the Andean region, the rural popular sectors were first incorporated as "peasants" and in most cases were unionized. Land reforms in Bolivia (1953) were carried out with the aim of weakening the rural oligarchy and incorporating the popular sectors into a corporatist system. Particularly in the highlands, the first incorporation neglected ethnic distinctions by emphasizing a class or "worker" identity (Yashar 2005: 59–65; Gotkowitz 2007: 282–87).

The first incorporation in Bolivia came about over the course of the 1952 revolution. Over the period 1953–64, the Revolutionary Nationalist Movement (MNR) promoted the corporatist incorporation of the rural popular sectors as members of peasant federations, following a course similar to that of the tin miners, who were organized into trade unions (Klein 2003: 209–22; Yashar 2005: 155–63). The enclave logic of the mining industry and the emergence of the strongest Trotskyist party in Latin America had shaped a radical trade unionist repertoire that lasted until 1953 (Angell 1998: 106–7). As a result, the first incorporation in Bolivia was carried out by a labor-mobilizing party and was limited to a large-scale extractive industry and the rural highland areas, where 90 percent of the indigenous population lived (Roberts 2002: 15; Yashar 2005: 155–63). At its peak, union density reached 24.8 percent of the working population, similar to Peru (Roberts 2002: 15, table 1). This issue is crucial for understanding why, during reincorporation struggles, the legacy of trade unionism has been stronger in Bolivia than in most other Andean countries, though lower than in Argentina.

The Demise of Corporatist Politics and Neoliberal Disincorporation

In Bolivia, the 1964 coup marked the end of first incorporation. An authoritarian populist military regime implemented what was known as the Military-Peasant Anti-Communist Pact as a way of dissolving the rural corporatist arrangements established by the MNR (Albó 1987; Yashar 2005: 163). In the 1960s and 1970s, this process provoked the emergence of a territorial movement that attempted to organize disincorporated peasants on the basis of their "indigenous" identity.

Following re-democratization, Bolivia applied one of the most far-reaching neoliberal reform programs in the region, which decimated the powerful unions in the mining sector and increased precariat among peasants. From 1985 to 1993, in response to 25,000 percent hyperinflation and a debt that reached 70 percent of exports, the democratic government promoted intensive neoliberal reforms that included a 17 percent decrease in the number of public sector employees and, in the first two years of reforms, a drop in the number of mine workers from 30,000 to 7,000 (Silva 2009: 106–7). In rural areas, the corporatist policies for peasants were mostly dismantled, including price controls and subsidies (Yashar 2005: 182).

As in Argentina, corporatist unions saw their power curtailed, and territorial movements of disincorporated popular sectors entered the political scene as the main contentious actors in the struggle for reincorporation. In Bolivia tin-mining unions were gradually debilitated, while the indigenous Katarist movement increased its power and expanded its influence, mainly among peasant unions (Healy and Paulson 2000; Klein 2003: ch. 9).[3] While in Argentina the *piqueteros* became more dynamic than the unions, in Bolivia coca growers and indigenous emerged as the strongest national actors after the neoliberal state reforms. In Argentina the popular sectors' suburban neighborhoods and shantytowns became the spaces for organizing, and in Bolivia the rural Incan *ayllus* have re-emerged as the locus of political organization for the indigenous-based National Council of Ayllus and Markas of Qullasuyu (CONAMAQ) (Fontana 2014: 6–7). This has implied a territorial cleavage, since ethnicity and place are intimately related, and the *ayllus* are based on kinship

[3] Emerging in the 1970s among urban Aymaras, Katarism was named after the 1700s indigenous leader Tupaj Katari. Katarism believes that indigenous Bolivians suffer a double oppression: ethnically as indigenous peoples and as a class due to their subaltern condition (Marxist influence). However, as happens with Peronism, it is a big movement that includes a multiplicity of SMOs, NGOs, unions, parties, and intellectuals. Katarism is as divided as Peronism, including moderates (that even supported neoliberalism in the 1990s) and radicals (some of them revolutionaries during the 1970s). Beyond their differences, the actors that consider themselves Katarists share a basic idea: that Bolivia is multicultural and plurilingual and must transcend the colonial legacies inherited from Spain (Albó 1987; Sanjinés 2004: ch. 4).

and geographical ties (Lucero 2008: 10). In 1994 municipal decentralization favored coca growers in their first attempts to participate in politics through elections (Van Cott 2005: 85–86).

Since the neoliberal state reforms, corporatist arrangements and most labor-based parties, like the MNR, have collapsed or undergone deep transformation. Neoliberalism has also altered the identification of popular sectors within party systems in the Andean region, spurred by the drive to recover identities that were not associated with the ISI model but are rather rooted, both territorially and ethnically, in the Andes (Van Cott 2005: ch. 3; Yashar 2005: 163–90; Lucero 2008). As part of these transformations, a new party, the Movement for Socialism (MAS), emerged from the joint efforts of leftist groups, trade unions, and the coca growers' movement to represent popular sector claims (Fontana 2013: 32).

Neoliberal reforms were associated with state decentralization. In Argentina decentralization provincialized the party system, making Greater Buenos Aires the main locus of contentious politics. In Bolivia, electoral reforms favored local and rural groups, such as indigenous communities. "In addition, the indigenous movement since the 1980s has been organized into territorially defined provincial-level federations that correspond to the country's provincial electoral districts" (Van Cott 2005: 119).

In general terms, the process of transition from the corporatist incorporation of peasants to indigenous territorial reincorporation in Bolivia was prompted by "state [neoliberal] reforms that left Indians politically marginalized as individual citizens, disempowered as corporatist peasant actors, and confronted with a challenge to local, political, and material autonomy. Their capacity to organize as Indians, however, has depended on transcommunity networks previously constructed by the state and other social actors" (Yashar 1998: 31) and on the support of external actors, particularly cooperation agencies and NGOs (Andolina et al. 2009). Similarly, in Argentina dense networks of activists and the heritage of first incorporation institutions played a crucial role in the constitution of the *piquetero* movement.

From Recognition of the "Indigenous Social Question" to the Legitimation of Reincorporation Movements

The subsequent struggles for the recognition of indigenous identities, institutions, territories, and socioeconomic claims were intimately related to collective resistance to the social consequences of neoliberal reforms.

However, as a Mayan leader put it, the struggle of indigenous movements in Latin America has mainly been for incorporation into the polity: "We do not want protection but effective participation in society and the economy" (*Latin American Weekly Reports*, 02/02/1993, cited by Yashar 2005: 291). In Bolivia, resistance dynamics have evolved into reincorporation struggles with the emergence of an "indigenous social question." In other words, organized popular sectors in Bolivia have been struggling for both the defeat of neoliberalism and the reshaping of the socio-political arena through the incorporation of the former corporatist "peasants" who had been excluded as a result of the recommodification of the rural economy as present-day "indigenous."

The socioeconomic recognition of the "indigenous question," though, was much harder to achieve than its political dimension, requiring greater contention than did the legitimation of the indigenous SMOs. While the indigenous movement has been organized into two main SMOs (the CONAMAQ and the Confederation of Indigenous Peoples of Eastern Bolivia, CIDOB), the peasants and coca growers' movement is split into six Federations of Coca Growers of the Cochabamba Valley and the Unified Confederation of Rural Workers of Bolivia (CSUTCB) (Lucero 2008: 11; Fontana 2014).

In 1998 the Gonzalo Sánchez de Lozada government recognized and legitimated the less contentious social movement sector of the indigenous movement. The same government that was promoting the second generation of neoliberal reforms won the election with a formula that included the first indigenous vice president.

As was the case in Argentina, recognition of a new "social question" is concomitant with state innovation in both social and repressive policies. In Bolivia, the government expanded repressive activities aimed at the more contentious coca growers' movement: in 1994 it instituted the Zero Coca eradication policy with US military support, and in 1995 it launched a 180-day state of siege against coca growers, teachers' unions, and other organizations, sparking intensive social unrest (Silva 2009: 120–22). Peasants perceived the intensive eradication efforts against coca cultivation during the 1990s as an additional source of impoverishment for those who had joined the coca growers' movement. Since the 1985 process of disincorporation in the mining industry an important migration of labor to more profitable coca production has occurred, involving around 7 percent of the economically active population (Yashar 2005: 184–85).

Parallel to this and following the indigenous march of 1992, Sánchez de Lozada created the Subsecretariat of Ethnic Affairs in 1993 and in 1995 granted constitutional recognition of the multicultural character of Bolivia (Yashar 2005: 215–16). From that point on, many state structures became, "among other things, terrains of struggle that [have been] reflect[ing] changing Indian-state relations" (Lucero 2008: 13).[4]

Second incorporation implies the re-routinization of rules and procedures. Based on institutions and practices belonging to the previous context, the second incorporation process is, on the movement side, built using a predominant repertoire of strategies. In Bolivia, this happened within a mostly Katarist repertoire of strategies, inherited from the sedimentation of a stock of legacies. As part of a process of resignification, the coca growers' movement adopted the indigenous Katarist repertoire of the 1970s and 1980s in its struggle against the neoliberal disincorporation of the countryside during the 1990s and 2000s. Katarism implied enriching the repertoire of strategies of peasant unions by combining class discourse with ethnic and cultural rights without rejecting European organizational forms (Healy and Paulson 2000). Coca growers gradually came to control the CSUTCB and effectively defended their production as part of the traditions and culture of the Aymara and Quechua peoples. Furthermore, the coca growers "did not necessarily emerge to defend local autonomy – as with the Kataristas before them – but soon came to talk about the needs and rights of their indigenous communities in the Chapare [in Cochabamba]. As such, they self-consciously started to talk about ethnicity as a key component of their political struggle" (Yashar 2005: 187). This process – in combination with the ethnic-based struggle for indigenous rights of CIDOB and CONAMAQ – gradually won recognition of the socioeconomic dimension of the "indigenous question."

As in Argentina, in order to mobilize territorially, left-wing leaders – coming from unions, guerrillas, CBCs, and political parties – had to go through a loosening of their class-based notions, introducing a territorial discourse that appealed to the popular sectors. With a Katarist strategy of ethnic-based territorial mobilization, the coca growers' movement promoted participation in party politics because electoral reforms favored the running of candidates by local communities. Under a left-wing banner, the movement was nationally legitimated in 1997 with the election of its first four deputies (Van Cott 2005: 86, table 3.4).

[4] In the relatively unpopulated Amazon region, indigenous struggles were mostly defensive against state penetration in a region weakly governed by state institutions (Yashar 2005: 187–88).

Within Argentina, the struggle for reincorporation has unfolded differently in Buenos Aires from the rest of the country. In Bolivia the dynamics have also evolved differently, depending on the geographical space of contention. The main difference has been between those spaces with a high density of popular sectors and the peripheral areas. In Bolivia the distinction has been between the Aymara and Quechua peoples (88 percent of the indigenous population according to the 2012 census) in the highlands and the other smaller indigenous groups in the Amazonian lowlands (Lucero 2008: 10, table 1).

The emergence of an indigenous movement and a coca growers' movement in Bolivia, both reincorporation movements that replaced corporatist rural and urban unions that arose during the first incorporation, was prompted by the disincorporation effects of the neoliberal reforms. Consequently, territorial political identities were central to the process. In class-based societies such as Argentina and Brazil, territorial identities have been constructed on the basis of the disincorporated condition of the popular sectors. In Argentina former "workers" have been called "unemployed workers," while in Brazil former "peasants" were termed "landless peasants." In ethnicity-based societies such as Bolivia's, the disincorporated popular sectors were defined by their non-corporatist condition: former "peasants" and "miners" are now "indigenous." As Lucero (2008) correctly asserts regarding Bolivia, this was not a natural process but rather a collective construction involving several actors, such as international NGOs, Protestants, and the Catholic Church as well as the left and unions. In Argentina, the equivalent process of constructing a "*piquetero*" identity did not involve international actors; it was instead closely linked to the reformulation of the left after re-democratization.

THE SECOND INCORPORATION IN BOLIVIA

The intensification of mobilization and economic restraints favored the emergence of post-neoliberal policies. In Bolivia, "Neoliberalism simultaneously provoked the resistance of rural people whose livelihoods were threatened and provided new opportunities for political incorporation through new policies of decentralization and ethno-development" (Lucero 2008: 78). In other words, the consequences of neoliberalism explain the popular sectors' quest for the return of the state as an articulator of social relationships. However, this second incorporation has occurred under conditions that differ from those of the first incorporation and with different sequential timing in each country.

In Bolivia, during the stage running from legitimation to reincorporation, there was an intensification of social unrest brought on by the attempts of popular movements to halt further neoliberal reforms. The first instance of this unrest was the protest against the privatization of the water supply, referred to as the "Water War of Cochabamba," which ended with the Katarist MAS winning seats in the national parliament for the first time. The privatization of local water companies was opposed by a coalition that included the CSUTCB, the Pachakuti Indigenous Movement (MIP), and other SMOs that organized roadblocks, mobilizations, and rallies from January to April 2000. Following severe repressive measures that included a ninety-day state of siege, the privatization law was finally repealed in 2000 (Perrault 2006). In the 2002 parliamentary elections, the MAS received the second-highest proportion of votes (20.94 percent), and Evo Morales, the main leader of the coca growers movement and the MAS, was re-elected as national parliamentarian.

In 2003, the recently re-elected Sánchez de Lozada announced his intention to sell gas to the United States via Chilean ports. This decision triggered a series of mobilizations similar to the resistance in 2000 to the privatization of water companies. In this case, however, the protest was nationalistic in nature: exporting the primary Bolivian commodity at subsidized prices through ports in a disputed territory was for many unacceptable.[5] Over two months, the CSUTCB, the MIP, and other SMOs organized thousands of roadblocks. As part of the general struggle for reincorporation, the so-called "Gas War" had three main consequences: Sánchez de Lozada's resignation in 2003, the introduction in 2004 of a new electoral law ending parties' monopoly of electoral representation, and Morales winning the 2005 presidential election with 53.7 percent of the vote.

The first government of Evo Morales promoted the same kind of neodevelopmental reforms as Néstor Kirchner did in Argentina. His program included the nationalization of crucial industries and services (water, mining, gas, and oil), the promotion of a social policy based on mass access to healthcare and food, and the initiation of political

[5] Although Bolivia lost its access to the Pacific Ocean after giving up land to Chile's Antofagasta region after the War of the Pacific (1879–83), it maintains its claim to these territories.

reincorporation on a territorial basis (Dunkerley 2007; Domingo 2009). One of the main changes in this regard was the 2009 constitutional reform, which integrated indigenous notions of plurinationality (Lupien 2011) in what might lead to a post-liberal democracy (Wolff 2013).

Building the Relationship between Reincorporation Movements and the State

In Bolivia as in Argentina, second incorporation implied the creation of institutions to formally and informally articulate popular sectors' claims in the reincorporation policy domain. Soon after the crises that put an end to the Sánchez de Lozada and De la Rúa governments, reincorporation began changing relationships between state institutions and popular sectors. Bolivian popular movements, for their part, built the MAS, a Katarist left-wing party in a plurinational-populist reincorporation coalition with social movements. The SMOs in the coalition do not respond entirely to the government even though the MAS and its allies sometimes mobilize them.

The relational construction of the reincorporation of poor people's movements in the state during the Morales presidencies, according to Zuazo (2010), went through three phases that moved from relative autonomy from the MAS and the state to gradual participation in a state-led agenda. The first phase involved the coordination of indigenous and peasant SMOs for the constitutional reform of 2007 (Zuazo 2010: 129, n. 8 for a full list of participants). The goal of what was known as the Unity Pact was to coordinate, from outside the MAS, the mobilization in support of the reform and then its final approval by referendum in 2009.

The second phase emerged during the Constitutional Assembly and produced the most enduring vehicle for reincorporation: the National Committee for Change (CONALCAM). The CONALCAM is an institutional structure to coordinate movements, unions, the presidency, and the parliament under Morales' leadership. The CONALCAM aims to put into practice the claim that the MAS has been producing "the government of social movements" as well as to unify actions to resist increasing opposition from the powerful eastern departments (Zuazo 2010: 130–32).[6] The CONALCAM includes around twenty federations and SMOs, in

[6] As was the case in Argentina during the 2008 rural lockout, since 2007 in Bolivia, second incorporation has faced intense resistance on the part of the richest regions against the economic and political costs of reincorporation.

2010 expanding to the subnational level with regional and departmental coordinating bodies.

The new Constitution establishes the neo-corporatist participation of social movements that are of a territorial nature. As a result, the third phase of the reincorporation process is the formalization of the incorporation of movements into the state apparatus through the establishment of the National Mechanism for Participation and Social Control providing opportunities to meet within each ministry according to an agenda established by public officials (Zuazo 2010: 133–34).

Contrary to Argentina, quite a few SMO leaders were able to achieve top-tier positions in Bolivia.[7] The most important has been the new Vice Ministry for the Coordination of Social Movements and Civil Society, given to the National Federation of Mining Cooperatives in 2006. That same year, the other most relevant positions given over to SMOs were the Ministry of Mining to the La Salvadora Mining Cooperative, the Ministry of Economic Development to the Federation of Peasant Women, and the national leaders of the coca growers' movement as Vice Minister of Coca and Integral Development and Vice Minister of Social Defense. Other movements were granted secondary positions in most ministries, such as the neighborhood groups of El Alto in the Ministry of Water and the home workers' federation in the Ministry of Justice. The Ministry of Labor was given to the Bolivian Workers' Union (COB), the first incorporation actor, as in Argentina (Cámara 2008; Tórrez et al. 2013: 173, n. 61). However, also like in Argentina, the role of movements remained subordinate (Tórrez et al. 2013: 173).

The second incorporation in Bolivia has been a territorial process because of the municipalization of politics, the recovery of indigenous-based traditional organizations, and the neoliberal weakening of corporatist unionism. Together these led to the emergence of a new territorialized cleavage for control over land, natural resources, and spaces of power between first incorporation (peasants) and second incorporation (indigenous) actors (Do Alto and Fontana 2013).[8]

[7] In parliament, the electoral success of the MAS also produced the mass inclusion of peasants in the House of Representatives (Zuazo 2009).

[8] This peasant-indigenous cleavage re-emerged with strength in 2011 with the conflict over the construction of a highway through the Isiboro Sécure National Park and Indigenous Territory, which had at its core the tension between the neo-developmental model supported by peasants and the preservation of natural resources prioritized by the indigenous communities (Tórrez et al. 2013: 175).

In the realm of social policies, cash transfer programs like the Juancito Pinto school vouchers and Juana Azurduy bonus for pregnant women and newborns were massively applied to improve social conditions. Some social policies were even developed with the participation of movements, such as the Dignity Rent pension program (Anria and Niedzwiecki 2015). Among other policies was the stimulation of land reform, benefiting 1,043,374 people between 2006 and 2012. In socioeconomic terms, Bolivia improved its Human Development Index, which went from 0.536 in 1990 to 0.662 in 2014; its Gini index also improved from 0.586 in 1999 to 0.471 in 2011, and poverty levels were reduced from 62.1 percent of the population in 1997 to 32.7 percent in 2013 (ECLAC 2014: 124, table II.A.2; ECLAC – Statistics Division 2015; UNDP 2015: 213, table 2). Although these are indirect means of measuring the effectiveness of government policy, they are nevertheless valid as bases for evaluating change.

The – so far open – reincorporation phase in Bolivia is experiencing some key challenges. The alliance between indigenous and peasants has practically finished, with coca growers still supportive of Morales but the indigenous peoples gradually looking toward right-wing allies. And territorialism has increased ethnized socio-political struggles in Bolivia (Do Alto and Fontana 2013).

BRAZIL'S FIRST INCORPORATION OF THE POPULAR SECTORS

A similar pattern can be observed in a society with a low percentage of indigenous people, such as Brazil. Here, the first incorporation took place under corporatist arrangements between 1930 and 1945 under Getúlio Vargas, not altering the unequal economic structure of the country (Cardoso 2010). The first incorporation was more an urban than a rural process for demobilization purposes under an authoritarian regime (Collier and Collier 1991: 185). In such a vast country, incorporation differed in each region. Depending on the degree of industrialization and unionization, incorporation was a massive or a limited process. Of all the states, São Paulo, Rio de Janeiro, and Rio Grande do Sul were where incorporation was mostly achieved (Collier and Collier 1991: 189; French 1992; Welch 1999). In less industrialized states like Pernambuco, first incorporation happened mainly through the sugarcane industry. Even though neither Vargas nor the following government of Juscelino Kubitschek altered the oligarchic rural social structure, a first incorporation of peasants was achieved in parts of Brazil mostly through the

National Confederation of Agricultural Workers (CONTAG), a situation that lasted until the demise of ISI (Maybury-Lewis 1994; Pereira 1997). After incorporation, peasant mobilizations increased with the support of the João Goulart's government, creating the first agrarian reform institutions, until he was expelled in a coup that put an end to incorporation efforts in 1964 (Collier and Collier 1991: 567–68; Fernandes 1998: 42–44;).

The process of disincorporation in Brazil began in the 1980s, bringing unemployment to 7.9 percent in 1981 and increasing impoverishment in the cities. With re-democratization in 1985, a weak relaunching of the ISI model was attempted. During José Sarney's government, a new Constitution in 1988 produced a legal framework for agrarian reform that focused on the social utility of land. However, his government did not change the modernist approach to agrarian reform inherited from the military regime. The strong ISI coalition that was built during the military regime between traditional landowners and industrialists remained powerful enough to block any attempt at implementing land reform (Branford and Rocha 2002: 34). In 1990, the failure of the relaunching of the ISI became apparent when inflation reached 1,000 percent.

The Emergence of the Reincorporation Movement

The landless peasants' movement includes around 110 SMOs (Feliciano 2011: 34–36), but unlike the *piqueteros*, there is a main one: the Rural Landless Workers Movement (MST). It was founded in 1984 out of the coordination of local peasant struggles for land. Inspired by Liberation Theology, the Catholic Church sought to organize peasants for land reform, with much more success than the urban CBCs in Argentina. The subsequent diffusion of land occupations in Southeastern Brazil laid the groundwork for the MST (Wright and Wolford 2003: 30–38). The MST's central claim is land tenure solely for those who cultivate and live on it (Harnecker 2002: 255). This communitarian perspective implied radical, non-capitalist land reform aiming to build a new political and socioeconomic order (Hammond and Rossi 2013). The stock of legacies of the MST and the other landless peasant SMOs is partially similar to the *piqueteros*, including CBCs and *basismo* and CONTAG's trade unionism but also the Peasant Leagues of the 1950s (Navarro 1994: 142–43; Pereira 1997: 165–66; Welch 2009).

Even though the MST emerged before the application of neoliberal reforms, most of the 110 SMOs in the Brazilian countryside appeared between 1994 and 1998 (Fernandes 2000: 257–58, tables 4.10 and 4.11). In a few cases they were the result of local divisions from the MST, but mostly they represented the emulation of the MST's successful formula for popular sectors' struggle for reincorporation in a context of massive and abrupt social exclusion. Overall, the MST has organized the majority of land occupations (Feliciano 2011: 41, graph 8).

Martins (1994: 156) argues that the struggle of the landless peasants' movement is not for agrarian reform but for their "recognition as not only workers, but as persons with the right to be paid for their work ... Peasants, thus, want social changes that lead to their recognition as members of society" (cited in Fernandes 2000: 21). In other words, their goals have been the same as those of the peasants and indigenous people in Bolivia and the *piqueteros* in Argentina: their reincorporation as wage-earners and citizens. Fernandes (1998: 47–48) argues that the growth of rural unrest was a response to the negative impacts of neoliberalism in the urban and rural popular sectors, enacting land occupations as a vehicle for socioeconomic integration. Moreover, Pereira (2003: 49–50) quotes sources that say that in the 1990s around 40 percent of the landless peasants who mobilized for land reform were previously unemployed urban dwellers of rural origin. In Argentina, resistance to neoliberalism and the quest for reincorporation were framed as an urban problem; in Bolivia the problem was as much rural as urban. In Brazil, the problem was framed in rural terms because there was a legal framework inherited from the first incorporation – mainly, the Land Statute of 1964 – that was consolidated with the Constitution of 1988, building a tradition of institutions and actors that made this policy area more favorable for reincorporation struggles than the urban one.

Neoliberal Reforms and the Re-emergence of a "Rural Social Question"

In 1991, president Fernando Collor controlled inflation and initiated the first generation of neoliberal reforms with a series of privatizations. However, Collor could not dismantle the ISI coalition, and his government became isolated as a result of policies that were affecting the middle classes (confiscation of savings), national and international banks (attempts to postpone debt moratoriums), and the traditional economic and political elites (verbally attacking them and trying to exercise autonomy from them). When in 1991 inflation returned and privatizations stalled, his power evaporated.

In 1992, Collor's political isolation, mounting street protests, and the threat of impeachment led him to resign. Vice president Itamar Franco's transitional government was very important for the legalization of the "rural question." The legal framework had not been updated following the Constitution of 1988, and the new articles it contained on agrarian issues had not been regulated. In 1993, Franco named Osvaldo Russo as president of the National Institute for Colonization and Agrarian Reform (INCRA), after consultation with the MST and CONTAG. Russo produced the legal framework that the INCRA needed to receive an annual budget and the legal power to expropriate land.

Franco's mandate demonstrated a relative openness to movements. He met with the MST's national leadership in February 1993, legitimizing the MST as a national political actor (Fernandes and Stédile 1999: 77). With the goal of reducing poverty, Franco implemented a Workers' Party (PT) proposal calling for the first National Council for Food Security, giving responsibility for its organization to the National Commission of Brazilian Bishops (CNBB) (*Correio Braziliense* 09/06/2011). At this meeting, neo-corporatist participation predominated, as several ministries, municipal governments, the Unitary Workers' Union (CUT), CONTAG, CNBB, and other organizations were formal members of this council, while SMOs like the MST were not.

After this interlude, first-generation neoliberal reforms resumed when Fernando Henrique Cardoso became Minister of the Economy. With his Real Plan, inflation was controlled and a new currency established. The plan's success also bolstered Cardoso's electoral ambitions, and he became president in 1994.

The Landless Peasants' Growing Territorial Resistance to Neoliberalism

President Cardoso continued with the privatization process initiated by Collor, and from 1994 to 1999, Brazil underwent the largest wave of denationalization in its history. During this period, unemployment grew – though never to the same extent as in Argentina – to levels double those of the previous two decades. While in 1986 unemployment was at its lowest levels (3.3 percent), under Franco it reached 6 percent (1993) and under Cardoso climbed further to 9.6 percent (1999). Cardoso's policies had the effect of dismantling the ISI model. Among the unintentional consequences of his policies was a reduction in the value of land by 45 percent (on average), economically weakening traditional landowners (Sallum

Jr. 2003: 196). In addition, the pressure from the landless peasants' movement and CONTAG for reincorporation in the rural sector called into question land distribution, one of the pillars of the ISI model in Brazil. During this period, several new organizations emerged emulating the MST. However, in contrast to what was happening in Argentina, the MST maintained its dominant position and avoided the fragmentation that the *piqueteros* suffered.

In 1995, as narrated to me by public officials, the National Council for Food Security was shut down, thus suffering the same fate of all the other neo-corporatist councils. Instead, the family-based cash transfer program Social Protection Network was instituted as the main social policy.

In 1995 and 1996, the expansion of the disruptive power of the landless peasants' movement and higher degrees of sub-national violence ended in two repressive situations that became turning points in the correlation of forces between the MST and the national government. In August 1995, in Corumbiara (Rondônia), at least ten peasants and two policemen were killed in a violent confrontation between rural unions and the police. One year later, in Eldorado dos Carajás (Pará), in another violent confrontation between the MST and the police, nineteen peasants were killed, provoking international condemnation of the Cardoso government's treatment of the "rural social question." The repercussions of these two events were such that for a second time a president of Brazil met with the MST's national leadership (May 1996). In addition, state repression was attenuated, paving the way for the national diffusion of the MST (Ondetti 2008: 150–55).

The "Rural Social Question" as a Reincorporation Policy

From 1996, the national government made several changes aimed at institutionalizing the "rural social question" and reducing levels of social unrest in what became Brazil's most ambitious land reform program, settling 375,453 families by the end of Cardoso's second mandate (Feliciano 2011: 22, graph 4). The program tried to accommodate two competing logics. On the one hand, it applied a model of expropriation based on the 1988 legal framework, a model defended by the landless peasants' movement. On the other hand, in 1998 the government implemented a program of negotiated or market-based land reform by which peasants could purchase land with the help of a flexible loan given by the state. This second model was designed by the World Bank and rejected by movements (Branford and Rocha 2002: 187–90; Navarro 2008: 10–11).

Thus, in Brazil the attempt to resolve the "rural social question" re-emerged as a compensatory policy for disincorporated workers instead of as a massive program of unemployment subsidies as implemented in Argentina. In Brazil, land reform was a result of a dense network of rural organizations struggling for land issues that could mobilize the mass of excluded urban workers, with no equivalent urban reincorporation movements. The pressure of the landless peasants' movement on the government led to the development of what Cardoso's Minister of Agrarian Development Raúl Jungmann called a "sponge" land reform program: "capitalism expels people [from the system], and you sponge it up, capitalism expels again, and you sponge it up" (interview 2008). This means that agrarian reform was carried out to reincorporate the disincorporated *urban and rural* popular sectors when the economic system could not absorb them on its own. During the 1980s to 2000s, those occupying lands were mostly urban unemployed workers (Ondetti 2008: 124).

In 1996, INCRA recovered its autonomy and budget and was moved from the landowner-controlled Ministry of Agriculture to the new Extraordinary Ministry of Land Policy. In the same period, the Cardoso administration passed two crucial laws for facilitating agrarian reform, one establishing the procedure for land expropriation and the other increasing taxation of unproductive land, which rose from 4.5 percent to 20 percent (Pereira 2003: 54). In addition, a Department of Agrarian Conflicts was created for the resolution of contentious events associated with the "rural social question" (Buainain 2008: 96).

Any attempt to address a "social question" includes two facets: the emergence of new social policies and of new policing techniques. The Cardoso administration was under pressure due to an increase in contentious actions organized by the landless peasants' movement. In an attempt to reduce land occupations, the government issued its Interministerial Ordinance (PI) 325 of 1998 establishing a procedure to limit the occupation of INCRA offices by landless peasant SMOs. In 2000, the Provisional Measure (MP) 2027 determined that each piece of land occupied would not be subject to expropriation for two years and, if occupied again, for four years.

THE SECOND INCORPORATION IN BRAZIL

By the time Luiz Inácio Lula da Silva, the first Brazilian president of worker origin, took power, the ISI model had been abandoned and replaced by a liberal-developmental model, the aim of which was "not to rebuild the entrepreneurial national State but to reform the State so that it might push private development and social equality" (Sallum Jr. 2003: 198–99). Cardoso had built a rather technocratic state structure that controlled the policy agenda without social participation. Lula's two mandates were mostly defined by continuity in economic terms. However, in political terms they represented a breaking point through the incorporation of social actors into the socio-political arena. The model of reincorporation initiated under Lula's PT government was a multi-sectoral state model that combined neo-corporatist and territorial dimensions.

Even though the MST, CONTAG, and other SMOs expressed their support for Lula's government, they saw the moderation in Lula's approach as symptomatic of an unwillingness to produce major transformations similar to the ones happening in Bolivia and Venezuela. The PT lacked a clear majority in parliament (though it was the main party, it had less than 20 percent of the Lower Chamber and Senate) and won governorships in only three peripheral states (Acre, Mato Grosso do Sul, and Piauí). As a result, the new government's potential to effect transformation was quite limited (Hunter 2010: 147). Finally, without a major crisis of neoliberalism – as had taken place in Argentina and Bolivia – there was no radical break with the past. For these reasons, the MST interpreted Lula's government as "a government under dispute" between a right-wing sector that would push for the preservation of the neoliberal path initiated by Collor and a left-wing sector that would push for the introduction of a new model of development.

In the years of 2003 and 2004 there was a huge increase in land occupations reflecting growing expectations of agrarian reform, the MST leadership's strategic decision of pushing the government toward the left to produce a rupture with the neoliberal path, and the government's decision not to apply MP2027. However, the government did not respond to this rise in occupations with more expropriations or settlements. In 2005 the government did begin settling more families, but soon after its re-election, settlement again abated, culminating in the lowest numbers of settlements and expropriations up to that time (Ondetti 2008: 201–7).

Under his coalition government, Lula distributed ministries to political parties and organizations according to the legislative, neo-corporatist, and territorial support they offered for his mandate. The coalition was so broad that the groups in government had overtly contradictory aims and perspectives, confirming – according to the movements – that this was a government under dispute amid two very different sectors. The first cabinet distributed ministries among the PT, the Communist Party of Brazil, the Liberal Party, the Brazilian Labor Party, the Green Party, and some business representatives. In the rural policy domain this logic was reproduced: the Ministry of Social Development was given to a CONTAG ally, INCRA to a MST ally, and the Ministry of Agriculture to the president of the Agribusiness Brazilian Society. The developmental-liberal coalition excluded the traditional landowners.

The critical moment in the tug-of-war over the direction Lula's government should take on the "rural question" and the role of the reincorporation movement in the coalition can be pinpointed to the campaign of the National Forum for Agrarian Reform and Justice in the Countryside for the application of the most ambitious agrarian reform in Brazilian history. The strategy was one of state colonization, pushing for the creation of a national agrarian reform program.

Even though during Cardoso's presidency the Ministry of Agrarian Development played a key role, during Lula became a state agency under permanent disputes among MST, CONTAG, other landless SMOs, and different PT tendencies. As a result, the INCRA presidency was the main state position occupied by an ally of the MST. At the end of 2003, facing increased rural unrest and after a year of vacillating on agrarian reform, Lula finally called on an MST ally to draft a plan for the reform. However, once the plan was drafted, the government considered it too ambitious. Instead of following it up, Lula continued with the same approach to the "social question" initiated by Cardoso in 1999, replacing agrarian reform with cash transfer policies as the main reincorporation policy. In 2003, Lula brought together three existing programs (School Allowance, Food Allowance, and Gas Help) along with a new one – called Food Card – to create the Family Allowance program. By the end of the year, the program had reached around 11,100,000 vulnerable families. As a key element of the reincorporation process, in 2004 the government created the Ministry of Social Development as the main institution for the administration of the "social question" (Fenwick 2009: 114–16).

The direction taken by the government did not please the landless peasants' movement, and it gradually distanced itself from the coalition. However, other policies for the "rural question" were applied, mainly in cooperation with CONTAG, such as the programs for family agriculture. By 2005 the MST had abandoned all its positions in the government and had become openly critical of it.[9] However, the lack of a total rupture with the government led to the emergence of other SMOs, such as the Land, Work, and Freedom Movement (MTL), which unified a series of smaller landless peasant SMOs linked to certain factions of the PT that had defected from the party to create the Socialism and Freedom Party (PSOL) from 2004 onward.

Reformulating Neo-corporatism

Lula cannot be considered a president who produced a total renewal of Brazilian politics. In Brazil, "modifications to corporatism are likely to be incremental, seeking to *overlie* rather than *replace* old corporatist institutions" (Doctor 2007: 135, italics in original).

In January and February 2003, several councils were created with the aim of integrating ministries with corporatist, territorial, and individual actors, building a participatory structure for the elaboration of social policies. The main council created was the Economic and Social Development Council (CDES). The goal of the CDES was to help in the production and implementation of social policy reforms. Gradually, however, it changed its focus to economic development. The underrepresentation of social movements – obtaining just sixteen of the ninety-one available seats (which included ten seats for ministries and one for Lula) – led to their informal organization into a subgroup for the articulation of their positions and tried to push the CDES toward the development of social policies that could produce policy recommendations in several areas (Doctor 2007: 135).

The "rural question" was partially addressed through the reopening of the National Council for Food Security. In 2003, this council had some movement participation, including the MST, unions like CONTAG, CUT, the General Labor Confederation of Brazil and the Syndical Force, and institutions of the CNBB, among others.

These were not the only councils. Indeed, by the end of Lula's second mandate there were thirty-four national councils, eighteen of them with social movement participation. Most of these councils were integrated into the structure of the ministries, like the new National Council for the Environment or the expanded National Council for Sustainable Rural Development. However, not all of these councils developed effective participatory policymaking processes. For instance, while the National

[9] CONTAG was also critical of the agrarian policies of the Lula governments.

Council for Public Security of the Ministry of Justice was a technocratic council, the National Council for Cities – during Minister for Cities Olívio Dutra's (PT) mandate – was highly participatory, with much involvement from urban movements. The participation of movements was also very important in the Ministry of the Environment until Marina Silva left government in 2008 (Abers et al. 2014). In other words, it was mostly in ministries created for dealing with territorial and reincorporation movements that the development of more participatory councils was possible.

Like in Argentina, the Secretariat-General of the Presidency played a central role in the government's informal relationship with the reincorporation movement. In 2003, its historical role of articulating the executive with the other branches of the state was transferred to the newly created Secretariat of Institutional Relations. Meanwhile, the National Secretariat for Social Articulation was created as a division of the Secretariat-General with the aim of coordinating the relationship of the state with social organizations. In contrast with Argentina's Secretariat-General, in Brazil no members of movements participated in this body, which included only public officials from the PT.

The End of the Second Incorporation Process

If movements still held out any hope that the PT government might alter its approach to the "rural question," the 2005 *mensalão* (installment) vote-buying corruption scandal dashed them. This breaking point introduced new divisions into the landless movement. The *mensalão* was an indication to movements that the PT had transformed into a catchall party and that the power of the left-wing sectors within the coalition had been significantly reduced (Wainwright and Branford 2006; Hunter 2010). However, MST and CONTAG dissatisfaction with the government had started *before* the *mensalão* because land reform was already at risk of failing as of earlier that year.

In terms of social policy, the reincorporation process played out in two stages: 1993 to 1999, when agrarian reform was the main reincorporation policy, and 1999 to 2012, when cash transfer programs like Family Allowance gradually replaced it. This process had two important consequences for the movement. The first was an increase in divisions within the movement as a result of the MST never totally rupturing with the PT and continuing to support PT presidential candidates. The second was a decrease in the number of land occupations due to the demobilization effects of Family Allowance. While between 2003 and 2005 there was an increase in the number of settlements, from 2006 to 2010 there was a steady decrease (Feliciano 2011: 22, graph 3). Meanwhile, the Family Allowance program steadily expanded its coverage between 2003 (3,600,000 families covered) and 2006 (11,100,000) and then growing even further between 2009 (12,400,000) and 2010 (12,900,000).[10]

The application of the first liberal-developmentalist Growth Acceleration Program (PAC) (January 2007–December 2010), which had not included agrarian reform as part of its goals, was a clear signal from the government of its strategic decision to abandon agrarian reform as a reincorporation policy.

Consolidation and Aftermath in Brazil

With the start of the first PAC and the development of specific mid-term policies consolidating the liberal-developmental model, the reincorporation process came to an end.[11] The period 2007–12 should be considered as the aftermath of the reincorporation period because it saw no substantial changes institutionally or in state-movement relations. Finally, the election of Dilma Rousseff (the main architect of the first PAC) as president in 2011 consolidated the direction initiated by Lula.

During its first two years, Rousseff's government was paralyzed by a series of corruption scandals that led to several cabinet reshuffles, and it has been very much limited in its transformative possibilities by the coalitional nature of Brazilian politics (von Bülow and Lassance 2012). The MST offered Rousseff critical support, as it customarily did with a PT president, but the relationship was more distant than with Lula. Social policy continued with the expansion of Family Allowance, reaching 13,400,000 families in 2011.[12] The expansion of cash transfer policies was done in a similar fashion to that of her predecessor: by combining pre-existing programs into a larger one that covered a greater number of vulnerable people. Meanwhile, agrarian reform was dismissed as a reincorporation policy. Due to the lack of budget for land expropriations, Rousseff's first year offered the lowest number of settlements (22,000 families) since re-democratization (*Brasil de Fato*, 04/04/2012

[10] Ministry of Social Development and Fight against Hunger (www.mds.gov.br/saladeimprensa/noticias/2012/outubro/imagens/19102012-evolucaoanualbf-9anos.jpg, viewed October 20, 2012).

[11] The second PAC began in January 2010 and ended in December 2014.

[12] Ibid., note 10.

and 08/06/2012). However, in socioeconomic terms, Brazil improved its Gini index from 0.640 in 1999 to 0.553 in 2013 and its Human Development Index from 0.608 in 1990 to 0.755 in 2014 (ECLAC 2014: 124, table II.A.2; UNDP 2015: 213, table 2). According to ECLAC, much more impressive is the reduction in poverty that was achieved: while in 1990 48 percent of the population was considered poor (reaching 70.6 percent in rural areas), in 2014 just 16.5 percent were poor (28.7 percent rural).

Finally, Rousseff did not redefine the roles of the main institutions responsible for the "social question" inherited from Lula's administration. Almost all councils were kept open and working as before. The informal relationship between social movements and the Secretariat-General of the Presidency continued to be structured as under Lula after an attempt to expand and institutionalize social participation within each ministry failed with the annulment by Congress of Decree 8,243 in October 2014.

CONCLUSION

The second wave of incorporation followed different paths in each country. In Brazil it was characterized by gradual metamorphosis, and in Argentina and Bolivia sharper ruptures and changes defined it. While in Brazil second incorporation featured a mix of neo-corporatist and territorial features, in Bolivia and Argentina it was mostly territorial.

The main reincorporation movement differed in each country too. In Argentina was an urban movement, in Brazil a rural one, while in Bolivia were mostly rural movements, but with an increasing participation of urban movements. There was also variation produced by the relevance of class or ethnicity in each society. While class-based societies such as Argentina and Brazil organized through the disincorporated condition of "unemployed workers" and "landless peasants," in an ethnic-based society as Bolivia, former "peasants" and "miners" were redefined as "indigenous." With the distinction between "class-based" and "ethnic-based" societies I do not attempt to propose an essentialist characterization of Argentina, Bolivia, and Brazil. As I showed throughout this chapter, the importance of class or ethnicity was a historical construction that is – at least – related to the characteristics of first and second incorporation.

In all three countries, however, first and second incorporation actors began sharing institutional spaces. In Brazil, these spaces were increasingly formalized and corporatized, leading to the gradual exclusion of the territorially based actors, while in Argentina and Bolivia this degree of formalization was not achieved. In all three countries, this new relationship with governments led to divisions within the reincorporation movements over the interpretation of the degree of change and continuity between the governments of the 1990s and those of the 2010s.

9

Conclusions

Since the end of the nineteenth century, the politics of Latin American poor people has been largely characterized by the two waves of incorporation. Incorporation waves represent major and prolonged historical processes of struggle between socioeconomic and political groups in their bids to expand or reduce the socio-political arena. The history of Latin America has been marked by these cyclical tensions between efforts to maintain a small polity delineated by an intimate relationship between economic and political power and pressure (sometimes from below) to expand this polity.

It is crucial to identify what Collier and Collier (1991) originally defined as "incorporation" as recursive in Latin America in order to understand how the region moves in waves that link the political regime with the economic system. However, this does not mean that this has been the only dynamic present in the region. Other major processes (not all focused on the popular sectors) have also unfolded in Latin American history, including nation-state building, democratization, revolution, civil war, and authoritarianism as among the most important. So far, the relationship between these other macro-dynamics and the waves of incorporation has been unexplored. Although these other dynamics emerge as contemporaneous and parallel to (dis)incorporation, research is still needed to understand if and how they might favor or inhibit these waves.

This book argued that neoliberalism has led to the emergence of a movement of disincorporated workers struggling to reincorporate the popular sectors into the socio-political arena as part of wage-earning society. Each historical period has been associated with different types of popular movements leading the efforts for social change. During the liberal period that preceded the first incorporation, the labor and/or peasant movements were the main organizers of the popular sectors in their claim for well-being through reform or revolution. For the second incorporation, a different type of movement emerged during the neoliberal period as the central popular actor in the drive to reverse the exclusionary consequences of authoritarianism and neoliberalism and claim the reincorporation of the popular sectors as citizens and wage-earners. The emergence of what I defined as the "reincorporation movement" – a type of movement that has built upon, but also decentered, labor-based actors – is the result of the important transformations analyzed in this book.

In Argentina, while the first incorporation was a corporatist process with trade unions as the main contentious actors, the second was a territorialized process in which the *piquetero* movement was the primary actor. It followed a multi-level (local, provincial, national) series of interactions centered around two main elements: the evolution of public policies and territorially based disputes between the movement and other political actors. The second incorporation in Argentina can be defined as a type of party territorial incorporation because it was carried out with the goal of channeling the territorial mobilization inherited from the movement of resistance to disincorporation into an electoral strategy of *kirchnerismo*.

As I showed in the comparisons with Bolivia and Brazil, the second wave of incorporation is a Latin American process. As with the first wave, the second did not cover all countries, but it did cover a large enough number of them to consider it a regional process (with national variants) (for the analysis of the second wave in more countries, cf. Silva and Rossi forthcoming). Even though incorporation is associated with the left's or populist accession to power, during the first wave this was not always true, and we should inquire whether this was also the case with the second wave. Further research should be carried out to understand the relationship between the accession to power of a particular ideological group and the type of (re)incorporation.

What this book has made clear is that even though the elites are important actors, they are as much the cause as the consequence of far bigger processes that led them to power in the first place. Moreover, the relational dynamics sometimes pushed non-leftist elites to apply wide-ranging incorporation policies or limited the capacity of leftists to steer the process in the desired direction. In other words, the relational approach positions elites as actors that are less central, depersonalizing many political decisions. By the same token, claims from below for expansion of the polity are frequently positioned as against capitalism and for revolutionary purposes. As could be seen in this book, actors' goals and strategies are not necessarily fulfilled even though huge changes may be achieved. Latin American history shows a pattern of claims asserted to resist or promote major transformations, resulting in massive or selective repression, the emergence of a "social question" that is translated into popular sectors reconnecting their lives to the state and capitalism, and a subsequent reversion to a partial or total contraction of the polity. In other words, there are no revolutions without both revolutionaries and counter-revolutionaries. But recognizing the importance of actors and of their stories, ideas, goals and strategies does not mean that history unfolds as contending humans expect it to.

History is as much the result of desired outcomes as it is the product of relational dynamics that are not totally under our control. However, the excessive structuralism that characterizes many studies overlooks the relational construction of macro-transformations. This book has followed Aminzade's (1992) concern for the need for bridging the relationship between the pace of long-term historical processes and the expectations of the actors involved in them. It is crucial that the narratives that are built take into consideration this subtle in-betweeness that is in fact at play when studying broad historical dynamics. This book applied this intermediate perspective, viewing actors' ideas and strategies as central but the dynamics as partially autonomous from them. As we were able to see, the second wave of incorporation in Argentina represented a partially satisfactory outcome of a series of semi-intended strategic actions. Reincorporation was neither the most rational option nor a result that was constrained by a specific reinforcing path. An open-ended relational dynamic emerged from actors who were aiming to achieve many other things. This book contradicts path-dependence as much as rational choice approaches, introducing the importance of a Tillyian relational approach that gives more weight to actors and their ideas.

The modified Tillyian perspective I implemented moves the focus away from the unsatisfactory debate about the primordial importance of agency or structure and onto the density of a theory-guided historical analysis. This book was concerned with the popular sectors' pressure from below for their reincorporation as citizens and wage-earners, and because of this, the *piquetero* movement was central in this narrative. However, this approach can be applied to any other kind of process and collection of actors in a comparative and historical approach to social change.

To achieve this relational perspective, this book proposed a refinement to the way strategic action has been typically analyzed in order to better understand the role of strategies from below in macro-historical change. In doing so, the analysis builds on and contributes to some of the general debates on historical institutionalism and to social movement studies. In other words, my intention was to situate actors' collective strategies within a non-determinist historical framework while specifying the components of the context of interaction and their relative spatial-temporal stability. This conceptual framework was then applied to a process-tracing analysis of the *piqueteros*' struggle for reincorporation in Argentina.

Another important contribution of this book is the attention it has paid to the importance of grasping and analyzing instances where movements have intentionally chosen not to perform public and/or contentious actions. The concepts of repertoire of strategies and stock of legacies help to bridge the artificial distinction between contentious and routine politics, viewing the picture as a dynamic interaction involving the selective use of strategies based on inherited legacies that limit the perceived options available for action. Recognizing the legitimacy of such a strategy avoids mistakenly taking the adoption of a non-contentious repertoire of strategies as indicative of movement dissolution. One of the main goals of this book was to produce a detailed narration of changes within a repertoire of strategies to see how the divisions between contentious and routine politics can be diluted. What I captured was the simultaneous performance of both types of repertoires by the same actor.

Concretely, in their struggle for reincorporation, the *piqueteros* commonly made use of picketing and insurrectional direct actions for moderate claims, such as access to unemployment subsidies. As I have shown, to understand the *piquetero* movement we need to study the left in Argentina. The *piqueteros*' repertoire of strategies has been enriched by a variety of legacies handed down to them from unions, CBCs, and guerrilla organizations whose predominant repertoire of strategies was composed of *basismo*, moderate *foquismo*, and trade unionist strategies, among others. The union legacies, together with territorialization, have also encouraged the constitution of mostly vertical SMOs – with the partial exception of the FPDS – loosely integrated within an increasingly diversified movement. Simultaneously, the positive re-evaluation of democracy narrowed the repertoire of strategies, eliminating armed struggle, coups, and other strategies from the list of perceived available alternatives for action, and electoral strategies were introduced with more centrality than was witnessed during the first incorporation. These factors explain why this movement has adopted radical methods of protest while remaining open to negotiation as a means of conflict resolution. In other words, the reincorporation movement, in its quest to bridge the gap between popular sectors and the state, restored the balance that had already existed between the unions' radical methods of protest during the pre-incorporation period and their more formal negotiations with the government (on the strategies used in the struggle for first incorporation, cf. Collier and Collier 1991: 336–44).

The proposed conceptual toolkit aims to preserve Charles Tilly's research tradition, enriched by input from other disciplines. The concepts of repertoire of strategies and stock of legacies can easily travel to other latitudes. These contributions to the general literature still need to be applied to other movements, as I have briefly done with Bolivia and Brazil. This book's efforts at bridging historical institutionalism and social movement studies open up a promising cross-fertilization research agenda that can help produce interesting new pathways in the comparative historical study of large-scale dynamics that integrates the actors' strategies into these processes. This book is an invitation to other scholars to explore the utility of these concepts and approach in their own work on other collective actors and macro-transformations around the world.

APPENDIX

Networks for the Constitution of the *Piquetero* Movement

Note 1: The words that appear in italics represent events (important protests, conflicts, coordination moments, electoral coalitions, political parties, etc.), those in bold are the main SMOs of the *piquetero* movement in the year they emerged, and those in normal font indicate all the other organizations.

Note 2: In Figures A and B the names of certain events and SMOs are repeated because both networks are relevant for the constitution of the *piquetero* movement.

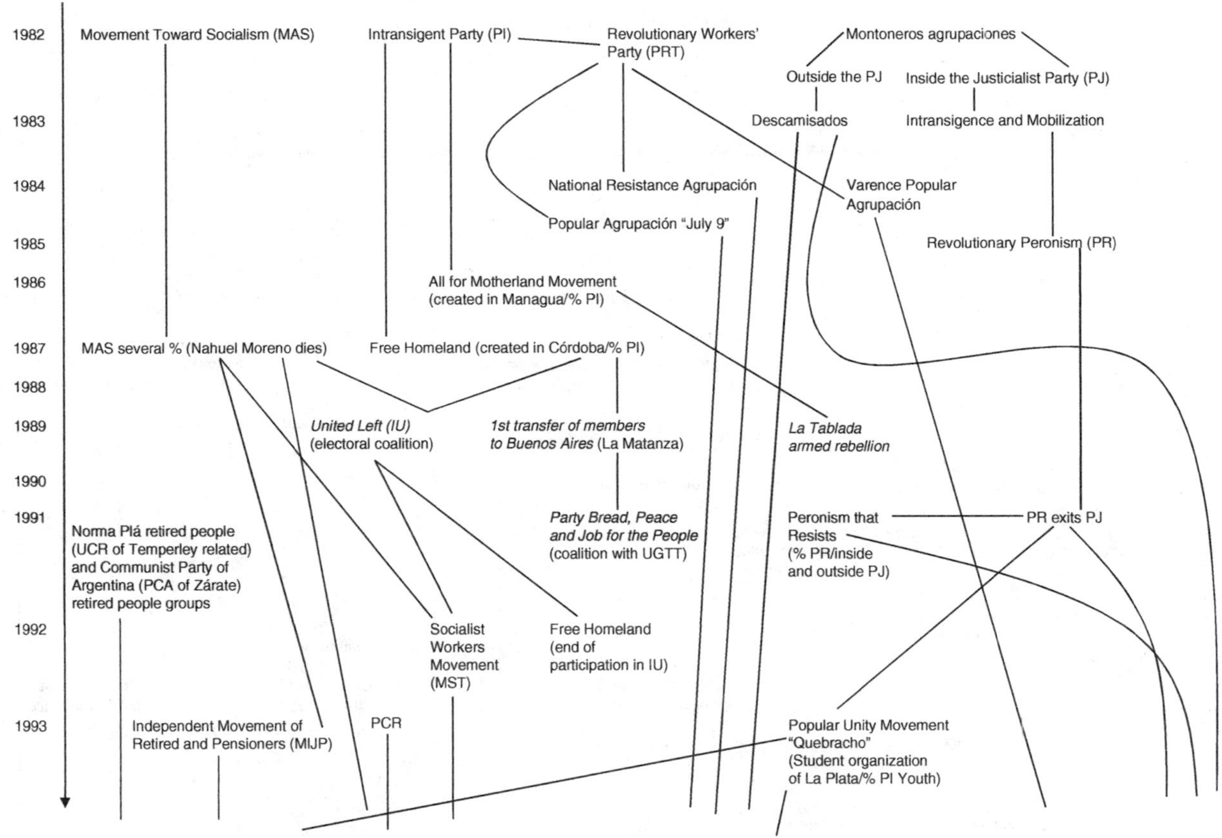

FIGURE A Left-Wing Parties and Organizations – Networks That Led to the Constitution of the *Piquetero* Movement

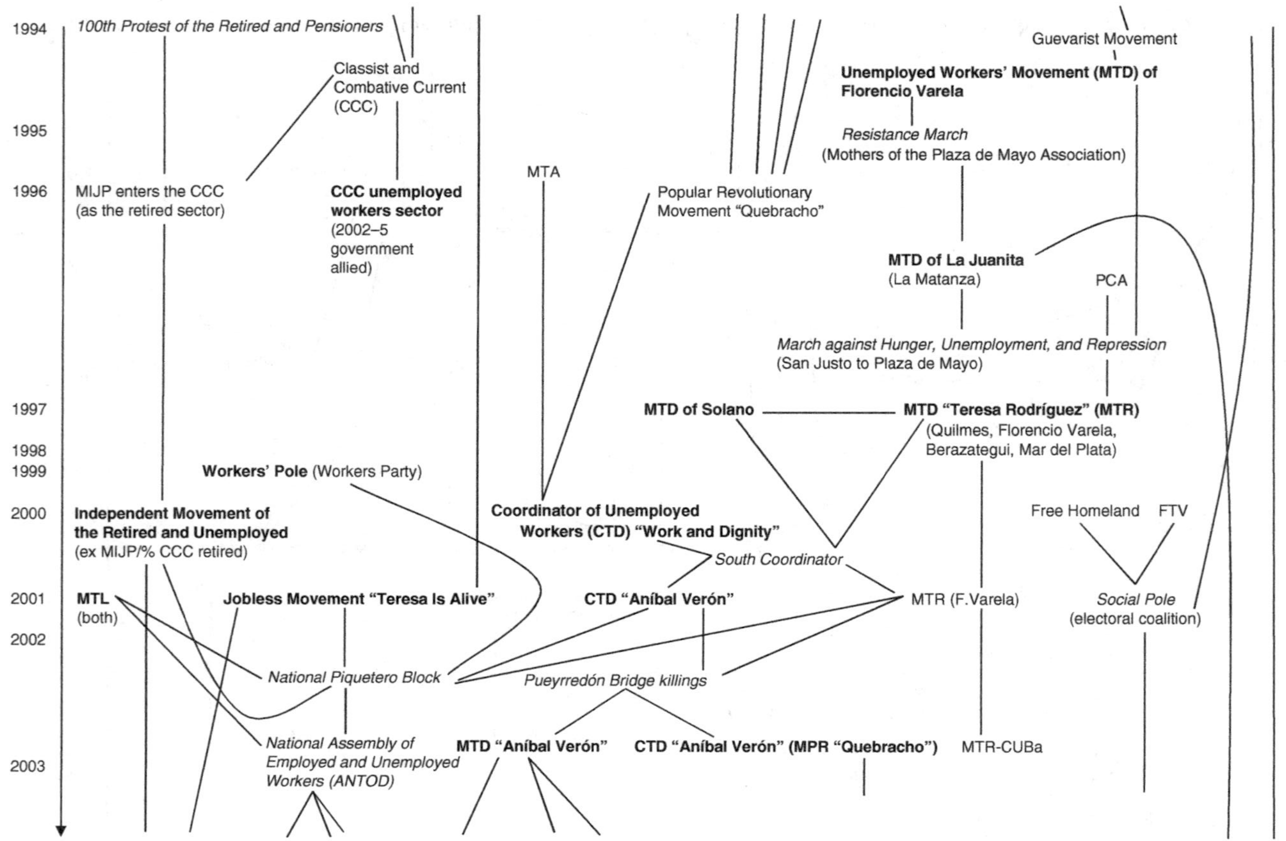

FIGURE A (cont.)

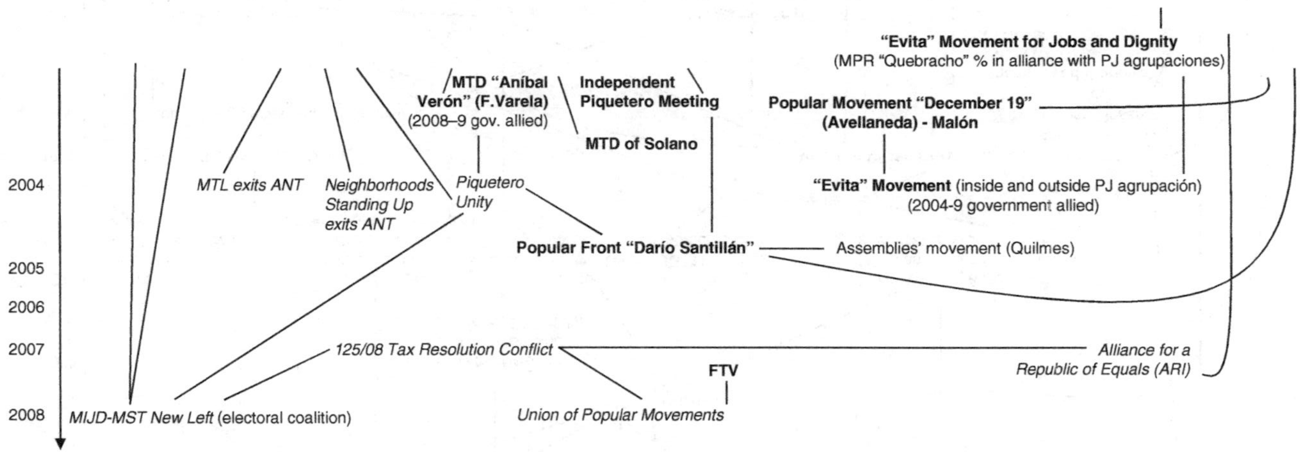

FIGURE A (cont.)

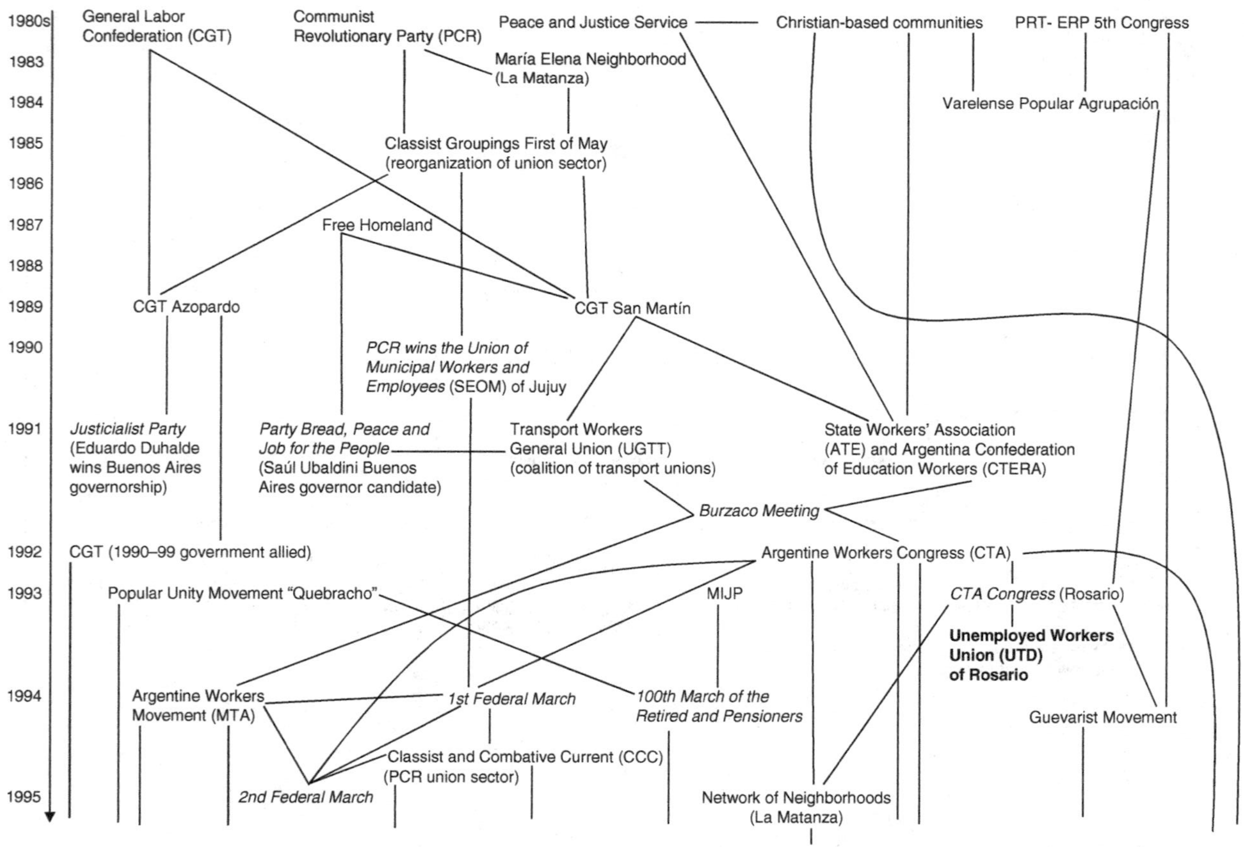

FIGURE B Unions Sector – Networks That Led to the Constitution of the *Piquetero* Movement

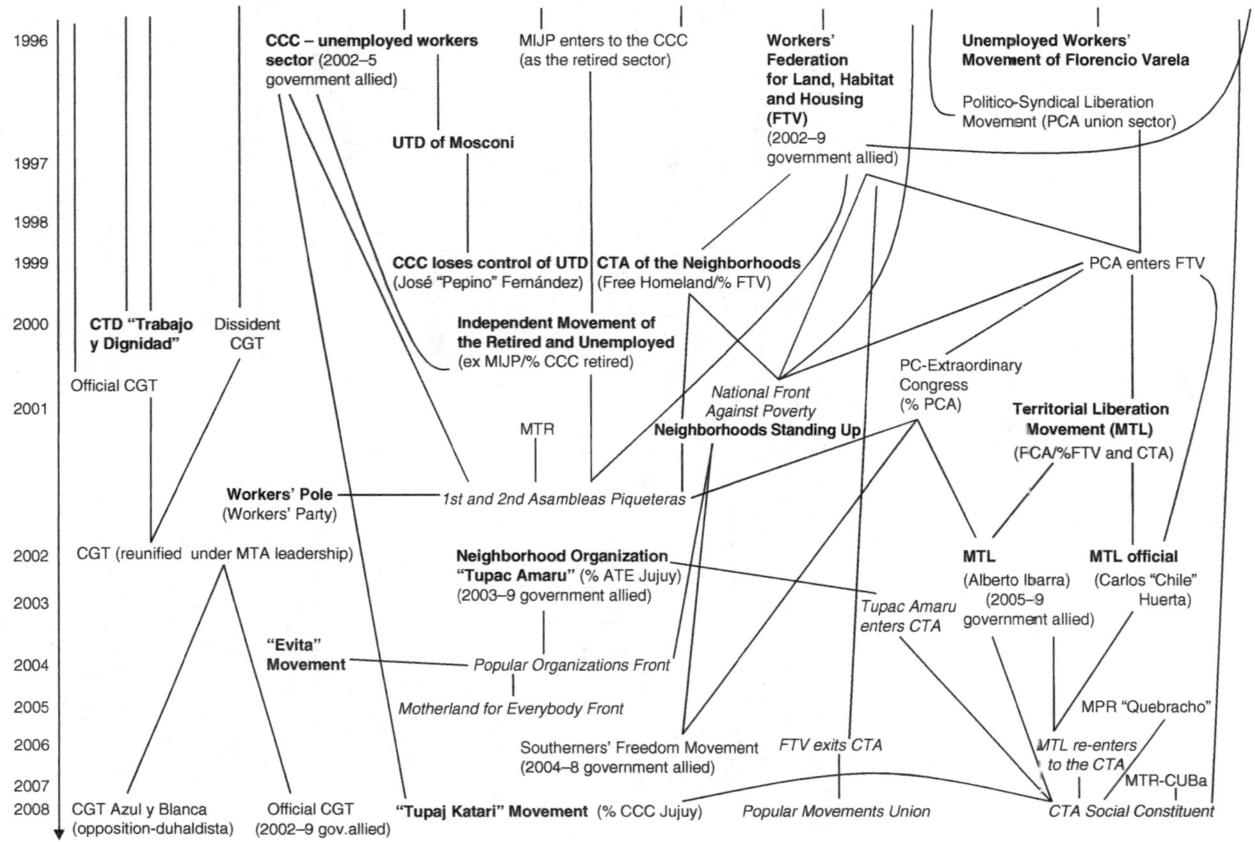

FIGURE B (cont.)

References

Abal Medina, Juan (2009), "The Rise and Fall of the Argentine Centre-Left: The Crisis of Frente Grande," *Party Politics*, 15 (3), 357–75.

Abers, Rebecca Neaera and Tatagiba, Luciana (2015), "Mobilizing for Women's Health from Inside the Brazilian Bureaucracy," in Federico M. Rossi and Marisa von Bülow (eds.), *Social Movement Dynamics: New Perspectives on Theory and Research from Latin America* (Farnham: Ashgate), 73–101.

Abers, Rebecca Neaera, Serafim, Lizandra, and Tatagiba, Luciana (2014), "Changing Repertoires of State-Society Interaction under Lula," in Fabio de Castro, Kees Koonings, and Marianne Wiesebron (eds.), *Brazil under the Workers' Party: Continuity and Change from Lula to Dilma* (New York: Palgrave-Macmillan), 36–61.

Acuña, Carlos (ed.) (1995), *La nueva matriz política argentina* (Buenos Aires: Ediciones Nueva Visión).

Albó, Xavier (1987), "From MNRistas to Kataristas to Katari," in Steve J. Stern (ed.), *Resistance, Rebellion, and Consciousness in the Andean Peasant World, 18th to 20th Centuries* (Madison: University of Wisconsin Press), 379–419.

Alcañiz, Isabella and Scheier, Melissa (2007), "New Social Movements with Old Party Politics: The MTL Piqueteros and the Communist Party in Argentina," *Latin American Perspectives*, 34 (153), 157–71.

Alderete, Juan Carlos and Gómez, Arnoldo (1999), *La desocupación en el infierno menemista* (Buenos Aires: Ágora).

Almeida, Paul D. (2007), "Defensive Mobilization: Popular Movements against Economic Adjustment Policies in Latin America," *Latin American Perspectives*, 34 (3), 123–39.

(2014), *Mobilizing Democracy: Globalization and Citizen Protest* (Baltimore: Johns Hopkins University Press).

Almeida, Paul D. and Johnston, Hank (2006), "Neoliberal Globalization and Popular Movements in Latin America," in Hank Johnston and Paul D. Almeida (eds.), *Latin American Social Movements: Globalization, Democratization, and Transnational Networks* (Boulder: Rowman & Littlefield), 3–18.

Altimir, Oscar and Beccaria, Luis (2001), "El persistente deterioro de la distribución del ingreso en la Argentina," *Desarrollo Económico*, 40 (160), 589–618.

Aminzade, Ronald (1992), "Historical Sociology and Time," *Sociological Methods & Research*, 20 (4), 456–80.

Aminzade, Ronald, Goldstone, Jack, McAdam, Doug, Perry, Elizabeth, Sewell, William H., Jr., Tarrow, Sidney, and Tilly, Charles (eds.) (2001), *Silence and Voice in the Study of Contentious Politics* (New York: Cambridge University Press).

Andolina, Robert, Laurie, Nina, and Radcliff, Sarah (2009), *Indigenous Development in the Andes: Culture, Power, and Transnationalism* (Durham: Duke University Press).

Angell, Alan (1998), "The Left in Latin America since c. 1920," in Leslie Bethell (ed.), *Latin America: Politics and Society since 1930* (Cambridge: Cambridge University Press), 75–144.

Anria, Santiago and Niedzwiecki, Sara (2015), "Social Movements and Social Policy: The Bolivian Renta Dignidad," *Studies in Comparative International Development*, 1–20 (First Online: DOI 10.1007/s12116-015-9207-1).

Antonello, Jucit (2004), *Consecuencia del saqueo en Argentina: la lucha piquetera* (Córdoba: Ferreyra Editor).

Armelino, Martín (2008), "Tensiones entre organización sindical y organización territorial: la experiencia de la CTA y la FTV en el período postcrisis," in Sebastián Pereyra, Germán Pérez, and Federico Schuster (eds.), *La huella piquetera. Avatares de las organizaciones de desocupados después de 2001* (La Plata: Ediciones Al Margen), 141–83.

Artese, Matías (2009), "Criminalización de la protesta en Argentina. Una construcción de lo delictivo más allá de la esfera jurídica," *América Latina Hoy*, 52, 149–69.

Auyero, Javier (2000), *Poor People's Politics: Peronist Survival Networks & the Legacy of Evita* (Durham: Duke University Press).

(2002), "Los cambios en el repertorio de la protesta social en la Argentina," *Desarrollo Económico*, 42 (166), 187–210.

(2003), *Contentious Lives: Two Argentine Women, Two Protests, and the Quest for Recognition* (Durham: Duke University Press).

(2007), *Routine Politics and Violence in Argentina: The Grey Zone of State Power* (Cambridge: Cambridge University Press).

Auyero, Javier and Moran, Timothy Patrick (2007), "The Dynamics of Collective Violence: Dissecting Food Riots in Contemporary Argentina," *Social Forces*, 85 (3), 1341–67.

Barbetta, Pablo and Lapegna, Pablo (2001), "Cuando la protesta toma forma: los cortes de ruta en el norte salteño," in Norma Giarracca (ed.), *La protesta social en la Argentina. Transformaciones económicas y crisis sociales en el interior del país* (Buenos Aires: Alianza), 231–57.

Barker, Colin, Johnson, Alan, and Lavalette, Michael (2001), "Leadership Matters: An Introduction," in Colin Barker, Alan Johnson, and Michael Lavalette (eds.), *Leadership and Social Movements* (Manchester: Manchester University Press), 1–23.

Barrientos, Armando (2014), "On the Distributional Implications of Social Protection Reforms in Latin America," in Giovanni Andrea Cornia (ed.), *Falling Inequality in Latin America: Policy Changes and Lessons* (Oxford: Oxford University Press), 340–60.

Barrientos, Armando and Santibáñez, Claudio (2009), "New Forms of Social Assistance and the Evolution of Social Protection in Latin America," *Journal of Latin American Studies*, 41 (1), 1–26.

Barros, Robert (1986), "The Left and Democracy: Recent Debates in Latin America," *Telos*, 68, 49–70.

Baschetti, Roberto (ed.) (1997), *Documentos de la Resistencia Peronista, 1955–1970* (La Plata: De la Campana).

Battezzati, Santiago (2012), "La Tupac Amaru: intermediación de intereses de los sectores populares informales en la provincia de Jujuy," *Desarrollo Económico*, 52 (205), 147–71.

Baud, Michiel and Rutten, Rosanne (eds.) (2004), *Popular Intellectuals and Social Movements: Framing Protest in Asia, Africa, and Latin America* (International Review of Social History, Cambridge: Cambridge University Press).

Beccaria, Luis and López, Néstor (eds.) (1996), *Sin trabajo: Las características del desempleo y sus efectos en la sociedad argentina* (Buenos Aires: Losada – UNICEF).

Becker, Marc (2011), *Pachakutik: Indigenous Movements and Electoral Politics in Ecuador* (Lanham: Rowman & Littlefield).

Belmartino, Susana (2005), *La atención médica argentina en el siglo XX: instituciones y procesos* (Buenos Aires: Siglo XXI).

Benclowicz, José Daniel (2011), "Repensando los orígenes del movimiento piquetero: Miseria y experiencias de lucha antes de las contrarreformas de la década de 1990 en el norte argentino," *Latin American Research Review*, 46 (2), 79–103.

(2013), *Estado de malestar y tradiciones de lucha. Genealogía del movimiento piquetero de Tartagal-Mosconi (1930–2001)* (Buenos Aires: Biblos).

Bergel, Pablo (2003), "Nuevas formas asociativas: asambleas vecinales y Movimientos de Trabajadores Desocupados (MTD)," in Inés González Bombal (ed.), *Nuevos movimientos sociales y ONGs en la Argentina de la crisis* (Buenos Aires: CEDES), 79–110.

Bidaseca, Karina and Rossi, Federico M. (2008), "Coaliciones nacionales contra procesos continentales de liberalización comercial: la Autoconvocatoria No al ALCA," in Alejandro Grimson and Sebastián Pereyra (eds.), *Conflictos globales, voces locales: movilización y activismo en clave transnacional* (Buenos Aires: UNRISD – Prometeo), 51–89.

Bonasso, Miguel (2002), *El palacio y la calle* (Buenos Aires: Planeta).

Borges, Jorge Luis (1996 [1960]), "Del rigor en la ciencia," *El Hacedor* (24th edn.; Buenos Aires: Emecé), 119.

Bosi, Lorenzo, Giugni, Marco and Uba, Katrin (eds.) (2016), *The Consequences of Social Movements* (Cambridge: Cambridge University Press).

Botana, Natalio and Gallo, Ezequiel (1997), *De la República posible a la República verdadera (1880–1910)* (Buenos Aires: Ariel).

Bourdieu, Pierre (1998), *Practical Reasons: On the Theory of Action* (Stanford: Stanford University Press).

(2000), *Pascalian Meditations* (Stanford: Stanford University Press).

Branford, Sue and Rocha, Jan (2002), *Cutting the Wire: The Story of the Landless Movement in Brazil* (London: Latin American Bureau).

Brennan, James P. (1988), "Industrialists and *Bolicheros*. Business and the Peronist Populist Alliance, 1943–1976," in James P. Brennan (ed.), *Peronism and Argentina* (Wilmington: SR Books), 79–123.

Buainain, Antônio Márcio (2008), "Reforma agrária por conflitos," in Antônio Márcio Buainain (ed.), *Luta pela Terra, Reforma Agrária e Gestão de Conflitos no Brasil* (Campinas: UNICAMP), 17–128.

Burdick, John, Oxhorn, Philip, and Roberts, Kenneth M. (eds.) (2009), *Beyond Neoliberalism in Latin America?: Societies and Politics at the Crossroads* (New York: Palgrave-Macmillan).

Burkart, Mara and Vázquez, Melina (2007), "Reflexiones sobre las experiencias de coordinación y/o articulación entre las organizaciones de trabajadores desocupados autónomas en Argentina," *V Congreso CEISAL 2007* (April 11–14, Bruxelles).

Burkart, Mara, Cobe, Lorena, Fornillo, Bruno, and Zipcioglu, Patricia (2008), "Las estrategias políticas de las organizaciones de desocupados a partir de la crisis de 2001," in Sebastián Pereyra, Germán Pérez, and Federico Schuster (eds.), *La huella piquetera. Avatares de las organizaciones de desocupados después de 2001* (La Plata: Ediciones Al Margen), 35–64.

Buzai, Gustavo D. and Marcos, Mariana (2012), "The Social Map of Greater Buenos Aires as Empirical Evidence of Urban Models," *Journal of Latin American Geography*, 11 (1), 67–78.

Calvo, Dolores (2006), *Exclusión y política. Estudio sociológico sobre la experiencia de la Federación de trabajadores por la Tierra, la Vivienda, y el Hábitat (1998–2002)* (Buenos Aires: Miño y Dávila).

Calvo, Ernesto and Escolar, Marcelo (2005), *La nueva política de los partidos en la Argentina: Crisis política, realineamientos partidarios y reforma electoral* (Buenos Aires: PENT-Prometeo).

Cámara, Gloria (2008), "Tres casos, tres formas de articulación: mineros, cocaleros y cívicos," in Yuri Tórrez Rubín de Celis (ed.), *Movimientos sociales en tiempos de poder: articulaciones y campos de conflicto en el gobierno del MAS (2006–2007)* (La Paz: Plural), 141–78.

Cameron, Maxwell A. and Hershberg, Eric (eds.) (2010), *Latin America's Left Turns: Politics, Policies, and Trajectories of Change* (Boulder: Lynne Rienner).

Cardoso, Adalberto (2010), "Uma Utopia Brasileira: Vargas e a Construção do Estado do Bem-Estar numa Sociedade Estruturalmente Desigual," *Dados*, 53 (4), 775–819.

Carr, Barry and Ellner, Steve (eds.) (1993), *The Latin American Left: From the Fall of Allende to the Perestroika* (Boulder: Westview Press).

Casaburi, Gabriel and Tussie, Diana (2000), "La sociedad civil y las agendas de los organismos de crédito," in Diana Tussie (ed.), *Luces y sombras de una nueva*

relación. El Banco Interamericano de Desarrollo, el Banco Mundial y la sociedad civil (Buenos Aires: Temas), 15–38.
Castañeda, Jorge (1993), *Utopia unarmed: The Latin American Left after the Cold War* (New York: Knopf).
Castelo, Fernando (2000), "'Todos unidos triunfaremos.' El entrismo morenista y sus caracterizaciones," *Razón y Revolución*, 6, www.razonyrevolucion.org .ar/textos/revryr/luchadeclases/ryr6Castelo.pdf.
Cavarozzi, Marcelo and Garretón, Manuel *Antonio* (1989), *Muerte y resurrección: los partidos políticos en el autoritarismo y las transiciones en el Cono Sur* (Santiago de Chile: FLACSO).
CELS (2003a), *El estado frente a la protesta social 1996–2002* (Buenos Aires: CELS – Siglo XXI).
(2003b), *Plan Jefes y Jefas ¿Derecho social o beneficio sin derechos?* (Buenos Aires: CELS).
Cerrutti, Marcela and Grimson, Alejandro (2004), "Buenos Aires, neoliberalismo y después. Cambios socioeconómicos y respuestas populares," *Working Paper Series* (The Center for Migration and Development: Princeton University).
Colectivo Situaciones (2001), "Por una política más allá de la política," in Colectivo Situaciones (ed.), *Contrapoder: Una introducción* (Buenos Aires: Ediciones de Mano en Mano), 19–46.
Colina, Jorge, Giordano, Osvaldo, Torres, Alejandra, and Cárdenas, Marcelo (2009), "Heads of household programme in Argentina: a human rights-based policy?," *International Social Science Journal*, 60 (197–98), 337–51.
Collier, David and Mahon, James (1993), "Conceptual 'Stretching' Revisited: Adapting Categories in Comparative Analysis," *American Political Science Review*, 87 (4), 845–55.
Collier, Ruth Berins and Collier, David (1991), *Shaping the Political Arena: Critical Junctures, the Labor Movement, and Regime Dynamics in Latin America* (Princeton: Princeton University Press).
Collier, Ruth Berins and Handlin, Samuel (eds.) (2009a), *Reorganizing Popular Politics: Participation and the New Interest Regime in Latin America* (University Park: Pennsylvania State University Press).
(2009b), "Situating the Analysis: Analytic Approach, Cases, and Historical Context," in Ruth Berins Collier and Samuel Handlin (eds.), *Reorganizing Popular Politics: Participation and the New Interest Regime in Latin America* (University Park: Pennsylvania State University Press), 32–60.
Connell, Raewyn and Dados, Nour (2014), "Where in the World Does Neoliberalism Come from?," *Theory and Society*, 43 (2), 117–38.
Cook, María Lorena (2007), *The Politics of Labor Reform in Latin America: Between Flexibility and Rights* (University Park: Pennsylvania State University Press).
Cornia, Giovanni Andrea (2014), Inequality Trends and Their Determinants: Latin America over 1990–2010," in Giovanni Andrea Cornia (ed.), *Falling Inequality in Latin America: Policy Changes and Lessons* (Oxford: Oxford University Press), 23–48.

Cravino, María Cristina (ed.) (2013), *Construyendo barrios. Transformaciones socioterritoriales a partir de los Programas Federales de Vivienda en el Área Metropolitana de Buenos Aires (2004–2009)* (Buenos Aires: UNGS – Ciccus).
Dagnino, Evelina (2003), "Citizenship in Latin America," *Latin American Perspectives*, 30, 221–25.
De Luca, Miguel (2008), "Political Recruitment and Candidate Selection in Argentina: Presidents and Governors, 1983 to 2006," in Peter Siavelis and Scott Morgenstern (eds.), *Pathways to Power: Political Recruitment and Candidate Selection in Latin America* (University Park: The Pennsylvania State University Press), 189–217.
De Luca, Miguel, Jones, Mark P., and Tula, María Inés (2002), "Back Rooms or Ballot Boxes?: Candidate Nomination in Argentina," *Comparative Political Studies*, 35 (4), 413–36.
Delamata, Gabriela (2002), "De los 'estallidos' provinciales a la generalización de la protesta en Argentina. Perspectiva y contexto en la significación de las nuevas protestas," *Nueva Sociedad*, 182, 121–37.
(2004), *Los barrios desbordados. Las organizaciones de desocupados del Gran Buenos Aires* (Buenos Aires: Centro Cultural Ricardo Rojas – EUDEBA).
(2005), "Las organizaciones de desocupados del Gran Buenos Aires y la(s) crisis," in Federico Schuster et al. (eds.), *Tomar la palabra. Estudios sobre protesta social y acción colectiva en la Argentina contemporánea* (Buenos Aires: Prometeo), 365–85.
Delgado, Nelson Giordano and Leite, Sergio Pereira (2011), "Políticas de Desenvolvimento Territorial no Meio Rural Brasileiro: Novas Institucionalidades e Protagonismo dos Atores," *Dados*, 54 (2), 431–73.
della Porta, Donatella and Diani, Mario (1999), *Social Movements: An Introduction* (Oxford: Blackwell).
Diani, Mario (1992), "The Concept of Social Movements," *The Sociological Review*, 40, 1–25.
Do Alto, Hervé and Fontana, Lorenza B. (2013), "Conflicto social y reterritorialización. Miradas cruzadas sobre movimientos rurales y regionalistas en Bolivia," *Trace*, 63, 24–34.
Doctor, Mahrukh (2007), "Lula's Development Council: Neo-Corporatism and Policy Reform in Brazil," *Latin American Perspectives*, 34 (6), 131–48.
Doherty, Brian (2013), "Tactics," in David Snow et al. (eds.), *The Wiley-Blackwell Encyclopedia of Social and Political Movements* (Oxford: Wiley-Blackwell), 1315–21.
Domingo, Pilar (2004), "Judicialization of Politics or Politicization of the Judiciary? Recent Trends in Latin America," *Democratization*, 11 (1), 104–26.
(2009), "Evo Morales, the MAS, and a Revolution in the Making," in Jean Grugel and Pía Riggirozzi (eds.), *Governance after Neoliberalism in Latin America* (New York: Palgrave Macmillan), 113–45.
Dunkerley, James (2007), "Evo Morales, and the Third Bolivian Revolution," *Journal of Latin American Studies*, 39 (01), 133–66.
ECLAC (2010), *Panorama social de América Latina 2010* (Santiago: ECLAC).
(2014), *Panorama social de América Latina 2014* (Santiago: ECLAC).

Ellner, Steve (2008), *Rethinking Venezuelan Politics: Class, Conflict, and the Chávez Phenomenon* (Boulder: Lynne Rienner).
Emirbayer, Mustafa (2010), "Tilly and Bourdieu," *The American Sociologist*, 41 (4), 400–22.
Epstein, Edward (1987), "Inflation and Public Policy in Argentina," *Boletín de Estudios Latinoamericanos y del Caribe*, 51, 81–97.
(2009), "Perpetuating Social Movements amid Declining Opportunity: The Survival Strategies of Two Argentine Piquetero Groups," *European Review of Latin American and Caribbean Studies*, 86 (April), 3–19.
Etchegaray, Fabián and Elrodi, Carlos (2001), "Public Opinion, Presidential Popularity, and Economic Reforms in Argentina, 1989–1996," in Susan Stokes (ed.), *Public Support for Market Reforms in New Democracies* (New York: Cambridge University Press), 187–214.
Etchemendy, Sebastián (2004), "Repression, Exclusion, and Inclusion: Government-Union Relations and Patterns of Labor Reform in Liberalizing Economies," *Comparative Politics*, 36 (3), 273–90.
(2005), "Old Actors in New Markets: Transforming the Populist/Industrial Coalition in Argentina, 1989–2001," in Steven Levitsky and María Victoria Murillo (eds.), *Argentine Democracy: The Politics of Institutional Weakness* (University Park: Pennsylvania State University Press), 62–87.
Etchemendy, Sebastián and Collier, Ruth Berins (2007), "Down but Not Out: Union Resurgence and Segmented Neocorporatism in Argentina (2003–2007)," *Politics & Society*, 35 (3), 363–401.
Falleti, Tulia (2010), *Decentralization and Subnational Politics in Latin America* (New York: Cambridge University Press).
(2011), "Varieties of Authoritarianism: The Organization of the Military State and Its Effects on Federalism in Argentina and Brazil," *Studies in Comparative International Development*, 46 (2), 137–62.
Fantasia, Rick (1988), *Culture of Solidarity: Consciousness, Action, and Contemporary American Workers* (Berkeley: University of California Press).
Fara, Luis (1985), "Luchas reivindicativas urbanas en un contexto autoritario. Los asentamientos de San Francisco Solano," in Elizabeth Jelin (ed.), *Los nuevos movimientos sociales* (2nd edn.; Buenos Aires: Centro Editor de América Latina), 120–39.
Farinetti, Marina (1999), "¿Qué queda del movimiento obrero? Las formas del reclamo laboral en la nueva democracia argentina," *Trabajo y Sociedad*, 1 (1), 1–34.
Feliciano, Carlos Alberto (ed.) (2011), *DATALUTA – Banco de Dados da Luta pela Terra: Relatório 2010* (12th edn.; Presidente Prudente: NERA – Núcleo de Estudos, Pesquisas e Projetos de Reforma Agrária).
Fenwick, Tracy Beck (2009), "Avoiding Governors: The Success of Bolsa Família," *Latin American Research Review*, 44 (1), 102–31.
Fernandes, Bernardo Mançano (1998), *Gênese e desenvolvimento do MST* (São Paulo: MST).
(2000), *A formação do MST no Brasil* (Petrópolis: Vozes).

Fernandes, Bernardo Mançano and Stédile, João Pedro (1999), *Brava Gente: A Trajetória do MST e a Luta Pela Terra no Brasil* (São Paulo: Fundação Perseu Abramo).
Ferraudi Curto, María Cecilia (2006), "Lucha y papeles en una organización piquetera del sur de Buenos Aires," in Daniel Míguez and Pablo Semán (eds.), *Entre santos, cumbias y piquetes: Las culturas populares en la Argentina reciente* (Buenos Aires: Biblos), 145–64.
Ferrer, Nelson (2005), *El MTA y la resistencia al neoliberalismo en los 90* (Buenos Aires: Dos Orillas).
Fligstein, Neil and McAdam, Doug (2011), "Toward a General Theory of Strategic Action Fields," *Sociological Theory*, 29 (1), 1–26.
Flores, Héctor "Toty" (ed.) (2005a), *De la culpa a la autogestión. Un recorrido del Movimiento de Trabajadores Desocupados de la Matanza* (Buenos Aires: Peña Lillo – Continente).
(2005b), "De la culpa a la autogestión," in Héctor "Toty" Flores (ed.), *De la culpa a la autogestión. Un recorrido del Movimiento de Trabajadores Desocupados de La Matanza* (Buenos Aires: Peña Lillo – Ediciones Continente), 13–45.
(2006), *Cuando con otros somos nosotros. La experiencia asociativa del Movimiento de Trabajadores Desocupados – MTD La Matanza –* (Buenos Aires: MTD Editora).
Flores-Macías, Gustavo (2012), *After Neoliberalism? The Left and Economic Reforms in Latin America* (New York: Oxford University Press).
Fontana, Lorenza B. (2013), "On the Perils and Potentialities of Revolution: Conflict and Collective Action in Contemporary Bolivia," *Latin American Perspectives*, 40 (3), 26–42.
(2014), "Indigenous Peasant 'Otherness': Rural Identities and Political Processes in Bolivia," *Bulletin of Latin American Research*, 33 (4), 436–51.
Fornillo, Bruno, García, Analía, and Vázquez, Melina (2008), "Las organizaciones de desocupados autónomas en la Argentina reciente. Redefiniciones político-ideológicas e identitarias en el Frente Popular Darío Santillán (2003–2007)," in Sebastián Pereyra, Germán Pérez, and Federico Schuster (eds.), *La huella piquetera. Avatares de las organizaciones de desocupados después de 2001* (La Plata: Ediciones Al Margen), 365–92.
Franceschelli, Ignacio and Ronconi, Lucas (2009), "The Effect of Workfare Policy on Social Movement Mobilizations," *Economics Letters*, 105 (3), 315–17.
Freedman, Lawrence (2013), *Strategy: A History* (New York: Oxford University Press).
French, John D. (1992), *The Brazilian Workers' ABC: Class Conflict and Alliances in Modern São Paulo* (Chapel Hill: University of North Carolina Press).
Gamson, William (1975), *The Strategy of Social Protest* (Homewood: The Dorsey Press).
Gamson, William and Meyer, David (1996), "Framing Political Opportunity," in Doug McAdam, John McCarthy, and Mayer Zald (eds.), *Comparative Perspectives on Social Movements: Political Opportunities, Mobilizing Structures, and Cultural Framings* (New York: Cambridge University Press), 275–90.

Ganz, Marshall (2000), "Resources and Resourcefulness: Strategic Capacity in the Unionization of California Agriculture, 1959–1966," *American Journal of Sociology*, 105 (4), 1003–62.

Gasparini, Leonardo and Cruces, Guillermo (2010), "A Distribution in Motion: The Case of Argentina," in Luis López-Calva and Nora Lustig (eds.), *Declining Inequality in Latin America: A Decade of Progress?* (New York: United Nations Development Program), 100–33.

Gaudio, Ricardo and Pilone, Jorge (1983), "El desarrollo de la negociación colectiva durante la etapa de modernización industrial en la Argentina. 1935–1943," *Desarrollo Económico*, 23 (90), 255–86.

(1984), "Estado y relaciones laborales en el período previo al surgimiento del peronismo, 1935–1943," *Desarrollo Económico*, 24 (94), 235–73.

George, Alexander and McKewon, Timothy (1985), "Case Studies and Theories of Organizational Decision Making," *Advances in Information Processing in Organizations*, 2, 21–58.

Gerchunoff, Pablo and Torre, Juan Carlos (1996), "La política de liberalización económica en la administración de Menem," *Desarrollo Económico*, 36 (143), 733–68.

Germani, Gino (1973), "El surgimiento del peronismo: el rol de los obreros y de los migrantes internos," *Desarrollo Económico*, 13 (51), 435–88.

Germano, Carlos (ed.) (2005), *Piqueteros. Nueva realidad social* (Buenos Aires: ACEP-Konrad Adenauer Stiftung).

Gibson, Edward and Calvo, Ernesto (2000), "Federalism and Low-Maintenance Constituencies: Territorial Dimensions of Economic Reform in Argentina," *Studies in Comparative International Development*, 35 (3), 32–55.

Giraudy, Agustina (2007), "The Distributive Politics of Emergency Employment Programs in Argentina (1993–2002)," *Latin American Research Review*, 42 (2), 33–55.

Giugni, Marco (1998a), "Social Movements and Change: Incorporation, Transformation, and Democratization," in Marco Giugni, Doug McAdam, and Charles Tilly (eds.), *From Contention to Democracy* (Lanham: Rowman & Littlefield), xi–xxiii.

(1998b), "Was It Worth the Effort? Outcomes and Consequences of Social Movements," *Annual Review of Sociology*, 98, 371–93.

Godio, Julio (2000), *Historia del movimiento obrero argentino 1880–2000*, 2 vols. (Buenos Aires: Corregidor).

Goldstone, Jack (2003), "Bridging Institutionalized and Noninstitutionalized Politics," in Jack Goldstone (ed.), *States, Parties, and Social Movements* (New York: Cambridge University Press), 1–24.

Gómez, Marcelo (2006), "Crisis y recomposición de la respuesta estatal a la acción colectiva desafiante en la Argentina 1989–2004," *Revista Argentina de Sociología*, 4 (6), 88–128.

Goodwin, Jeff and Jasper, James M. (1999), "Caught in a Winding, Snarling Vine: The Structural Bias of Political Process Theory," *Sociological Forum*, 14 (1), 27–54.

(eds.) (2012), *Contention in Context: Political Opportunities and the Emergence of Protest* (Stanford: Stanford University Press).

Gorriarán Merlo, Enrique (2003), *Memorias de Enrique Gorriarán Merlo: De los setenta a La Tablada* (Buenos Aires: Planeta).
Gotkowitz, Laura (2007), *A Revolution for Our Rights: Indigenous Struggles for Land and Justice in Bolivia, 1880–1952* (Durham: Duke University Press).
Grimson, Alejandro (2003), "Piquetes en la ciénaga. Los bloqueos políticos de los cortes de ruta," *El Rodaballo* (15), 8–11.
Grugel, Jean and Riggirozzi, Pía (2009), *Governance after Neoliberalism in Latin America* (New York: Palgrave-Macmillan).
(eds.) (2012), "Post-Neoliberalism in Latin America: Rebuilding and Reclaiming the State after Crisis," *Development & Change*, 43 (1), 1–21.
Guevara, Ernesto "Che" (1997 [1963]), *Obras completas* (Buenos Aires: MACLA).
Haggard, Stephan and Kaufman, Robert R. (1995), *The Political Economy of Democratic Transitions* (Princeton: Princeton University Press).
Hammond, John L. and Rossi, Federico M. (2013), "Landless Workers Movement (MST) Brazil," in David Snow et al. (eds.), *The Wiley-Blackwell Encyclopedia of Social and Political Movements* (2nd edn.; Oxford: Wiley-Blackwell), 680–83.
Hardt, Michael and Negri, Antonio (2000), *Empire* (Cambridge: Harvard University Press).
Harnecker, Marta (2002), *Sin Tierra: construyendo movimiento social* (Madrid: Siglo XXI).
Healy, Kevin and Paulson, Susan (2000), "Political economies of identity in Bolivia, 1952–1998," *Journal of Latin American and Caribbean Anthropology*, 5 (2), 2–29.
Helmke, Gretchen and Levitsky, Steven (2006), "Introduction," in Gretchen Helmke and Steven Levitsky (eds.), *Informal Institutions and Democracy: Lessons from Latin America* (Baltimore: Johns Hopkins University Press), 1–30.
Herrera, María Rosa (2008), "La contienda política en Argentina 1997–2002: un ciclo de protesta," *América Latina Hoy*, 48, 165–89.
Hilb, Claudia (2007), "La Tablada: el último acto de la guerrilla setentista," *Lucha Armada en la Argentina*, 3 (9), 4–22.
Hilb, Claudia and Lutzky, Daniel (1984), *La nueva izquierda argentina: 1960–1980* (Buenos Aires: Centro Editor de América Latina).
Hobsbawm, Eric (1994), *The Age of Extremes: The Short Twentieth Century, 1914–1991* (London: Abacus).
Hobson, Barbara (2003), "Introduction," in Barbara Hobson (ed.), *Recognition Struggles and Social Movements: Contested Identities, Agency and Power* (Cambridge: Cambridge University Press), 1–17.
Holloway, John (2002), *Change the World without Taking Power* (London: Pluto Press).
Honneth, Axel (1995), *The Struggle for Recognition: The Moral Grammar of Social Conflicts* (Cambridge: Polity Press).
Huber, Evelyne and Stephens, John D. (2012), *Democracy and the Left: Social Policy and Inequality in Latin America* (Chicago: University of Chicago Press).

Hunter, Wendy (2010), *The Transformation of the Workers' Party in Brazil, 1989–2009* (New York: Cambridge University Press).

Ichaso, Josefina (2013) *Indicadores de conflictividad social (1980–2012)*, Centro de Estudios para la Nueva Mayoría, http://nuevamayoria.com/images/stories/celaforum/bases1212.pdf.

Isman, Raúl (2004), *Los piquetes de La Matanza: de la aparición del movimiento social a la construcción de la unidad popular* (Buenos Aires: Nuevos Tiempos).

Isuani, Ernesto (1985), *Los orígenes conflictivos de la seguridad social argentina* (Buenos Aires: Centro Editor de América Latina).

James, Daniel (1988), *Resistance and Integration: Peronism and the Argentine Working Class, 1946–1976* (Cambridge: Cambridge University Press).

Jasper, James M. (2004), "A Strategic Approach to Collective Action: Looking for Agency in Social Movement Choices," *Mobilization*, 9 (1), 1–16.

(2006), *Getting Your Way: Strategic Dilemmas in the Real World* (Chicago: University of Chicago Press).

(2012), "Choice Points, Emotional Batteries, and Other Ways to Find Strategic Agency at the Microlevel," in Gregory M. Maney et al. (eds.), *Strategies for Social Change* (Minneapolis: University of Minnesota Press), 23–42.

Jenness, Valerie, Meyer, David, and Ingram, Helen (2005), "Conclusion. Social Movements, Public Policy, and Democracy: Rethinking the Nexus," in David Meyer, Valerie Jenness, and Helen Ingram (eds.), *Routing the Opposition: Social Movements, Public Policy, and Democracy* (Minneapolis: The University of Minnesota Press), 288–306.

Karush, Matthew B. and Chamosa, Oscar (eds.) (2010), *The New Cultural History of Peronism: Power and Identity in Mid-twentieth-century Argentina* (Durham: Duke University Press).

Keifman, Saúl N. and Maurizio, Roxana (2014), "Changes in Labour Market Conditions and Policies and Their Impact on Wage Inequality during the Last Decade," in Giovanni Andrea Cornia (ed.), *Falling Inequality in Latin America: Policy Changes and Lessons* (Oxford: Oxford University Press), 251–73.

Klein, Herbert S. (2003), *A Concise History of Bolivia* (New York: Cambridge University Press).

Kohan, Aníbal (2002), *¡A las calles! Una historia de los movimientos piqueteros y caceroleros del '90 al 2002* (Buenos Aires: Colihue).

Korol, Claudia (2006), "Guerras y emancipaciones en las tierras del petróleo," in Claudia Korol (ed.), *Mosconi: cortando las rutas del petróleo* (Buenos Aires: Ediciones Madres de Plaza de Mayo), 51–84.

Krinsky, John and Mische, Ann (2013), "Formations and Formalisms: Charles Tilly and the Paradox of the Actor," *Annual Review of Sociology*, 39 (1), 1–26.

Kurtz, Marcus J. (2013), *Latin American State Building in Comparative Perspective: Social Foundations of Institutional Order* (New York: Cambridge University Press).

Lee Mudge, Stephanie (2008), "What Is Neo-liberalism?," *Socio-Economic Review*, 6 (4), 703–31.

Levitsky, Steven (2001), "An 'Organised Disorganisation': Informal Organisation and the Persistence of Local Party Structures in Argentine Peronism," *Journal of Latin American Studies*, 33 (1), 29–66.

(2003a), "From Labor Politics to Machine Politics: The Transformation of Party-Union Linkages in Argentine Peronism, 1983–1999," *Latin American Research Review*, 38 (3), 3–36.

(2003b), *Transforming Labor-Based Parties in Latin America: Argentine Peronism in Comparative Perspective* (Cambridge: Cambridge University Press).

Levitsky, Steven and Murillo, María Victoria (2003), "Argentina Weathers the Storm," *Journal of Democracy*, 14 (4), 152–66.

(2005), "Introduction," in Steven Levitsky and María Victoria Murillo (eds.), *The Politics of Institutional Weakness: Argentine Democracy* (University Park: Pennsylvania State University Press), 1–17.

Levitsky, Steven and Roberts, Kenneth M. (2011), "Latin America's 'Left Turn': A Framework for Analysis," in Steven Levitsky and Kenneth M. Roberts (eds.), *The Resurgence of the Latin American Left* (Baltimore: Johns Hopkins University Press), 1–28.

Linz, Juan J. (1978), *The Breakdown of Democratic Regimes: Crisis, Breakdown and Reequilibration* (Baltimore: Johns Hopkins University Press).

Llanos, Mariana (2002), *Privatization and Democracy in Latin America: An Analysis of President-Congress Relations* (New York: Palgrave).

Lodola, Germán (2005), "Protesta popular y redes clientelares en la Argentina: el reparto federal del Plan Trabajar (1996–2001)," *Desarrollo Económico*, 44 (176), 515–16.

Lucero, José Antonio (2008), *Struggles of Voice: The Politics of Indigenous Representation in the Andes* (Pittsburgh: University of Pittsburgh Press).

Luna, Juan Pablo and Filgueira, Fernando (2009), "The Left Turns as Multiple Paradigmatic Crises," *Third World Quarterly*, 30 (2), 371–95.

Lupien, Pascal (2011), "The Incorporation of Indigenous Concepts of Plurinationality into the New Constitutions of Ecuador and Bolivia," *Democratization*, 18 (3), 774 –96.

Lustig, Nora, Gray-Molina, George, Higgins, Sean, Jaramillo, Miguel, Jiménez, Wilson, Paz, Verónica, Pereira, Claudiney, Pessino, Carola, Scott, John, and Yañez, Ernesto (2012), "The Impact of Taxes and Social Spending on Inequality and Poverty in Argentina, Bolivia, Brazil, Mexico, and Peru: A Synthesis of Results," CEQ Working Paper 3 (Commitment to Equity: Tulane University), www.commitmentoequity.org/publications_files/Latin%20America/CEQWPNo3%20SocSpendSynthesisResults%20Jan%202013.pdf.

Mahoney, James (2000), "Path Dependence in Historical Sociology," *Theory and Society*, 29 (4), 507–48.

(2001), *The Legacies of Liberalism: Path Dependence and Political Regimes in Central America* (Baltimore: Johns Hopkins University Press).

Mahoney, James and Thelen, Kathleen (2010), "A Theory of Gradual Institutional Change," in James Mahon and Kathleen Thelen (eds.), *Explaining Institutional Change: Ambiguity, Agency, and Power* (New York: Cambridge University Press), 1–37.

Maney, Gregory M., Andrew, Kenneth T., Kutz-Flamenbaum, Rachel V., Rohlinger, Deana A., and Goodwin, Jeff (2012), "An Introduction to Strategies for Social Change," in Gregory M. Maney et al. (eds.), *Strategies for Social Change* (Minneapolis: University of Minnesota Press), xi–xxxviii.

Manin, Bernard (1992), "Metamorfosis de la representación," in Mario Dos Santos (ed.), *¿Qué queda de la representación política?* (Caracas: CLACSO-Nueva Sociedad), 9–40.

Mao, Tse-Tung (1965 [1940]), "Current Problems of Tactics in the Anti-Japanese United Front," in Tse-Tung Mao (ed.), *Selected Works of Mao Tse-Tung* (2nd edn.; Beijing: Foreign Language Press), 421–30.

Martins, Jose de Souza (1994), *O Poder do Atraso: Ensaios de Sociologia da História Lenta* (São Paulo: Hucitec).

Marx, Karl (1926 [1852]), *The Eighteenth Brumaire of Louis Bonaparte* (New York: International Publishers).

Massetti, Astor (2006), "'Piqueteros eran los de antes': sobre las transformaciones en la protesta piquetera," *Lavboratorio*, 8 (19), 29–36.

(2009), "Cuando los movimientos se institucionalizan. Las organizaciones territoriales urbanas en el gobierno de la ciudad de Buenos Aires," in Gabriela Delamata (ed.), *Movilizaciones sociales: ¿nuevas ciudadanías?* (Buenos Aires: Biblos), 205–35.

Mauro, Sebastián and Rossi, Federico M. (2015), "The Movement of Popular and Neighborhood Assemblies in the City of Buenos Aires, 2002–2011," *Latin American Perspectives*, 42 (2), 107–24.

Maybury-Lewis, Biorn (1994), *The Politics of the Possible: The Brazilian Rural Workers' Trade Union Movement, 1964–1985* (Philadelphia: Temple University Press).

Mazzeo, Miguel (2004), *Piqueteros: Notas para una tipología* (Buenos Aires: FISyP – Manuel Suárez).

McAdam, Doug (1982), *Political Process and the Development of Black Insurgency, 1930–1970* (Chicago: University of Chicago Press).

(1983), "Tactical Innovation and the Pace of Insurgency," *American Sociological Review*, 48 (6), 735–54.

(1996), "Conceptual Problems, Current Problems, Future Directions," in Doug McAdam, John McCarthy, and Mayer Zald (eds.), *Comparative Perspectives on Social Movements: Political Opportunities, Mobilizing Structures, and Cultural Framings* (New York: Cambridge University Press), 23–40.

McAdam, Doug, Tarrow, Sidney, and Tilly, Charles (2001), *Dynamics of Contention* (New York: Cambridge University Press).

(2008), "Methods for Measuring Mechanisms of Contention," *Qualitative Sociology*, 31 (4), 307–31.

McGuire, James (1997), *Peronism without Perón: Unions, Parties and Democracy in Argentina* (Stanford: Stanford University Press).

Melucci, Antonio (1989), *Nomads of the Present. Social Movements and Individual Needs in Contemporary Society* (Philadelphia: Temple University Press).

Merklen, Denis (1991), *Asentamientos en La Matanza: La terquedad de lo nuestro* (Buenos Aires: Catálogos).

(2005), *Pobres Ciudadanos. Las clases populares en la era democrática (Argentina, 1983–2003)* (Buenos Aires: Gorla).

Meyer, David and Minkoff, Debra (2004), "Conceptualizing Political Opportunities," *Social Forces*, 82 (4), 1457–92.

Meyer, David and Staggenborg, Suzanne (2012), "Thinking about Strategy," in Gregory M. Maney et al. (eds.), *Strategies for Social Change* (Minneapolis: University of Minnesota Press), 3–22.

Mignone, Emilio (2006), *Iglesia y dictadura. El papel de la iglesia a la luz de sus relaciones con el régimen militar* (2nd edn.; Buenos Aires: Colihue).

Moreno, Nahuel (1980), *Tesis sobre las revoluciones del siglo XX. Actualización del programa de transición* (Buenos Aires: Antídoto).

Motta, Sara C. (2009), "New Ways of Making and Living Politics: The Movimiento de Trabajadores Desocupados de Solano and the 'Movement of Movements,'" *Bulletin of Latin American Research*, 28 (1), 83–101.

Moyano, María José (1992), "Going Underground in Argentina. A Look at the Founders of a Guerrilla Movement," in Donatella della Porta (ed.), *International Social Movement Research* (4th edn.; Greenwich: JAI Press), 105–29.

MTD de Solano and Colectivo Situaciones (2002), *La hipótesis 891. Más allá de los piquetes* (Buenos Aires: Ediciones de Mano en Mano).

Murillo, María Victoria (1999), "Recovering Political Dynamics: Teachers' Unions and the Decentralization of Education in Argentina and Mexico," *Journal of Interamerican Studies and World Affairs*, 41 (1), 31–57.

(2005), "Partisanship amidst Convergence: The Politics of Labor Reform in Latin America," *Comparative Politics*, 37 (4), 441–58.

Natalucci, Ana (2008a), "De los barrios a la plaza. Desplazamientos en la trayectoria del Movimiento Evita," in Sebastián Pereyra, Germán Pérez, and Federico Schuster (eds.), *La huella piquetera. Avatares de las organizaciones de desocupados después de 2001* (La Plata: Ediciones Al Margen), 117–40.

(2008b), "Las estrategias de las orgánicas de izquierda frente a la crisis de 2001. El caso del Polo Obrero," in Sebastián Pereyra, Germán Pérez, and Federico Schuster (eds.), *La huella piquetera. Avatares de las organizaciones de desocupados después de 2001* (La Plata: Ediciones Al Margen), 205–31.

Navarro, Zander (1994), "Democracy, Citizenship and Representation: Rural Social Movements in Southern Brazil, 1978–1990," *Bulletin of Latin American Research*, 13 (2), 129–54.

(2008), "Social Movements of the Past Confront the Present: The Brazilian Landless Movement (MST) and the Challenges of Mobilising the Rural Poor in Neoliberal Times," Conference: "Social Movements and the Politics of Neoliberalism: International Perspectives on the MENA Region" (March 12–15, Florence & Montecatini Terme: European University Institute).

Neffa, Julio (2008), *Desempleo, pobreza y políticas públicas. Fortalezas y debilidades del Plan Jefes y Jefas de Hogar Desocupados* (Buenos Aires: Miño y Dávila).

Negri, Antonio (2001), "Contrapoder," in Colectivo Situaciones (ed.), *Contrapoder: una introducción* (Buenos Aires: Ediciones de Mano en Mano), 83–92.

Nepstad, Sharon Erickson and Vinthagen, Stellan (2012), "Strategic Choices in Cross-National Movements: A Comparison of the Swedish and British Plowshares Movements," in Gregory M. Maney et al. (eds.), *Strategies for Social Change* (Minneapolis: University of Minnesota Press), 263–84.

Novaro, Marcos (2009), *Argentina en el fin de siglo. Democracia, mercado y nación (1983–2001)* (Buenos Aires: Paidós).

Novaro, Marcos and Palermo, Vicente (2003), *La dictadura militar, 1976–1983: del golpe de estado a la restauración democrática* (Buenos Aires: Paidós).

O'Donnell, Guillermo (1973), *Modernization and Bureaucratic-Authoritarianism: Studies in South American Politics* (Berkeley: Institute of International Studies, University of California).

(1988), *Bureaucratic Authoritarianism: Argentina, 1966–1973, in Comparative Perspective* (Berkeley: University of California Press).

Ollier, María Matilde (2001), *Las coaliciones políticas en la Argentina: el caso de la Alianza* (Buenos Aires: Fondo de Cultura Económica).

(2009), *De la revolución a la democracia: cambios privados, públicos y políticos de la izquierda argentina* (Buenos Aires: Siglo XXI).

Ondetti, Gabriel (2008), *Land, Protest, and Politics: The Landless Movement and the Struggle for Agrarian Reform in Brazil* (University Park: Pennsylvania State University Press).

Orlansky, Dora (1998), "Las políticas de descentralización," *Desarrollo Económico*, 38 (151), 827–44.

Oszlak, Oscar (2003), "El mito del estado mínimo: una década de reforma estatal en la Argentina," *Desarrollo Económico*, 42 (168), 519–43.

Oviedo, Luis (2000), *Una historia del movimiento piquetero. De las primeras coordinadoras a las asambleas nacionales* (1st edn.; Buenos Aires: Rumbo).

(2004), *Una historia del movimiento piquetero. De las primeras coordinadoras al Argentinazo* (2nd edn.; Buenos Aires: Rumbos).

Oxhorn, Philip (1998), "Is the Century of Corporatism Over? Neoliberalism and the Rise of Neopluralism," in Philip Oxhorn and Graciela Ducatenzeiler (eds.), *What Kind of Democracy? What Kind of Market? Latin America in the Age of Neoliberalism* (University Park: Pennsylvania State University Press), 195–217.

Pacheco, Mariano (2004), *Del piquete al movimiento. Parte 1: De los origenes al 20 de diciembre de 2001* (Buenos Aires: Cuadernos de la FISYP).

Palermo, Vicente and Novaro, Marcos (1996), *Política y poder en el gobierno de Menem* (Buenos Aires: Norma).

Panizza, Francisco (2009), *Contemporary Latin America: Development and Democracy beyond the Washington Consensus* (London: Zed Books).

Pereira, Anthony (1997), *The End of the Peasantry: The Rural Labor Movement in Northeast Brazil, 1961–1988* (Pittsburgh: University of Pittsburgh Press).

(2003), "Brazil's Agrarian Reform: Democratic Innovation or Oligarchic Exclusion Redux?," *Latin American Politics and Society*, 45 (2), 41–65.

Perelmiter, Luisina (2012), "Fronteras inestables y eficaces. El ingreso de organizaciones de desocupados a la burocracia asistencial del Estado. Argentina (2003–2008)," *Estudios Sociológicos*, 30 (89), 431–58.

Pereyra, Sebastián, Pérez, Germán, and Schuster, Federico (eds.) (2008), *La huella piquetera. Avatares de las organizaciones de desocupados después de 2001* (La Plata: Ediciones Al Margen).

Pérez, Germán and Natalucci, Ana (eds.) (2012), *"Vamos las bandas": organizaciones y militancia kirchnerista* (Buenos Aires: Nueva Trilce).

Perrault, Thomas (2006), "From the *Guerra del Agua* to the *Guerra del Gas*: Resource Governance, Popular Protest and Social Justice in Bolivia," *Antipode*, 38, 150–72.

Peruzzotti, Enrique (2005), "Demanding Accountable Government: Citizens, Politicians, and the Perils of Representative Democracy in Argentina," in Steven Levitsky and María Victoria Murillo (eds.), *Argentine Democracy: The Politics of Institutional Weakness* (University Park: Pennsylvania State University Press), 229–49.

Pierson, Paul (2000), "Not Just What, but *When*: Timing and Sequence in Political Processes," *Studies in American Political Development*, 14, 72–92.

(2004), *Politics in Time: History, Institutions, and Social Analysis* (Princeton: Princeton University Press).

Piven, Frances and Cloward, Richard (1979), *Poor People's Movements: Why They Succeed, How They Failed* (New York: Vintage Books).

Plotkin, Mariano (2003), *Mañana es San Perón: A Cultural History of Perón's Argentina* (Wilmington: SR Books).

Poli, Christian (2007), *Movimiento Territorial Liberación: piquetes, organización, poder popular* (Buenos Aires: Ediciones del CCC).

Portes, Alejandro and Hoffmann, Kelly (2003), "Latin American Class Structures: Their Composition and Change during the Neoliberal Era," *Latin American Research Review*, 38 (1), 41–82.

Prévôt-Schapira, Marie-France (1993), "La consolidación municipal en el Gran Buenos Aires: tensiones y ambigüedades," *Estudio Sociológicos*, 11 (33), 769–98.

(1996), "Las políticas de lucha contra la pobreza en la periferia de Buenos Aires, 1984–1994," *Revista Mexicana de Sociología*, 58 (2), 73–94.

(1999), "From Utopia to Pragmatism: The Heritage of Basismo in Local Government in the Greater Buenos Aires Region," *Bulletin of Latin American Research*, 18 (2), 227–39.

Quirós, Julieta (2006), *Cruzando la Sarmiento: Una etnografía sobre piqueteros en la trama social sur del Gran Buenos Aires* (Buenos Aires: Antropofagia-IDES).

Rabotnikof, Nora, Riggirozzi, María Pía, and Tussie, Diana (2000), "Los organismos internacionales frente a la sociedad civil: las agendas en juego," in Diana Tussie (ed.), *Luces y sombras de una nueva relación. El Banco Interamericano de Desarrollo, el Banco Mundial y la sociedad civil* (Buenos Aires: Temas), 39–72.

Reiss, Matthias and Perry, Matt (eds.) (2011), *Unemployment and Protest: New Perspectives on Two Centuries of Contention* (Oxford: Oxford University Press).

Repetto, Fabián (2000), "Gestión pública, actores e institucionalidad: las políticas frente a la pobreza en los '90,' *Desarrollo Económico*, 39 (156), 597–618.

Reygadas, Luis and Filgueira, Fernando (2010), "Inequality and the Incorporation Crisis: The Left's Social Policy Toolkit," in Maxwell A. Cameron and Eric Hershberg (eds.), *Latin America's Left Turns: Politics, Policies, and Trajectories of Change* (Boulder: Lynne Rienner), 171–91.

Roberts, Kenneth M. (1998), *Deepening Democracy? The Modern Left and Social Movements in Chile and Peru* (Stanford: Stanford University Press).

(2002), "Social Inequalities without Class Cleavages in Latin America's Neoliberal Era," *Studies in Comparative International Development*, 36 (4), 3–33.

(2008), "The Mobilization of Opposition to Economic Liberalization," *Annual Review of Political Science*, 11 (1), 327–49.

(2013), "Market Reform, Programmatic (De)alignment, and Party System Stability in Latin America," *Comparative Political Studies*, 46 (11), 1422–52.

Rodríguez Blanco, Maricel (2002), "La parte de los que no tienen parte. La dimensión simbólica y política de las protestas sociales: la experiencia de los piqueteros en Jujuy," *Cuadernos de Trabajo* (Buenos Aires: Centro Cultural de la Cooperación).

Rossi, Federico M. (2005a), "Aparición, auge y declinación de un movimiento social: las asambleas vecinales y populares de Buenos Aires, 2001–2003," *European Review of Latin American and Caribbean Studies*, 78 (April), 67–88.

(2005b), "Crisis de la República Delegativa. La constitución de nuevos actores políticos en la Argentina (2001–2003): las asambleas vecinales y populares," *América Latina Hoy*, 39, 195–216.

(2006), "Movimientos Sociales," in Luis Aznar and Miguel De Luca (eds.), *Política. Cuestiones y Problemas* (1st edn.; Buenos Aires: Ariel), 235–74.

(2013a), "Peronism," in David Snow et al. (eds.), *The Wiley-Blackwell Encyclopedia of Social and Political Movements* (3rd edn.; Oxford: Willey-Blackwell), 925–28.

(2013b), "*Piqueteros* (Workers/Unemployment Movement in Argentina)," in David Snow et al. (eds.), *The Wiley-Blackwell Encyclopedia of Social and Political Movements* (3rd edn.; Oxford: Wiley-Blackwell), 929–32.

(2015a), "Beyond Clientelism: The Piquetero Movement and the State in Argentina," in Paul Almeida and Allen Cordero Ulate (eds.), *Handbook of Social Movements across Latin America* (New York: Springer), 117–28.

(2015b), "Conceptualizing Strategy Making in a Historical and Collective Perspective," in Federico M. Rossi and Marisa von Bülow (eds.), *Social Movement Dynamics: New Perspectives on Theory and Research from Latin America* (The Mobilization Series on Social Movements, Protest and Culture; Farnham: Ashgate), 15–41.

(2015c), "The Second Wave of Incorporation in Latin America: A Conceptualization of the Quest for Inclusion Applied to Argentina," *Latin American Politics and Society*, 57 (1), 1–28.

Rot, Gabriel (2007), "El Partido Comunista y la lucha armada," *Lucha Armada en la Argentina*, 3 (7), 14–25.

Rubio, Leticia and Del Grossi, Leonardo (eds.) (2005), *Habla Quebracho: una mirada histórica* (Buenos Aires: Movimiento Patriótico Revolucionario "Quebracho").

Ruggeri, Andrés (ed.) (2010), *Las empresas recuperadas en la Argentina 2010* (Buenos Aires: Programa Facultad Abierta – Universidad de Buenos Aires).

Russo, Sandra (2010), *Milagro Sala: Jallalla. La Tupac Amaru, utopía en construcción* (Buenos Aires: Colihue).

Saad-Filho, Alfredo, Iannini, Francesca, and Molinari, Elizabeth Jean (2007), "Neoliberalism, Democracy and Economic Policy in Latin America," in Philip Arestis and Malcolm Sawyer (eds.), *Political Economy of Latin America: Recent Economic Performance* (New York: Palgrave-Macmillan), 1–35.

Sain, Marcelo Fabián (2006), "Police, Politics, and Society in the Province of Buenos Aires," in Edward Epstein and David Pion-Berlin (eds.), *Broken Promises? The Argentine Crisis and Argentine Democracy* (Lanham: Lexington Books), 51–70.

Sallum Jr., Brasilio (2003), "The Changing Role of the State: New Patterns of State-Society Relations in Brazil at the End of the Twentieth Century," in Maria D'Alva Kinzo and James Dunkerley (eds.), *Brazil since 1985: Politics, Economy and Society* (London: Institute of Latin American Studies), 179–99.

Sánchez, Pilar (2000), *Correntinazo itéva* (Cuadernos; Buenos Aires: Editorial Agora).

(1997), *El Cutralcazo: la pueblada de Cutral Co y Plaza Huincul* (Cuadernos; Buenos Aires: Editorial Agora).

Sanjinés C., Javier (2004), *Mestizaje Upside-Down: Aesthetic Politics in Modern Bolivia* (Pittsburgh: University of Pittsburgh Press).

Santillán, Carlos "Perro" and Olmedo, Jesús (1998), *El "Perro" Santillán. Diálogo con Jesús Olmedo* (Buenos Aires: Ediciones Populares).

Schefner, Jon, Pasdirtz, George, and Blad, Cory (2006), "Austerity Protests and Immiserating Growth in Mexico and Argentina," in Hank Johnston and Paul Almeida (eds.), *Latin American Social Movements: Globalization, Democratization and Transnational Networks* (Lanham: Rowman & Littlefield), 19–41.

Schmitter, Philippe C. (1974), "Still the Century of Corporatism?," *The Review of Politics*, 36, 85–131.

Schuster, Federico, Pérez, Germán, Pereyra, Sebastián, Armesto, Melchor, Armelino, Martín, García, Analía, Natalucci, Ana, Vázquez, Melina, and Zipcioglu, Patricia (2006), *Transformaciones en la protesta social en Argentina 1989–2003* (Documentos de Trabajo; Buenos Aires: IIGG-Universidad de Buenos Aires).

Schutz, Alfred (1967), *The Phenomenology of the Social World* (Evanston: Northwestern University Press).

Schvarzer, Jorge (1998), "Economic Reform in Argentina: Which Social Forces for What Aims?," in Philip Oxhorn and Graciela Ducatenzeiler (eds.), *What Kind of Democracy? What Kind of Market?* (University Park: Pennsylvania State University Press), 61–88.

Scribano, Adrián (1999), "Argentina 'cortada': cortes de ruta y visibilidad social en el contexto del ajuste," in Margarita López Maya (ed.), *Lucha popular, democracia, neoliberalismo: protesta popular en América Latina en los años del ajuste* (Caracas: Editorial Nueva Sociedad), 45–71.

Sewell, William H., Jr. (2005), *Logics of History* (Chicago: The Chicago University Press).

(2008), "The Temporalities of Capitalism," *Socio-Economic Review*, 6 (3), 517–37.

Silva, Eduardo (2009), *Challenging Neoliberalism in Latin America* (New York: Cambridge University Press).

Silva, Eduardo and Rossi, Federico M. (eds.) (forthcoming), *Reshaping the Political Arena in Latin America: From Resisting Neoliberalism to the Second Incorporation* (Pittsburgh: University of Pittsburgh Press).

Smith, William C., Acuña, Carlos H., and Gamarra, Eduardo A. (eds.) (1994), *Latin American Political Economy in the Age of Neoliberal Reform: Theoretical and Comparative Perspectives for the 1990s* (Coral Gables: North-South Center – Transaction Publishers).

Smithey, Lee A. (2009), "Social Movement Strategy, Tactics, and Collective Identity," *Sociology Compass*, 3 (4), 658–71.

Smulovitz, Catalina (2005), "Petitioning and Creating Rights: Judicialization in Argentina," in Rachel Sieder, Line Schjolden, and Alan Angell (eds.), *The Judicialization of Politics in Latin America* (New York: Palgrave MacMillan), 161–85.

Snow, David, Soule, Sarah, and Kriesi, Hanspeter (2004), "Mapping the Terrain," in David Snow, Sarah Soule, and Hanspeter Kriesi (eds.), *The Blackwell Companion to Social Movements* (Oxford: Blackwell), 3–16.

Sorel, Georges (1999 [1908]), *Reflections on Violence* (Cambridge: Cambridge University Press).

Staggenborg, Suzanne (1991), *The Pro-Choice Movement: Organization and Activism in the Abortion Conflict* (New York: Oxford University Press).

Stener Carlson, Eric (2006), "The Gendarmen's Response to Social Protest in Argentina," in Edward Epstein and David Pion-Berlin (eds.), *Broken Promises? The Argentine Crisis and Argentine Democracy* (Lanham: Lexington Books), 181–202.

Suriano, Juan (1988), *Trabajadores, anarquismo y Estado represor: de la Ley de Residencia a la Ley de Defensa Social (1902–1910)* (Buenos Aires: Centro Editor de América Latina).

(ed.) (2000), *La cuestión social en Argentina, 1870–1943* (Buenos Aires: La Colmena).

Svampa, Maristella (2003), "Organizaciones de trabajadores desocupados. El modelo General Mosconi. Un estudio de caso," in Inés González Bombal (ed.), *Nuevos movimientos sociales y ONGs en la Argentina de la ciris* (Buenos Aires: CEDES), 51–78.

(2005), *La sociedad excluyente: la Argentina bajo el signo del neoliberalismo* (Buenos Aires: Taurus).

(2006), "La experiencia de la UTD," in Claudia Korol (ed.), *Mosconi: cortando las rutas del petróleo* (Buenos Aires: Ediciones Madres de Plaza de Mayo), 151–57.

Svampa, Maristella and Pandolfi, Claudio (2004), "Las vías de la criminalización de la protesta en Argentina," *Revista del Observatorio Social de América Latina*, 14, 285–96.

Svampa, Maristella and Pereyra, Sebastián (2003), *Entre la ruta y el barrio: la experiencia de las organizaciones piqueteras* (1st edn.; Buenos Aires: Biblos).

Tarcus, Horacio (1996), *El marxismo olvidado en la Argentina: Silvio Frondizi y Milcíades Peña* (Buenos Aires: El Cielo por Asalto).

Tarrow, Sidney (1989), *Democracy and Disorder. Protest and Politics in Italy, 1965–1975* (Cambridge: Cambridge University Press).

(1994), *Power in Movement: Social Movements, Collective Action, and Politics* (1st edn.; New York: Cambridge University Press).

(1998), *Power in Movement: Social Movements and Contentious Politics* (2nd edn.; Cambridge: Cambridge University Press).

(2012), *Strangers at the Gates: Movements and States in Contentious Politics* (Cambridge: Cambridge University Press).

Taylor, Verta and Van Dyke, Nella (2004), "'Get Up, Stand Up': Tactical Repertoires of Social Movements," in David Snow, Sarah Soule, and Hanspeter Kriesi (eds.), *The Blackwell Companion to Social Movements* (Oxford: Blackwell), 262–93.

Thelen, Kathleen (1999), "Historical Institutionalism in Comparative Perspective," *Annual Review of Political Science*, 2, 369–404.

Tilly, Charles (1984), *Big Structures, Large Processes, Huge Comparisons* (New York: Russell Sage Foundation).

(1986), *The Contentious French* (Cambridge: Harvard University Press).

(1995), "Contentious Repertoires in Great Britain, 1758–1834," in Mark Traugott (ed.), *Repertoires and Cycles of Collective Action* (Durham: Duke University Press), 15–42.

(2004), *Social Movements, 1768–2004* (Boulder: Paradigm).

(2006), *Regimes and Repertoires* (Chicago: University of Chicago Press).

(2008), *Contentious Performances* (New York: Cambridge University Press).

Tilly, Charles and Tarrow, Sidney (2006), *Contentious Politics* (Boulder: Paradigm).

Tokman, Victor E. and O'Donnell, Guillermo (1998), *Poverty and Inequality in Latin America: Issues and New Challenges* (Notre Dame: University of Notre Dame Press).

Torre, Juan Carlos (1990), *Perón y la Vieja Guardia Sindical. Los orígenes del peronismo* (Buenos Aires: Sudamericana).

(2004), "Prólogo," in Juan Carlos Torre (ed.), *El gigante invertebrado. Los sindicatos en el gobierno, 1973–1976* (Buenos Aires: Siglo XXI), VII–XVIII.

Torre, Juan Carlos and Pastoriza, Elisa (2002), "La democratización del bienestar," in Juan Carlos Torre (ed.), *Los años peronistas (1943–1955)* (Nueva Historia Argentina, 8th edn.; Buenos Aires: Sudamericana), 257–312.

Torres, Fernanda (2006), *Todavía piqueteros: la CTD Aníbal Verón* (La Plata: Editorial de la Universidad de La Plata).

Tórrez, Yuri F., Jáuregui, Luciana, Mamani, Juan Víctor, and García, Mildred (2013), *La izquierda en el poder: o cuando los gobiernos progresistas lidian*

con lo popular en Bolivia (1943–2011) (Cochabamba: Centro Cuarto Intermedio).
Traverso, Enzo (2006), *Il passato: istruzioni per l'uso. Storia, memoria, politica.* (Verona: Ombre Corte).
Tussie, Diana (ed.) (2000), *Luces y sombras de una nueva relación. El Banco Interamericano de Desarrollo, el Banco Mundial y la sociedad civil* (Buenos Aires: Temas).
UNDP (2015), *Human Development Report 2015* (New York: UNDP).
Van Cott, Donna (2005), *From Movements to Parties in Latin America: The Evolution of Ethnic Politics* (New York: Cambridge University Press).
Vommaro, Pablo (2008), "El trabajo territorial y comunitario de las organizaciones de desocupados: el caso del MTD de Solano," in Germán Pérez, Sebastián Pereyra, and Federico Schuster (eds.), *La huella piquetera. Avatares de las organizaciones de desocupados después de 2001* (La Plata: Ediciones Al Margen), 355–64.
von Bülow, Marisa and Lassance, Antônio (2012), "Brasil después de Lula: ¿más de lo mismo?," *Revista de Ciencia Política*, 32 (1), 49–64.
Wainwright, Hilary and Branford, Sue (2006), *En el ojo del huracán: visiones de militantes de izquierda sobre la crisis política de Brasil* (Amsterdam: TNI).
Weitz-Shapiro, Rebecca (2006), "Partisanship and Protest: The Politics of Workfare Distribution in Argentina," *Latin American Research Review*, 41 (3), 122–47.
Welch, Cliff (1999), *The Seed Was Planted: The São Paulo Roots of Brazil's Rural Labor Movement, 1924–1964* (Pennsylvania: Pennsylvania State University Press).
(2009), "Camponeses: Brazil's Peasant Movement in Historical Perspective (1946–2004)," *Latin American Perspectives*, 36 (4), 126–55.
Wenger, Etienne (1998), *Communities of Practice: Learning, Meaning, and Identity* (Cambridge: Cambridge University Press).
Weyland, Kurt Gerhard, Madrid, Raúl L., and Hunter, Wendy (eds.) (2010), *Leftist Governments in Latin America: Successes and Shortcomings* (New York: Cambridge University Press).
Wolff, Jonas (2007), "(De-)Mobilising the Marginalised: A Comparison of the Argentine Piqueteros and Ecuador's Indigenous Movement," *Journal of Latin American Studies*, 39 (01), 1–29.
(2013), "Towards Post-Liberal Democracy in Latin America? A Conceptual Framework Applied to Bolivia," *Journal of Latin American Studies*, 45 (01), 31–59.
Woods, Marcela (2007), "Modalidades y límites de la intervención de la Iglesia Católica en conflictos sociales territoriales. De la mediación a la confrontación en la diócesis de Quilmes," in María Cristina Cravino (ed.), *Resistiendo en los barrios. Acción colectiva y movimientos sociales en el Área Metropolitana de Buenos Aires* (Buenos Aires: UNGS), 77–99.
World Bank (2000), *Implementation Report 41950-AR. Buenos Aires* (Washington: World Bank).
Wright, Angus and Wolford, Wendy (2003), *To Inherit the Earth: The Landless Movement and the Struggle for a New Brazil* (Oakland: Food First Books).

Yashar, Deborah (1998), "Contesting Citizenship: Indigenous Movements and Democracy in Latin America," *Comparative Politics*, 31 (1), 23–42.

(2005), *Contesting Citizenship in Latin America: The Rise of Indigenous Movements and the Postliberal Challenge* (New York: Cambridge University Press).

Zuazo, Moira (2009), *¿Ciómo nació el MAS? La ruralizaciión de la política en Bolivia. Entrevistas a 85 parlamentarios del partido* (2nd edn.; La Paz: Friedrich Ebert Stiftung).

(2010), "¿Los movimientos sociales en el poder? El gobierno del MAS en Bolivia," *Nueva Sociedad*, 227 (May–June), 120–34.

Index

Books in the Series (*continued from p. ii*)

Donatella della Porta, *Where Did the Revolution Go?: Contentious Politics and the Quality of Democracy*
Mario Diani, *The Cement of Civil Society: Studying Networks in Localities*
Todd A. Eisenstadt, *Politics, Identity, and Mexico's Indigenous Rights Movements*
Daniel Q. Gillion, *The Political Power of Protest: Minority Activism and Shifts in Public Policy*
Jack A. Goldstone, editor, *States, Parties, and Social Movements*
Jennifer Hadden, *Networks in Contention: The Divisive Politics of Climate Change*
Michael T. Heaney and Fabio Rojas, *Party in the Street: The Antiwar Movement and the Democratic Party after 9/11*
Tamara Kay, *NAFTA and the Politics of Labor Transnationalism*
Neil Ketchley, *Egypt in a Time of Revolution: Contentious Politics and the Arab Spring*
Joseph Luders, *The Civil Rights Movement and the Logic of Social Change*
Doug McAdam and Hilary Boudet, *Putting Social Movements in Their Place: Explaining Opposition to Energy Projects in the United States, 2000–2005*
Doug McAdam, Sidney Tarrow, and Charles Tilly, *Dynamics of Contention*
Holly J. McCammon, *The U.S. Women's Jury Movements and Strategic Adaptation: A More Just Verdict*
Sharon Nepstad, *Religion and War Resistance and the Plowshares Movement*
Kevin J. O'Brien and Lianjiang Li, *Rightful Resistance in Rural China*
Silvia Pedraza, *Political Disaffection in Cuba's Revolution and Exodus*
Héctor Perla Jr., *Sandinista Nicaragua's Resistance to US Coercion*
Eduardo Silva, *Challenging Neoliberalism in Latin America*
Erica S. Simmons, *Meaningful Resistance: Market Reforms and the Roots of Social Protest in Latin America*
Sarah Soule, *Contention and Corporate Social Responsibility*
Sherrill Stroschein, *Ethnic Struggle, Coexistence, and Democratization in Eastern Europe*
Yang Su, *Collective Killings in Rural China during the Cultural Revolution*
Sidney Tarrow, *The Language of Contention: Revolutions in Words, 1688–2012*
Sidney Tarrow, *The New Transnational Activism*
Wayne P. Te Brake, *Religious War and Religious Peace in Early Modern Europe*
Ralph A. Thaxton Jr., *Catastrophe and Contention in Rural China: Mao's Great Leap Forward Famine and the Origins of Righteous Resistance in Da Fo Village*
Ralph A. Thaxton Jr., *Force and Contention in Contemporary China: Memory and Resistance in the Long Shadow of the Catastrophic Past*
Charles Tilly, *Contention and Democracy in Europe, 1650–2000*

Charles Tilly, *Contentious Performances*
Charles Tilly, *The Politics of Collective Violence*
Marisa von Bülow, *Building Transnational Networks: Civil Society and the Politics of Trade in the Americas*
Lesley J. Wood, *Direct Action, Deliberation, and Diffusion: Collective Action after the WTO Protests in Seattle*
Stuart A. Wright, *Patriots, Politics, and the Oklahoma City Bombing*
Deborah Yashar, *Contesting Citizenship in Latin America: The Rise of Indigenous Movements and the Postliberal Challenge*
Andrew Yeo, *Activists, Alliances, and Anti-U.S. Base Protests*